ZIG☆ZAG™

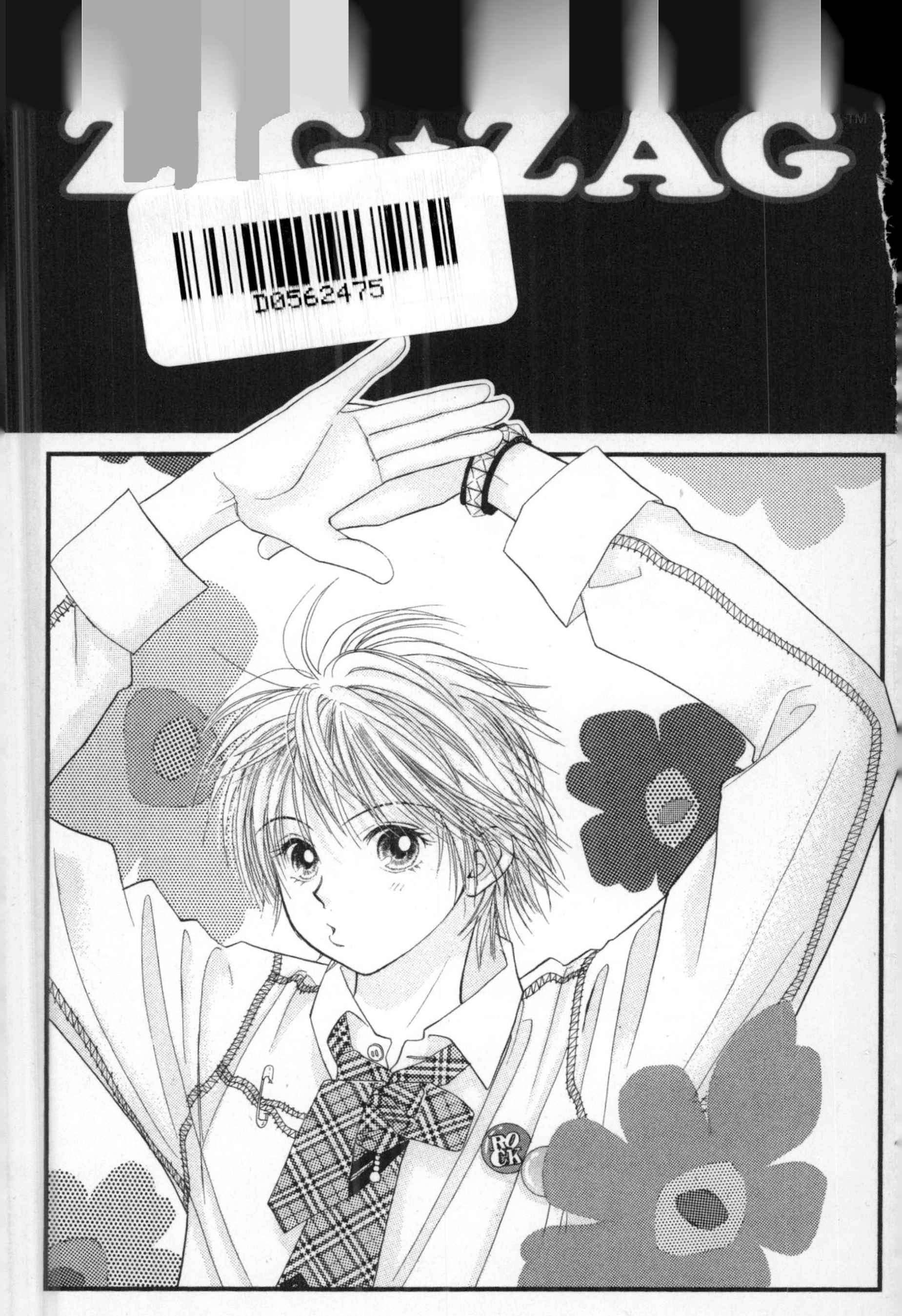
ROCK

ZIG★ZAG Volume 1
Created by Yuki Nakaji

Translation - Jonathan Lee
English Adaptation - Gina Lee Ferenzi
Retouch and Lettering - Star Print Brokers
Production Artist - Vicente Rivera, Jr.
Graphic Designer - James Lee

Editor - Peter Ahlstrom
Digital Imaging Manager - Chris Buford
Pre-Production Supervisor - Erika Terriquez
Production Manager - Elisabeth Brizzi
Managing Editor - Vy Nguyen
Creative Director - Anne Marie Horne
Editor-in-Chief - Rob Tokar
Publisher - Mike Kiley
President and C.O.O. - John Parker
C.E.O. and Chief Creative Officer - Stuart Levy

A **TOKYOPOP** Manga

TOKYOPOP Inc.
5900 Wilshire Blvd. Suite 2000
Los Angeles, CA 90036

E-mail: info@TOKYOPOP.com
Come visit us online at www.TOKYOPOP.com

ISBN: 978-1-4278-0308-5

First TOKYOPOP printing: November 2007
10 9 8 7 6 5 4 3 2 1
Printed in the USA

ZIG☆ZAG™

Volume 1

by

Yuki Nakaji

TOKYOPOP®

HAMBURG // LONDON // LOS ANGELES // TOKYO

ZIG☆ZAG ™

Contents

Chapter 1 6

Chapter 2 57

Chapter 3 101

Chapter 4 141

Caramel Photo Studio III 184

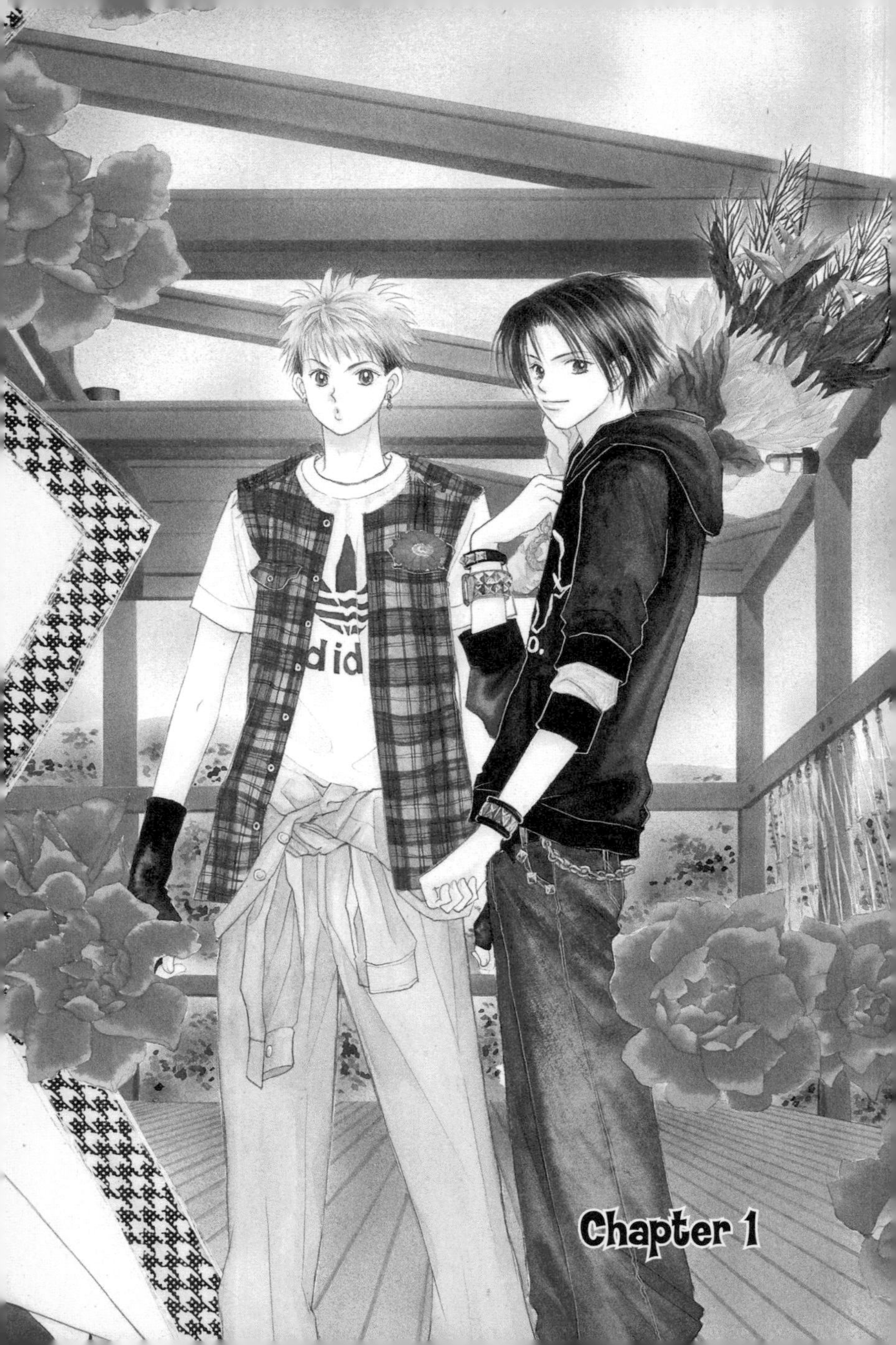
Chapter 1

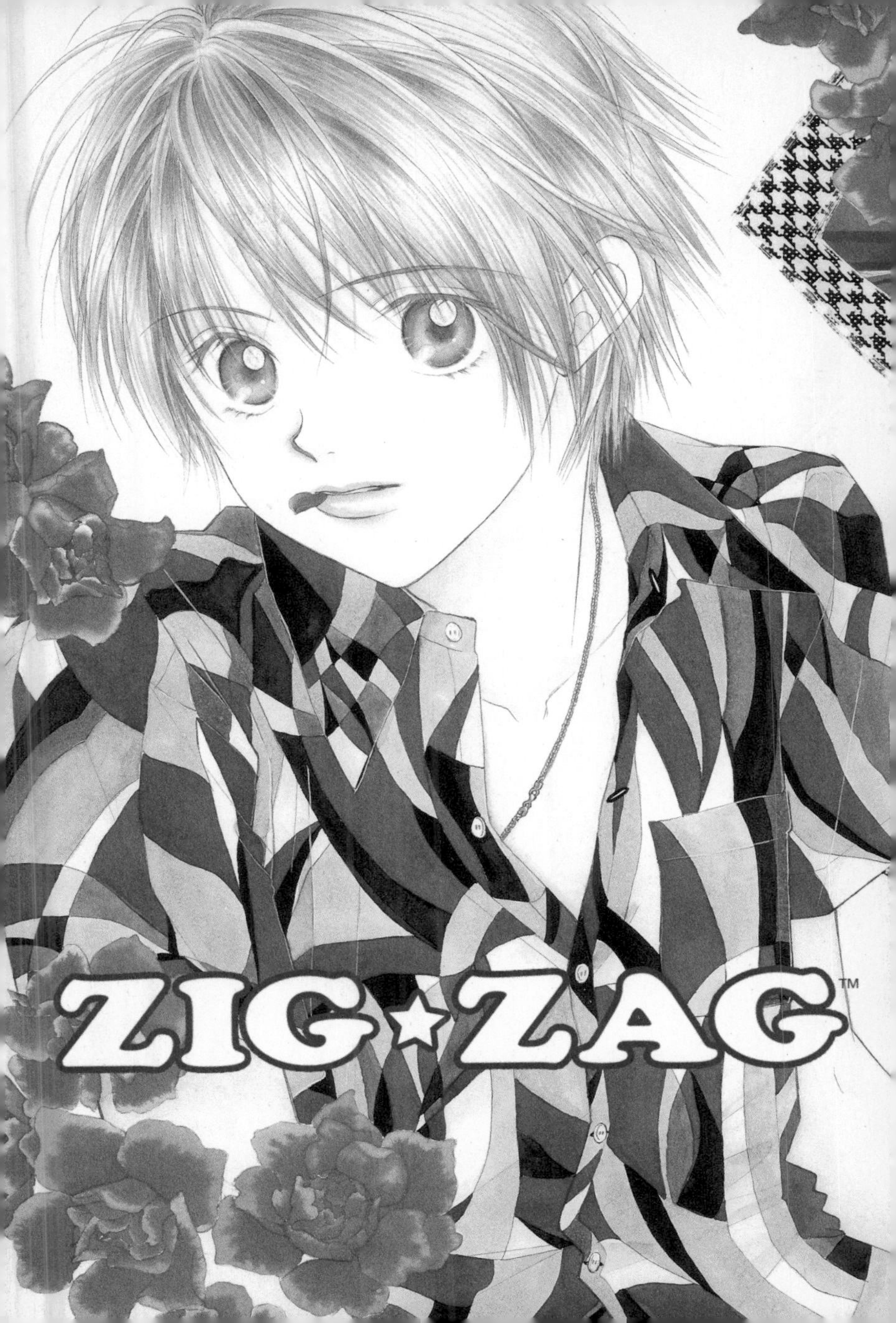
ZIG★ZAG™

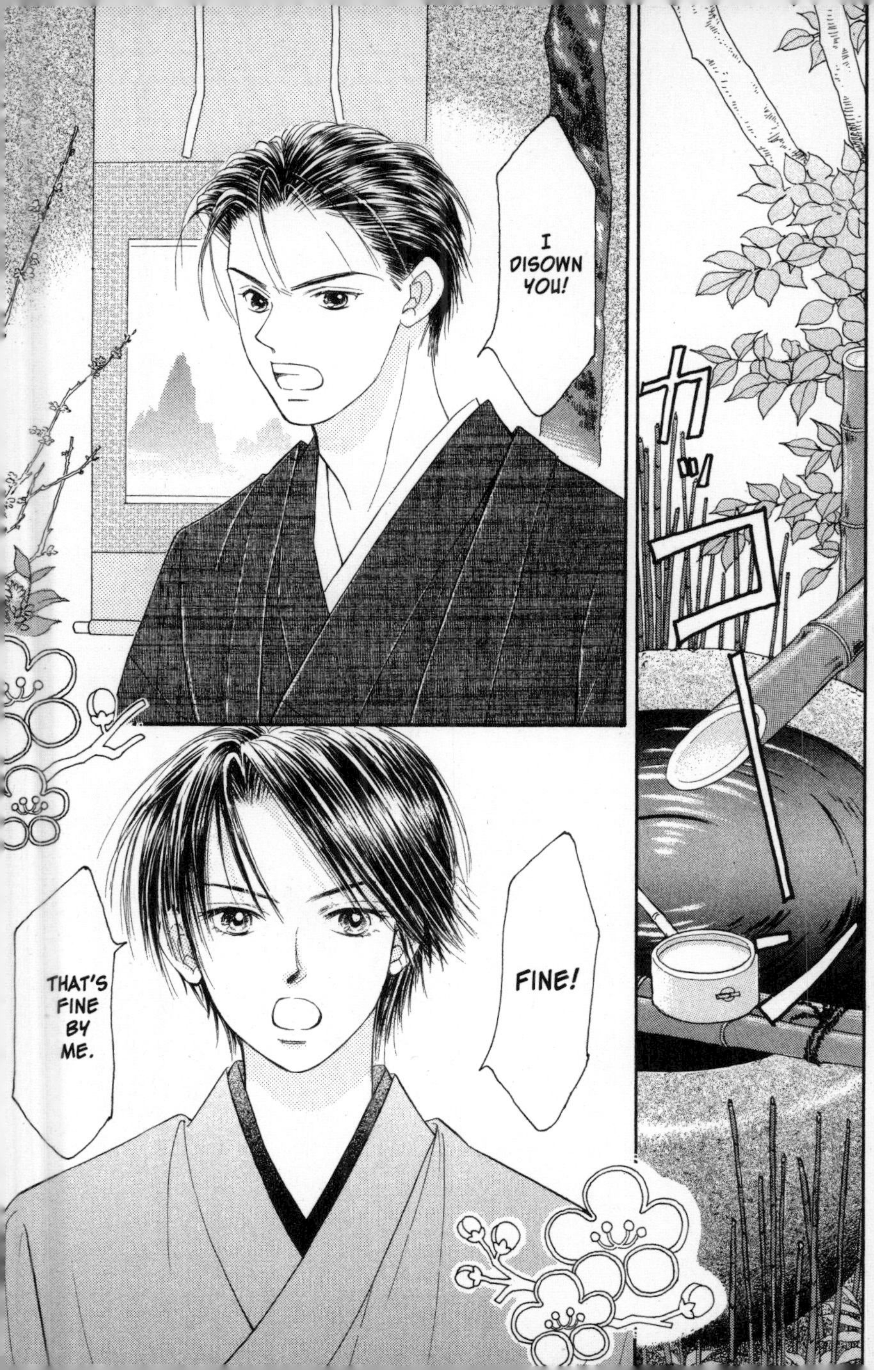
カッコー
I DISOWN YOU!
FINE!
THAT'S FINE BY ME.

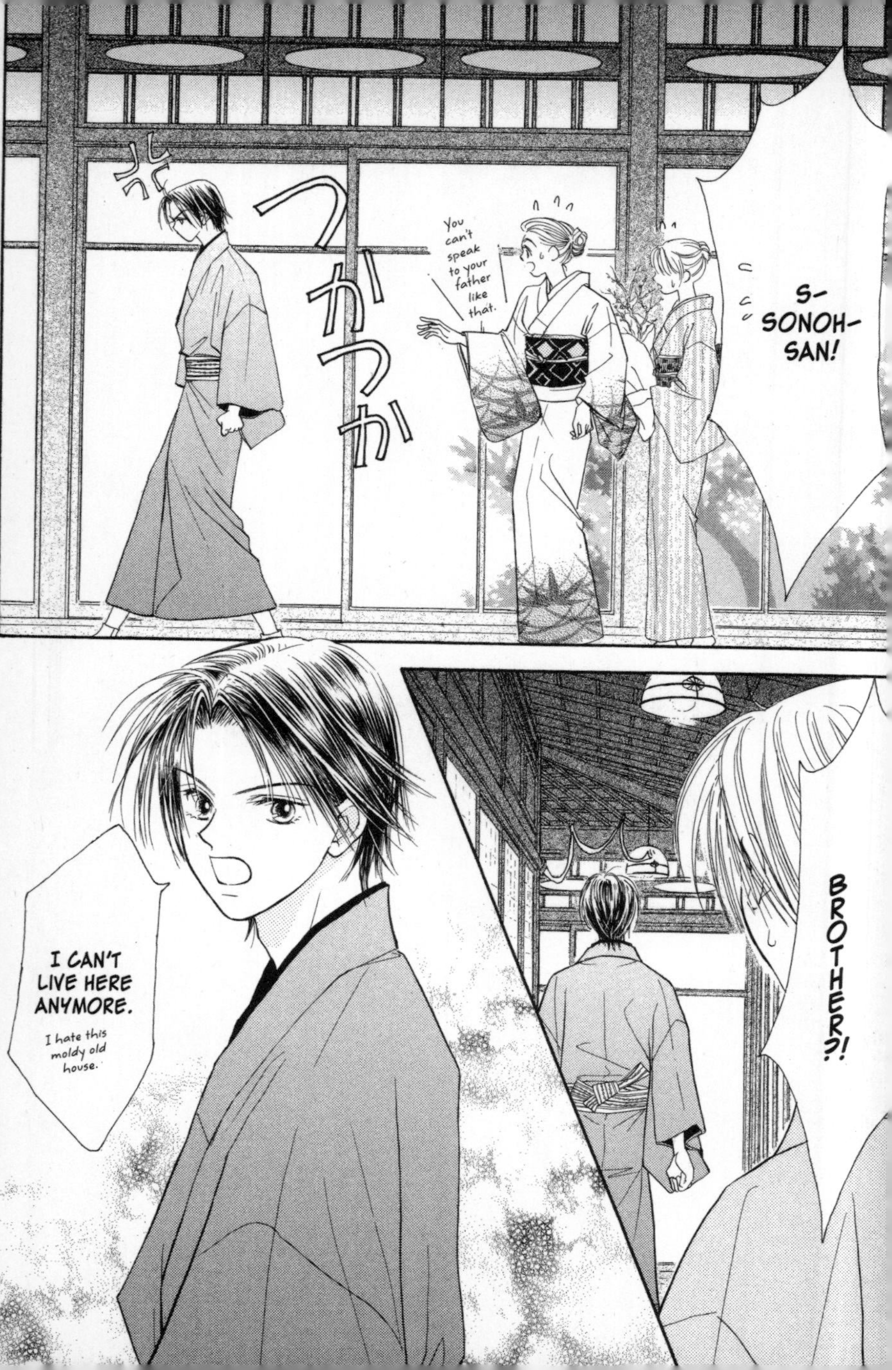
S-SONOH-SAN!
You can't speak to your father like that.
つかつか
BROTHER?!
I CAN'T LIVE HERE ANYMORE.
I hate this moldy old house.

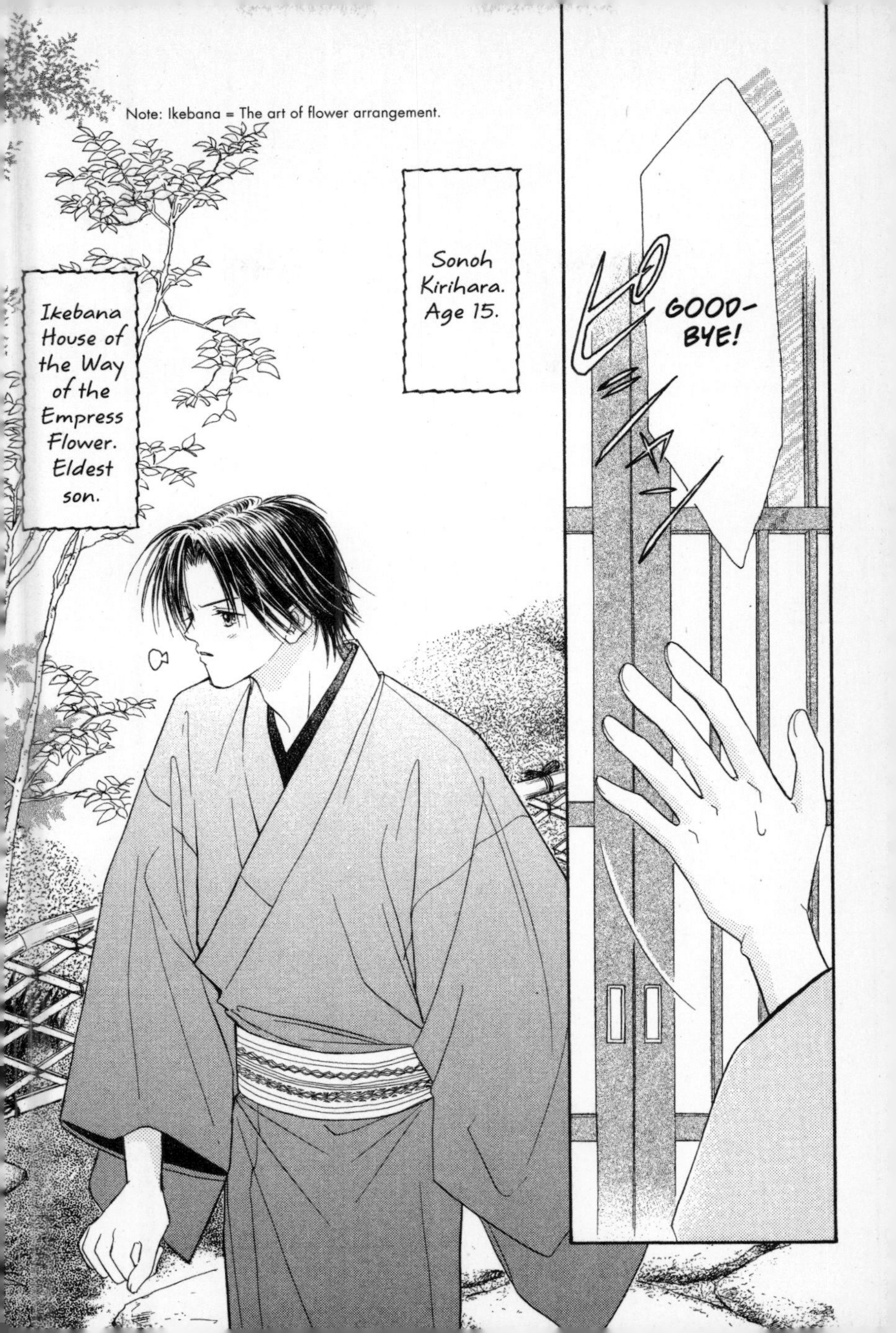
GOOD-BYE!
Sonoh Kirihara. Age 15.
Ikebana House of the Way of the Empress Flower. Eldest son.
Note: Ikebana = The art of flower arrangement.

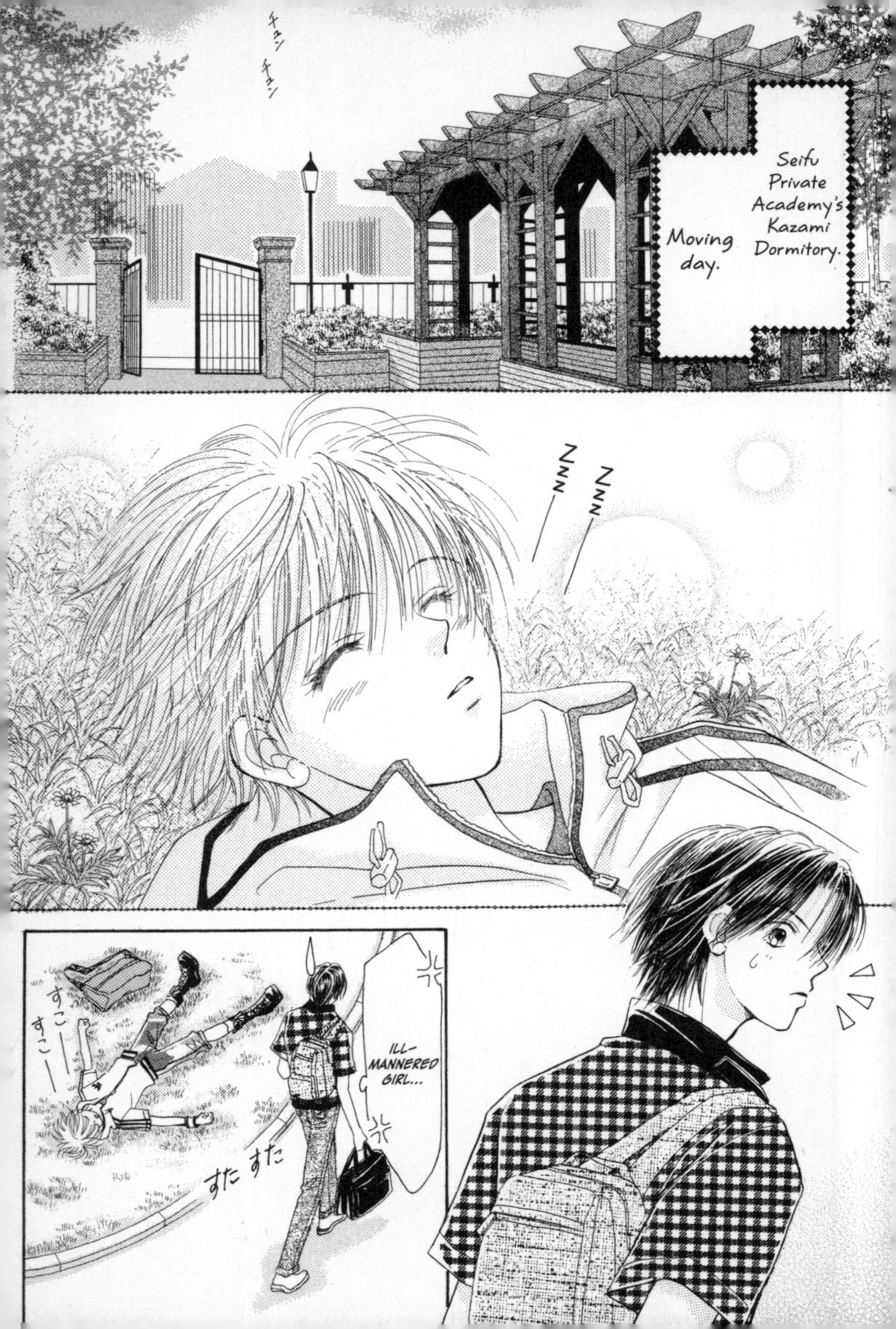
チュン チュン
Seifu Private Academy's Kazami Dormitory.
Moving day.
Zzz
Zzz
ILL-MANNERED GIRL...
すこー すこー
すた すた

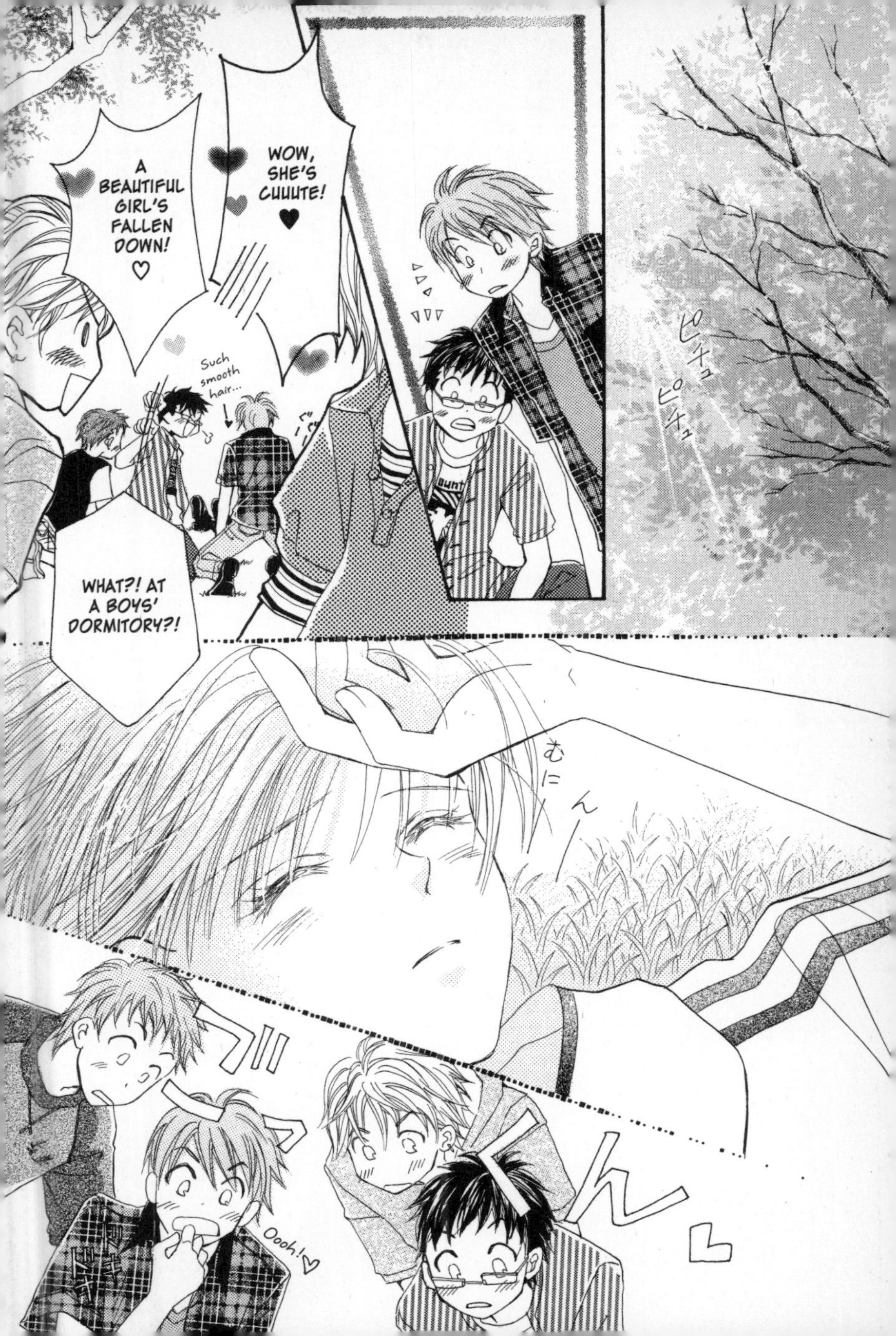

ピチュ
ピチュ
WOW, SHE'S CUUUTE! ♥
A BEAUTIFUL GIRL'S FALLEN DOWN! ♡
Such smooth hair...
WHAT?! AT A BOYS' DORMITORY?!
むにん
Oooh! ♡

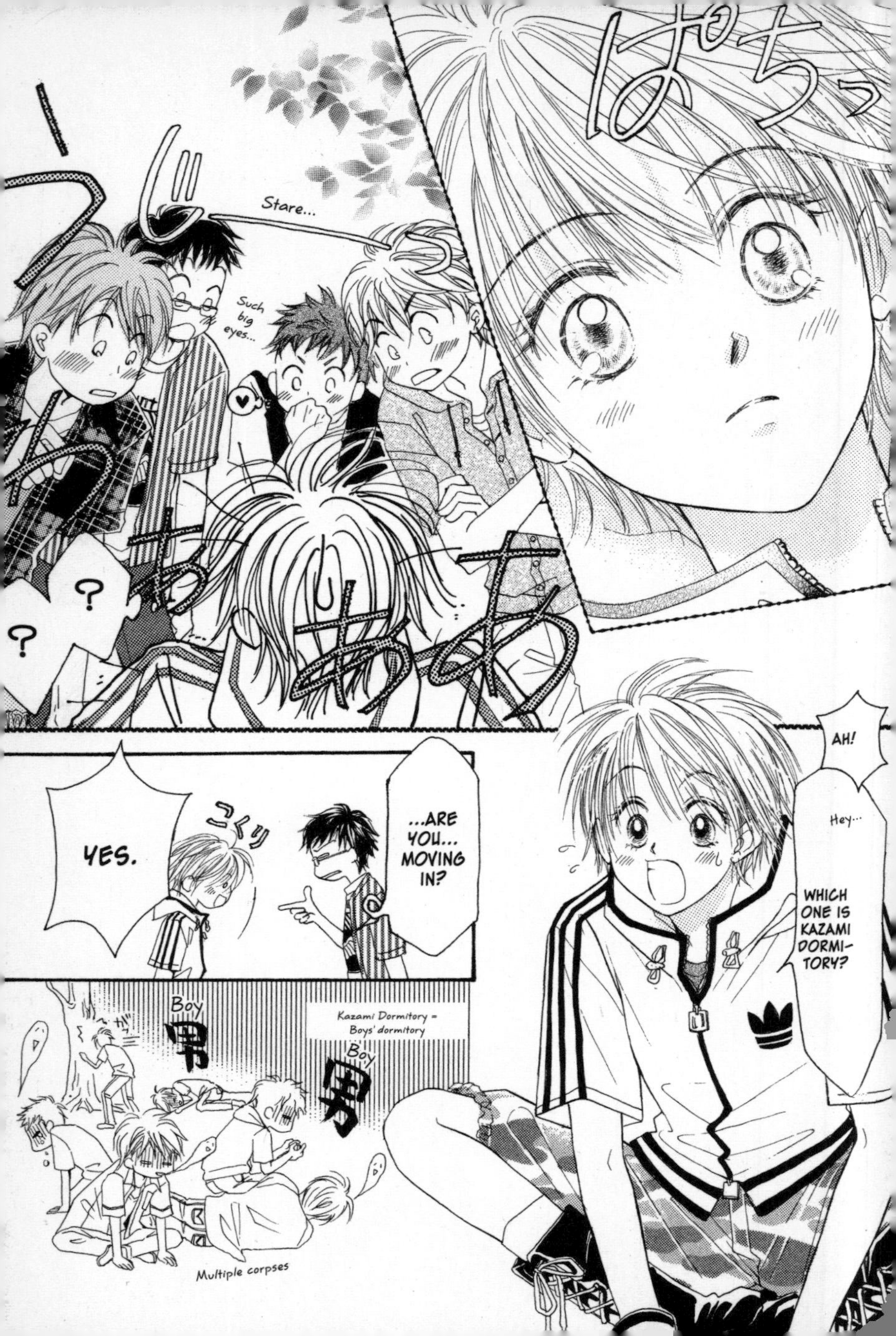

ぱちっ
じーっ
Stare...
Such big eyes...
?
?
AH!
Hey...
WHICH ONE IS KAZAMI DORMITORY?
...ARE YOU... MOVING IN?
こくり
YES.
Kazami Dormitory = Boys' dormitory
Boy
男
Boy
男
Multiple corpses

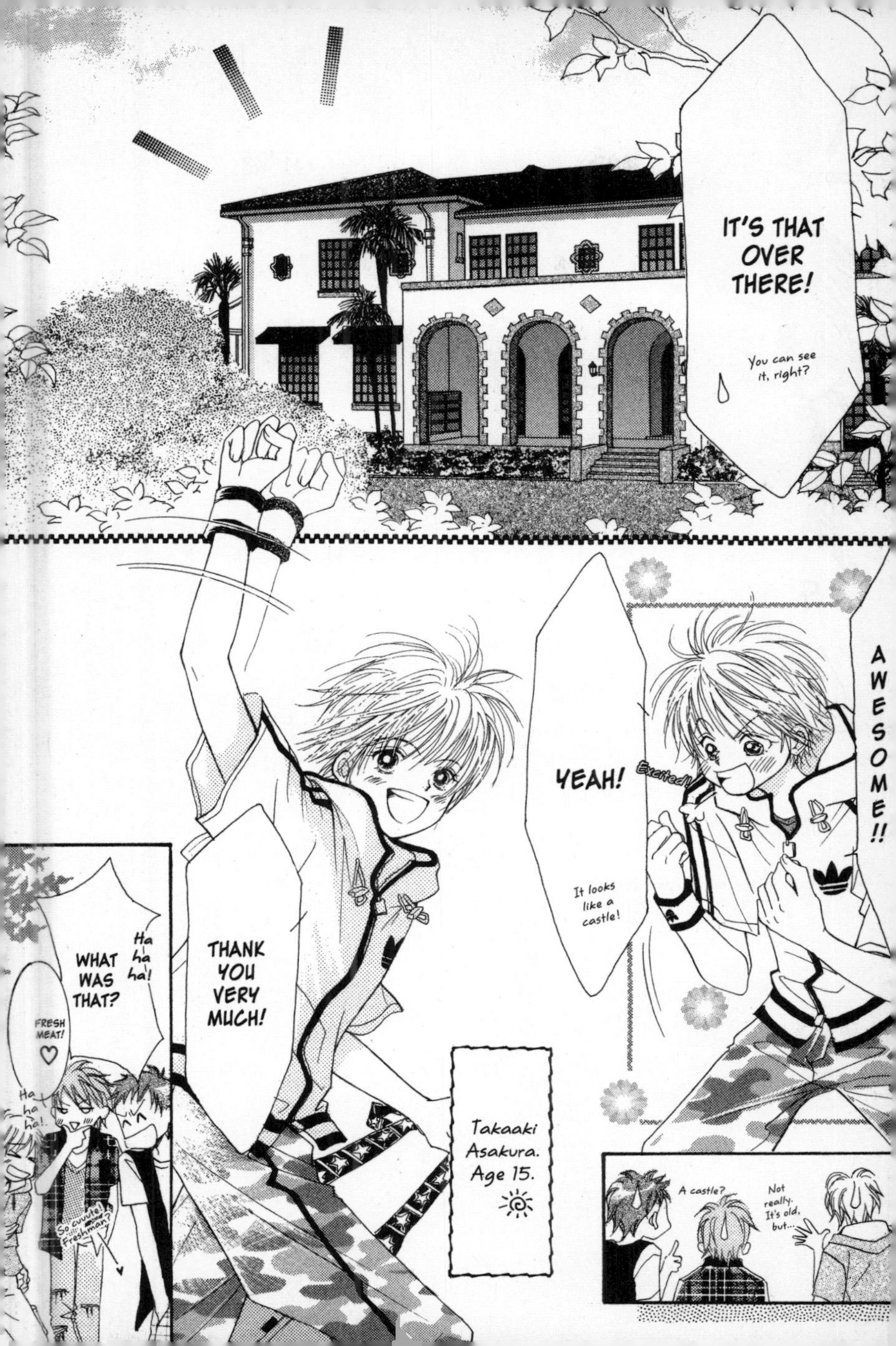

IT'S THAT OVER THERE!
You can see it, right?
AWESOME!!
YEAH!
Excited!
It looks like a castle!
Not really. It's old, but...
A castle?
THANK YOU VERY MUCH!
Takaaki Asakura. Age 15.
Ha ha ha!
WHAT WAS THAT?
FRESH MEAT! ♡
Ha ha ha!
So cuuute! Freshman?

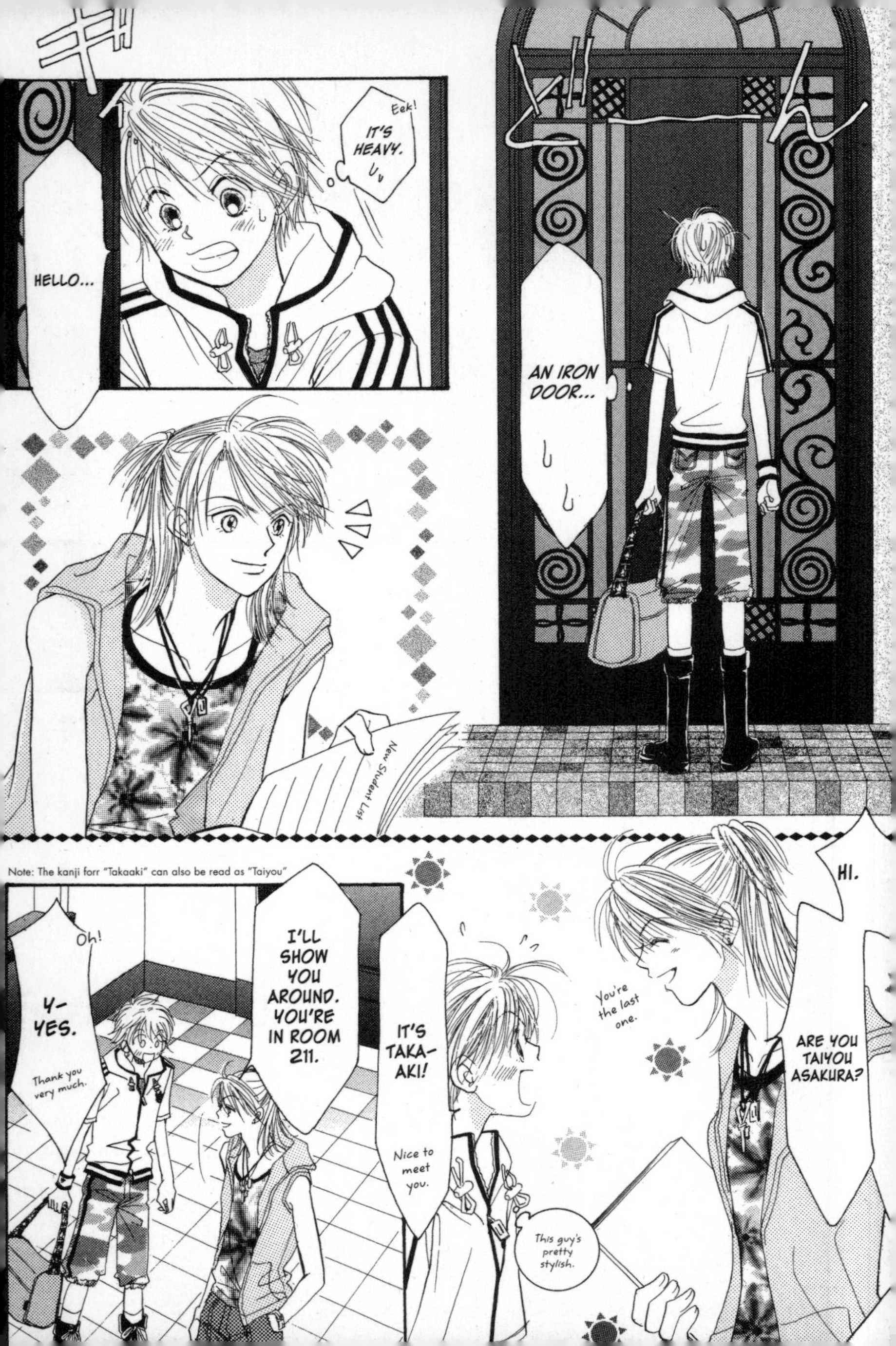
AN IRON DOOR...
Eek!
IT'S HEAVY.
HELLO...
New Student List
Note: The kanji forr "Takaaki" can also be read as "Taiyou"
HI.
ARE YOU TAIYOU ASAKURA?
You're the last one.
IT'S TAKA-AKI!
Nice to meet you.
This guy's pretty stylish.
I'LL SHOW YOU AROUND. YOU'RE IN ROOM 211.
Oh!
Y-YES.
Thank you very much.

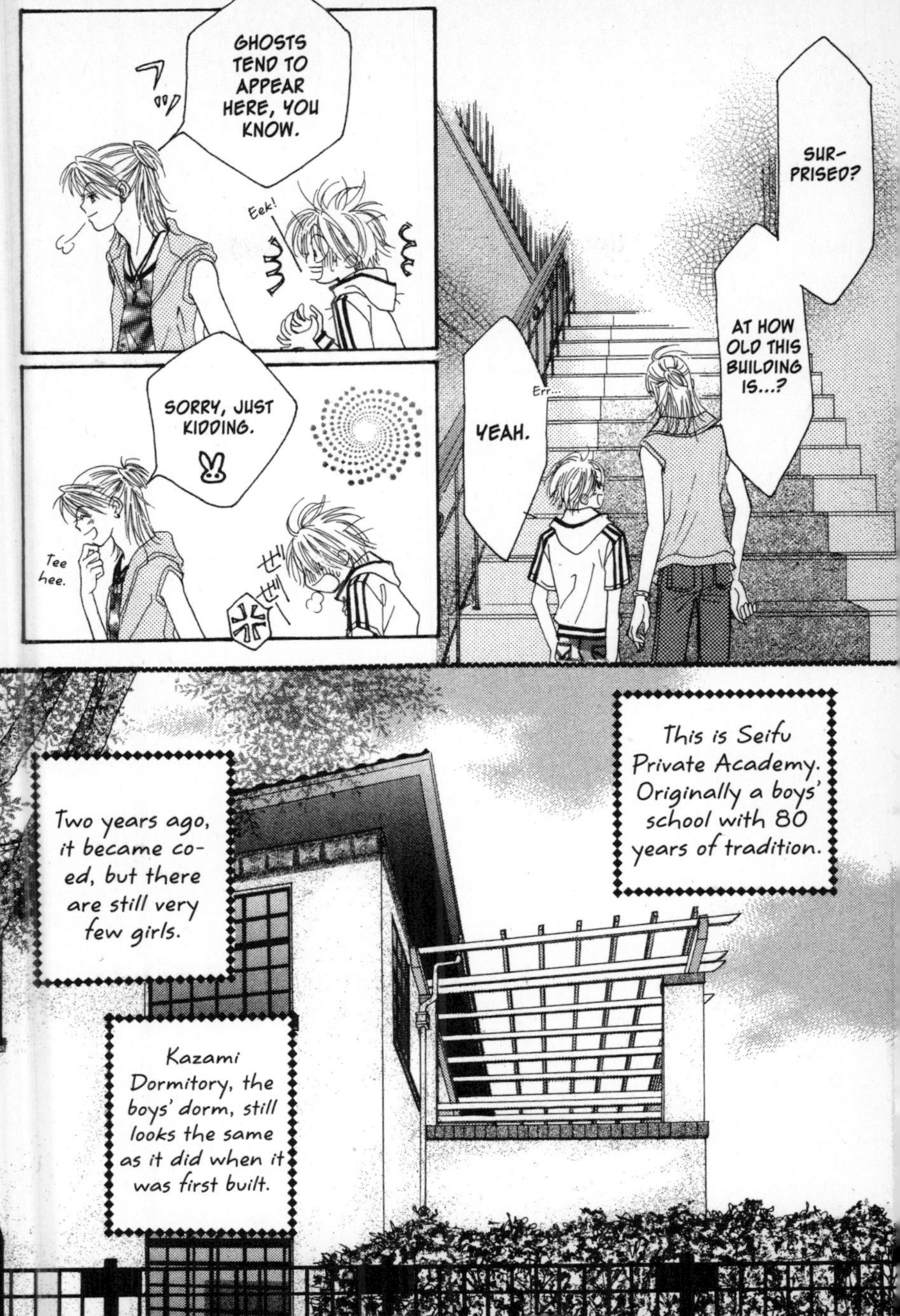
SUR-PRISED?
AT HOW OLD THIS BUILDING IS...?
Err...
YEAH.
GHOSTS TEND TO APPEAR HERE, YOU KNOW.
Eek!
SORRY, JUST KIDDING.
Tee hee.
This is Seifu Private Academy. Originally a boys' school with 80 years of tradition.
Two years ago, it became co-ed, but there are still very few girls.
Kazami Dormitory, the boys' dorm, still looks the same as it did when it was first built.

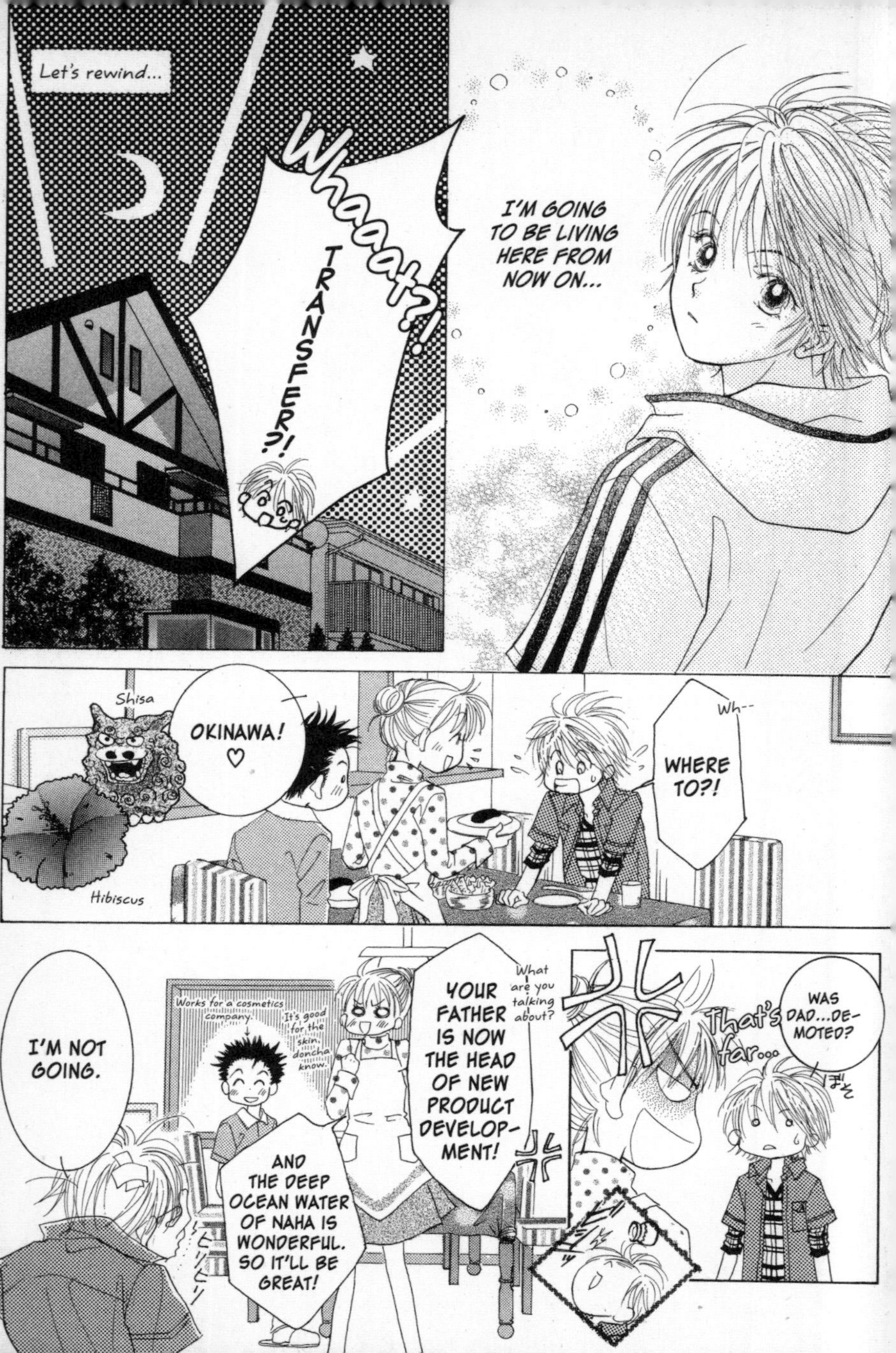
I'M GOING TO BE LIVING HERE FROM NOW ON...
Let's rewind...
Whaaat?!
TRANSFER?!
Wh--
WHERE TO?!
OKINAWA! ♡
Shisa
Hibiscus
WAS DAD...DE-MOTED?
ぼそ
That's far...
What are you talking about?
YOUR FATHER IS NOW THE HEAD OF NEW PRODUCT DEVELOPMENT!
It's good for the skin, doncha know.
Works for a cosmetics company.
AND THE DEEP OCEAN WATER OF NAHA IS WONDERFUL. SO IT'LL BE GREAT!
I'M NOT GOING.

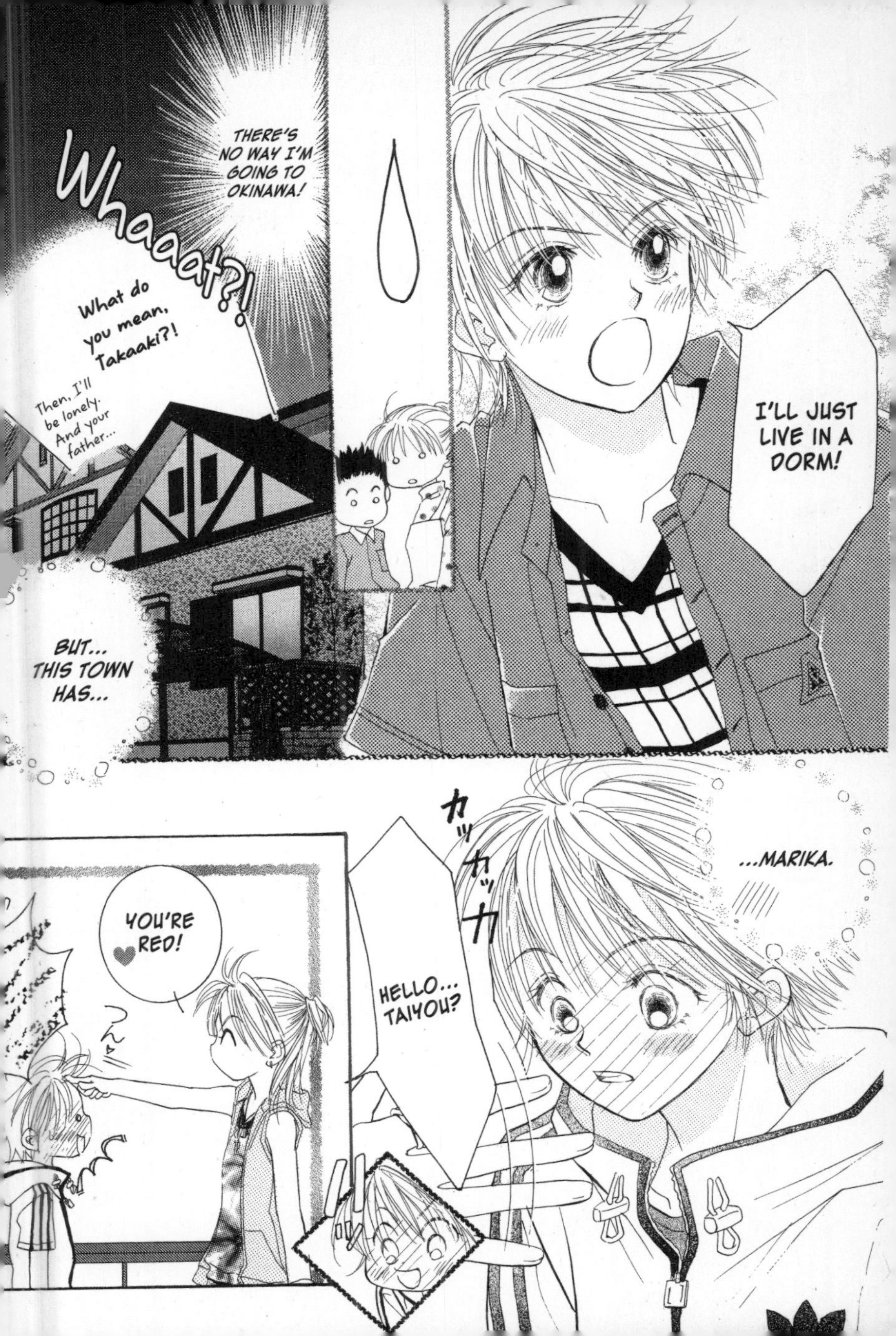
I'LL JUST LIVE IN A DORM!
THERE'S NO WAY I'M GOING TO OKINAWA!
Whaaat?!
What do you mean, Takaaki?!
Then, I'll be lonely. And your father...
BUT... THIS TOWN HAS...
...MARIKA.
カッカッカ
HELLO... TAIYOU?
YOU'RE RED!

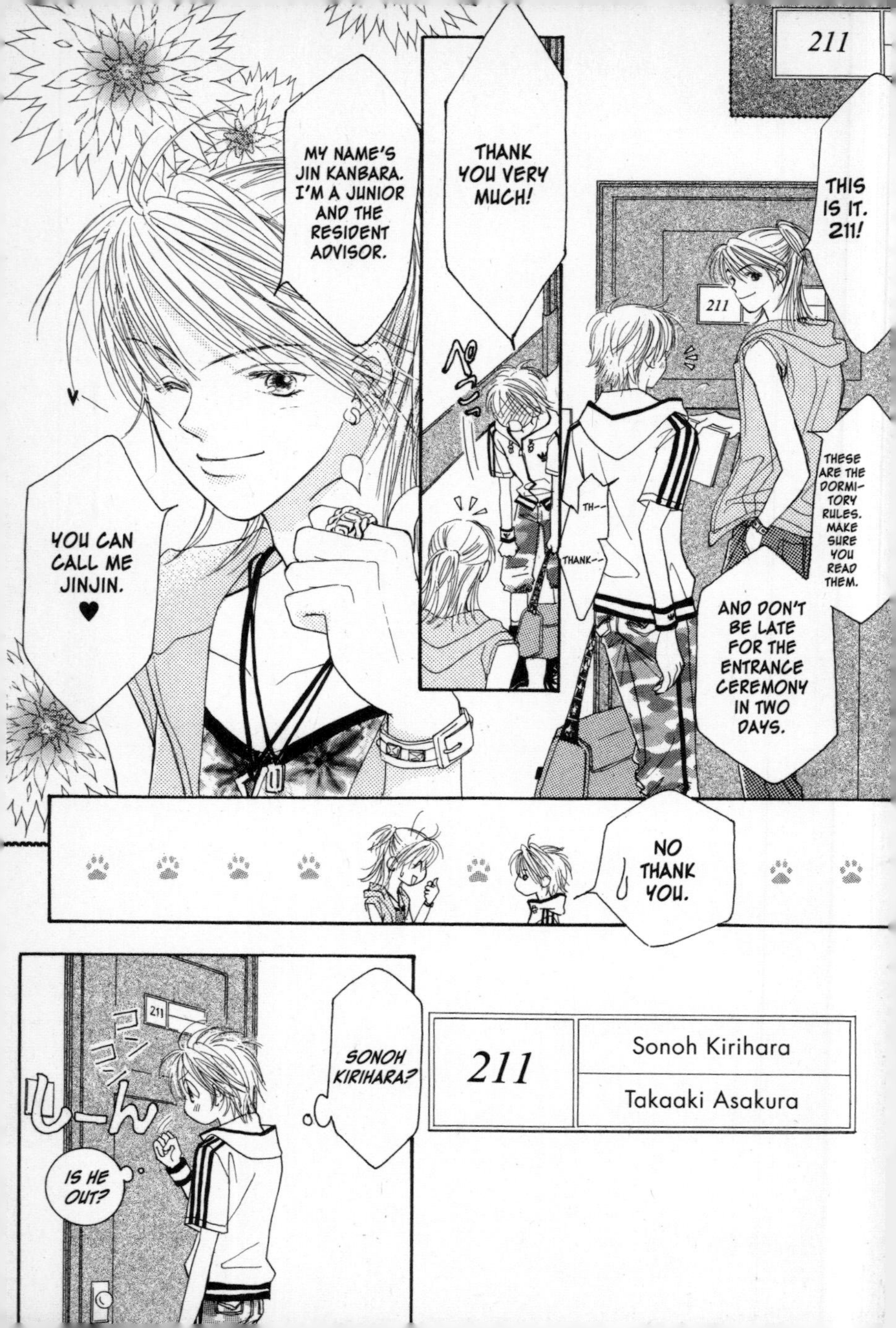
211
THIS IS IT. 211!
THESE ARE THE DORMITORY RULES. MAKE SURE YOU READ THEM.
AND DON'T BE LATE FOR THE ENTRANCE CEREMONY IN TWO DAYS.
TH--
THANK--
THANK YOU VERY MUCH!
MY NAME'S JIN KANBARA. I'M A JUNIOR AND THE RESIDENT ADVISOR.
YOU CAN CALL ME JINJIN. ♥
NO THANK YOU.
211
211
Sonoh Kirihara
Takaaki Asakura
SONOH KIRIHARA?
しーん
IS HE OUT?

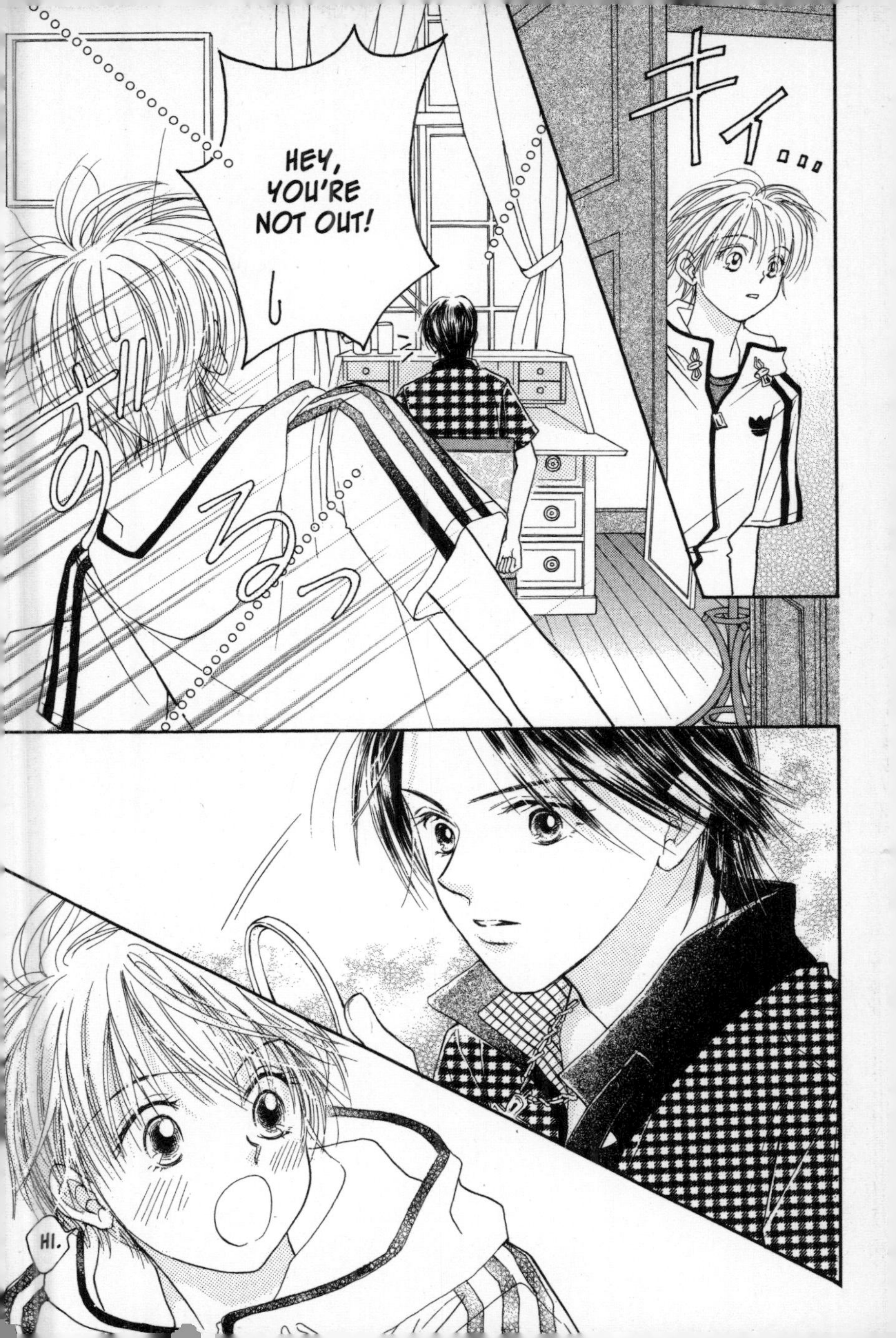
キィ...
HEY, YOU'RE NOT OUT!
HI.

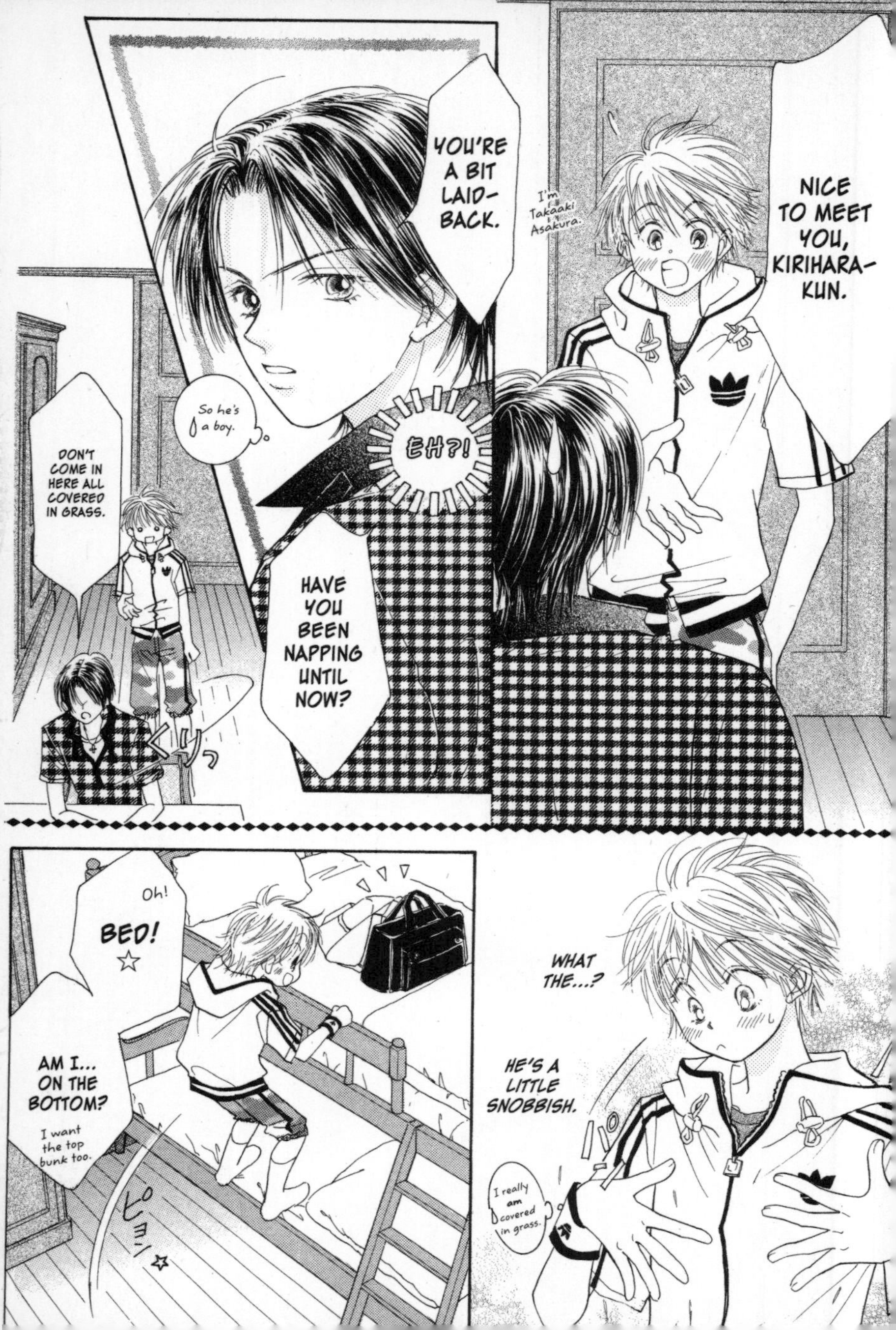
NICE TO MEET YOU, KIRIHARA-KUN.
I'm Takaaki Asakura.
YOU'RE A BIT LAID-BACK.
EH?!
So he's a boy.
HAVE YOU BEEN NAPPING UNTIL NOW?
DON'T COME IN HERE ALL COVERED IN GRASS.
WHAT THE...?
HE'S A LITTLE SNOBBISH.
I really am covered in grass.
Oh!
BED! ☆
AM I... ON THE BOTTOM?
I want the top bunk too.

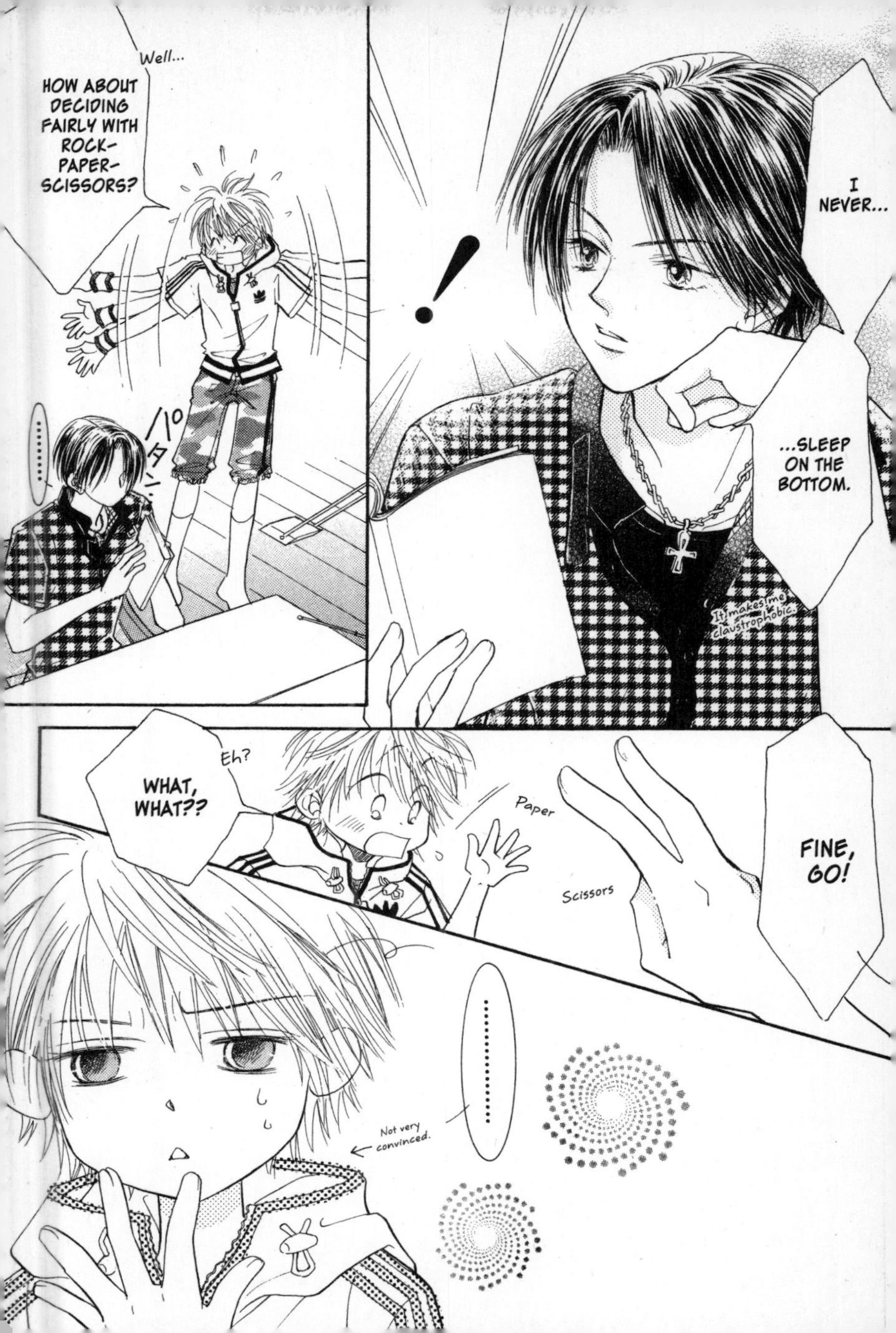
I NEVER...
...SLEEP ON THE BOTTOM.
It makes me claustrophobic.
!
Well...
HOW ABOUT DECIDING FAIRLY WITH ROCK-PAPER-SCISSORS?
......
パタン
FINE, GO!
Paper
Scissors
Eh?
WHAT, WHAT??
......
Not very convinced.

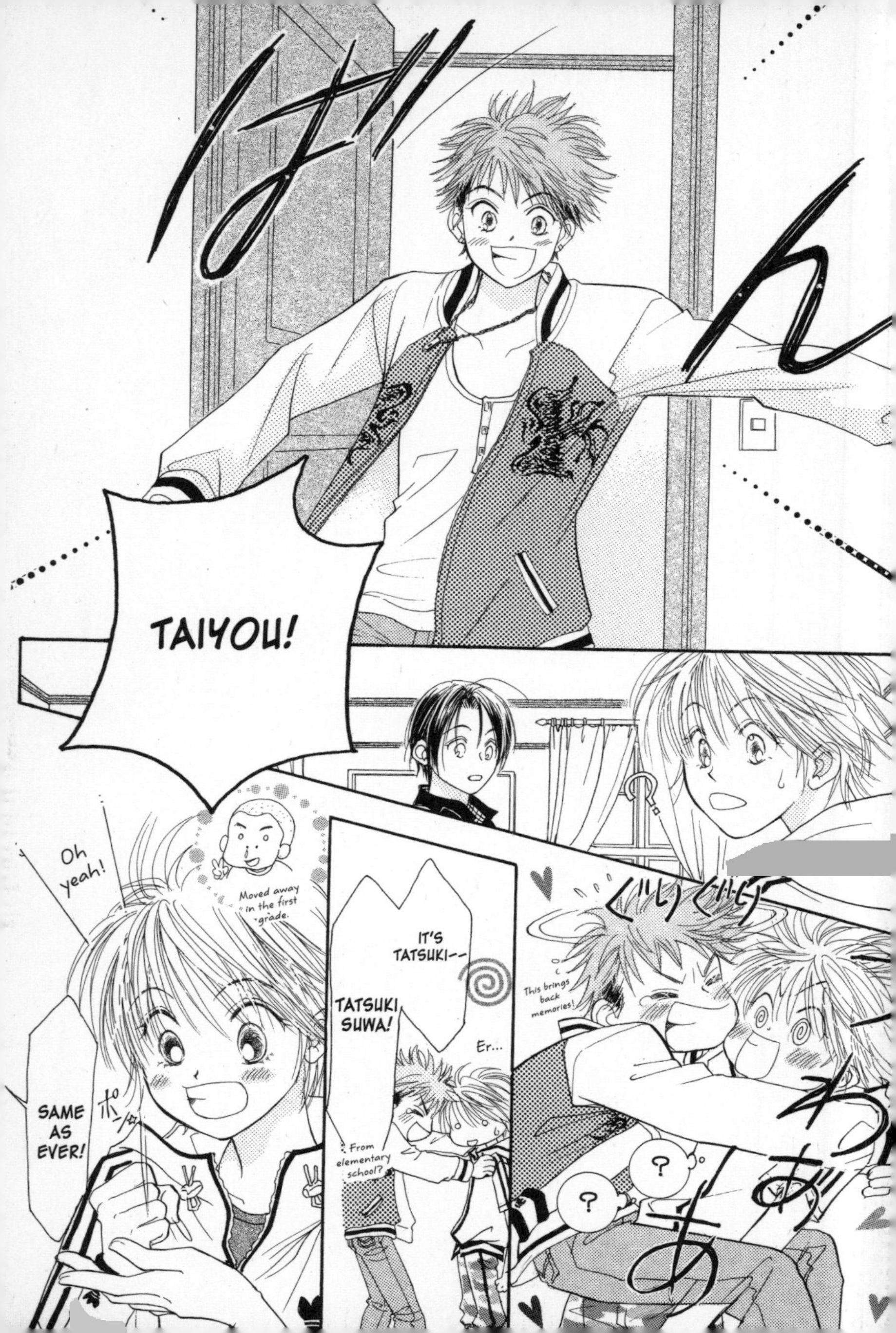
ばん
TAIYOU!
ぐりぐり
This brings back memories!
わああ
IT'S TATSUKI--
TATSUKI SUWA!
Er...
From elementary school?
Oh yeah!
Moved away in the first grade.
SAME AS EVER!
ポン☆

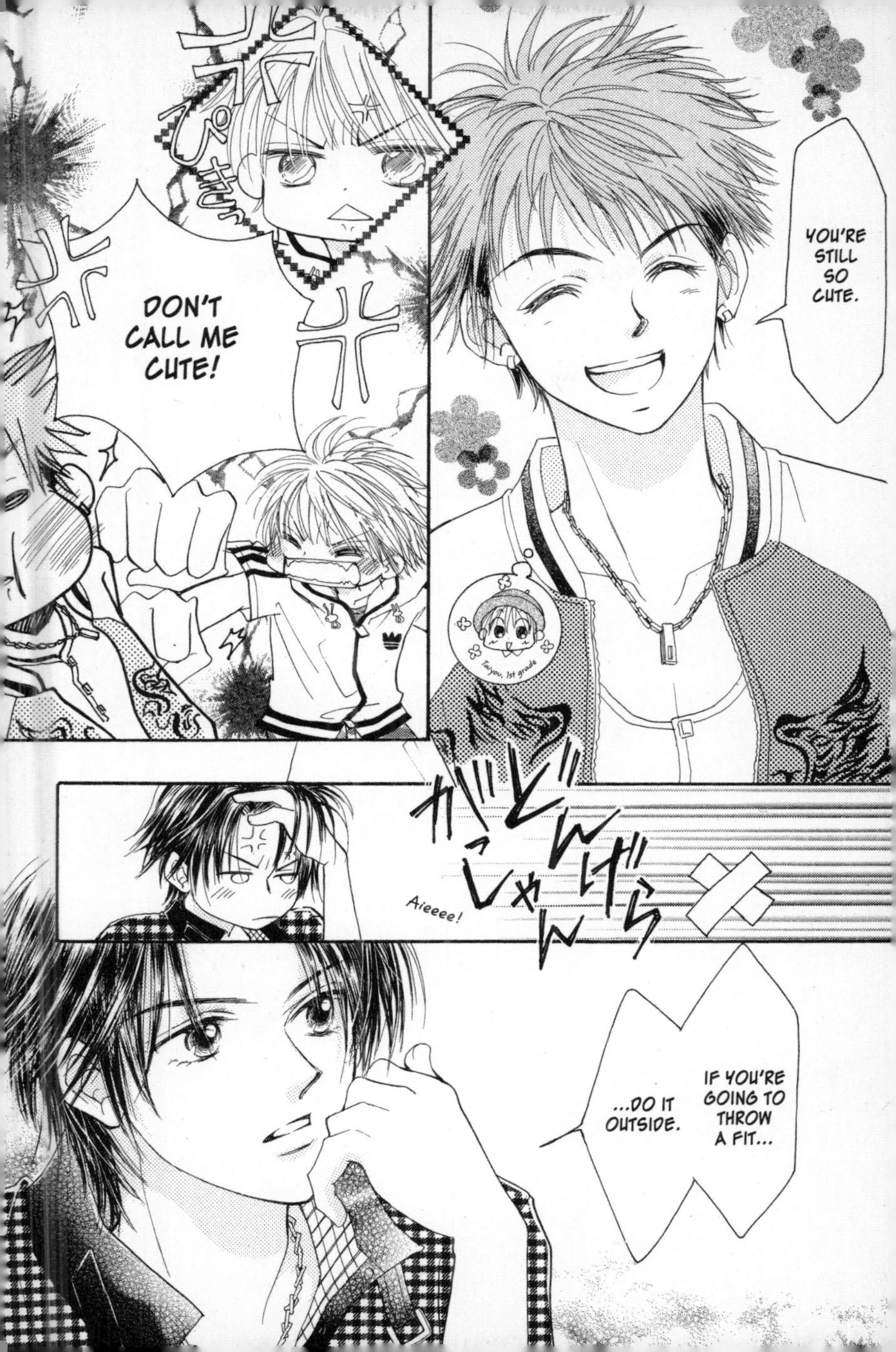
YOU'RE STILL SO CUTE.
Taiyou, 1st grade
DON'T CALL ME CUTE!
Aieeee!
IF YOU'RE GOING TO THROW A FIT...
...DO IT OUTSIDE.

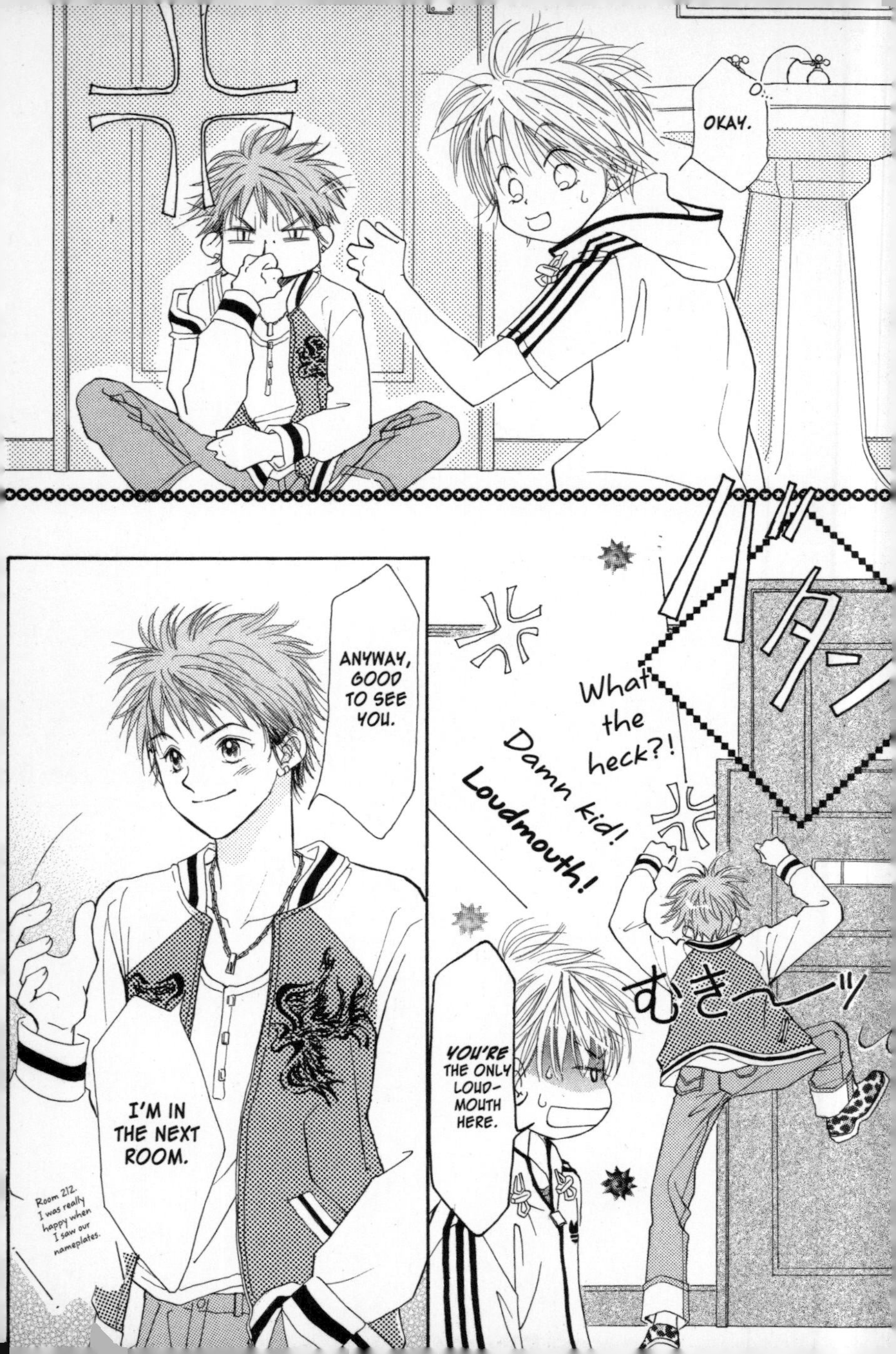
OKAY.
バタン
What the heck?!
Damn kid!
Loudmouth!
むきーッ
YOU'RE THE ONLY LOUD-MOUTH HERE.
ANYWAY, GOOD TO SEE YOU.
I'M IN THE NEXT ROOM.
Room 212. I was really happy when I saw our nameplates.

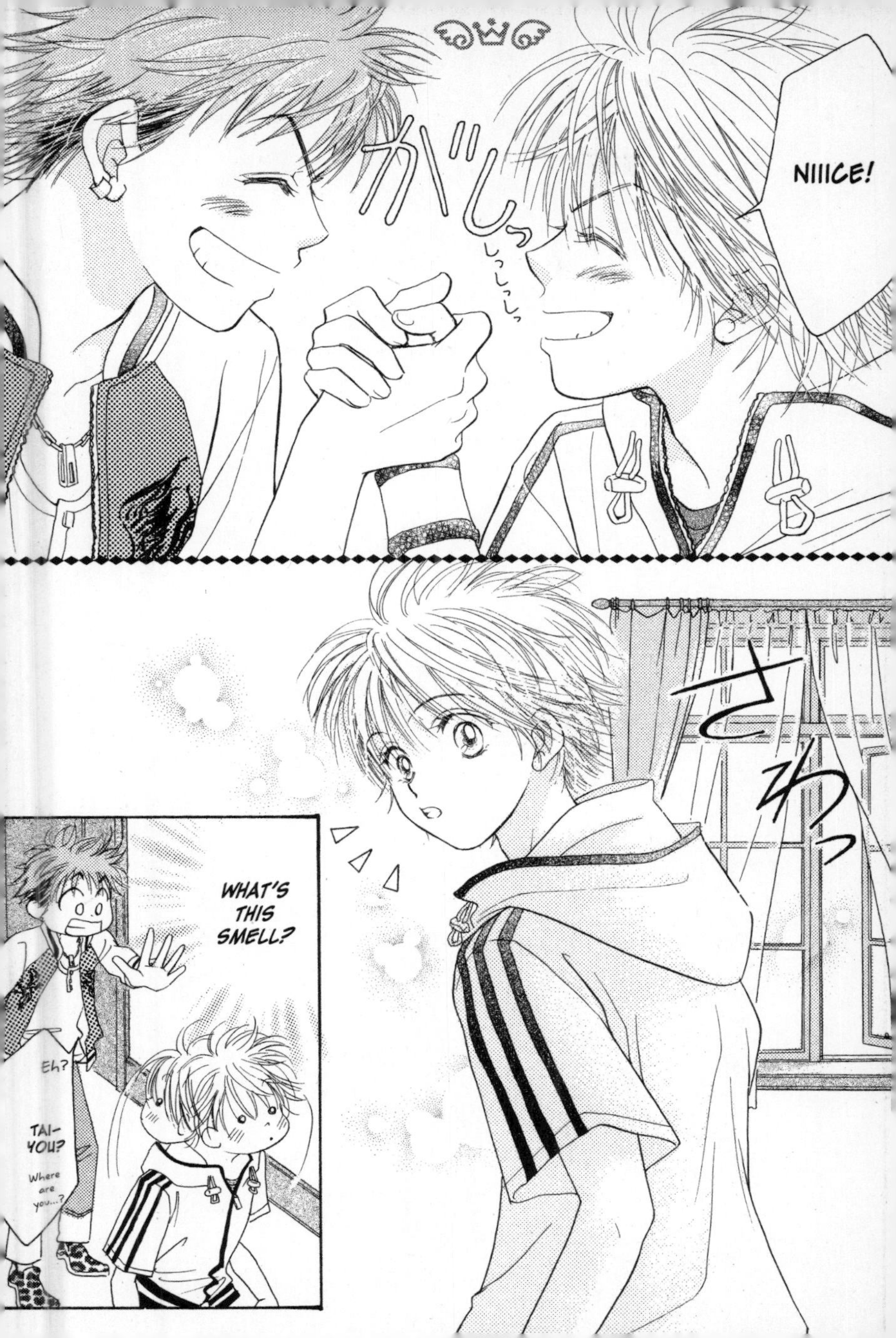
がしっ
しっしっしっ
NIIICE!
さわっ
WHAT'S THIS SMELL?
Eh?
TAI-YOU?
Where are you...?

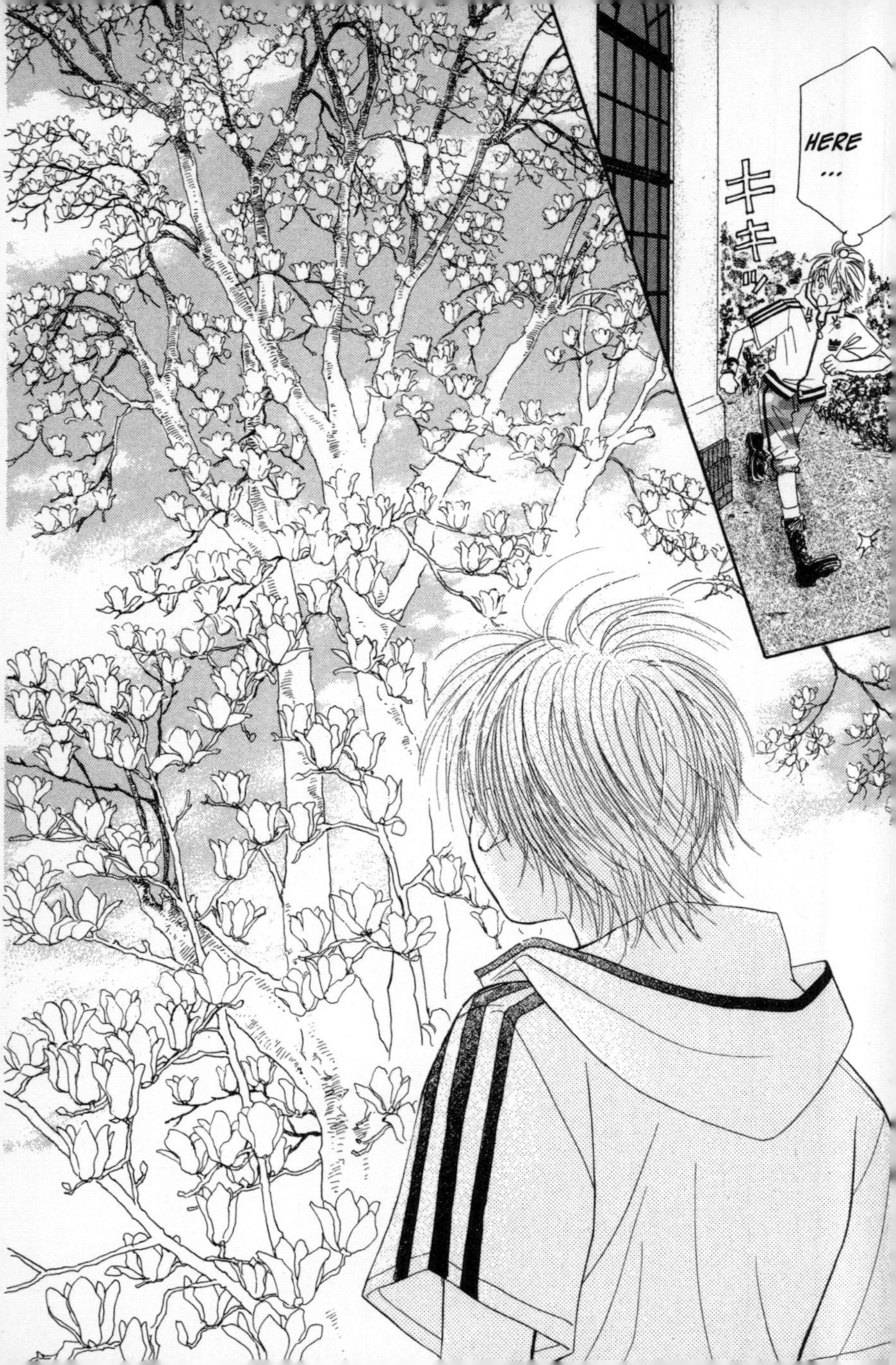
HERE ...
キキッ

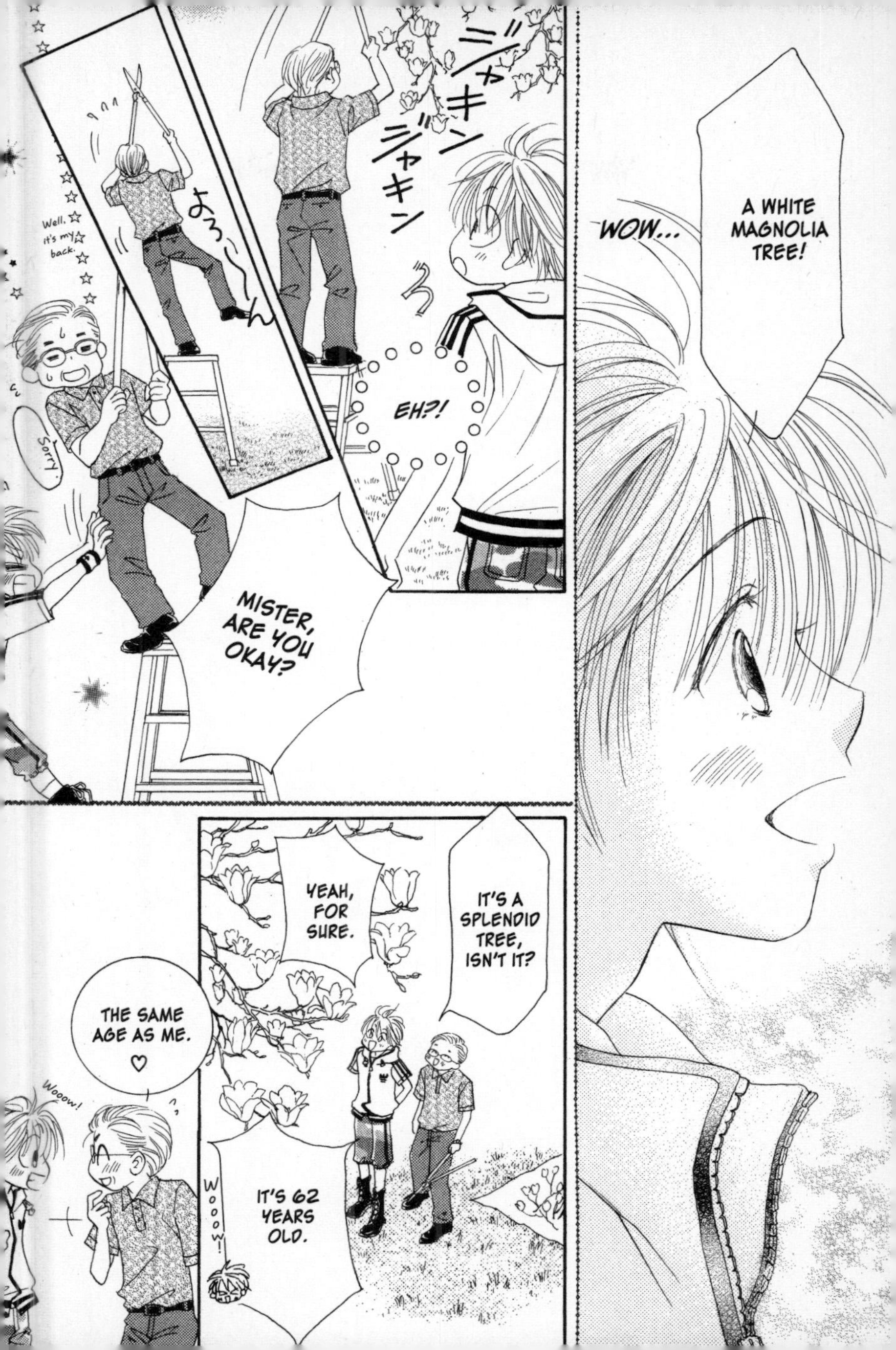
A WHITE MAGNOLIA TREE!
WOW...
ジャキン
ジャキン
EH?!
よろ～ん
Well, it's my back.
Sorry.
MISTER, ARE YOU OKAY?
IT'S A SPLENDID TREE, ISN'T IT?
YEAH, FOR SURE.
IT'S 62 YEARS OLD.
Wooow!
THE SAME AGE AS ME. ♡
Wooow!

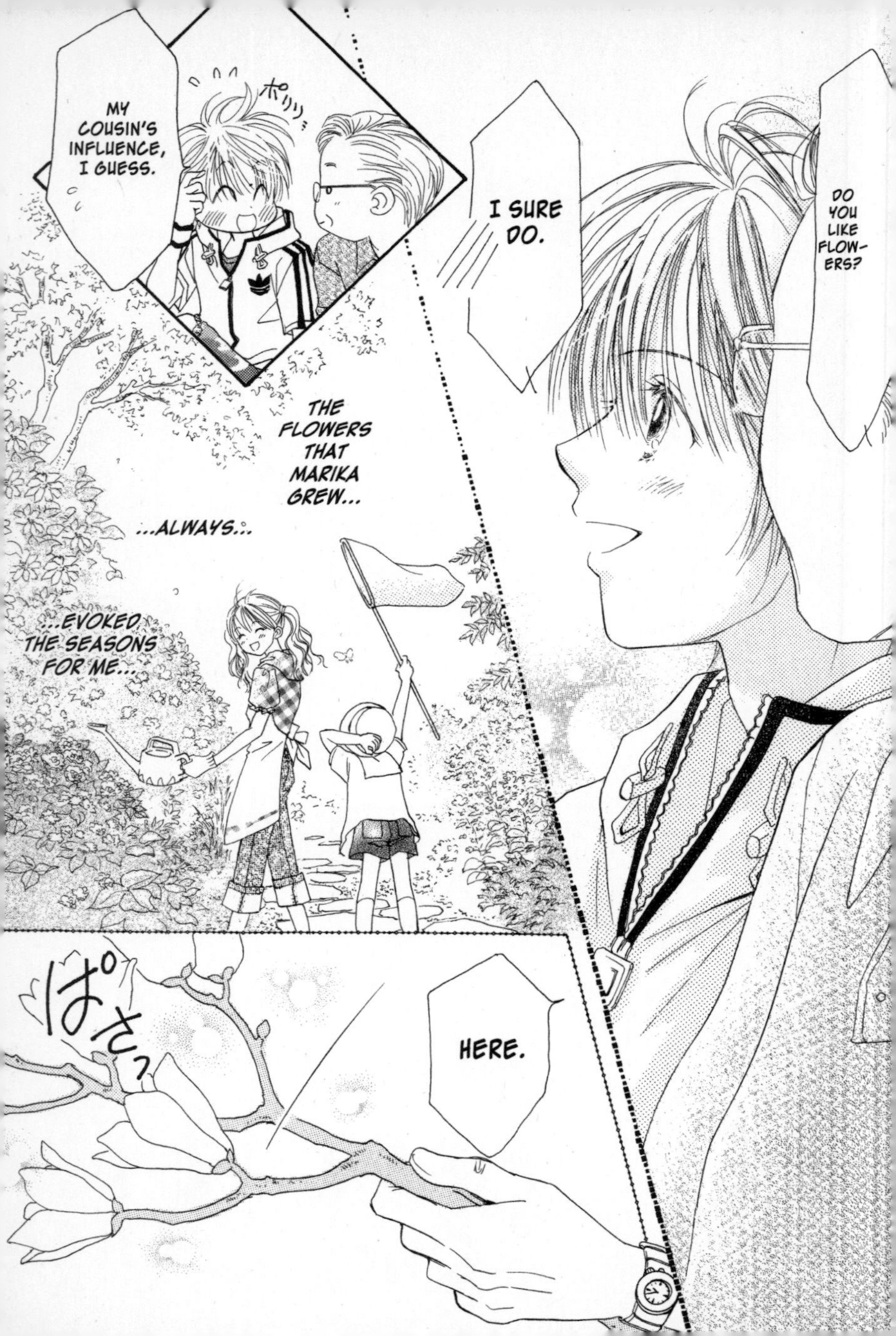
DO YOU LIKE FLOWERS?
I SURE DO.
MY COUSIN'S INFLUENCE, I GUESS.
ポリリ
THE FLOWERS THAT MARIKA GREW...
...ALWAYS...
...EVOKED THE SEASONS FOR ME...
HERE.
ぱさっ

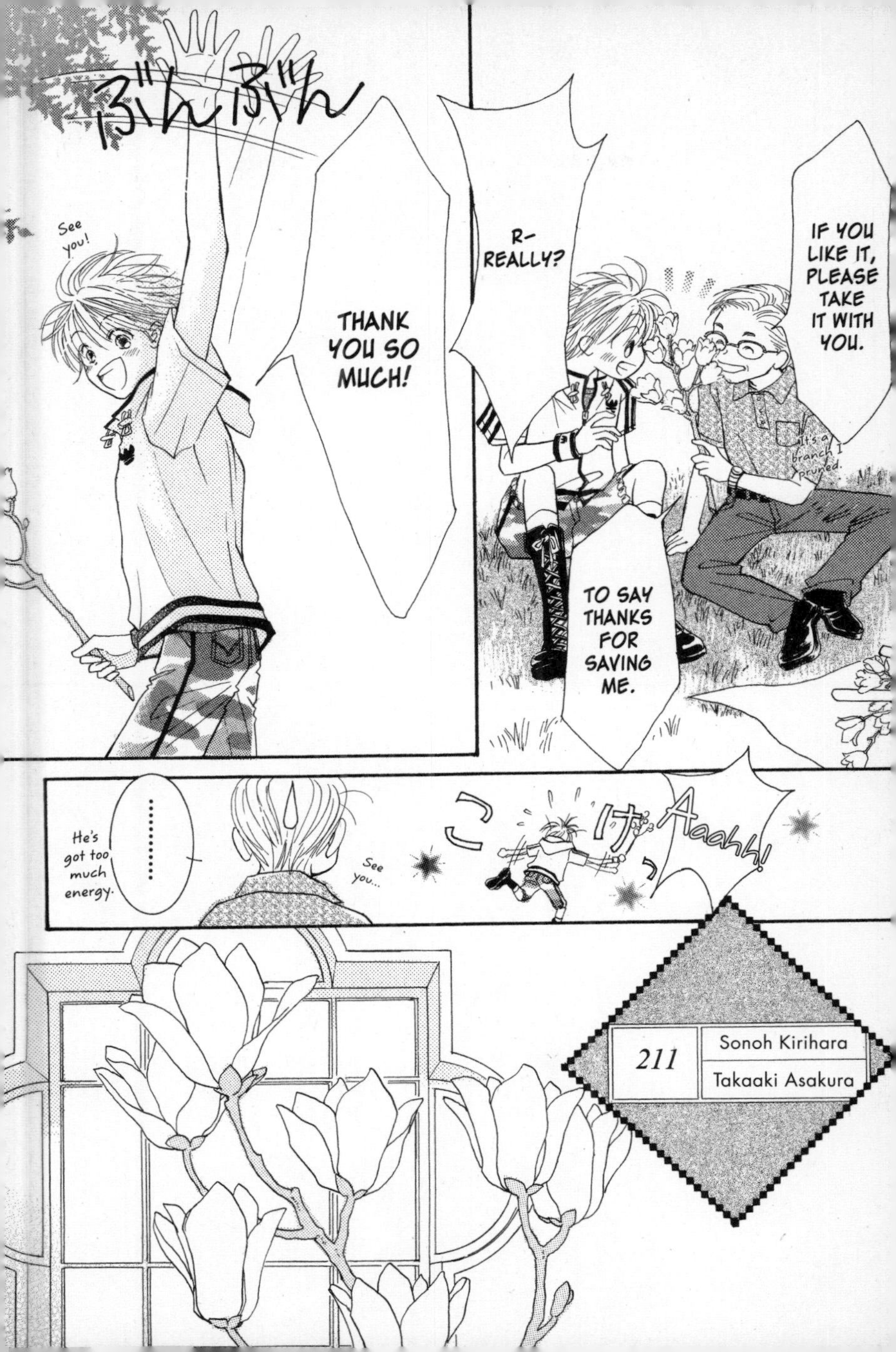
IF YOU LIKE IT, PLEASE TAKE IT WITH YOU.
It's a branch I pruned.
R-REALLY?
TO SAY THANKS FOR SAVING ME.
ぶんぶん
THANK YOU SO MUCH!
See you!
Aaahh!
こけっ
See you...
......
He's got too much energy.
211
Sonoh Kirihara
Takaaki Asakura

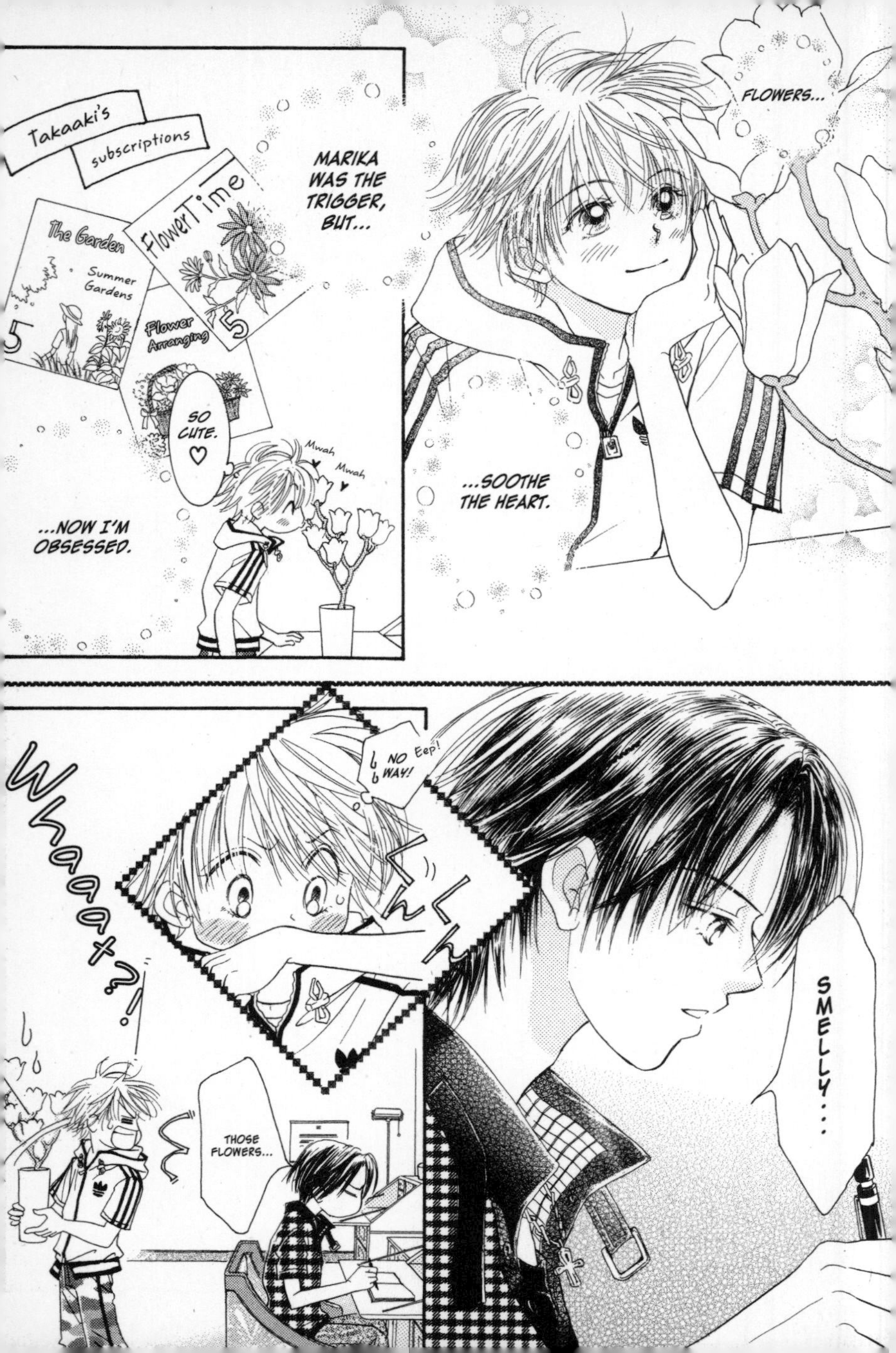
FLOWERS...
...SOOTHE THE HEART.
Takaaki's subscriptions
MARIKA WAS THE TRIGGER, BUT...
FlowerTime 5
The Garden
Summer Gardens
5
Flower Arranging
SO CUTE. ♥
Mwah Mwah
...NOW I'M OBSESSED.
Eep!
NO WAY!
Whaaat?!
SMELLY...
THOSE FLOWERS...

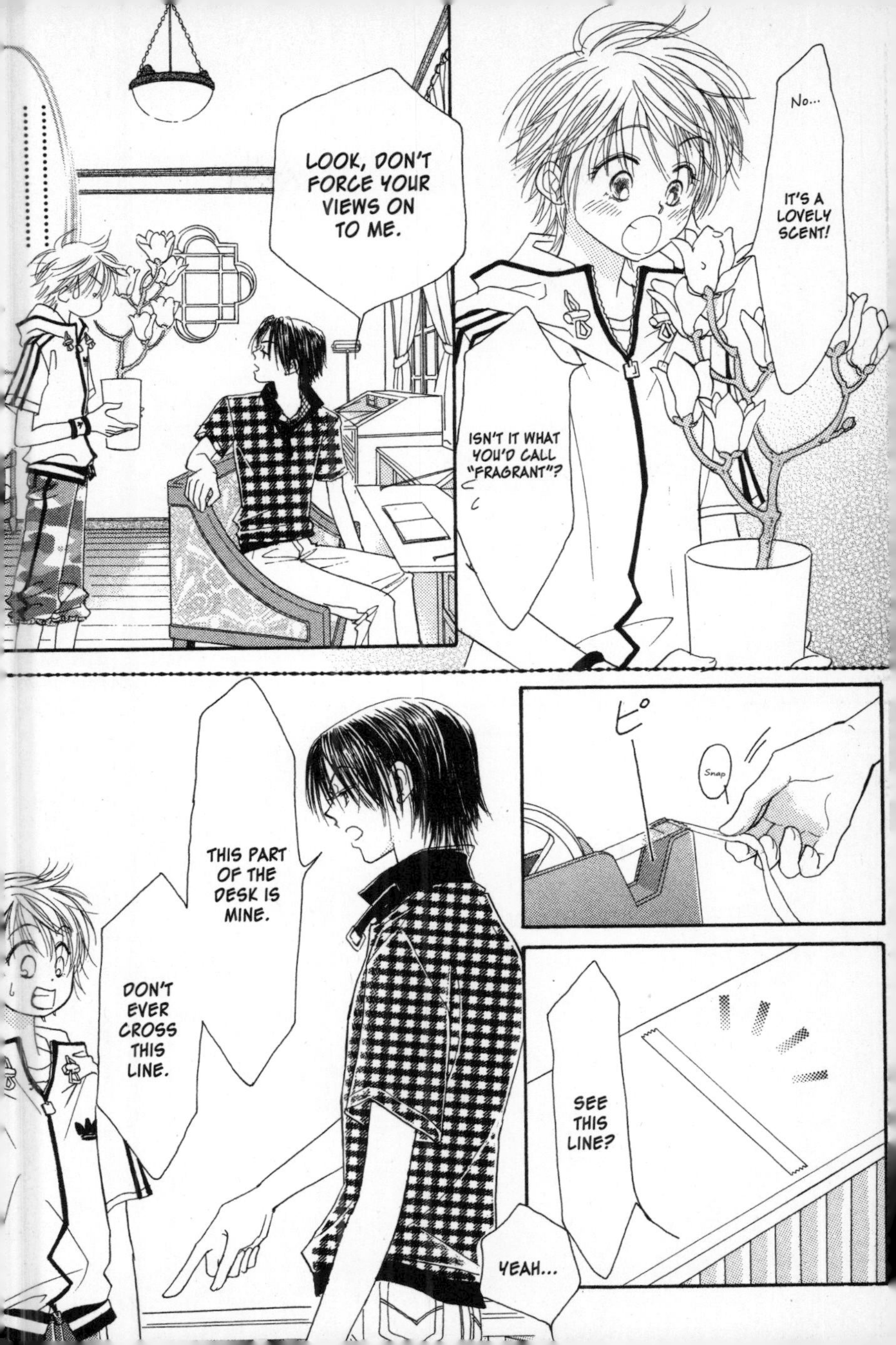
No...
IT'S A LOVELY SCENT!
ISN'T IT WHAT YOU'D CALL "FRAGRANT"?
LOOK, DON'T FORCE YOUR VIEWS ON TO ME.
ピ
Snap
SEE THIS LINE?
YEAH...
THIS PART OF THE DESK IS MINE.
DON'T EVER CROSS THIS LINE.

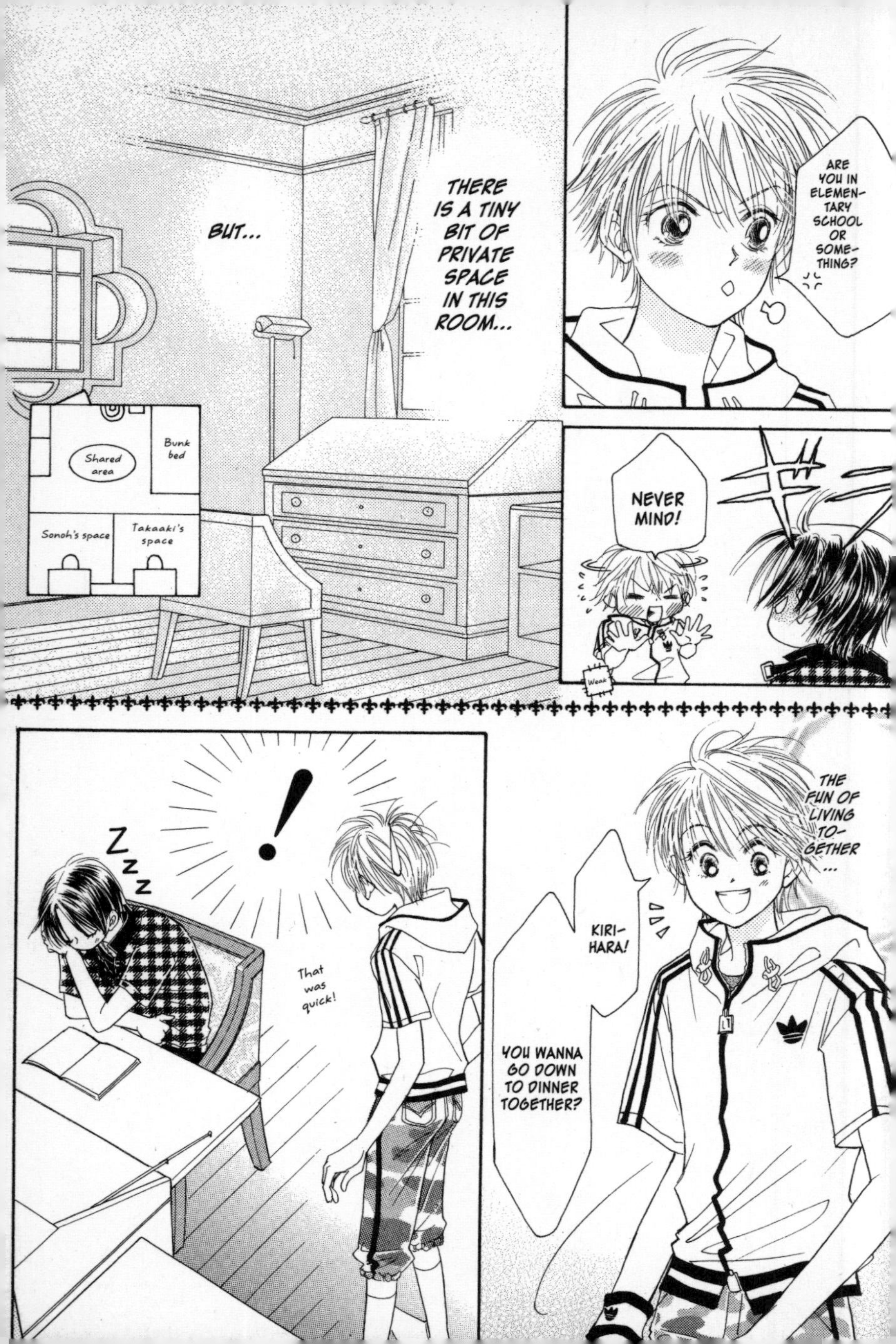
ARE YOU IN ELEMENTARY SCHOOL OR SOMETHING?
NEVER MIND!
Weak
THERE IS A TINY BIT OF PRIVATE SPACE IN THIS ROOM...
BUT...
Bunk bed
Shared area
Sonoh's space
Takaaki's space
THE FUN OF LIVING TOGETHER...
KIRIHARA!
YOU WANNA GO DOWN TO DINNER TOGETHER?
!
ZZZ
That was quick!

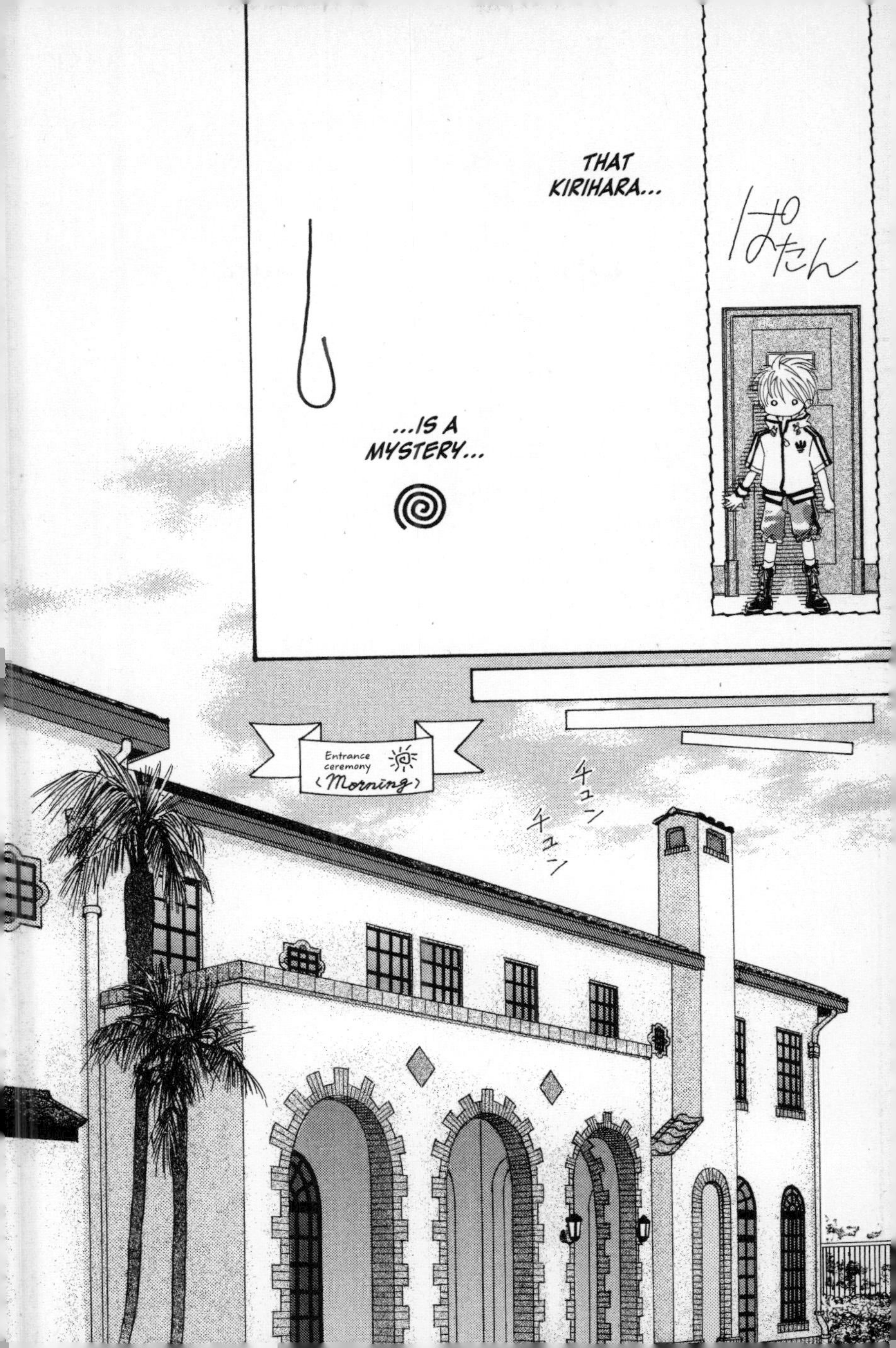
ぱたん
THAT KIRIHARA...
...IS A MYSTERY...
Entrance ceremony ‹Morning›
チュン
チュン

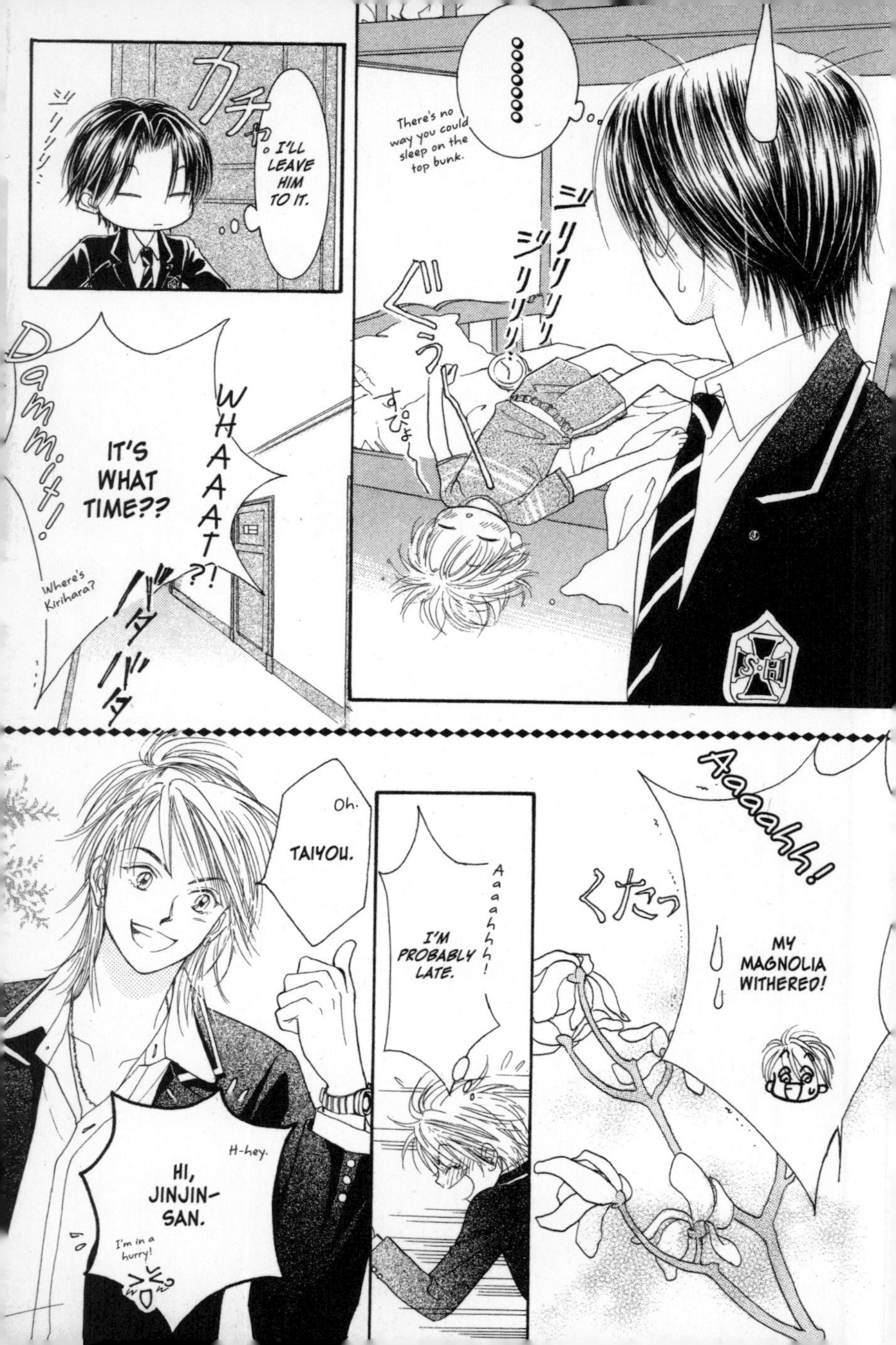

There's no way you could sleep on the top bunk.
ジリリリリ ジリリリリ
すぴょ~
カチャ
I'LL LEAVE HIM TO IT.
WHAAAAT?!
IT'S WHAT TIME??
Dammit!
Where's Kirihara?
バタバタ
Aaaahh!
くたっ
MY MAGNOLIA WITHERED!
Aaaahhh!
I'M PROBABLY LATE.
Oh.
TAIYOU.
H-hey.
HI, JINJIN-SAN.
I'm in a hurry!

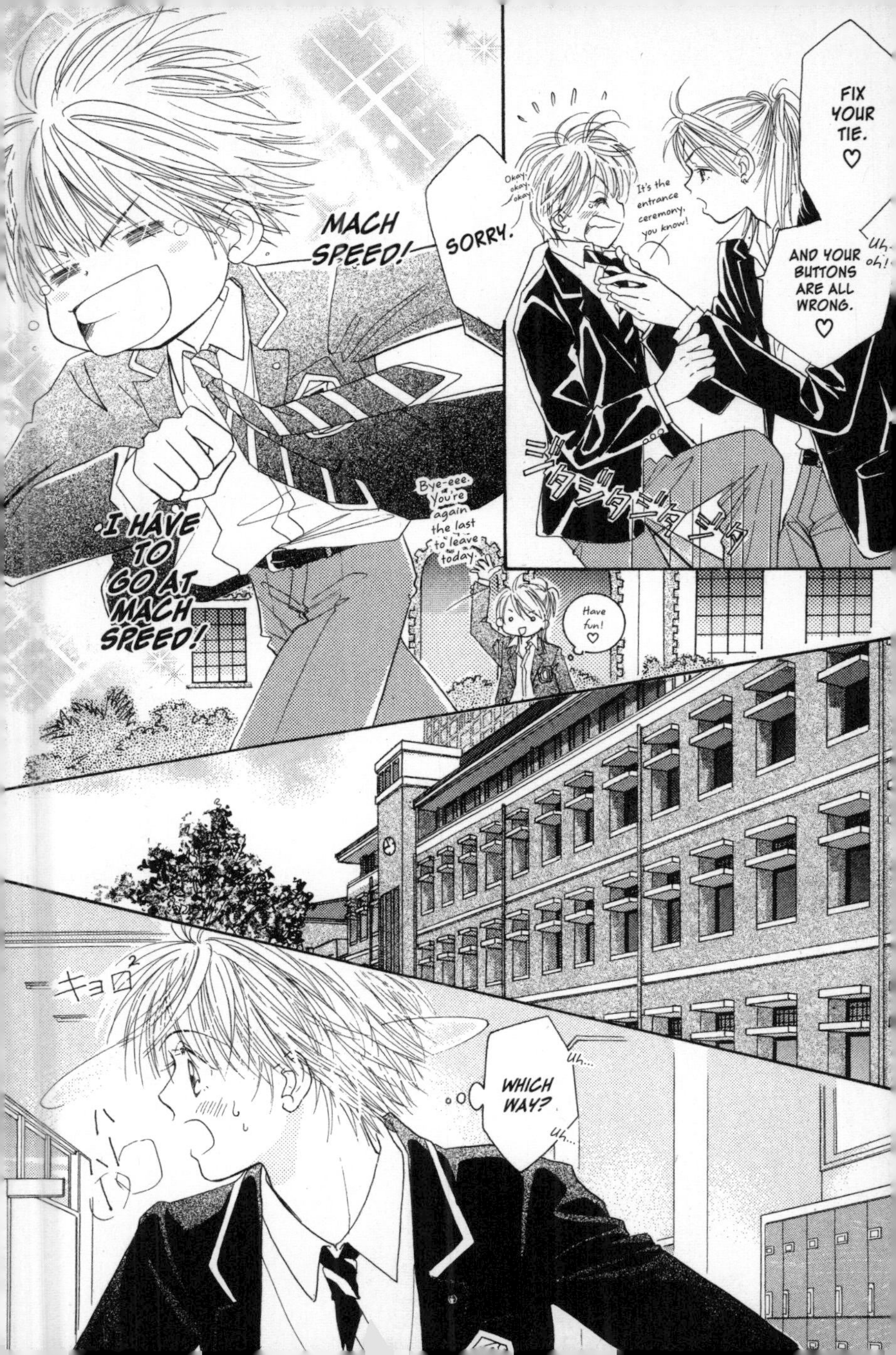
FIX YOUR TIE. ♡
Uh-oh!
AND YOUR BUTTONS ARE ALL WRONG. ♡
It's the entrance ceremony, you know!
Okay, okay, okay.
SORRY.
MACH SPEED!
I HAVE TO GO AT MACH SPEED!
Bye-eee. You're again the last to leave today.
Have fun! ♡
キョロ^2
Uh...
WHICH WAY?
Uh...

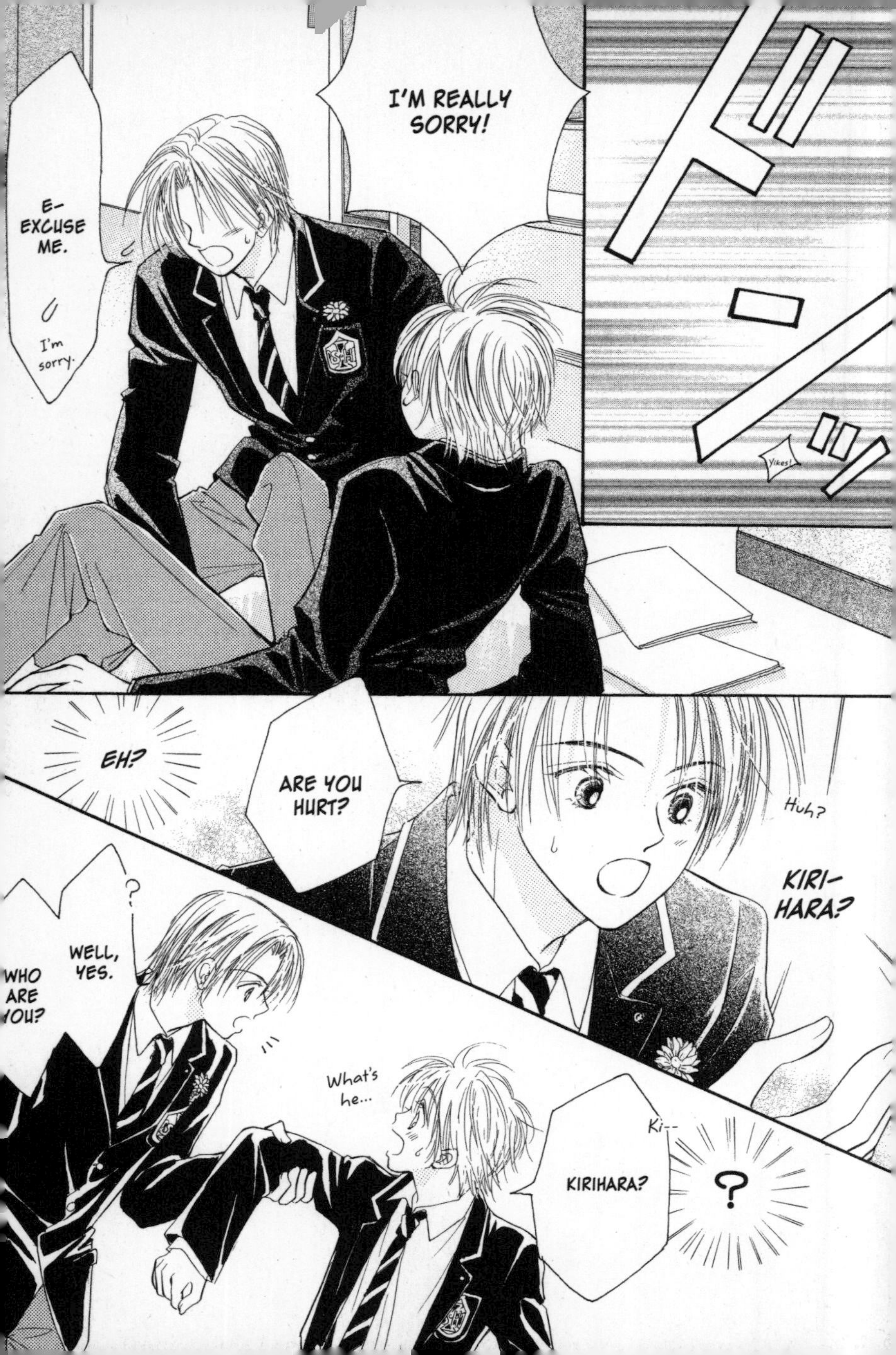
Yikes!
I'M REALLY SORRY!
E-EXCUSE ME.
I'm sorry.
Huh?
KIRI-HARA?
ARE YOU HURT?
EH?
KIRIHARA?
Ki--
?
What's he...
WELL, YES.
WHO ARE YOU?

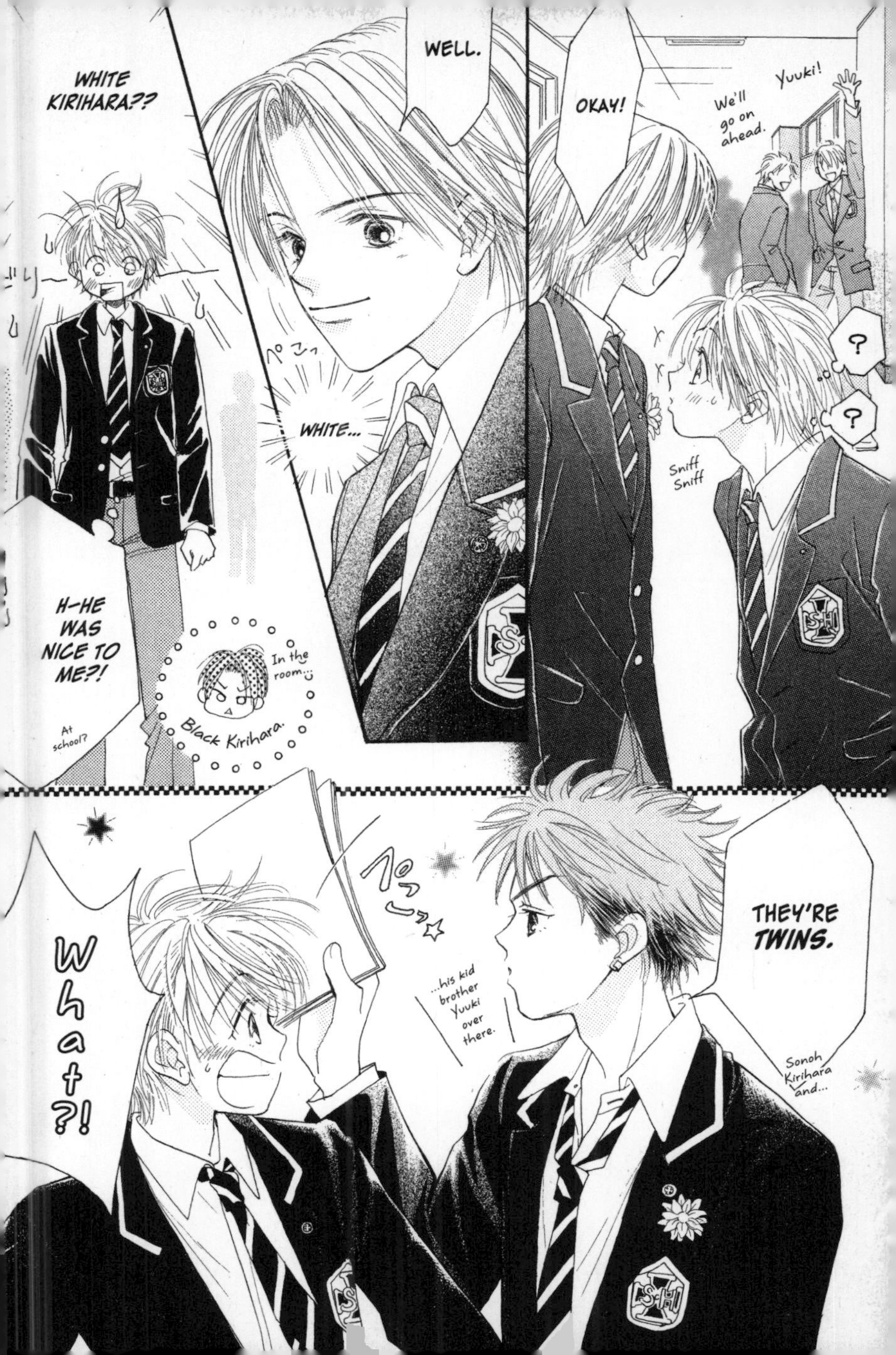
OKAY!
Yuuki!
We'll go on ahead.
Sniff Sniff
?
?
WELL.
WHITE...
WHITE KIRIHARA??
H-HE WAS NICE TO ME?!
At school?
In the room...
Black Kirihara.
Sonoh Kirihara and...
...his kid brother Yuuki over there.
THEY'RE TWINS.
What?!

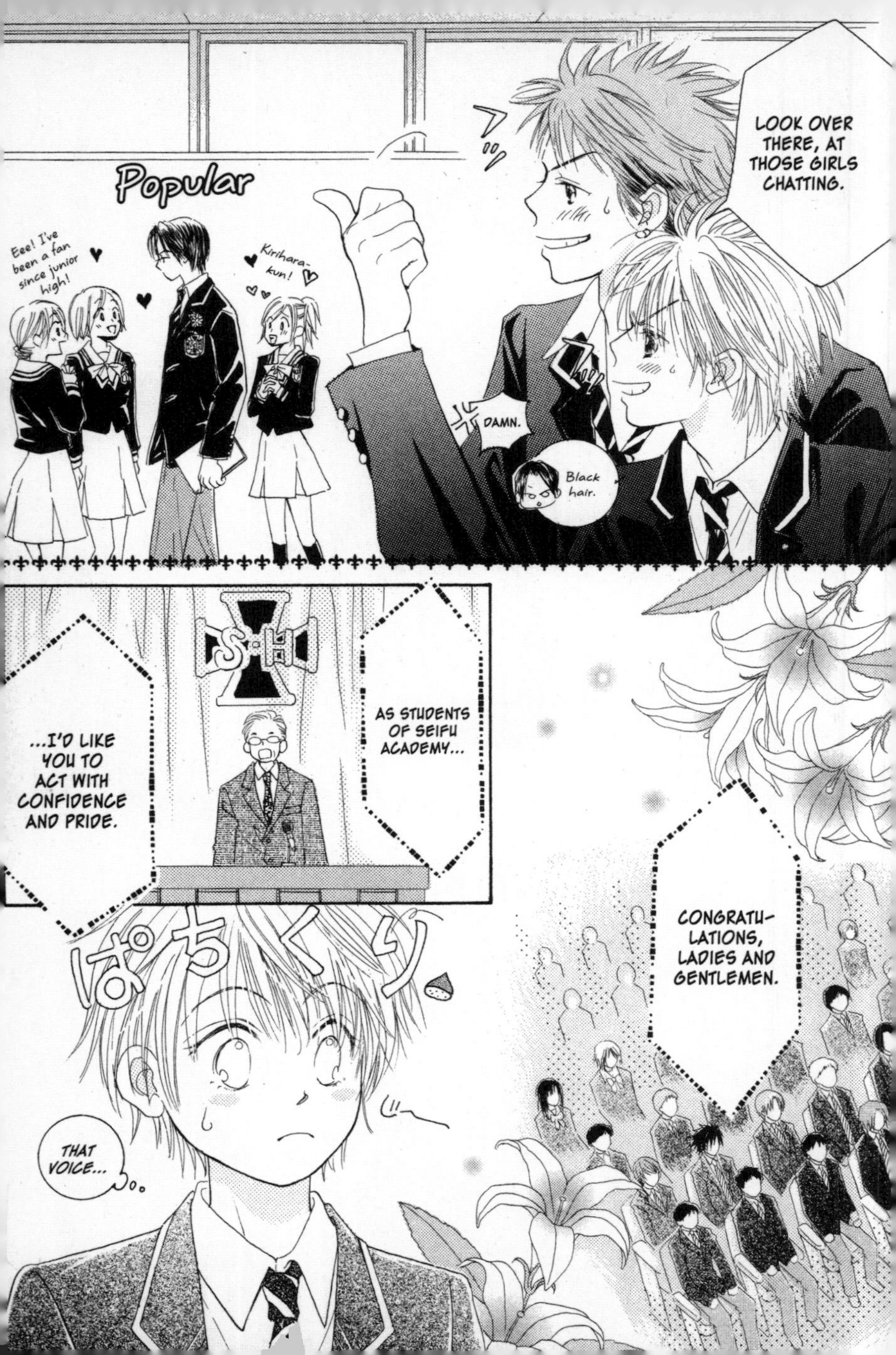
LOOK OVER THERE, AT THOSE GIRLS CHATTING.
DAMN.
Black hair.
Popular
Kirihara-kun!
Eee! I've been a fan since junior high!
CONGRATULATIONS, LADIES AND GENTLEMEN.
AS STUDENTS OF SEIFU ACADEMY...
...I'D LIKE YOU TO ACT WITH CONFIDENCE AND PRIDE.
ぱちくり
THAT VOICE...

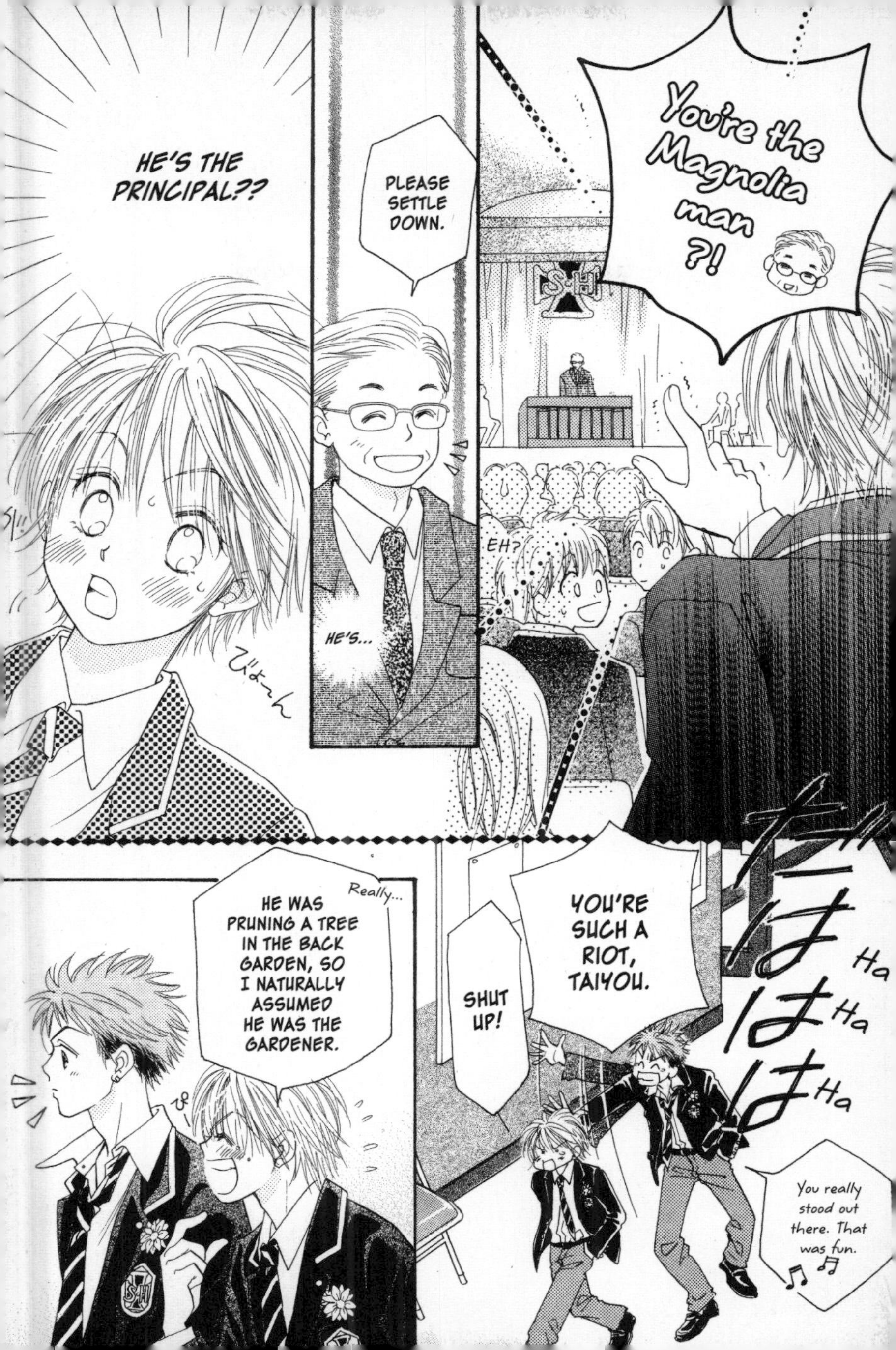

You're the Magnolia man ?!
EH?
PLEASE SETTLE DOWN.
HE'S...
HE'S THE PRINCIPAL??
Ha Ha Ha
YOU'RE SUCH A RIOT, TAIYOU.
SHUT UP!
You really stood out there. That was fun.
Really...
HE WAS PRUNING A TREE IN THE BACK GARDEN, SO I NATURALLY ASSUMED HE WAS THE GARDENER.

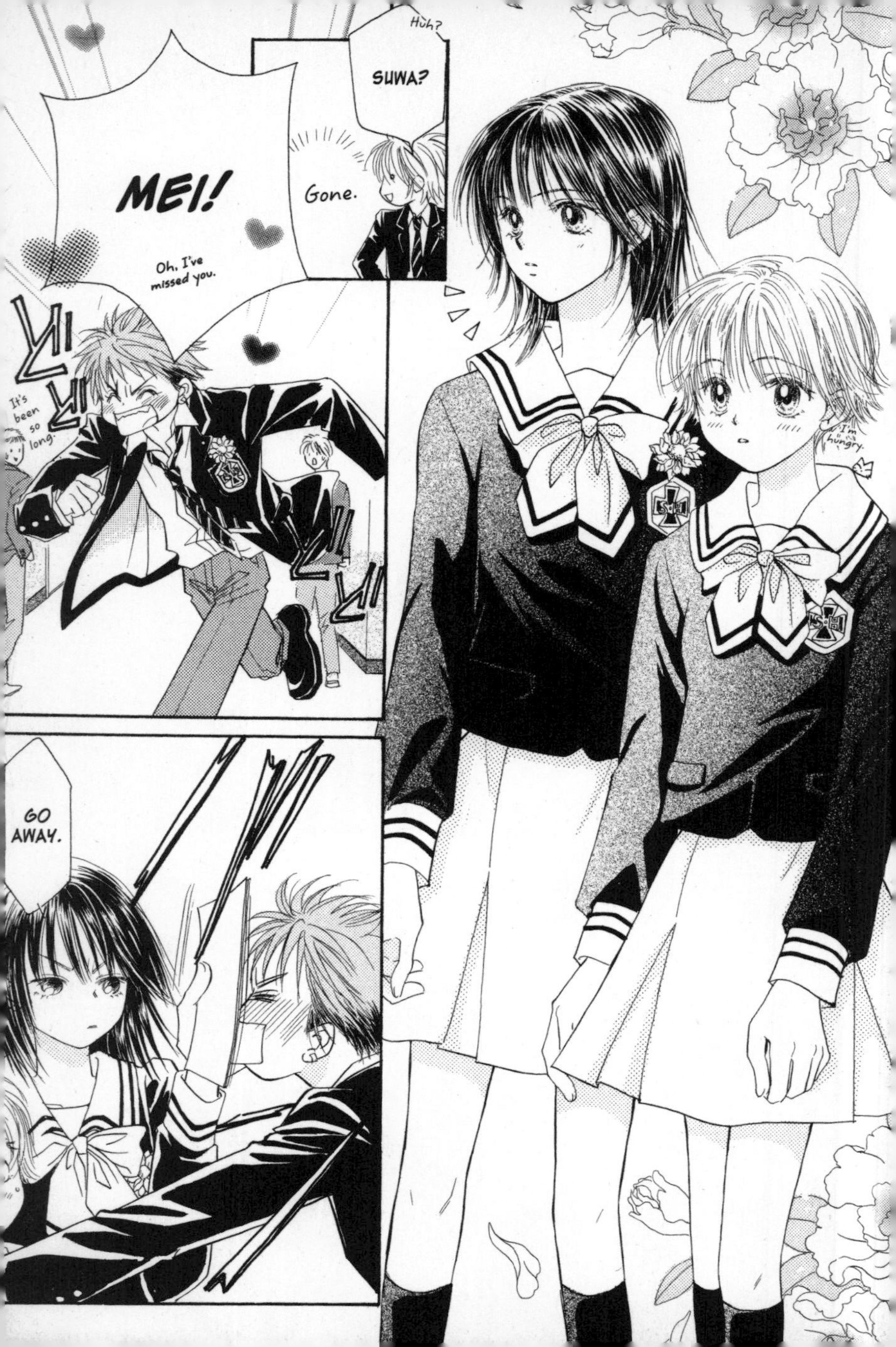
I'm hungry.
Huh?
SUWA?
Gone.
MEI!
Oh, I've missed you.
It's been so long.
GO AWAY.

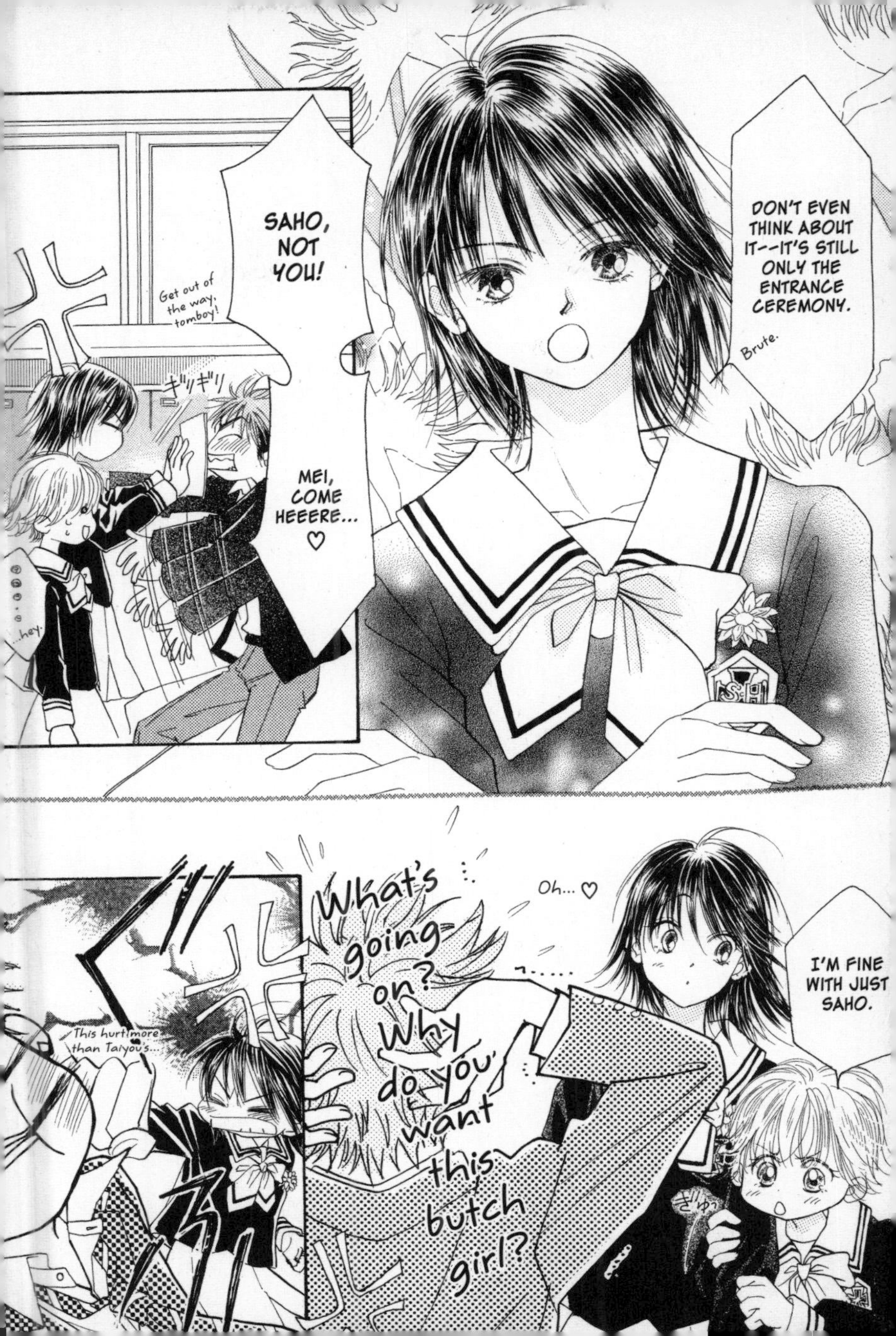
DON'T EVEN THINK ABOUT IT--IT'S STILL ONLY THE ENTRANCE CEREMONY.
Brute.
SAHO, NOT YOU!
Get out of the way, tomboy!
MEI, COME HEEERE... ♡
...hey.
I'M FINE WITH JUST SAHO.
Oh... ♡
What's going on? Why do you want this butch girl?
This hurt more than Taiyou's...

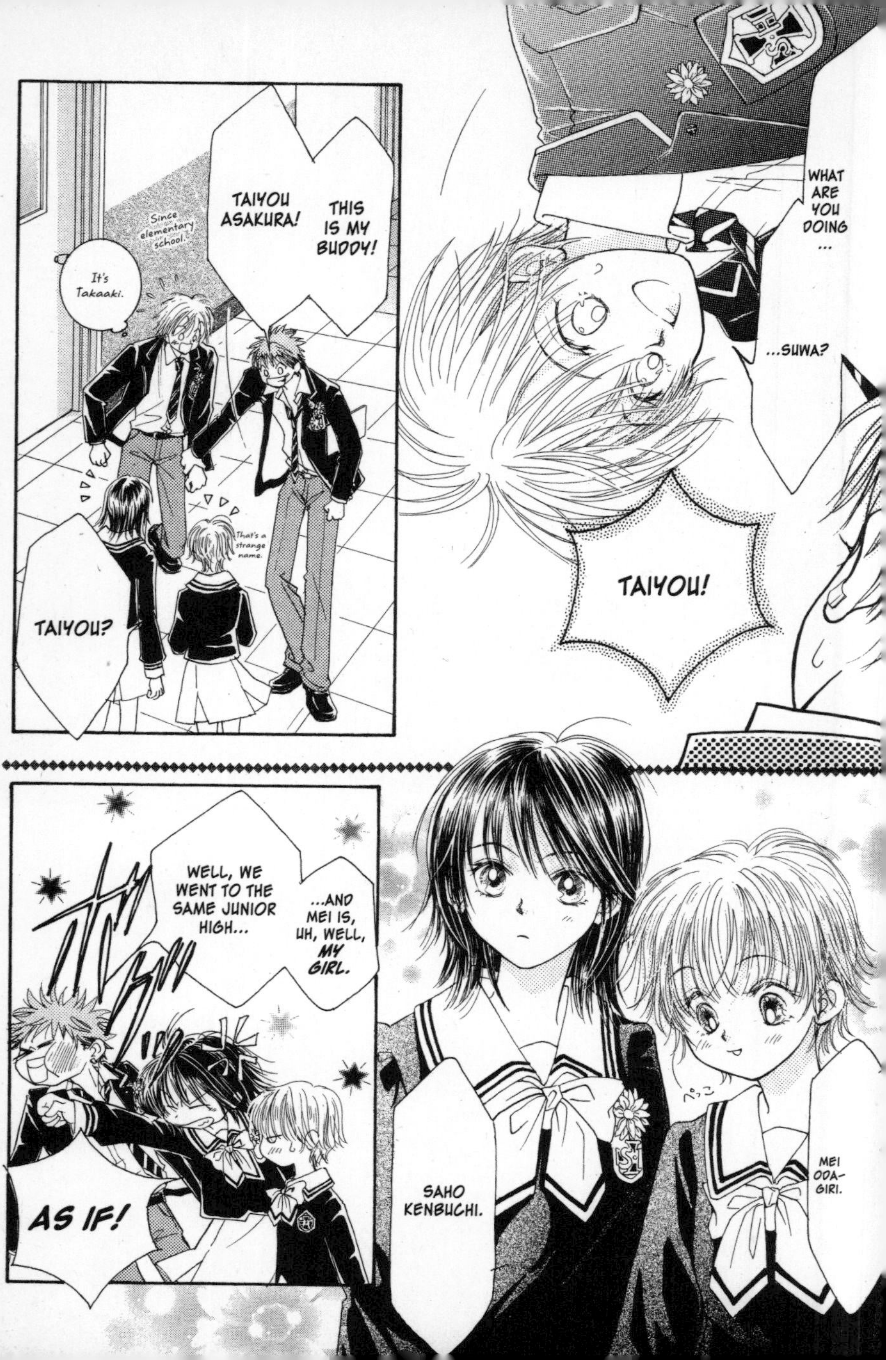
WHAT ARE YOU DOING ...
...SUWA?
TAIYOU!
TAIYOU ASAKURA!
THIS IS MY BUDDY!
Since elementary school.
It's Takaaki.
That's a strange name.
TAIYOU?
MEI ODA-GIRI.
SAHO KENBUCHI.
WELL, WE WENT TO THE SAME JUNIOR HIGH...
...AND MEI IS, UH, WELL, MY GIRL.
AS IF!

Hello,

this is Nakaji.

Long time no see!

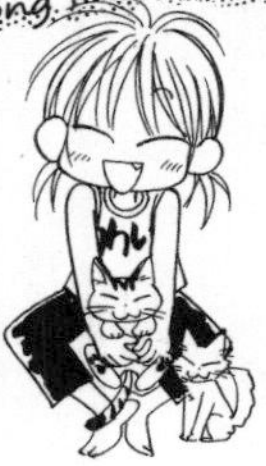

Have you been well? Thank you very much for picking up the first volume of Zig☆Zag. This is actually my first comic in nine months. It's been a while since I've drawn uniforms, which was fun. ♡ (Announcement: I think I'd like to draw the other versions of uniforms I haven't used yet.) ♡

¼ Space

Contents

1. Characters who's who #1
   Taiyou-kun, of course.
2. Characters who's who #2
   This is maybe...Sonoh.
3. Caramel Paradise.

Side ¼ Bookmark x 2
Accessory Road 1

Supplement:
Caramel photo showcase III

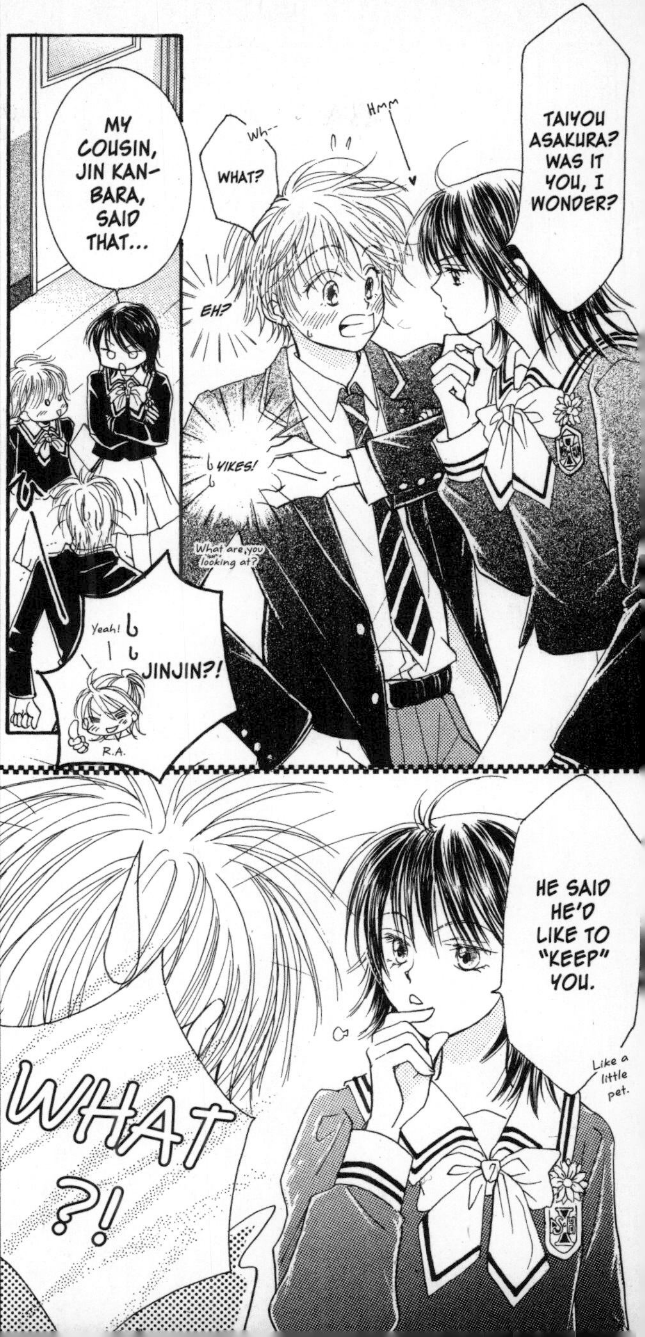
TAIYOU ASAKURA? WAS IT YOU, I WONDER?
HMM
Wh-- WHAT?
EH?
YIKES!
What are you looking at?
MY COUSIN, JIN KANBARA, SAID THAT...
Yeah!
JINJIN?!
R.A.
HE SAID HE'D LIKE TO "KEEP" YOU.
Like a little pet.
WHAT?!

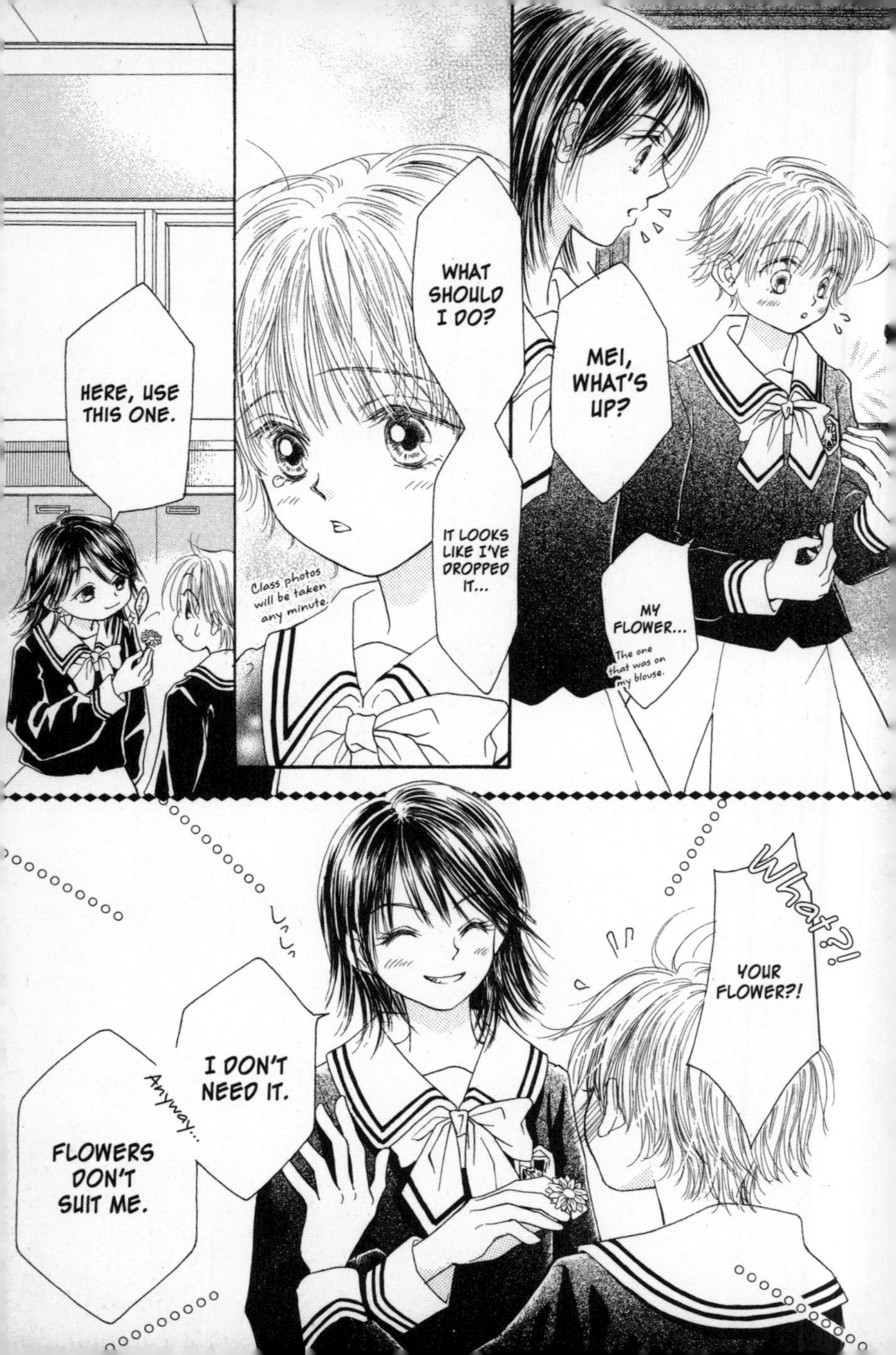
MEI, WHAT'S UP?
MY FLOWER...
The one that was on my blouse.
WHAT SHOULD I DO?
IT LOOKS LIKE I'VE DROPPED IT...
Class photos will be taken any minute.
HERE, USE THIS ONE.
What?!
YOUR FLOWER?!
I DON'T NEED IT.
Anyway...
FLOWERS DON'T SUIT ME.

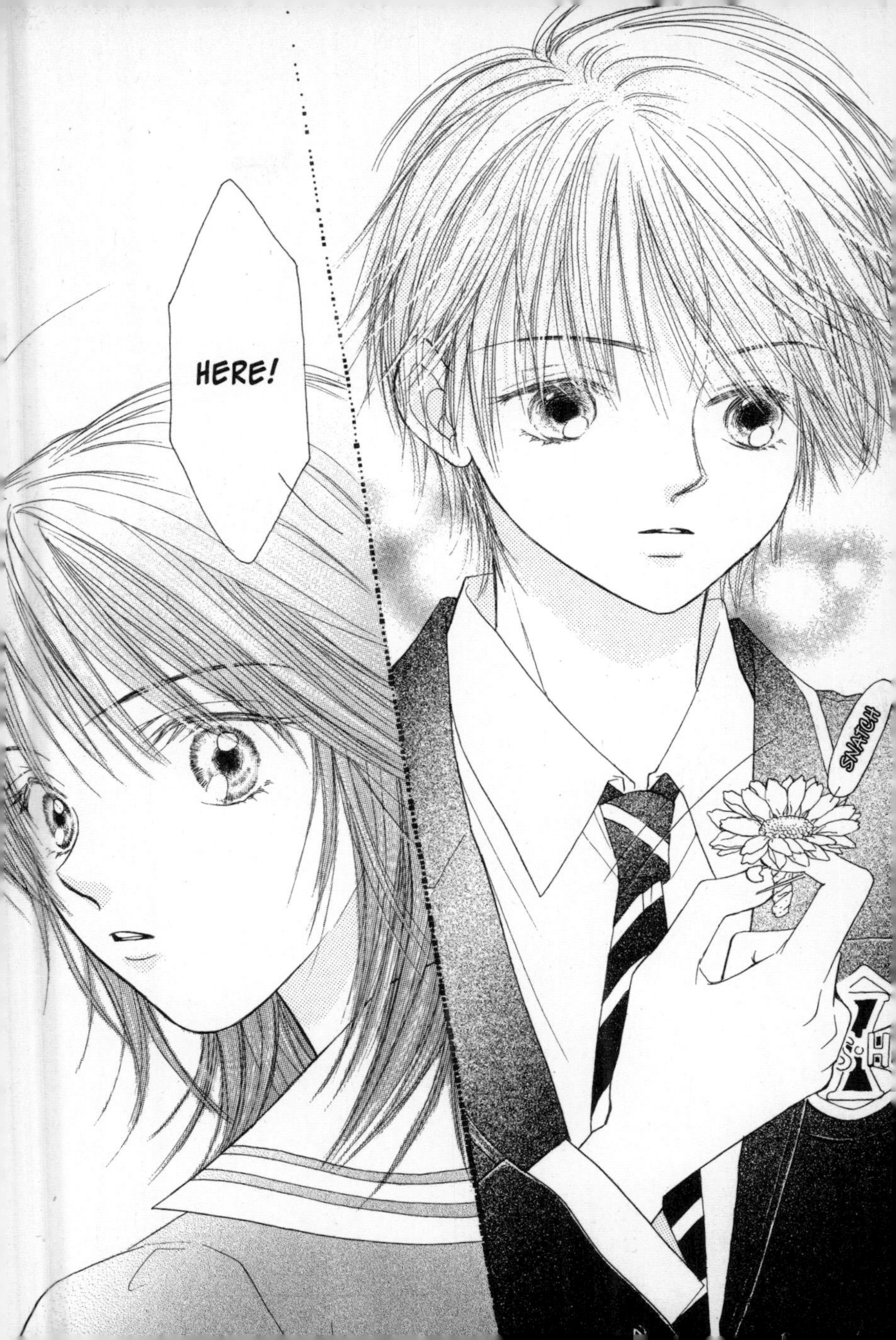
SNATCH
HERE!

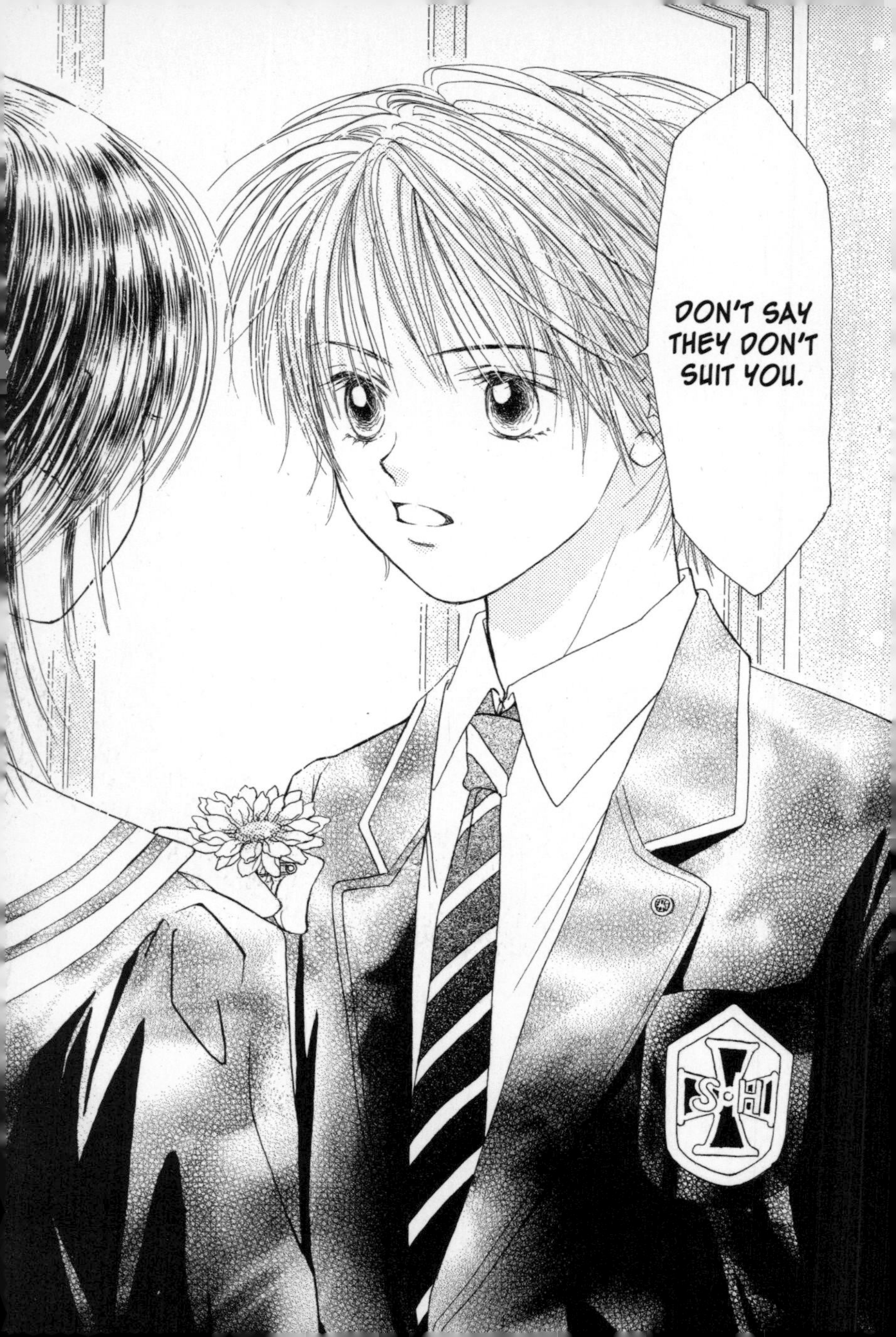
DON'T SAY THEY DON'T SUIT YOU.

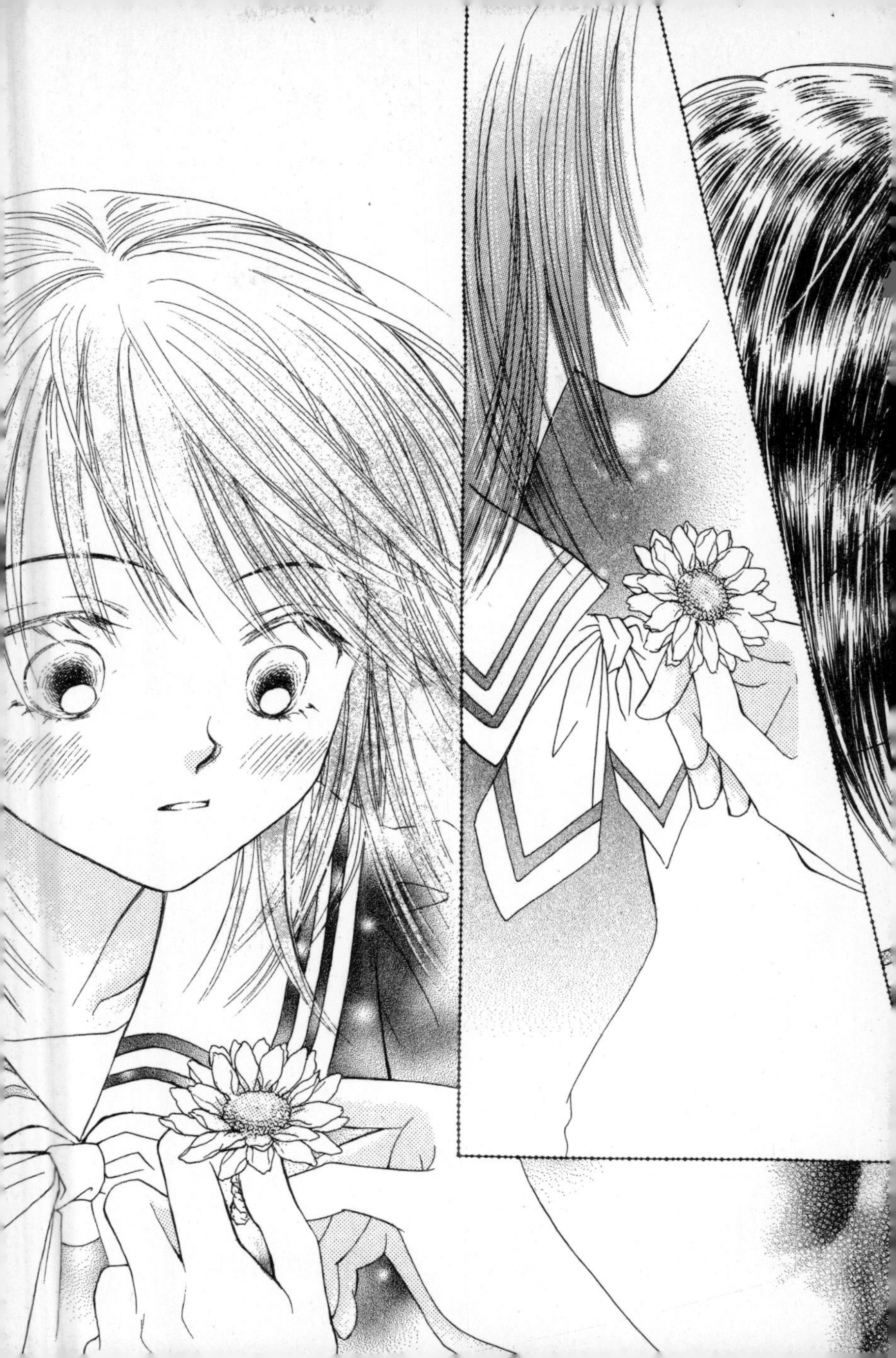

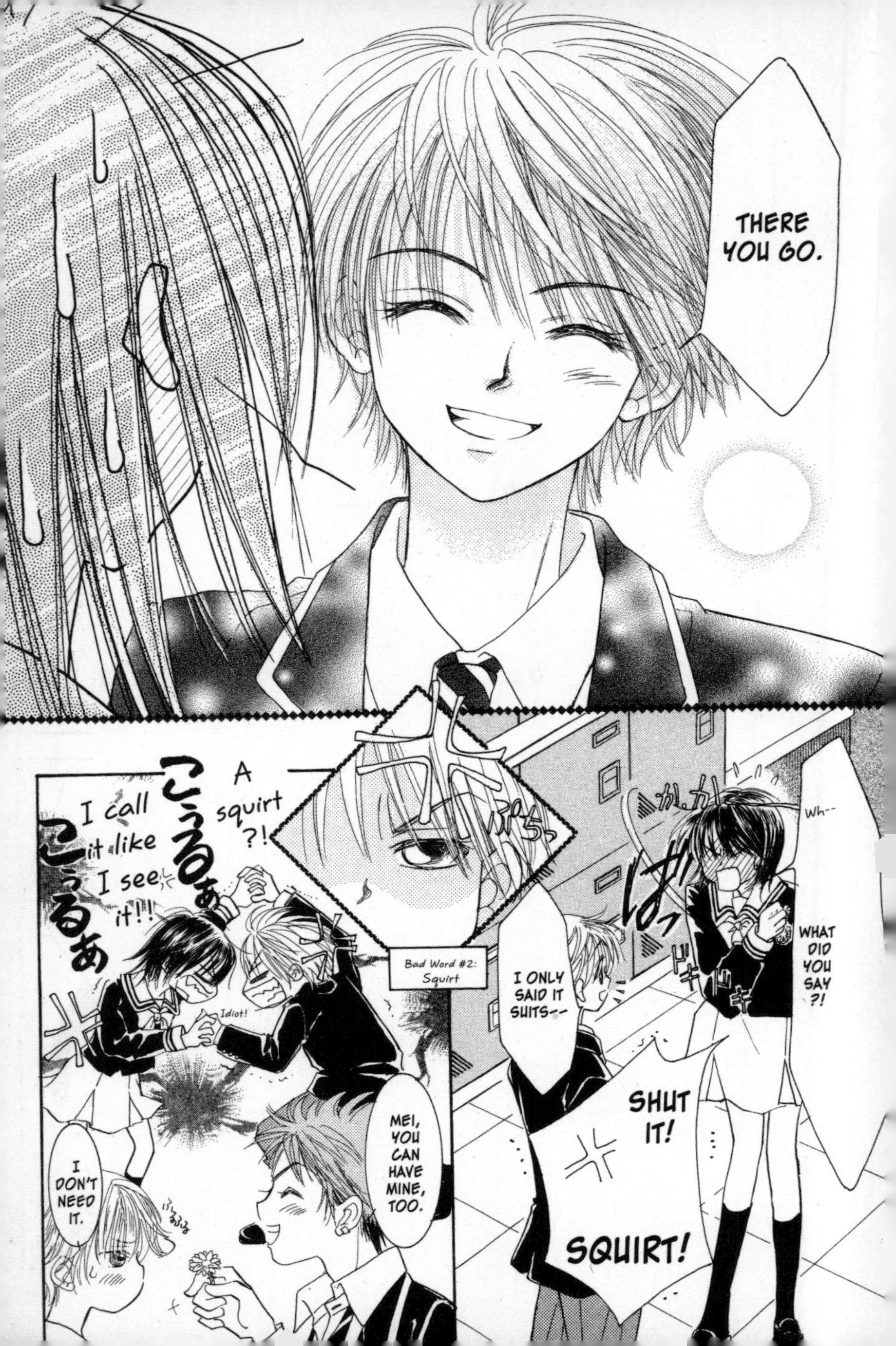

THERE YOU GO.
Wh--
WHAT DID YOU SAY ?!
I ONLY SAID IT SUITS--
SHUT IT!
SQUIRT!
A squirt ?!
こぅるぁ
I call it like I see it!!
こぅるぁ
Bad Word #2: Squirt
Idiot!
MEI, YOU CAN HAVE MINE, TOO.
I DON'T NEED IT.

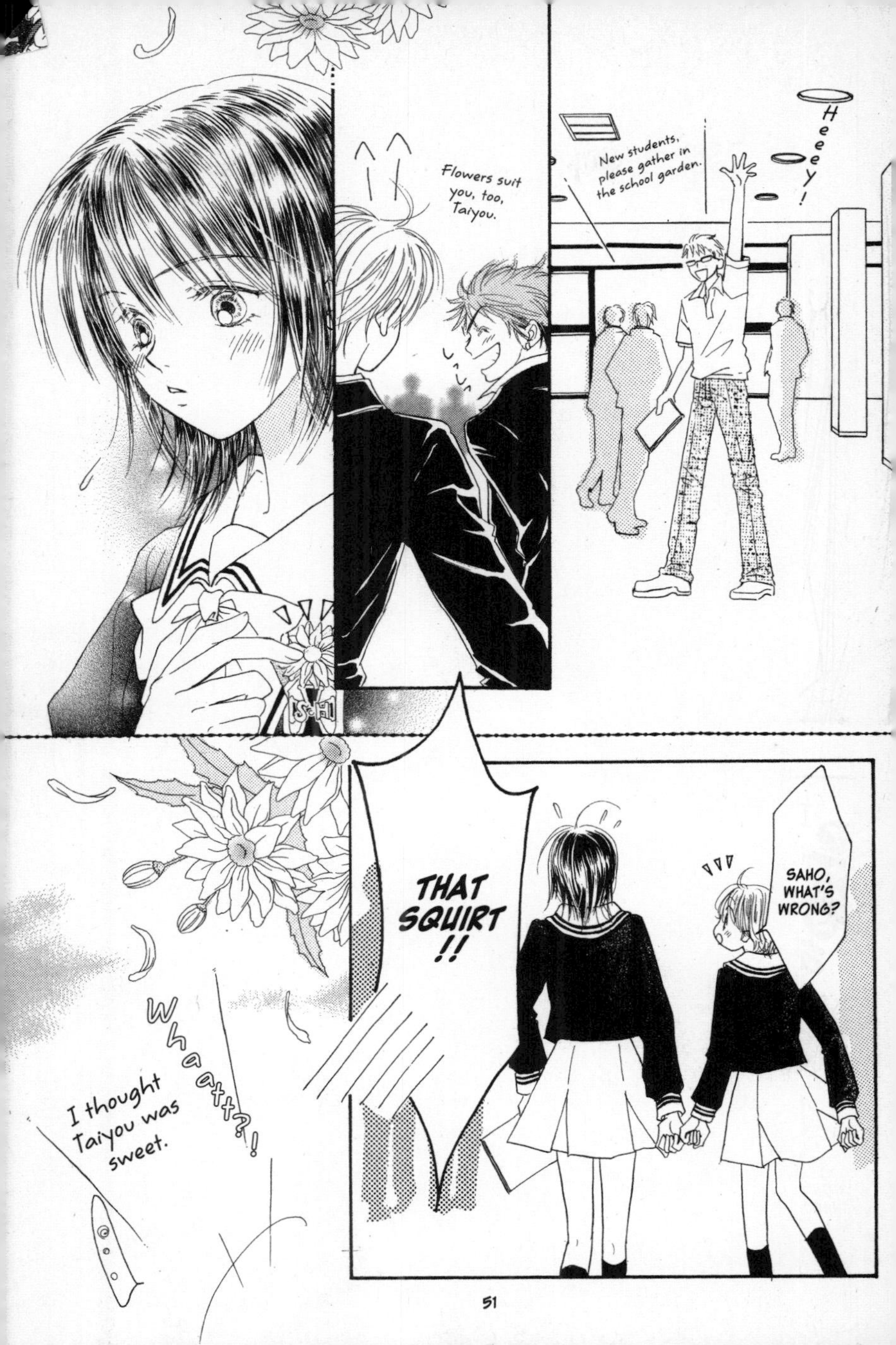
Heeey!
New students, please gather in the school garden.
Flowers suit you, too, Taiyou.
SAHO, WHAT'S WRONG?
THAT SQUIRT!!
Whaatt?!
I thought Taiyou was sweet.

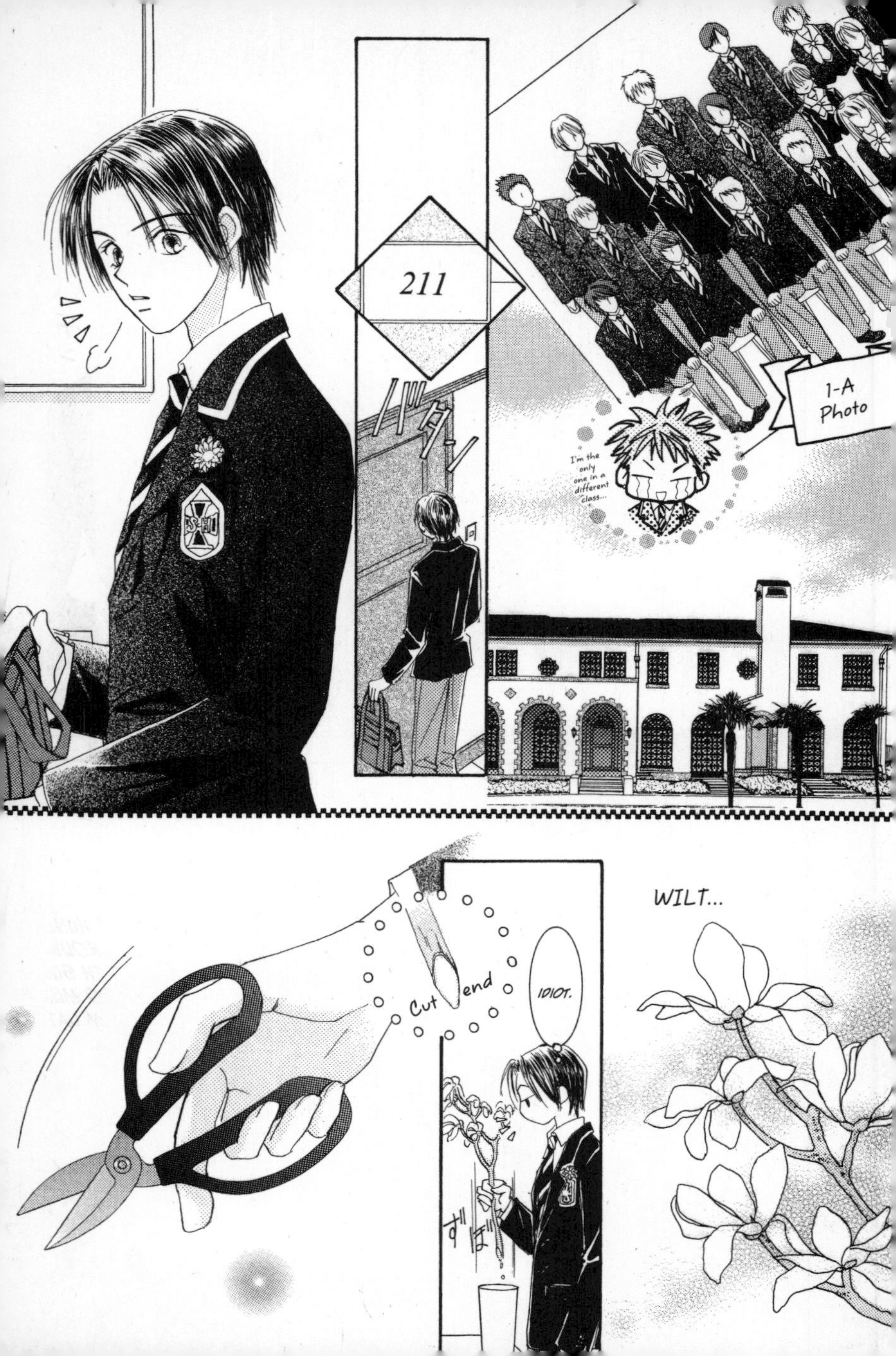
1-A Photo
I'm the only one in a different class...
211
バターン
WILT...
IDIOT.
Cut end
ずぼ

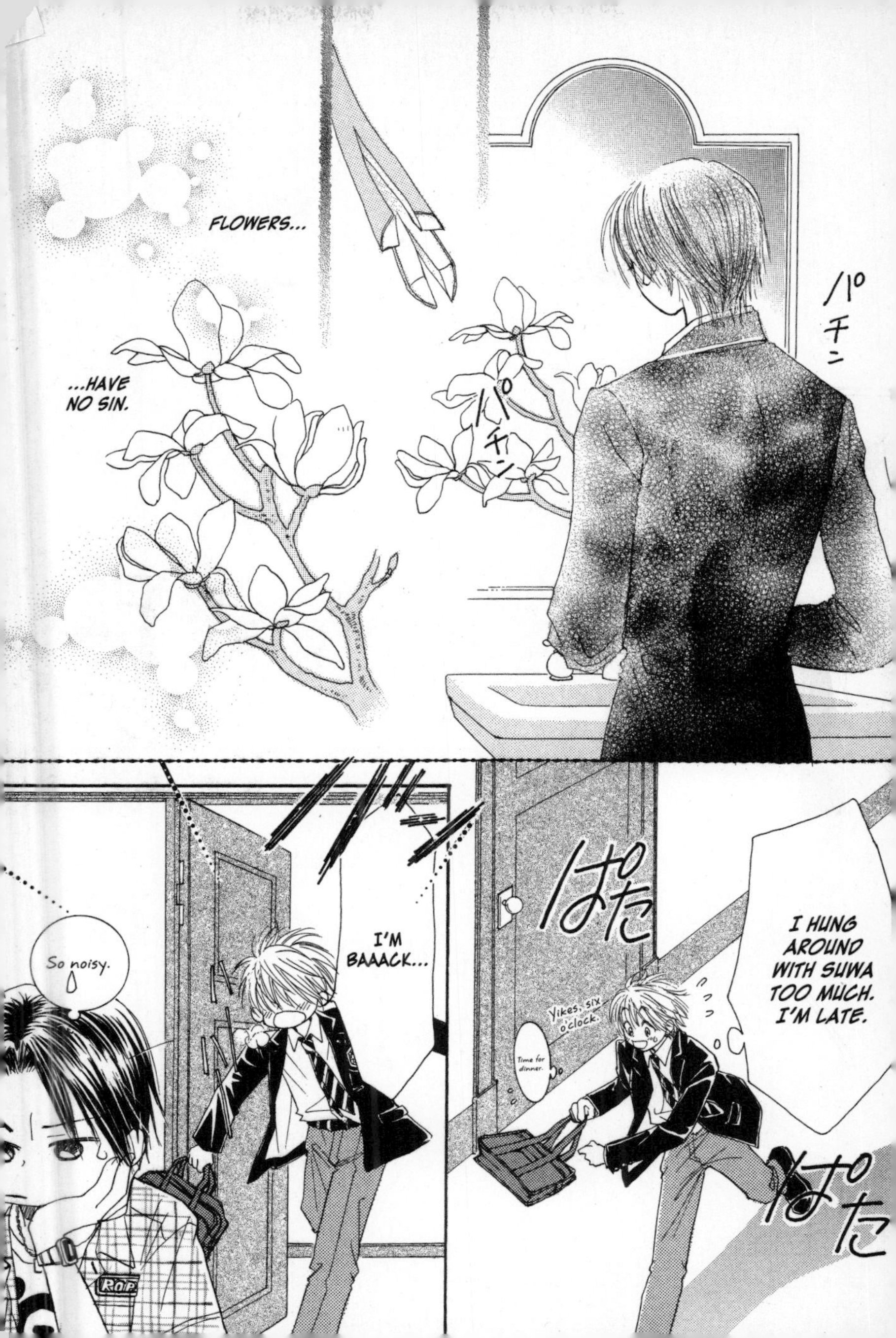

パチン
FLOWERS...
パチン
...HAVE NO SIN.
I HUNG AROUND WITH SUWA TOO MUCH. I'M LATE.
ぱた
Yikes, six o'clock.
Time for dinner.
ぱた
I'M BAAACK...
So noisy.

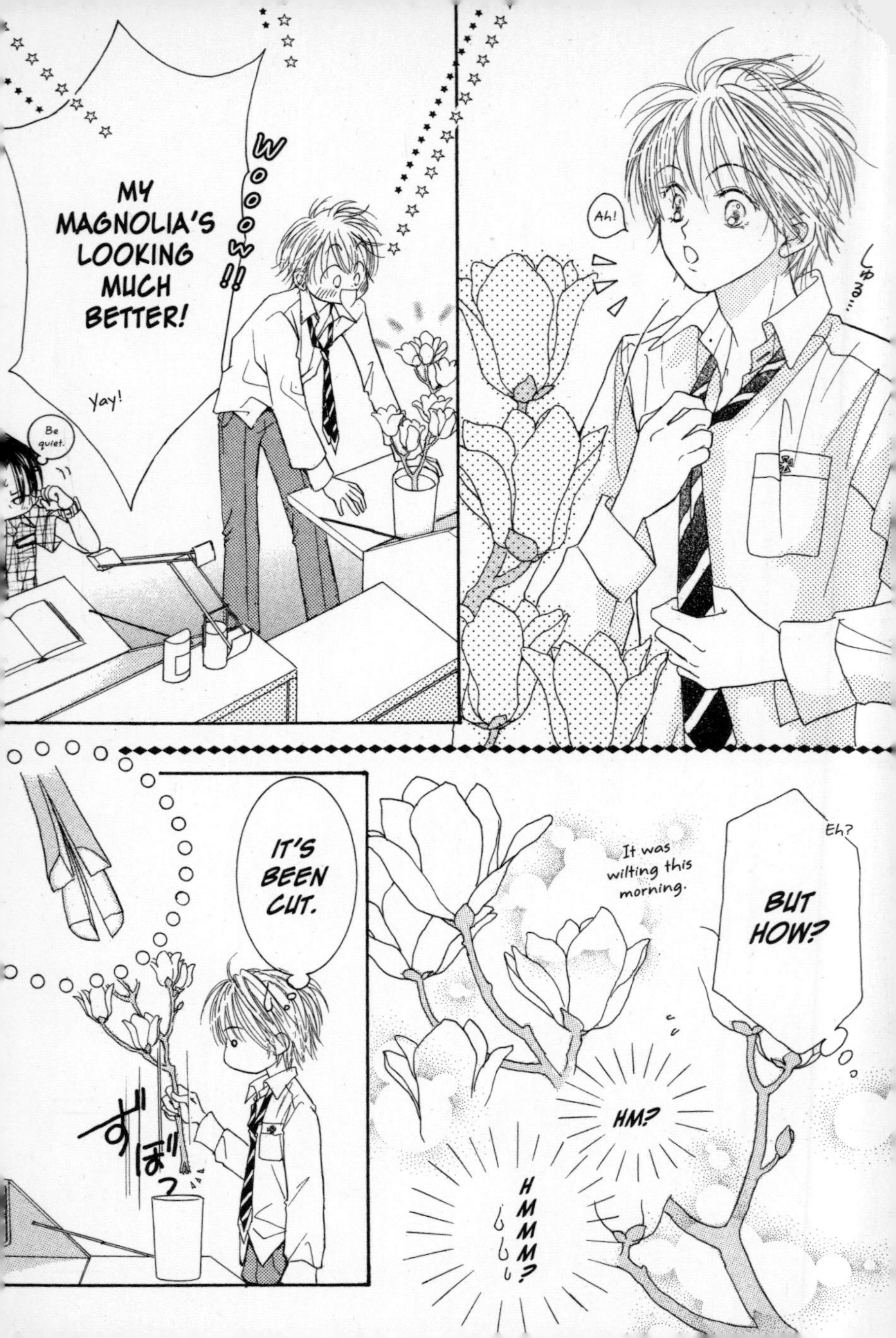
Ah!
しゅる…
MY MAGNOLIA'S LOOKING MUCH BETTER!
WOOOOW!!
Yay!
Be quiet.
Eh?
BUT HOW?
It was wilting this morning.
HM?
HMMM?
IT'S BEEN CUT.
ずぼっ

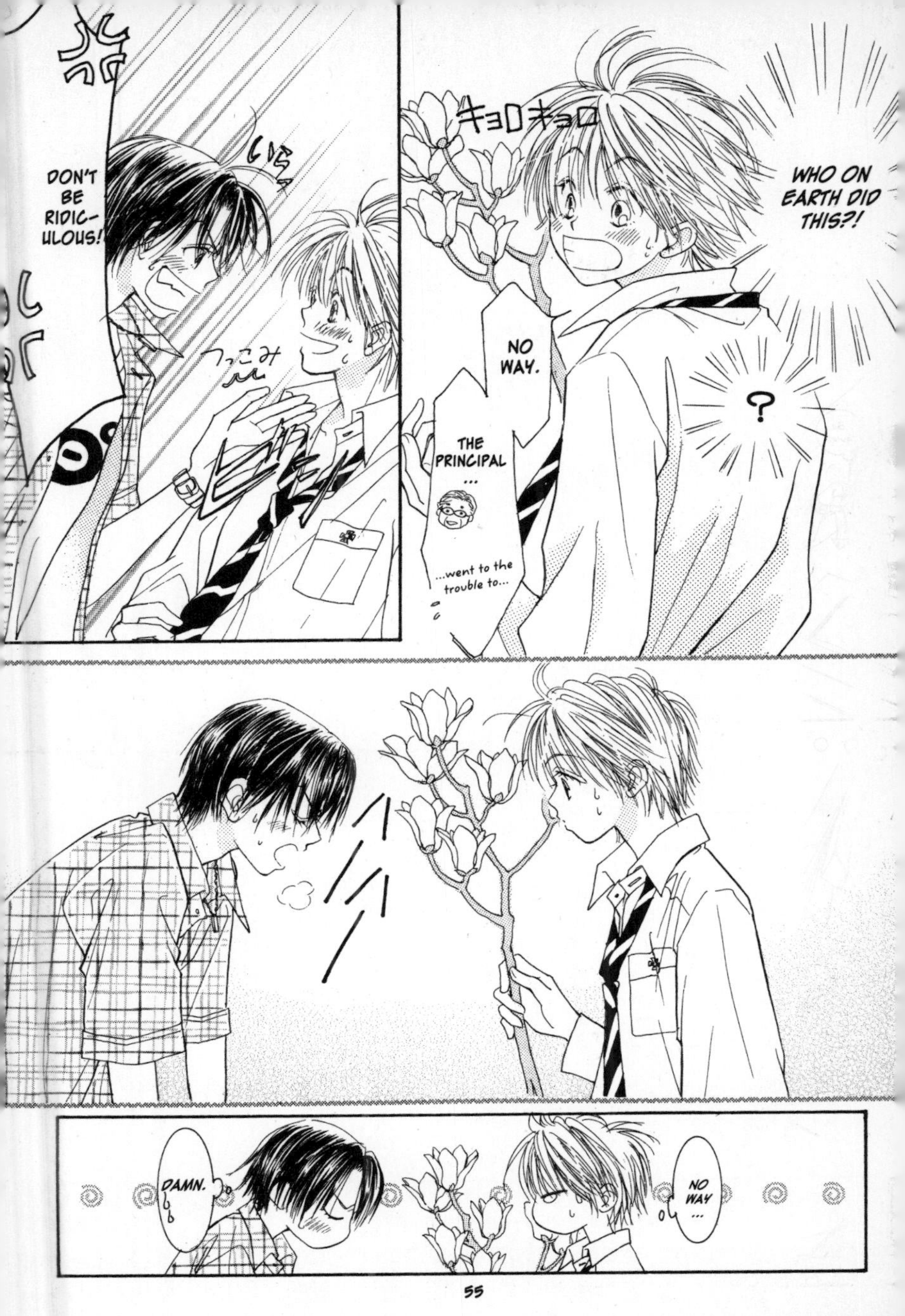

WHO ON EARTH DID THIS?!
キョロキョロ
?
NO WAY.
THE PRINCIPAL ...
...went to the trouble to...
DON'T BE RIDIC-ULOUS!
つっこみ
NO WAY ...
DAMN.

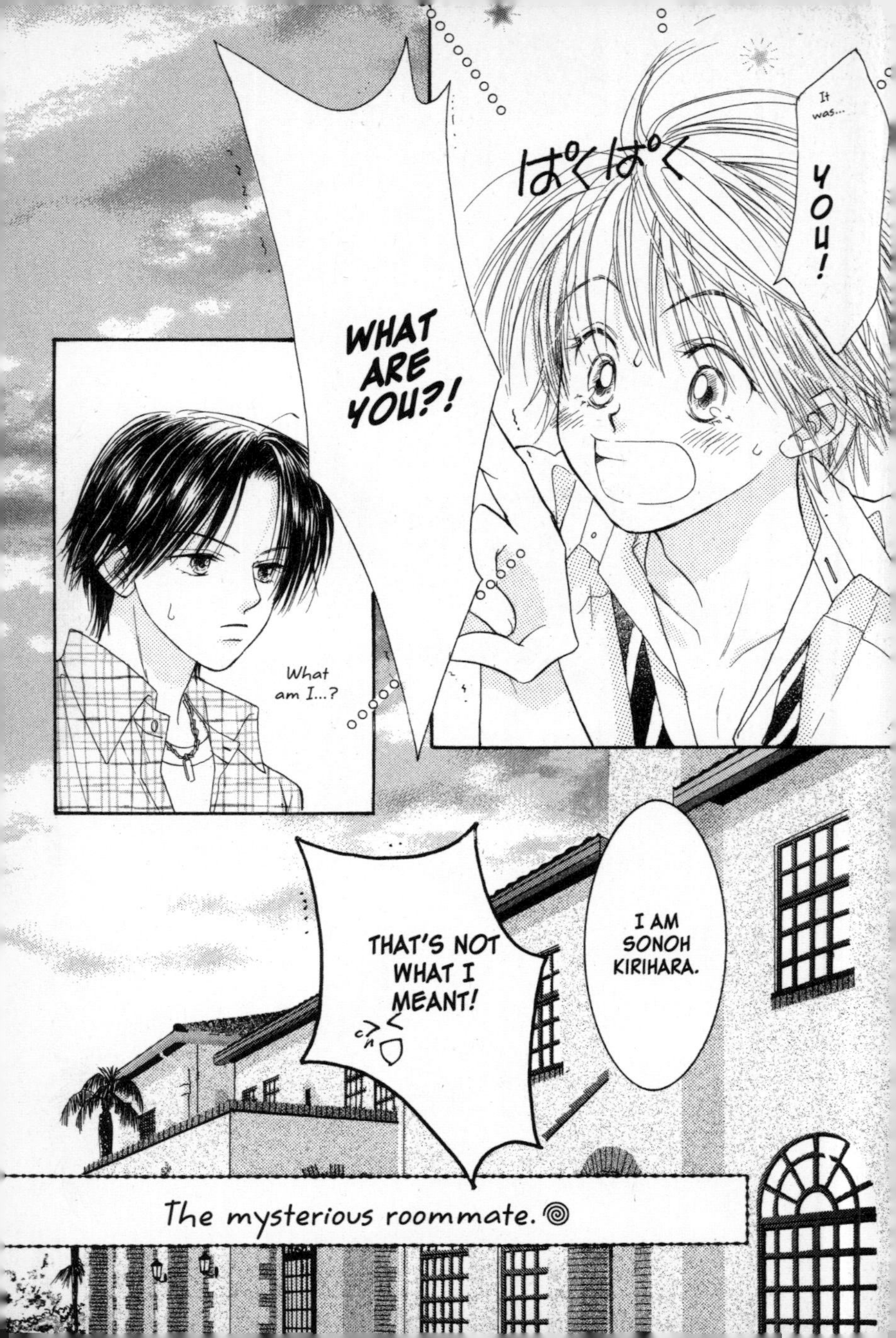
It was... YOU!
ぱくぱく
WHAT ARE YOU?!
What am I...?
I AM SONOH KIRIHARA.
THAT'S NOT WHAT I MEANT!
The mysterious roommate.

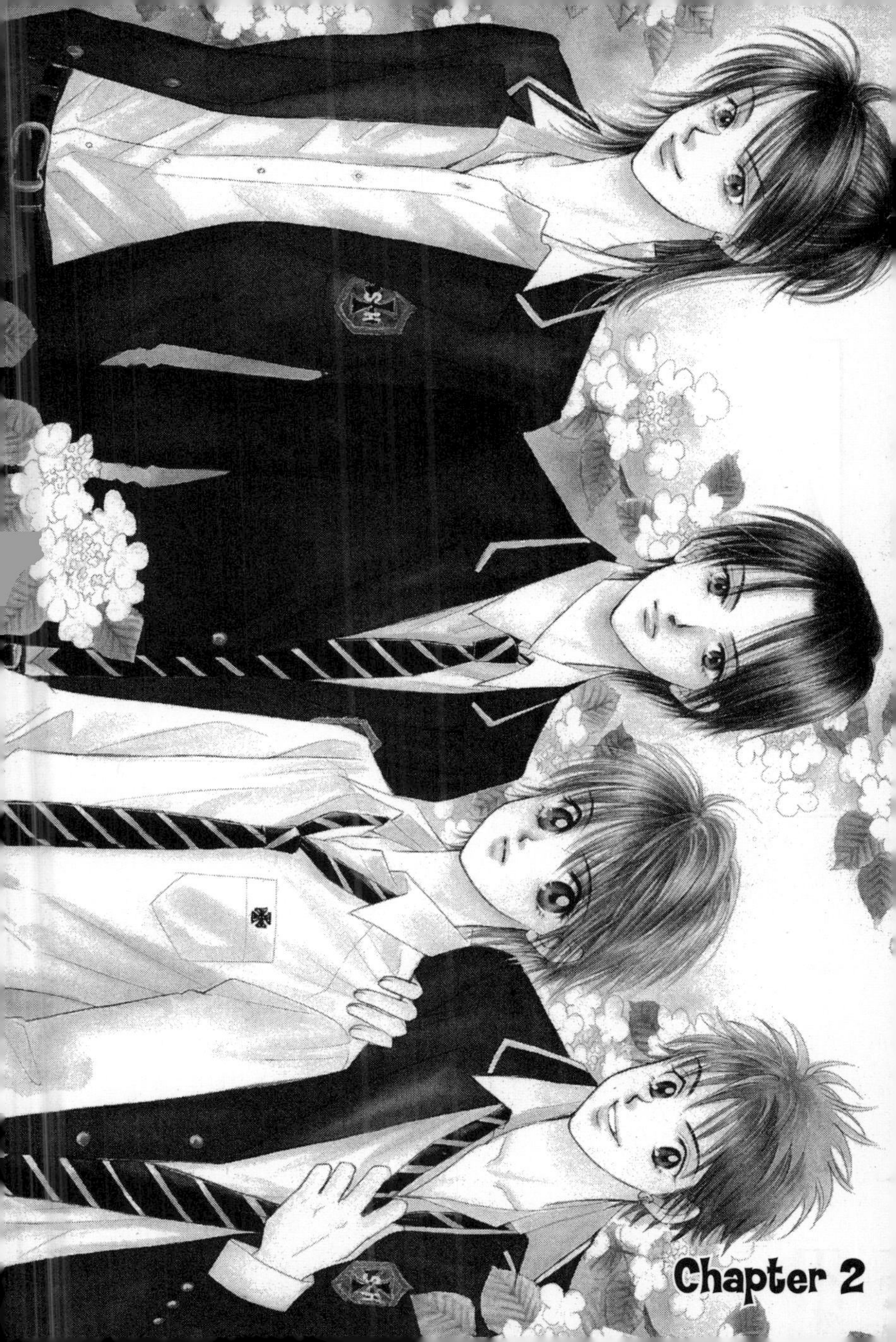
Chapter 2

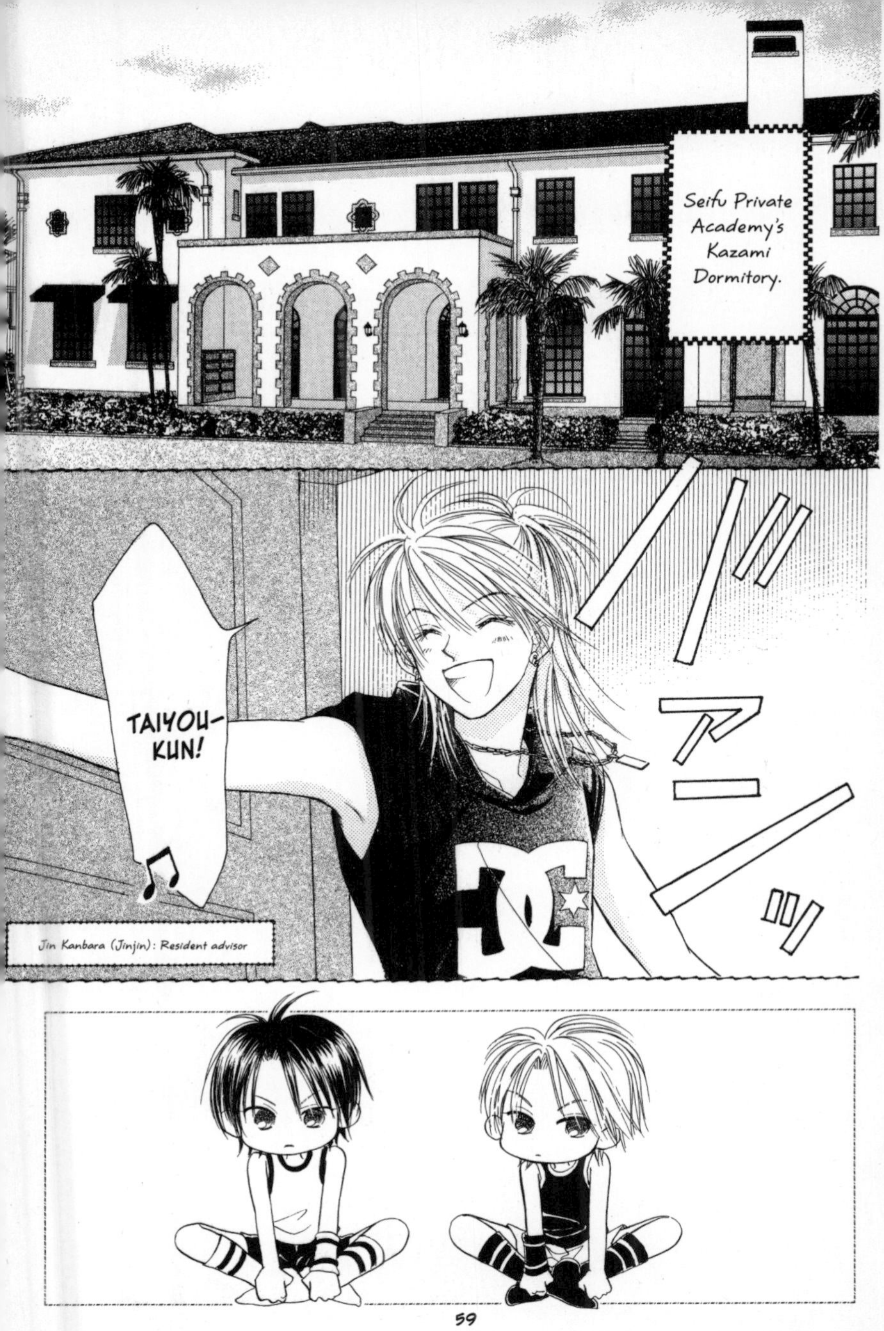
Seifu Private Academy's Kazami Dormitory.
TAIYOU-KUN! ♪
Jin Kanbara (Jinjin): Resident advisor

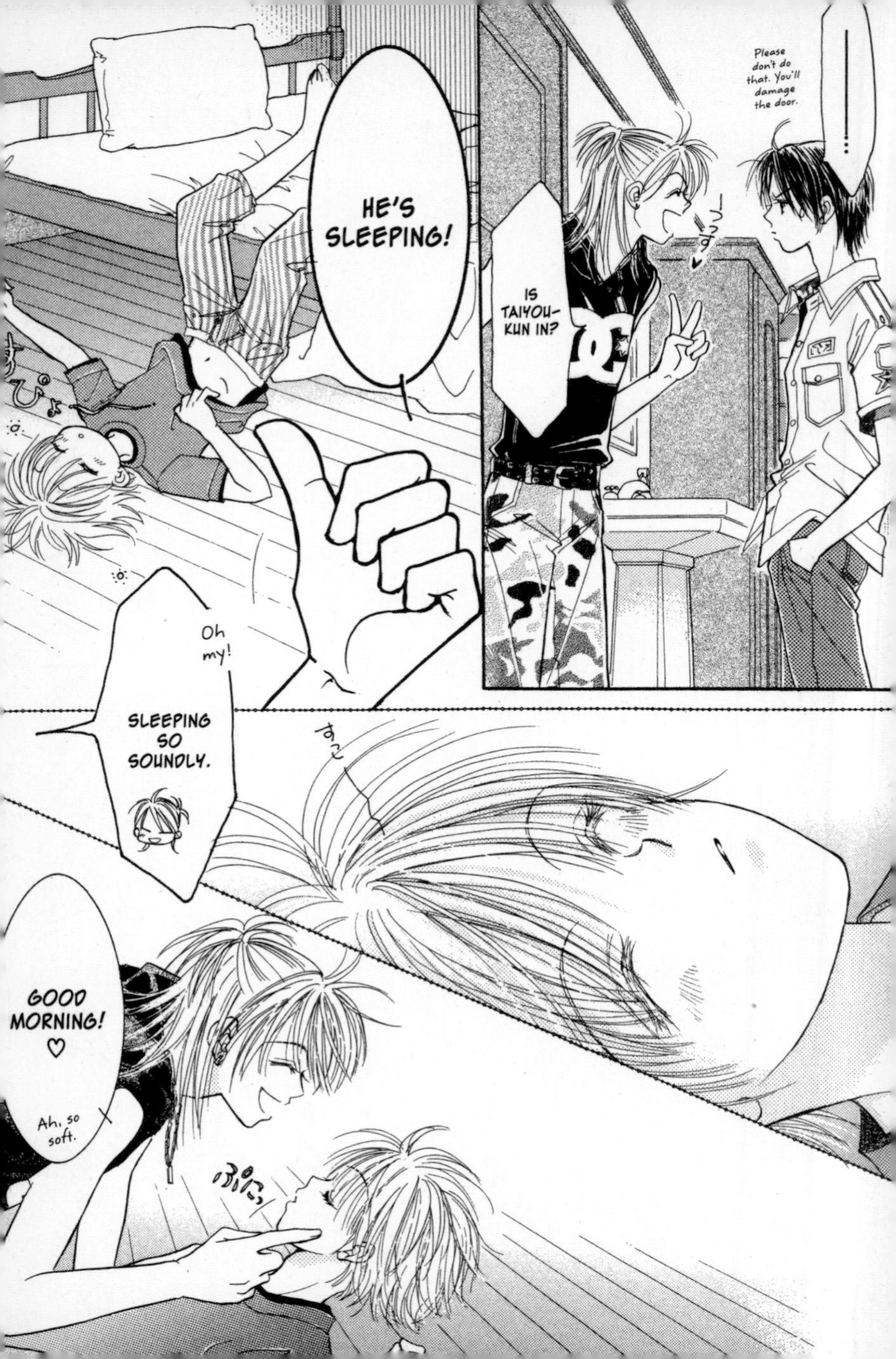

!......
Please don't do that. You'll damage the door.
IS TAIYOU-KUN IN?
HE'S SLEEPING!
Oh my!
SLEEPING SO SOUNDLY.
GOOD MORNING! ♡
Ah, so soft.

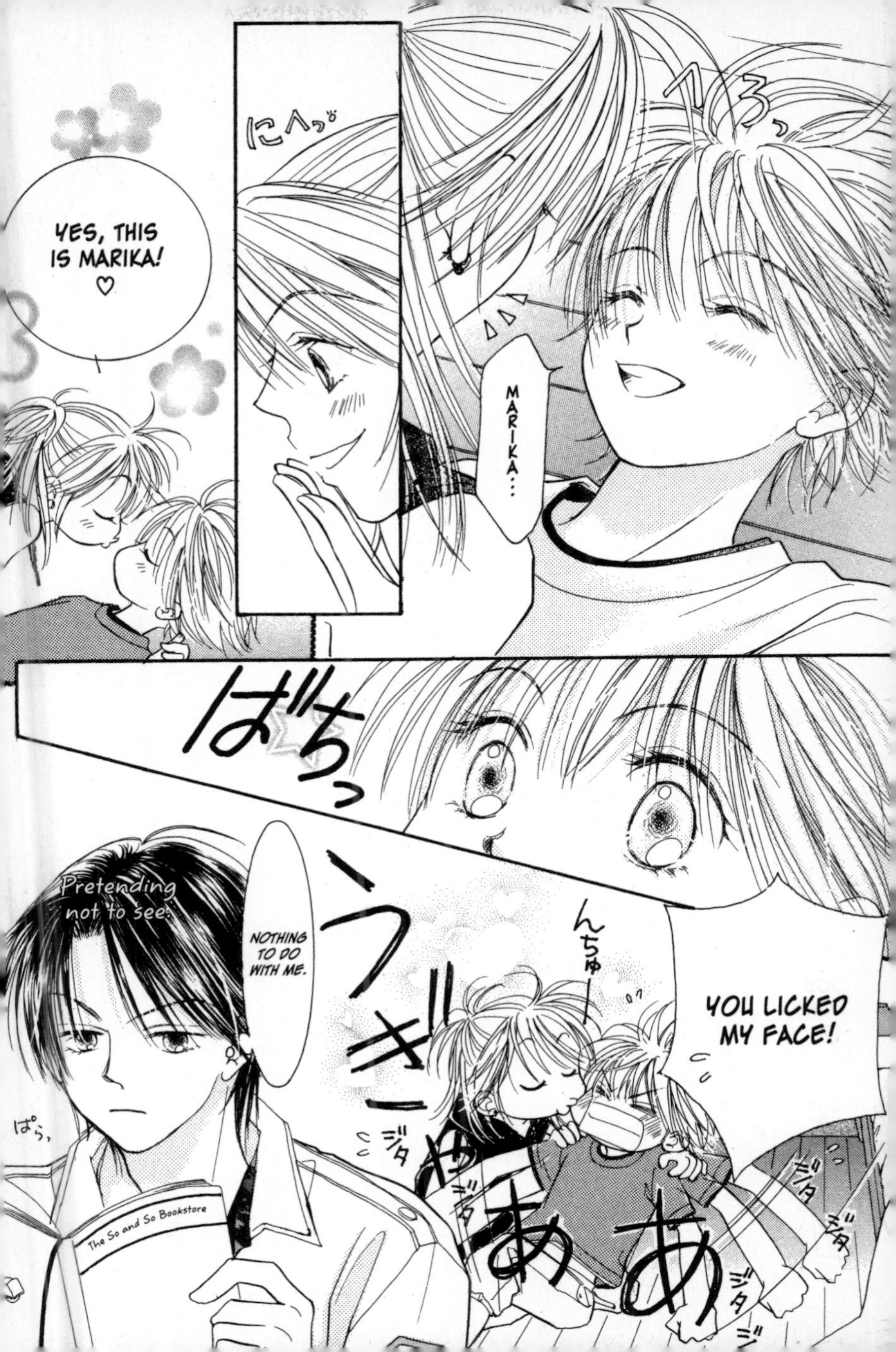
へろっ
MARIKA...
にへっ
YES, THIS IS MARIKA! ♡
ぱちっ
YOU LICKED MY FACE!
んちゅー
うぎゃああ
ジタ
ジタ
ジタ
ジタ
ジタ
NOTHING TO DO WITH ME.
Pretending not to see.
ぱらっ
The So and So Bookstore

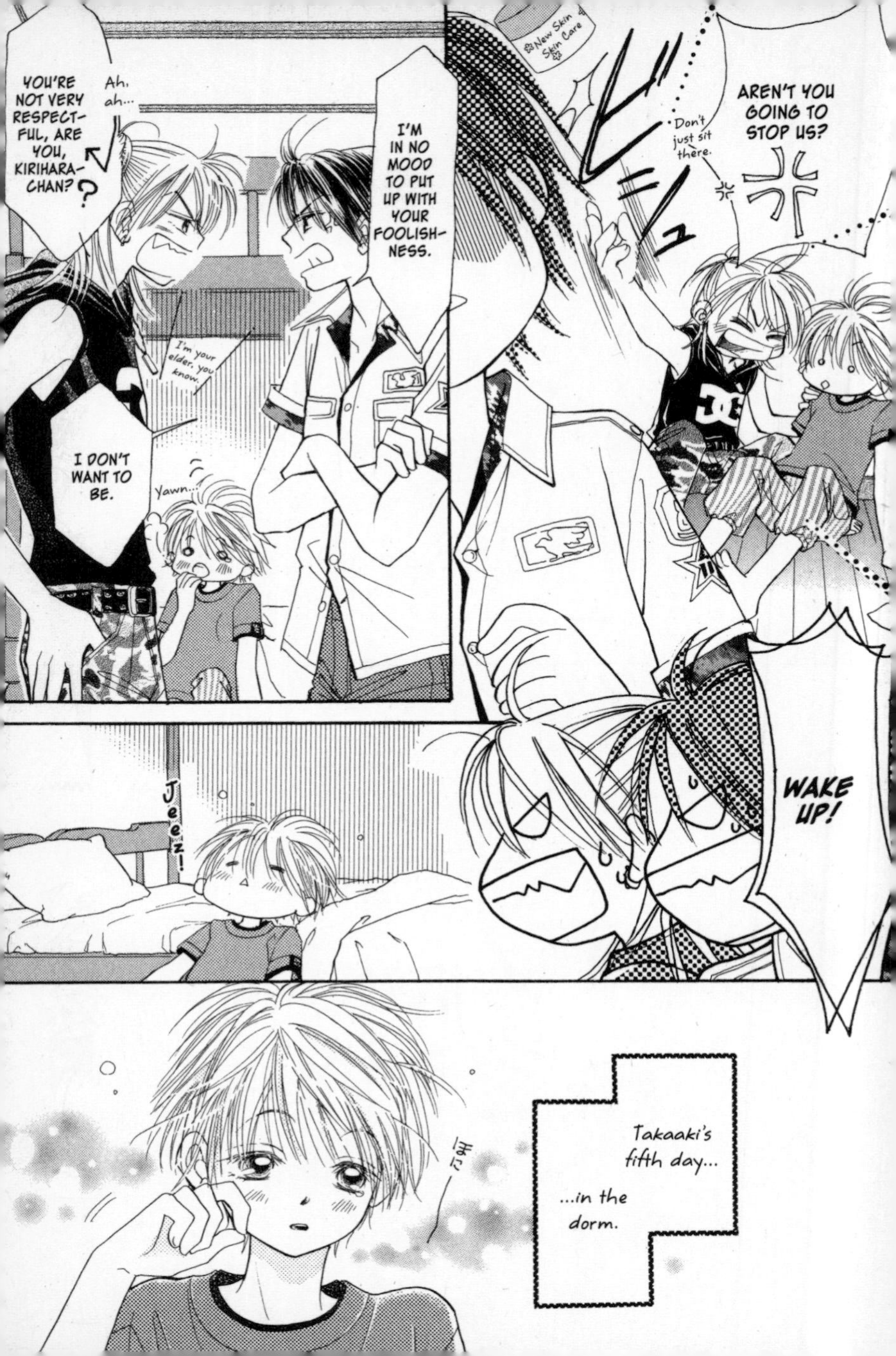
New Skin Skin Care
AREN'T YOU GOING TO STOP US?
Don't just sit there.
I'M IN NO MOOD TO PUT UP WITH YOUR FOOLISHNESS.
Ah, ah...
YOU'RE NOT VERY RESPECTFUL, ARE YOU, KIRIHARA-CHAN?
I'm your elder, you know.
I DON'T WANT TO BE.
Yawn...
WAKE UP!
Jeez!
Takaaki's fifth day...
...in the dorm.

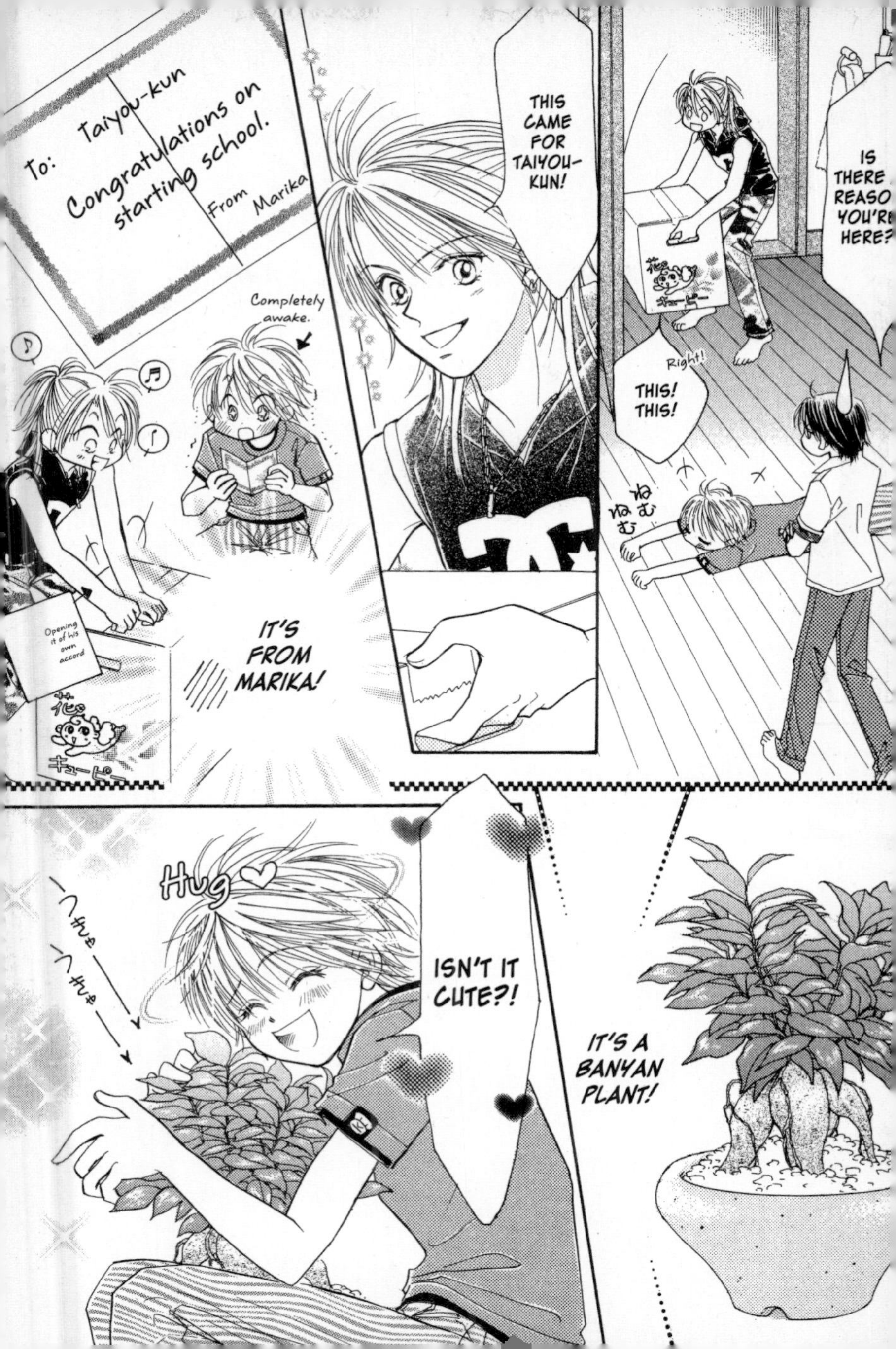
IS THERE REASO YOU'RE HERE?
Right!
THIS! THIS!
ねむねむ
THIS CAME FOR TAIYOU-KUN!
To: Taiyou-kun
Congratulations on starting school.
From Marika
Completely awake.
IT'S FROM MARIKA!
Opening it of his own accord
IT'S A BANYAN PLANT!
ISN'T IT CUTE?!
Hug

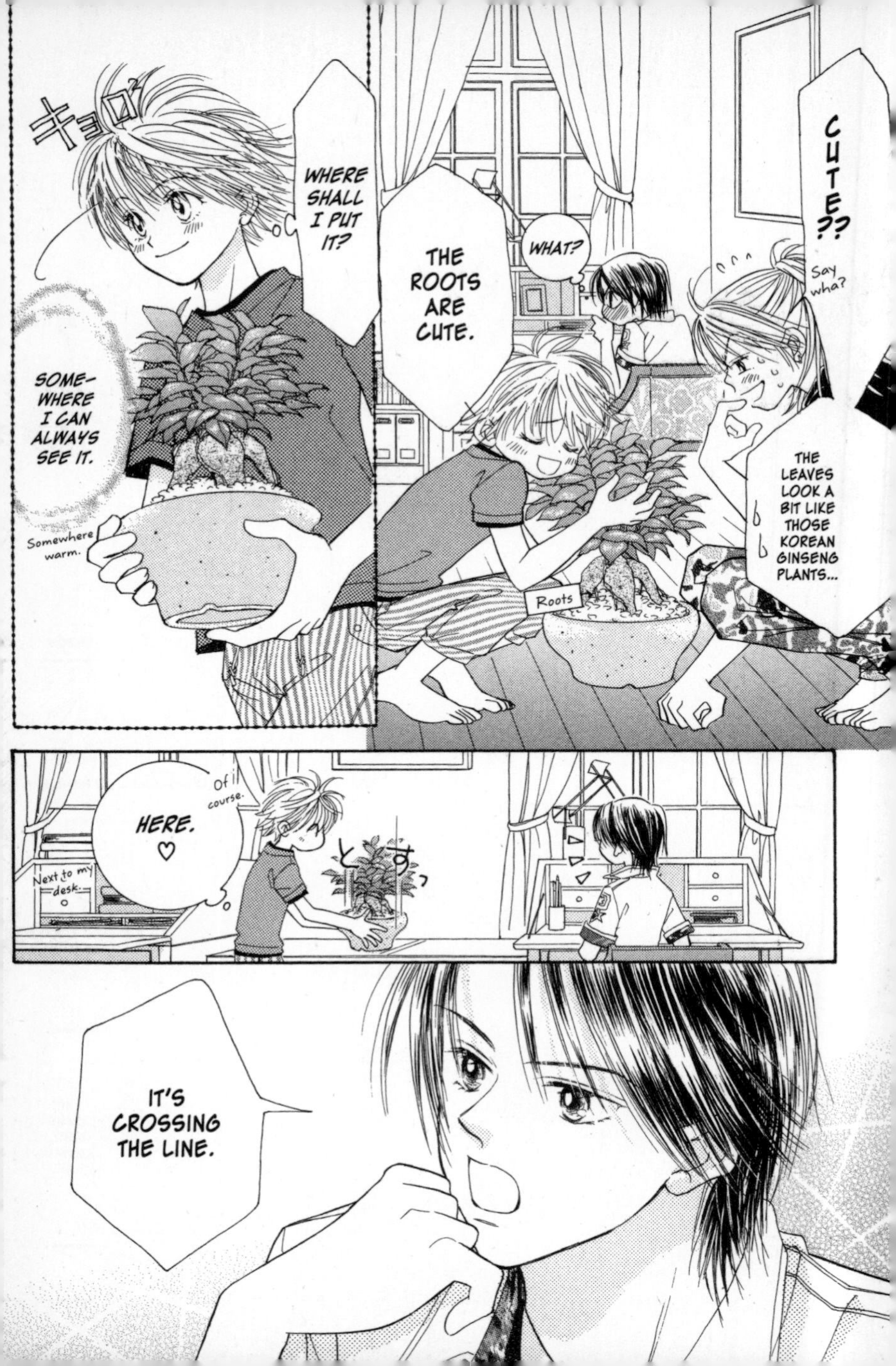
THE ROOTS ARE CUTE.
WHAT?
CUTE??
Say wha?
THE LEAVES LOOK A BIT LIKE THOSE KOREAN GINSENG PLANTS...
Roots
WHERE SHALL I PUT IT?
キョロ
SOME-WHERE I CAN ALWAYS SEE IT.
Somewhere warm.
HERE. ♡
Of course.
Next to my desk.
とす
IT'S CROSSING THE LINE.

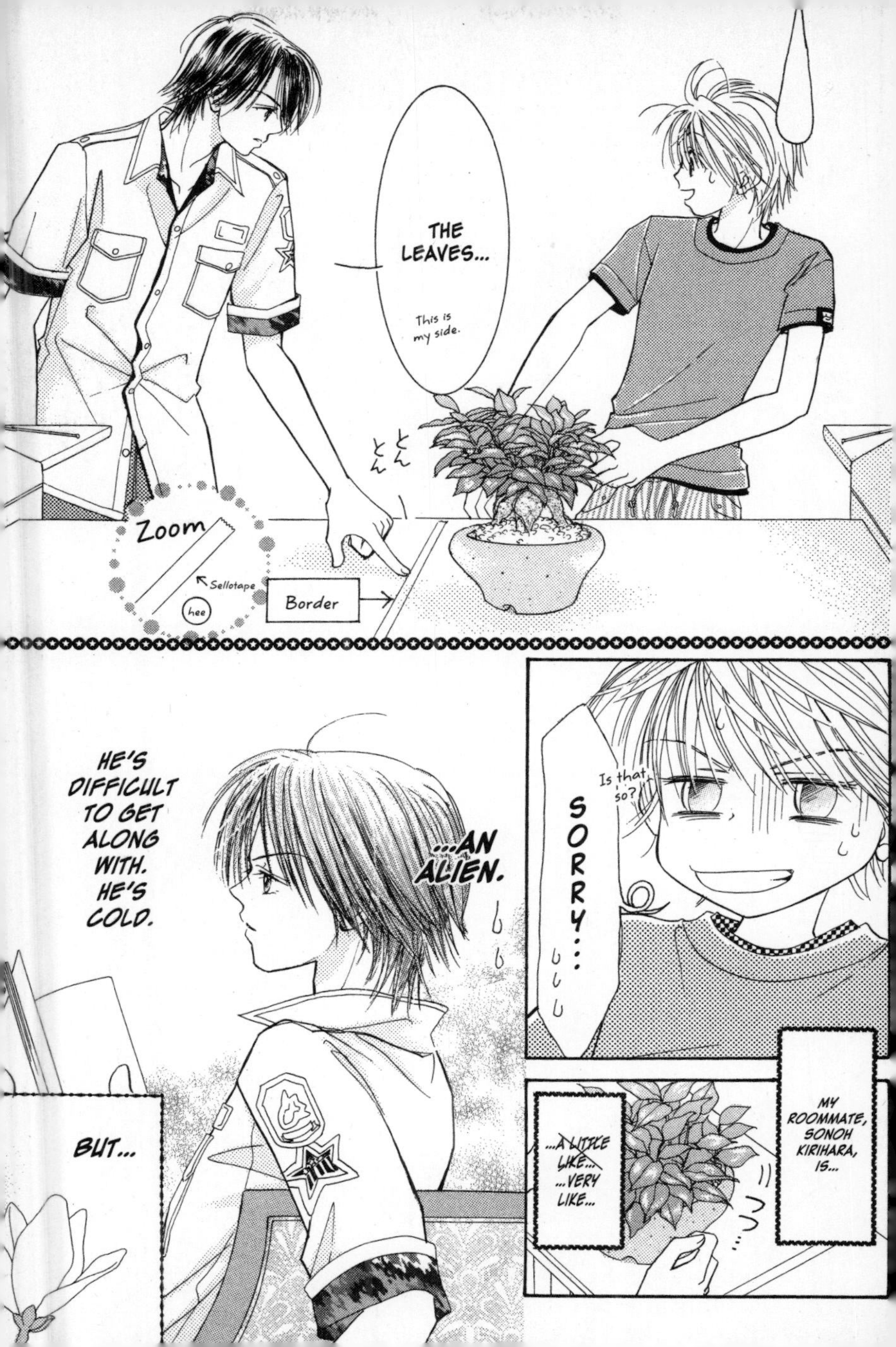
THE LEAVES...
This is my side.
とんとん
Zoom
Sellotape
hee
Border
Is that so?
SORRY...
MY ROOMMATE, SONOH KIRIHARA, IS...
...A LITTLE LIKE... ...VERY LIKE...
...AN ALIEN.
HE'S DIFFICULT TO GET ALONG WITH. HE'S COLD.
BUT...

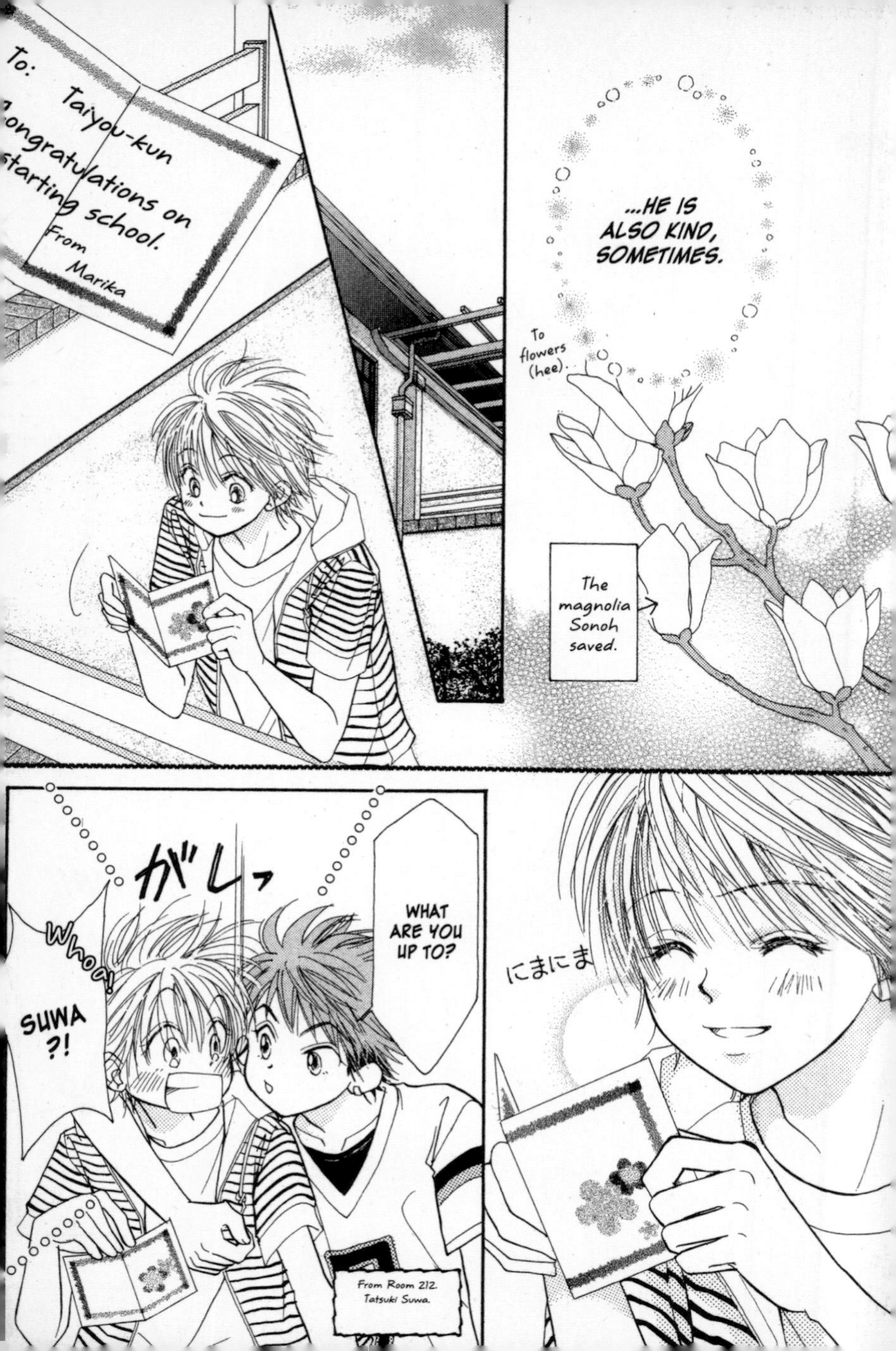
...HE IS ALSO KIND, SOMETIMES.
To flowers (hee).
The magnolia Sonoh saved.
To:
Taiyou-kun
ongratulations on
tarting school.
From
Marika
にまにま
WHAT ARE YOU UP TO?
がしっ
Whoa!
SUWA ?!
From Room 212. Tatsuki Suwa.

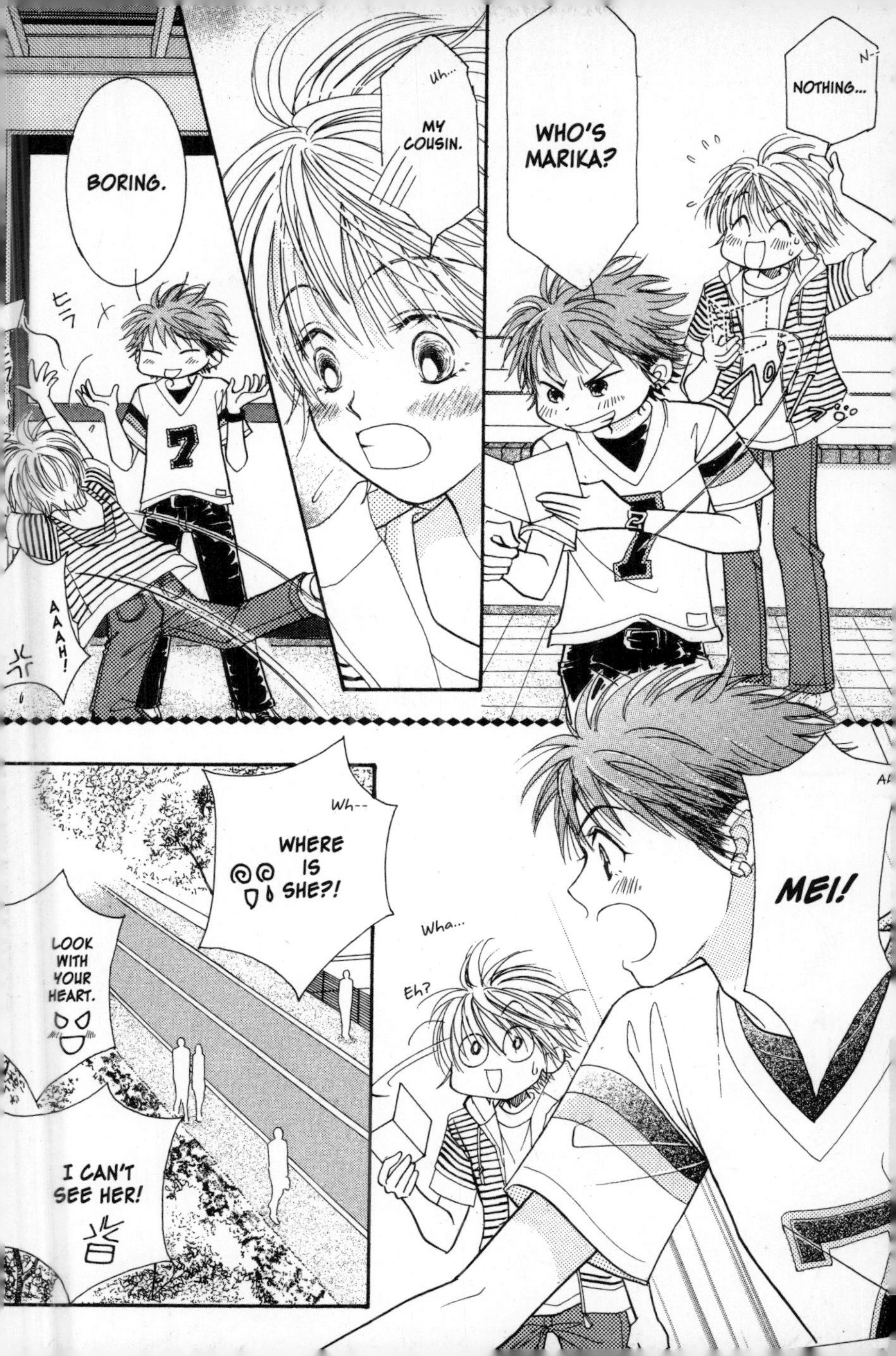

N-- NOTHING...
WHO'S MARIKA?
Uh... MY COUSIN.
BORING.
AAAAH!
MEI!
Wha...
Eh?
Wh-- WHERE IS SHE?!
LOOK WITH YOUR HEART.
I CAN'T SEE HER!

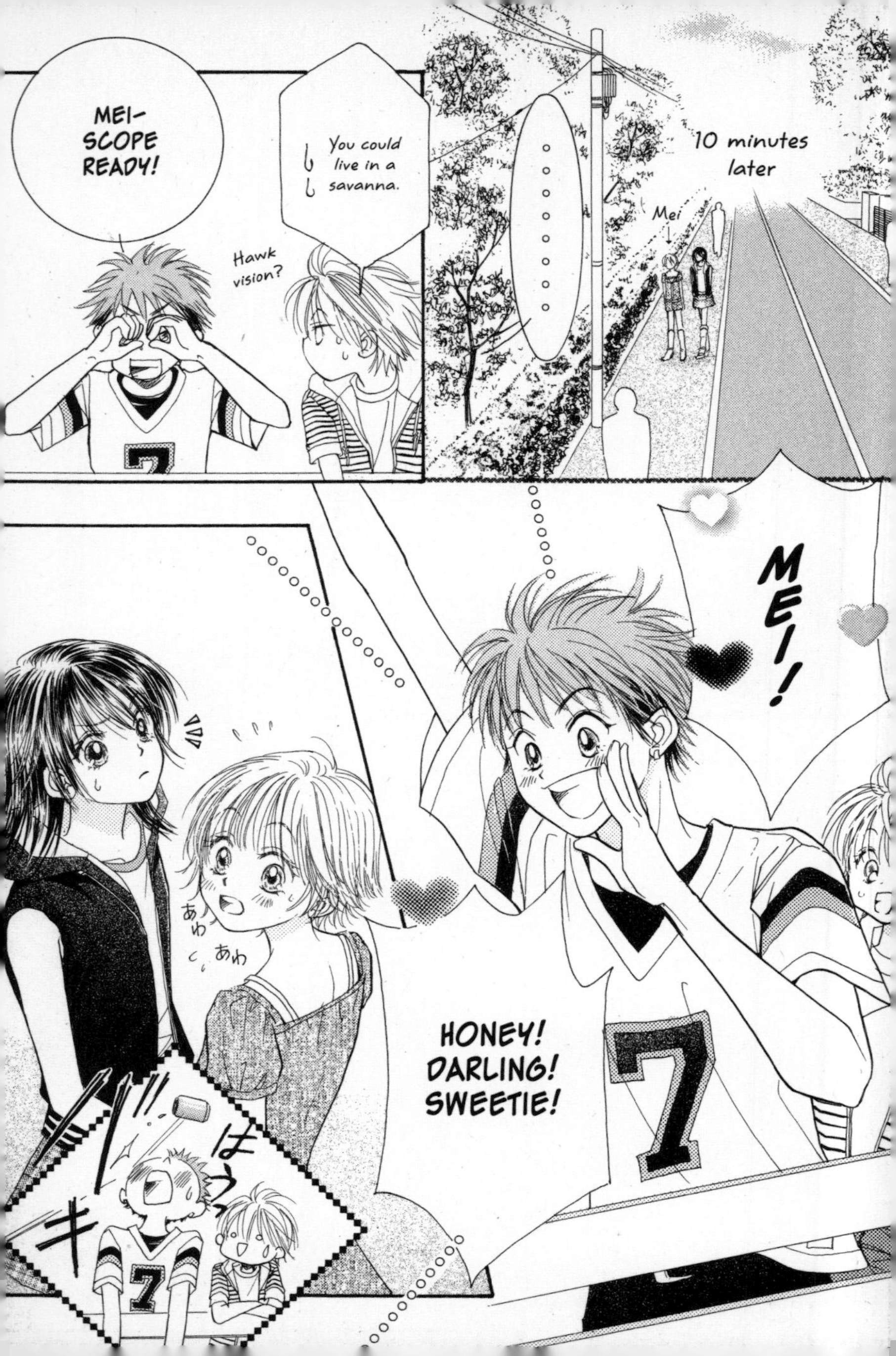
10 minutes later
Mei
......
You could live in a savanna.
MEI-SCOPE READY!
Hawk vision?
MEI!!
HONEY! DARLING! SWEETIE!
あわ
あわ
はっ

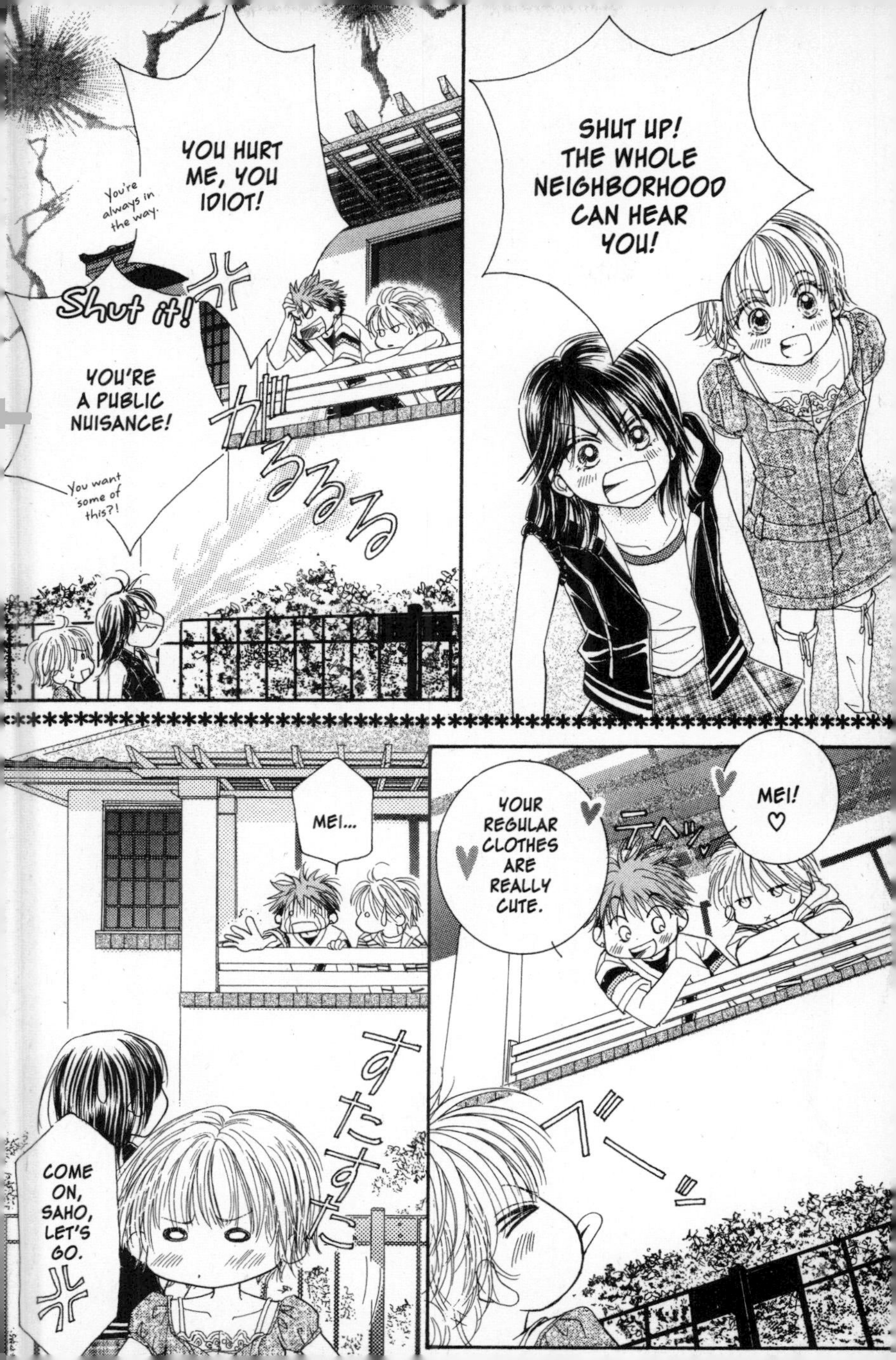
SHUT UP! THE WHOLE NEIGHBORHOOD CAN HEAR YOU!
YOU HURT ME, YOU IDIOT!
You're always in the way.
Shut it!
YOU'RE A PUBLIC NUISANCE!
You want some of this?!
MEI! ♡
YOUR REGULAR CLOTHES ARE REALLY CUTE.
MEI...
COME ON, SAHO, LET'S GO.
すたすた

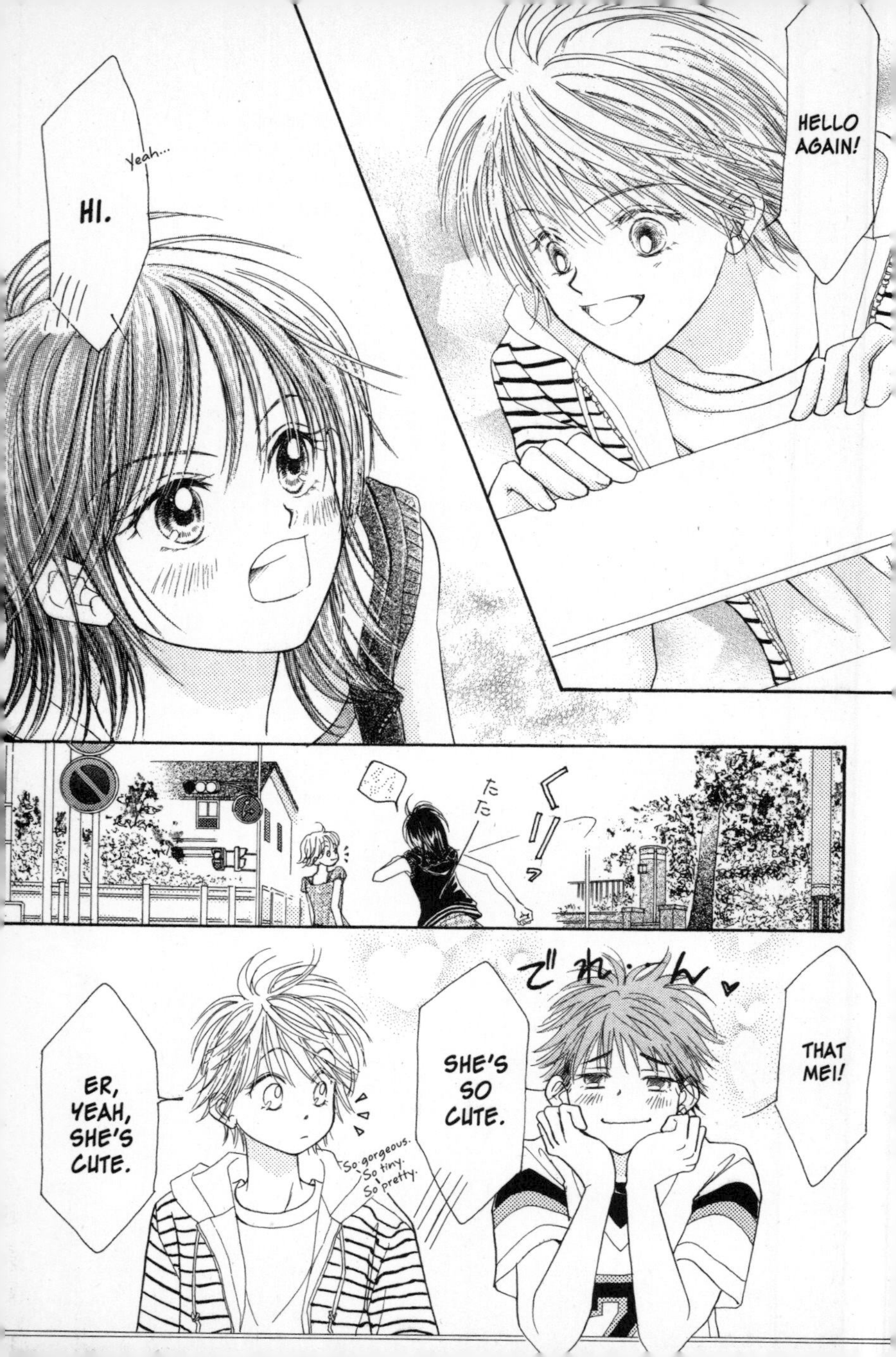
HELLO AGAIN!
HI.
Yeah...
たた
でれ～ん
THAT MEI!
SHE'S SO CUTE.
So gorgeous.
So tiny.
So pretty.
ER, YEAH, SHE'S CUTE.

Characters who's who? ①

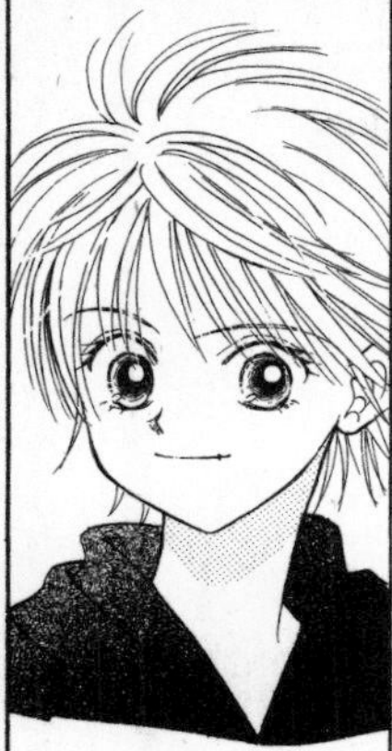

Takaaki Asakura

First-year in high school

- Main character.
- Nickname: Taiyou.
- Loves Marika.
- Also loves flowers.
- Wants to be tall. Only 157cm. Hopes to be 180cm. ←Wild hope A bit in his own world.

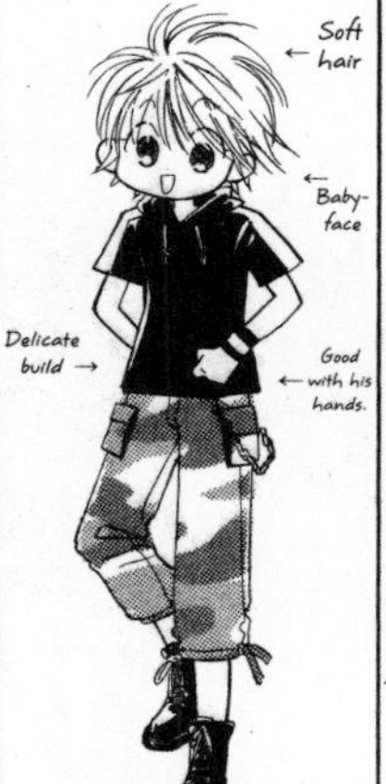
Soft hair
Baby-face
Delicate build
Good with his hands.

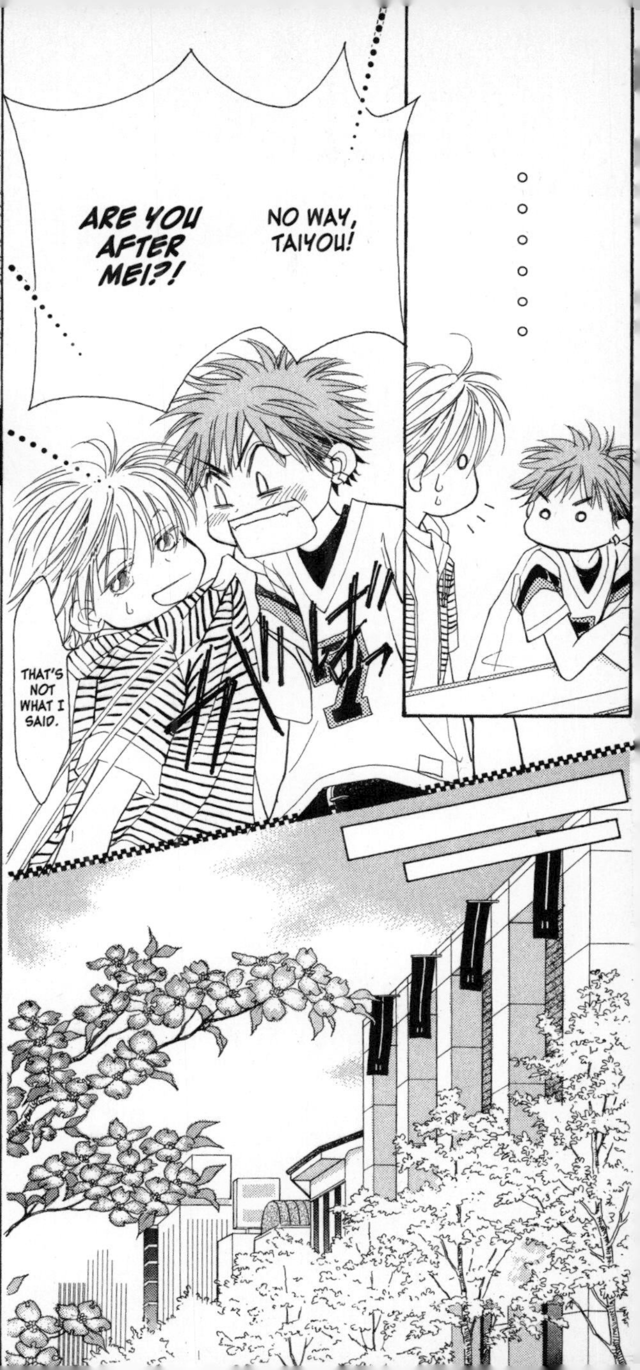
NO WAY, TAIYOU!
ARE YOU AFTER MEI?!
THAT'S NOT WHAT I SAID.

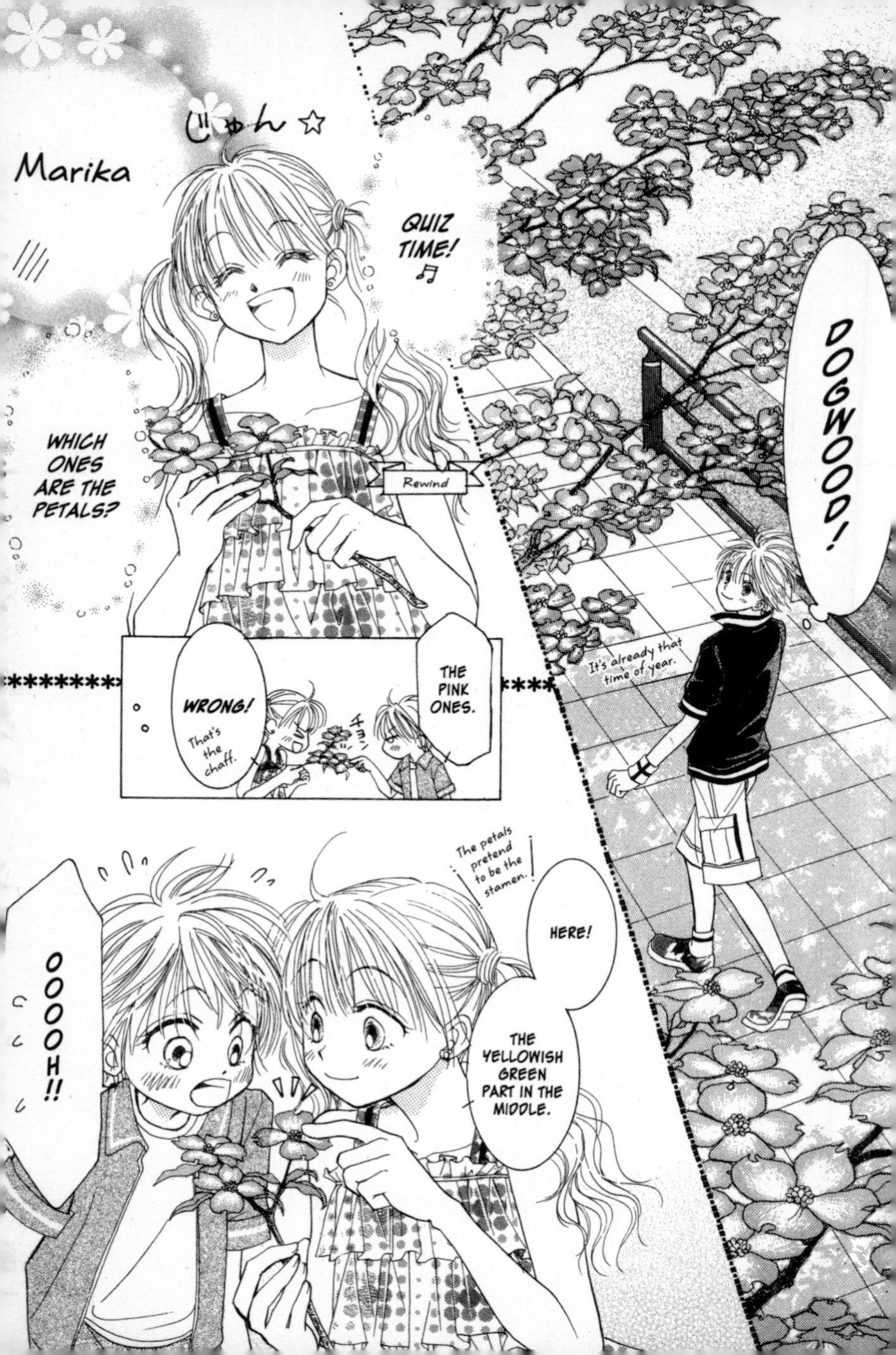

DOGWOOOD!
It's already that time of year.
じゅん☆
Marika
QUIZ TIME! ♫
WHICH ONES ARE THE PETALS?
Rewind
THE PINK ONES.
WRONG!
That's the chaff.
HERE!
The petals pretend to be the stamen.
THE YELLOWISH GREEN PART IN THE MIDDLE.
OOOOH!!

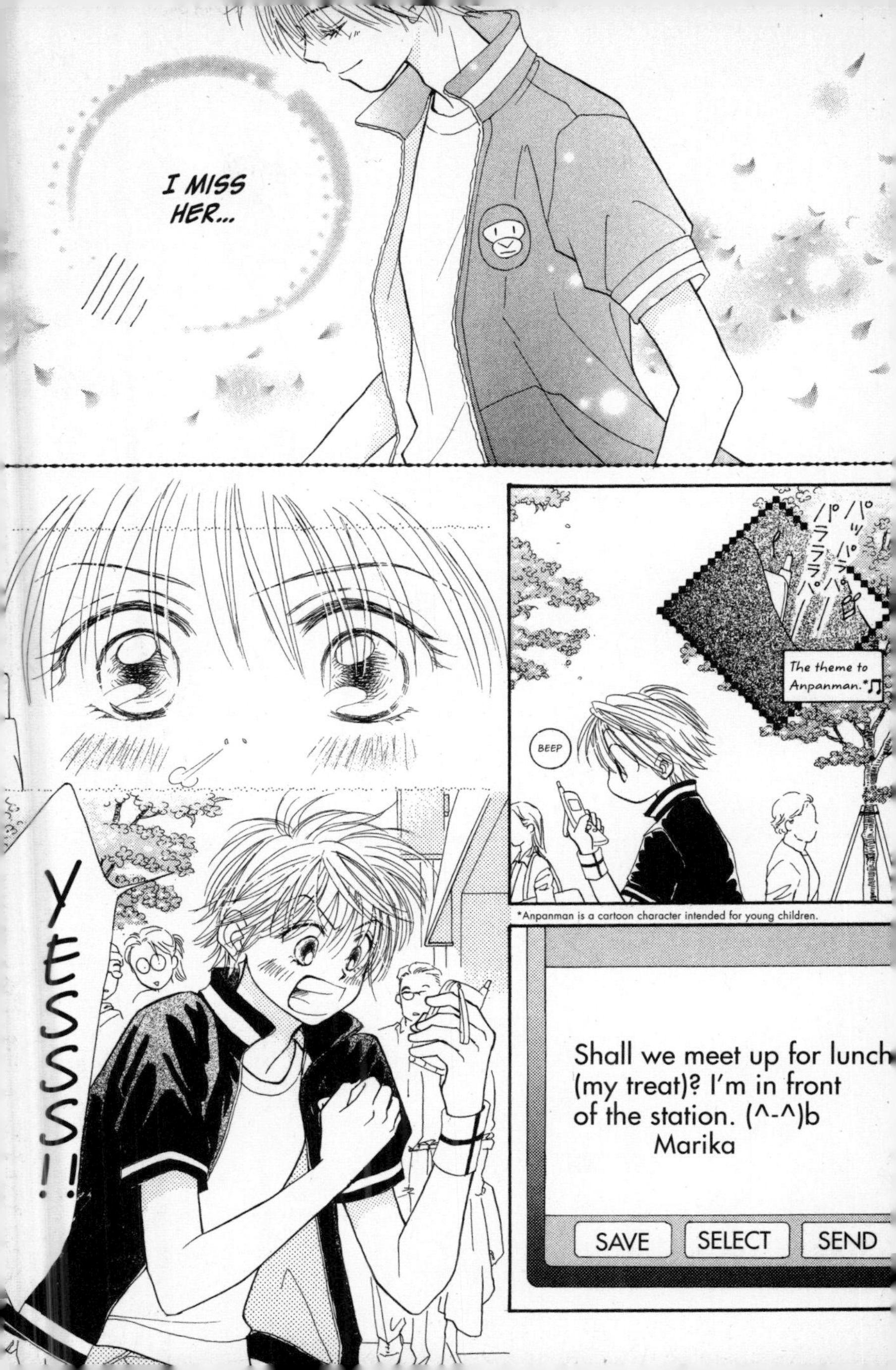
I MISS HER...
BEEP
The theme to Anpanman.*♫
Shall we meet up for lunch (my treat)? I'm in front of the station. (^-^)b
Marika
SAVE
SELECT
SEND
YESSS!!
*Anpanman is a cartoon character intended for young children.

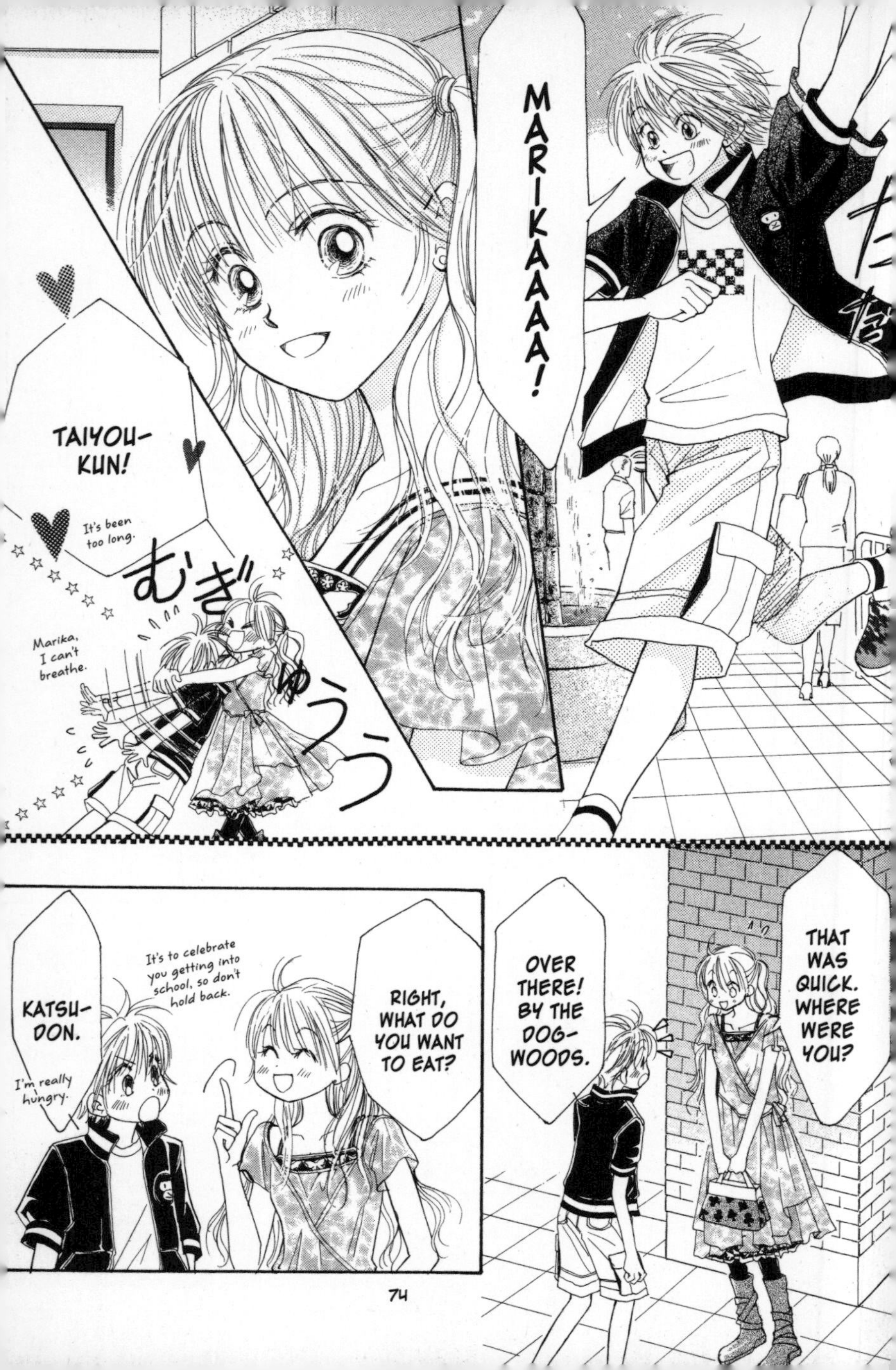
MARIKAAAA!
TAIYOU-KUN!
It's been too long.
むぎゅううう
Marika, I can't breathe.
THAT WAS QUICK. WHERE WERE YOU?
OVER THERE! BY THE DOG-WOODS.
RIGHT, WHAT DO YOU WANT TO EAT?
It's to celebrate you getting into school, so don't hold back.
KATSU-DON.
I'm really hungry.

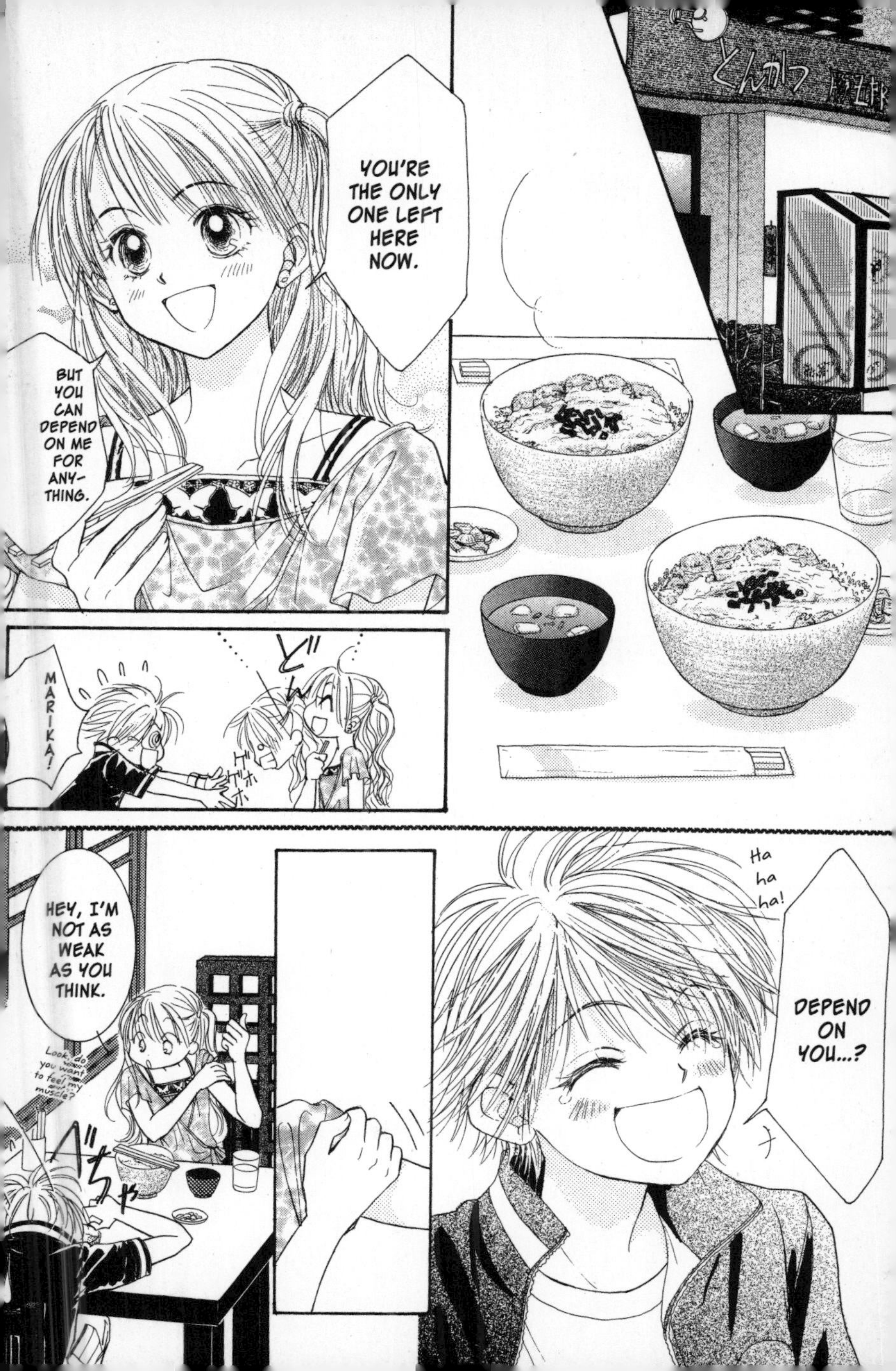
とんかつ
YOU'RE THE ONLY ONE LEFT HERE NOW.
BUT YOU CAN DEPEND ON ME FOR ANY-THING.
MARIKA!
Ha ha ha!
DEPEND ON YOU...?
HEY, I'M NOT AS WEAK AS YOU THINK.
Look, do you want to feel my muscle?

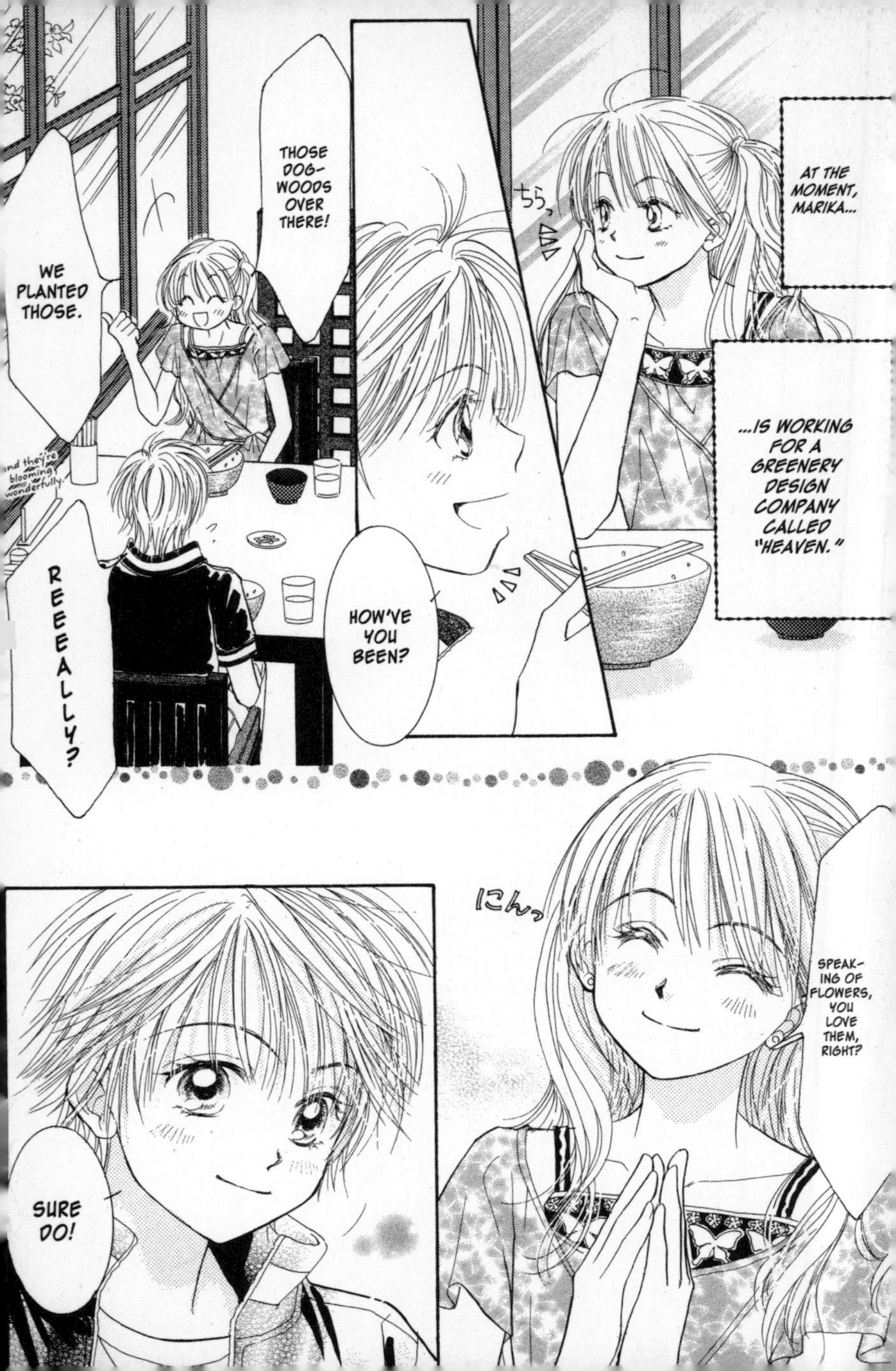
ちら
AT THE MOMENT, MARIKA...
...IS WORKING FOR A GREENERY DESIGN COMPANY CALLED "HEAVEN."
HOW'VE YOU BEEN?
THOSE DOG-WOODS OVER THERE!
WE PLANTED THOSE.
and they're blooming wonderfully.
REEEALLY?
にんっ
SPEAK-ING OF FLOWERS, YOU LOVE THEM, RIGHT?
SURE DO!

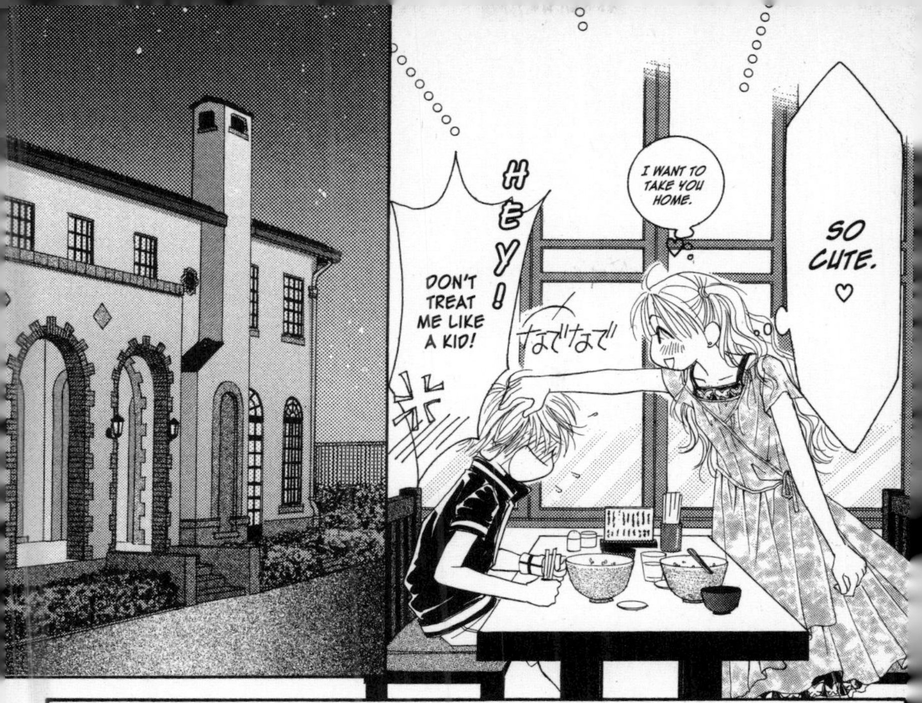
SO CUTE. ♡
I WANT TO TAKE YOU HOME. ♡
Hey!
DON'T TREAT ME LIKE A KID!
なでなで

Bath

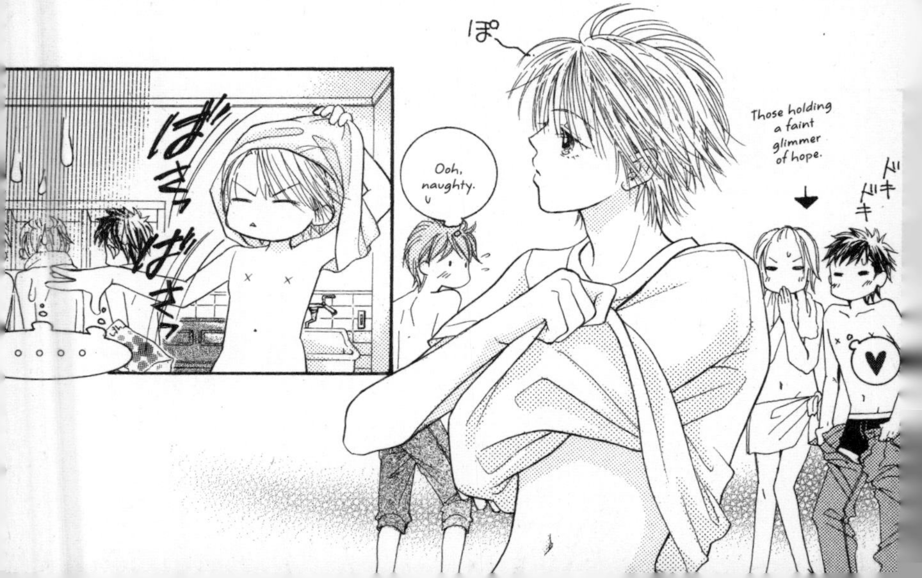
ドキドキ
Those holding a faint glimmer of hope.
ぽ
Ooh, naughty.
ばさっばさっ

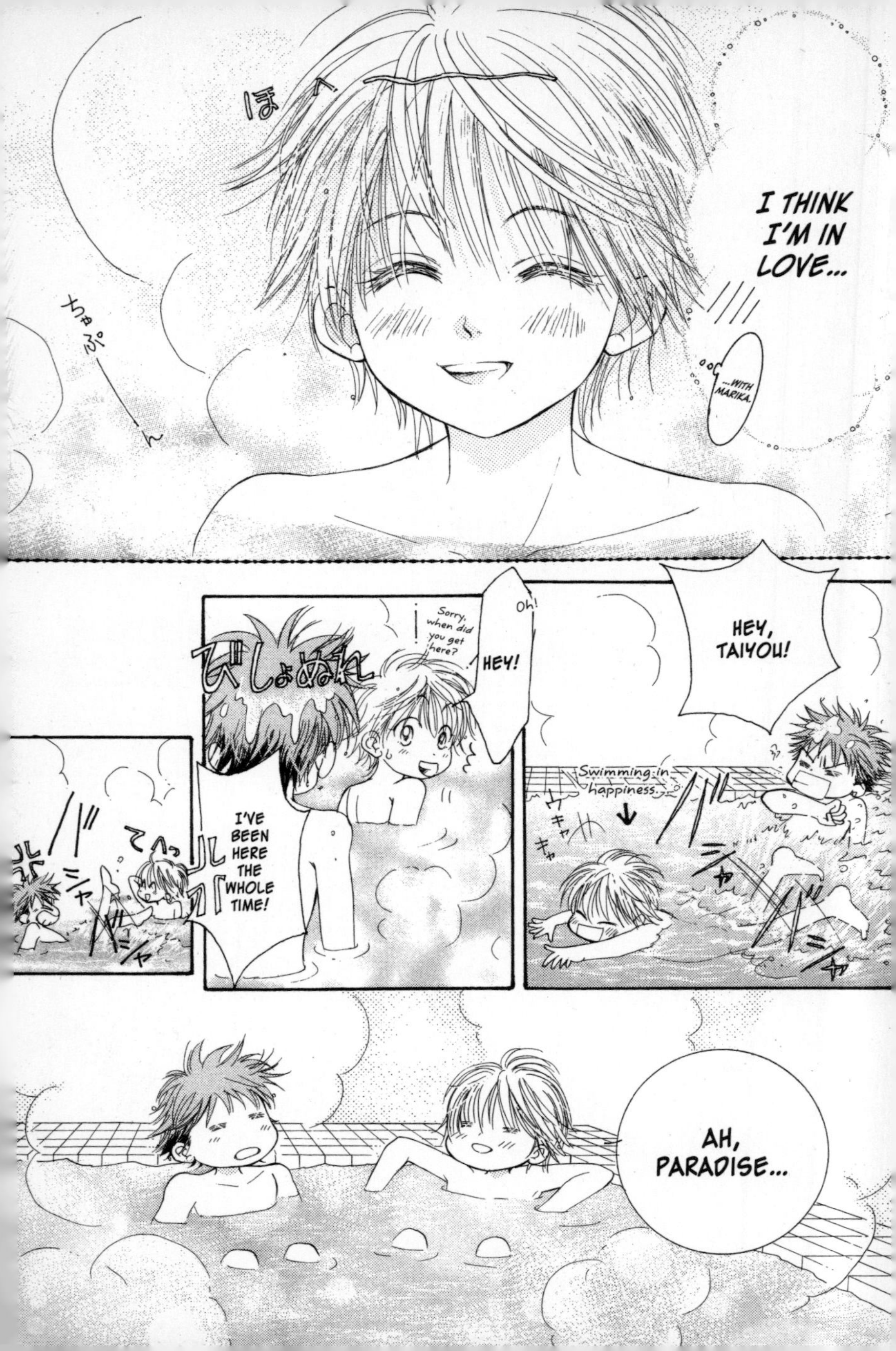
ほへ
I THINK I'M IN LOVE...
...WITH MARIKA.
ちゅぷーん
HEY, TAIYOU!
Swimming in happiness.
Oh!
HEY!
Sorry, when did you get here?
びしょぬれ
I'VE BEEN HERE THE WHOLE TIME!
AH, PARADISE...

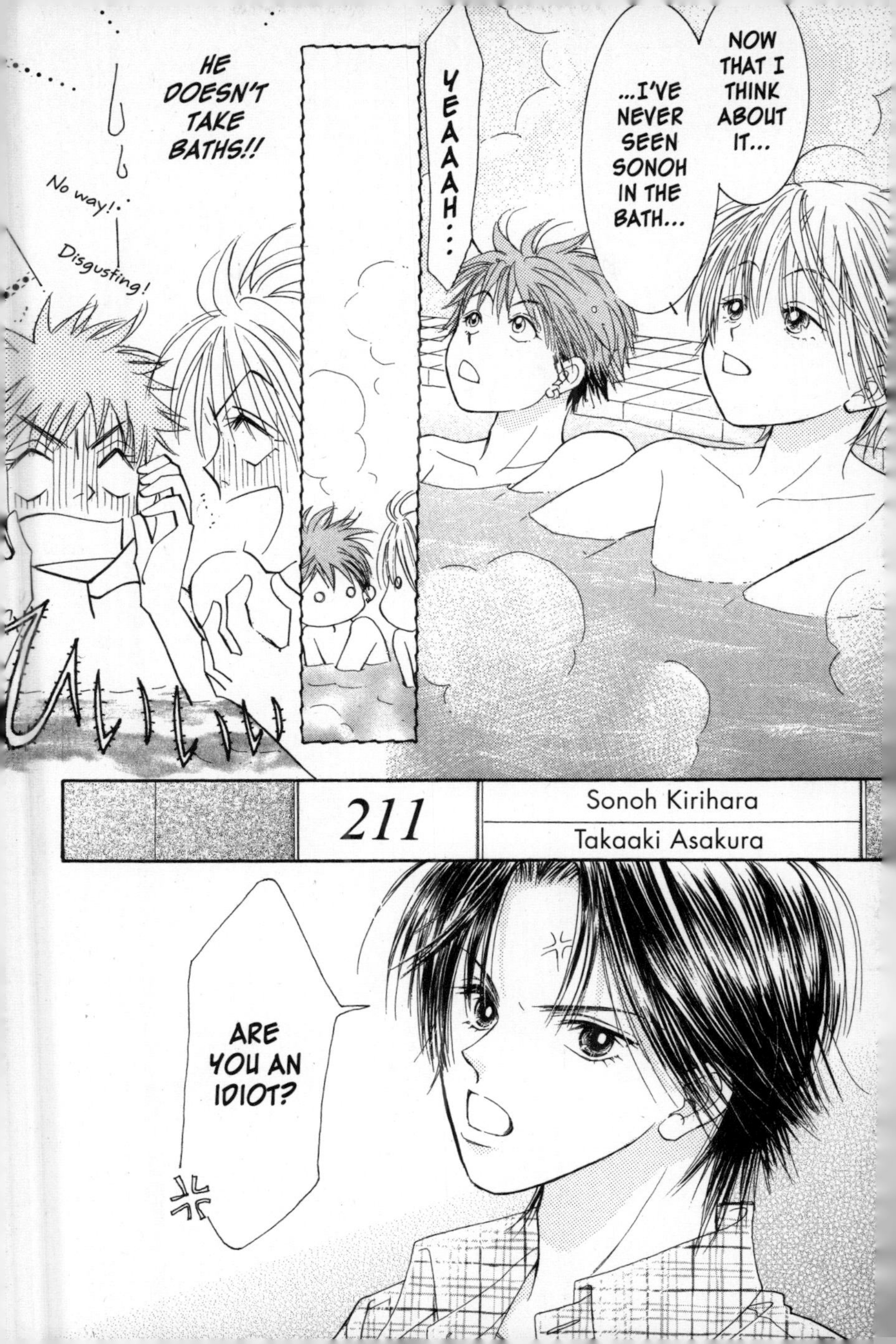
NOW THAT I THINK ABOUT IT...
...I'VE NEVER SEEN SONOH IN THE BATH...
YEAAAAH...
HE DOESN'T TAKE BATHS!!
No way!
Disgusting!
211
Sonoh Kirihara
Takaaki Asakura
ARE YOU AN IDIOT?

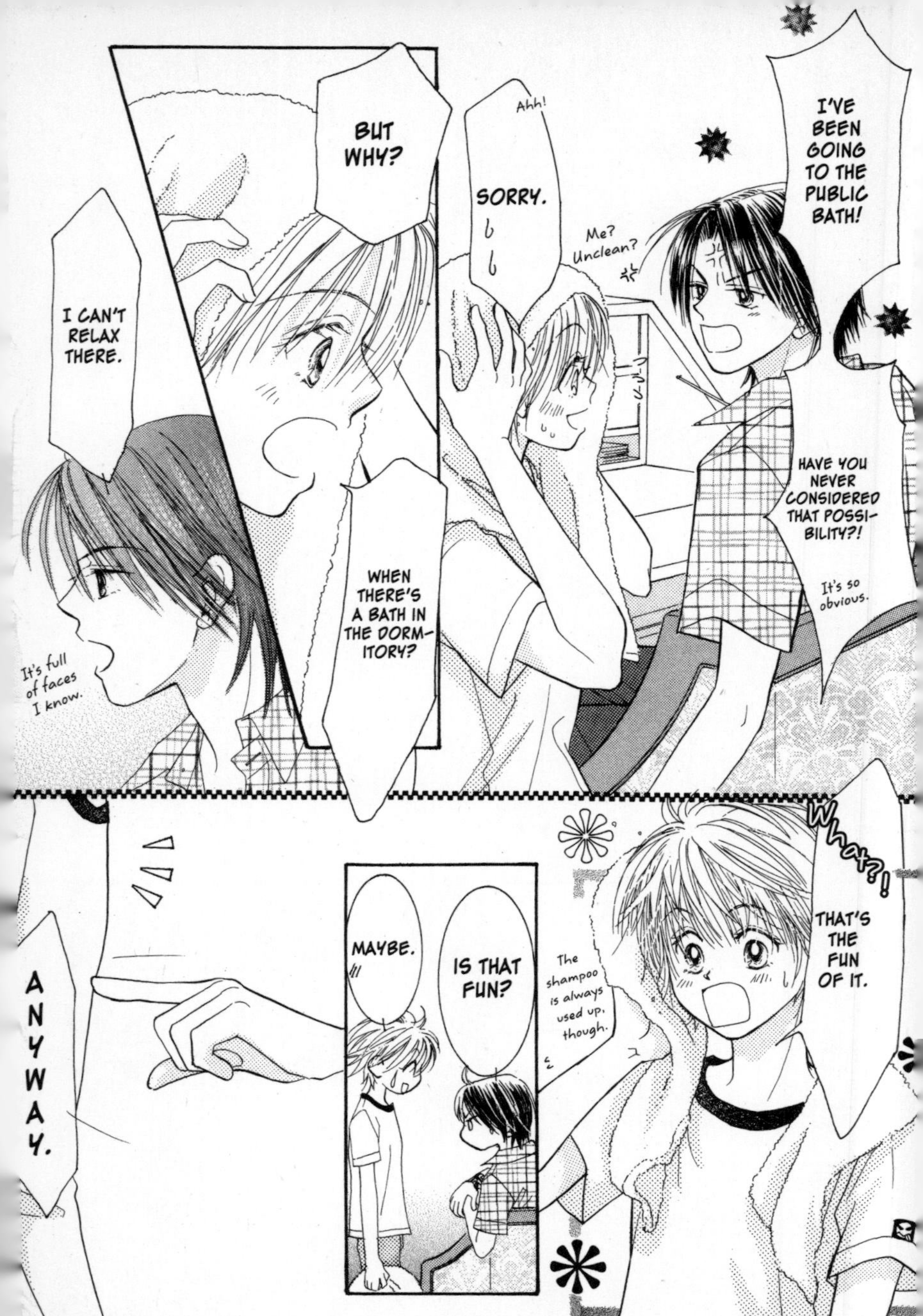
I'VE BEEN GOING TO THE PUBLIC BATH!
Me? Unclean?
HAVE YOU NEVER CONSIDERED THAT POSSI-BILITY?!
It's so obvious.
Ahh!
SORRY.
BUT WHY?
WHEN THERE'S A BATH IN THE DORM-ITORY?
I CAN'T RELAX THERE.
It's full of faces I know.
What?!
THAT'S THE FUN OF IT.
The shampoo is always used up, though.
IS THAT FUN?
MAYBE.
ANYWAY.

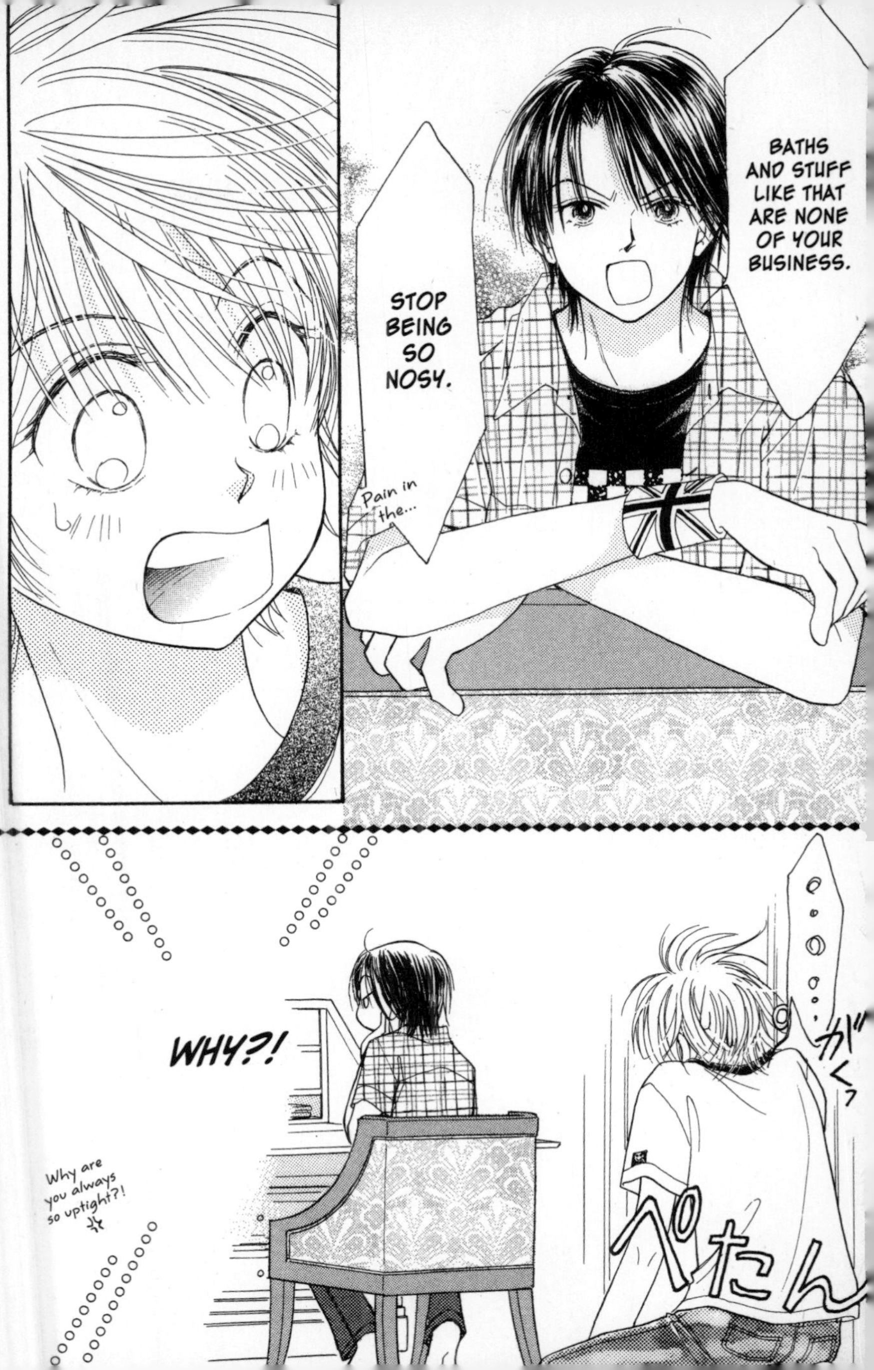
BATHS AND STUFF LIKE THAT ARE NONE OF YOUR BUSINESS.
STOP BEING SO NOSY.
Pain in the...
がくっ
WHY?!
ぺたん
Why are you always so uptight?!

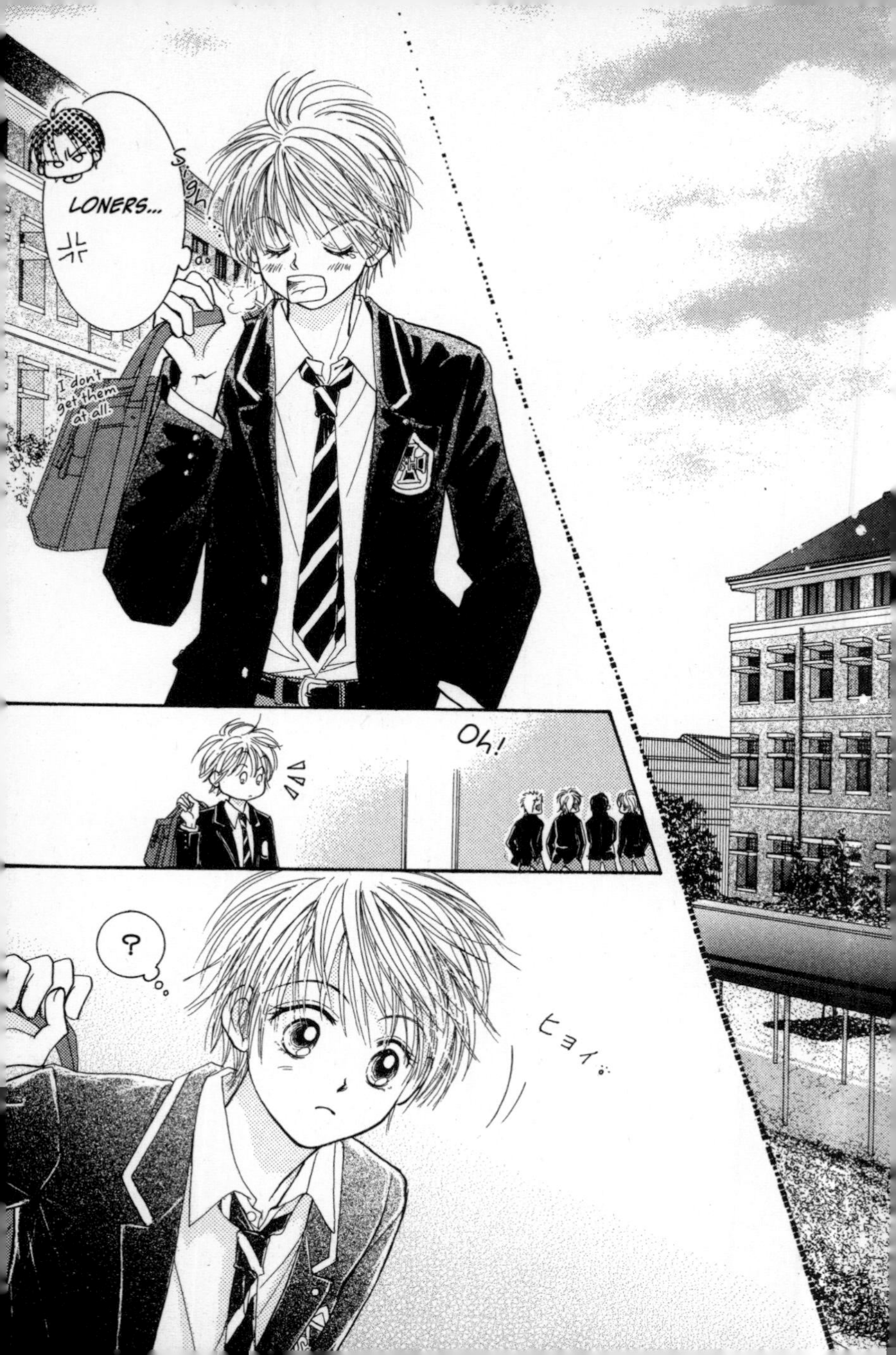

Sigh
LONERS...
I don't get them at all.
Oh!
?
ヒョイ

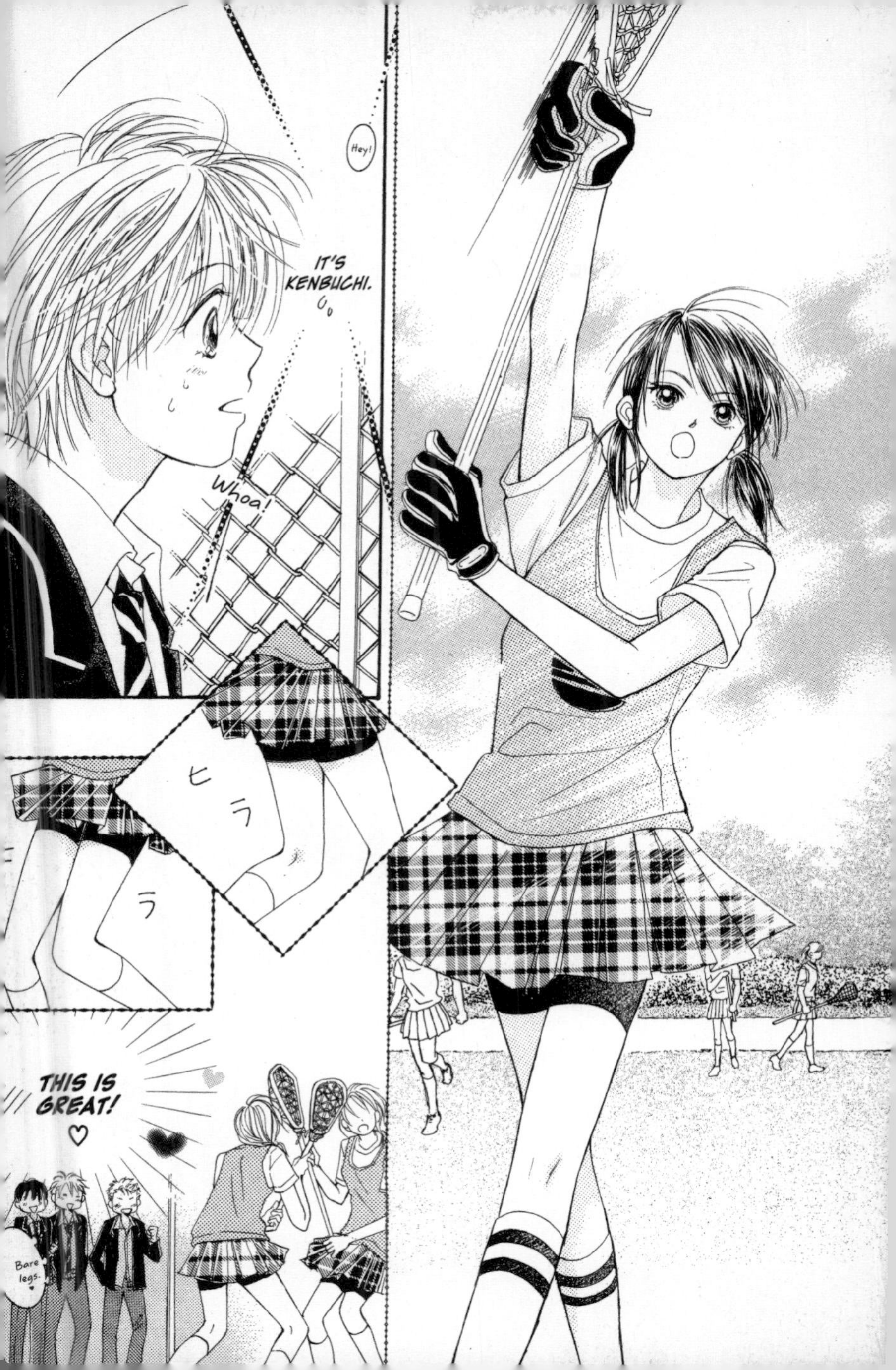
Hey!
IT'S KENBUCHI.
Whoa!
ヒラ
ラ
THIS IS GREAT! ♡
Bare legs.

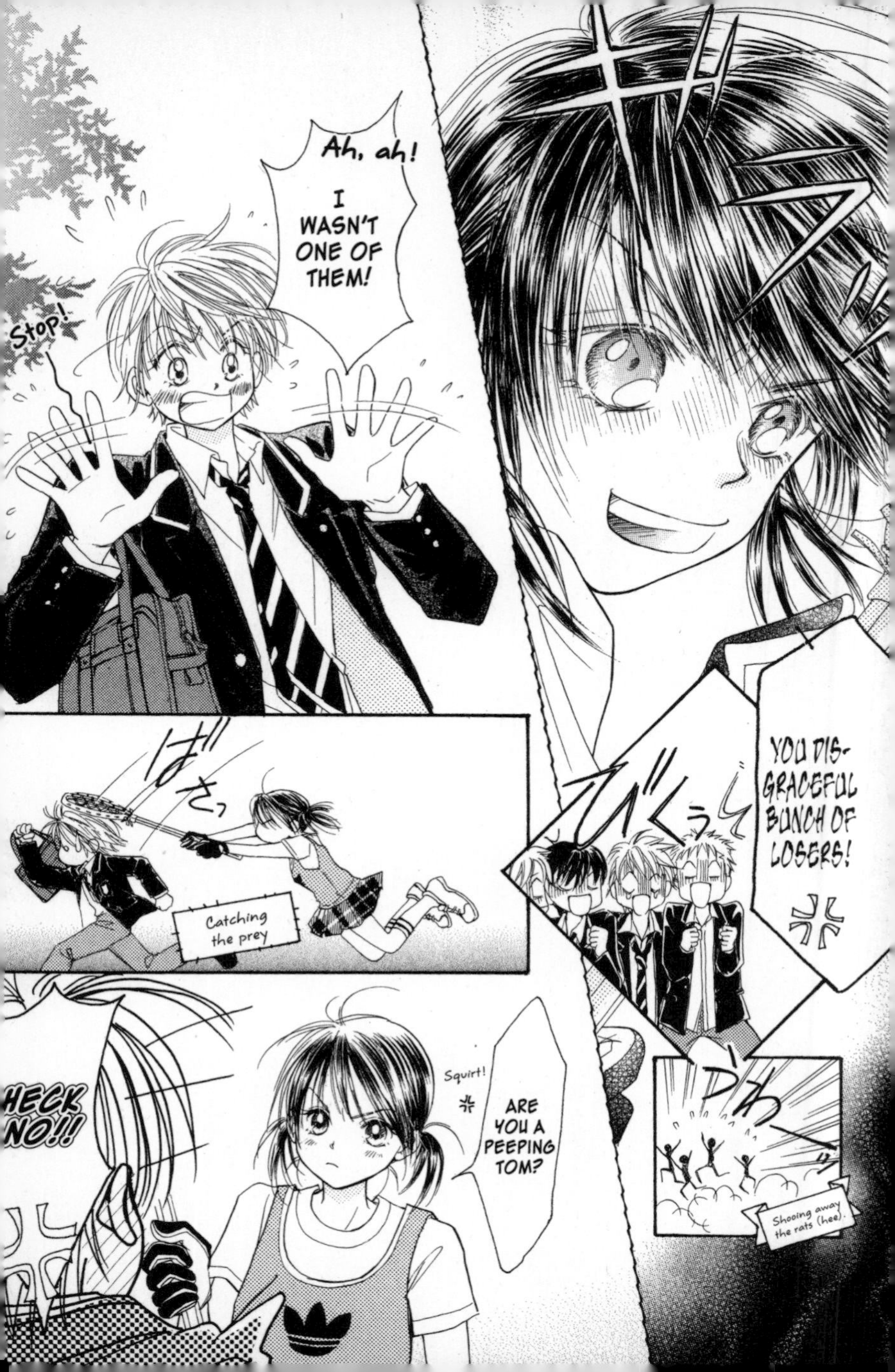

YOU DIS-GRACEFUL BUNCH OF LOSERS!
Shooing away the rats (hee).
Ah, ah!
I WASN'T ONE OF THEM!
Stop!
Catching the prey
ARE YOU A PEEPING TOM?
Squirt!
HECK NO!!

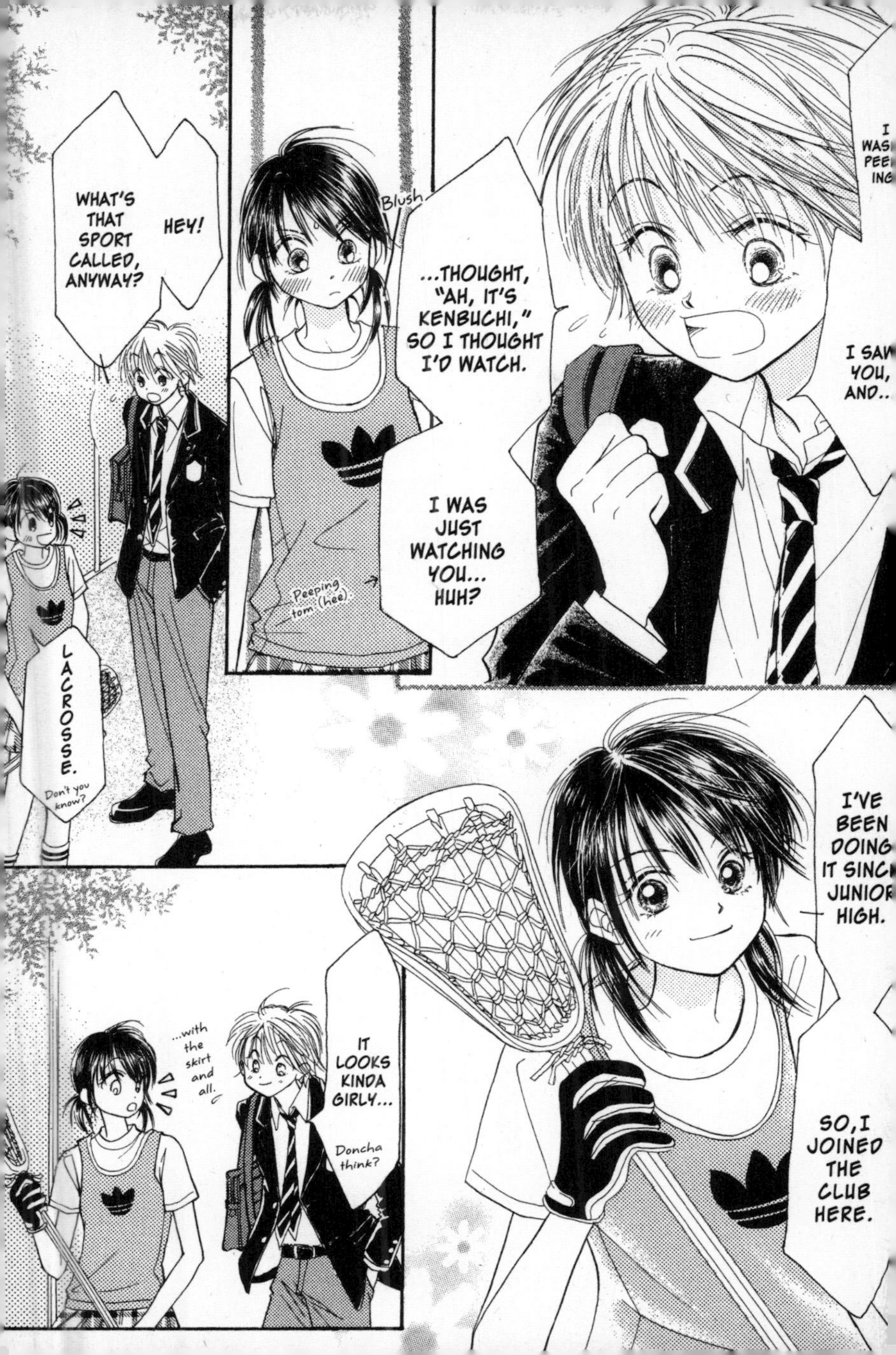

I WAS PEE ING
I SAW YOU, AND..
...THOUGHT, "AH, IT'S KENBUCHI," SO I THOUGHT I'D WATCH.
I WAS JUST WATCHING YOU... HUH?
Blush
Peeping tom (hee)
HEY!
WHAT'S THAT SPORT CALLED, ANYWAY?
LACROSSE.
Don't you know?
I'VE BEEN DOING IT SINC JUNIOR HIGH.
SO, I JOINED THE CLUB HERE.
IT LOOKS KINDA GIRLY...
...with the skirt and all.
Doncha think?

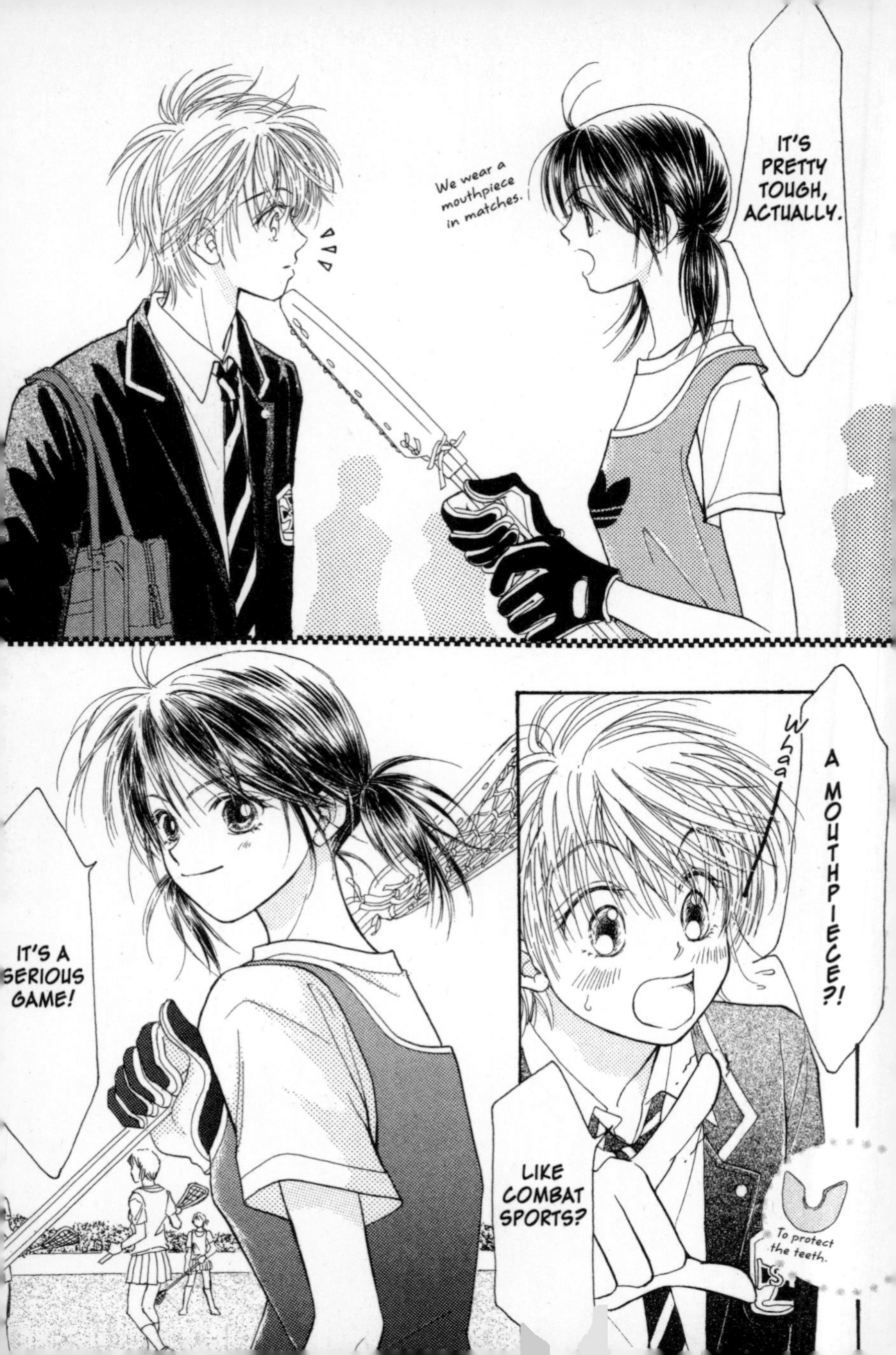
IT'S PRETTY TOUGH, ACTUALLY.
We wear a mouthpiece in matches.
A MOUTHPIECE?!
Whaa
To protect the teeth.
LIKE COMBAT SPORTS?
IT'S A SERIOUS GAME!

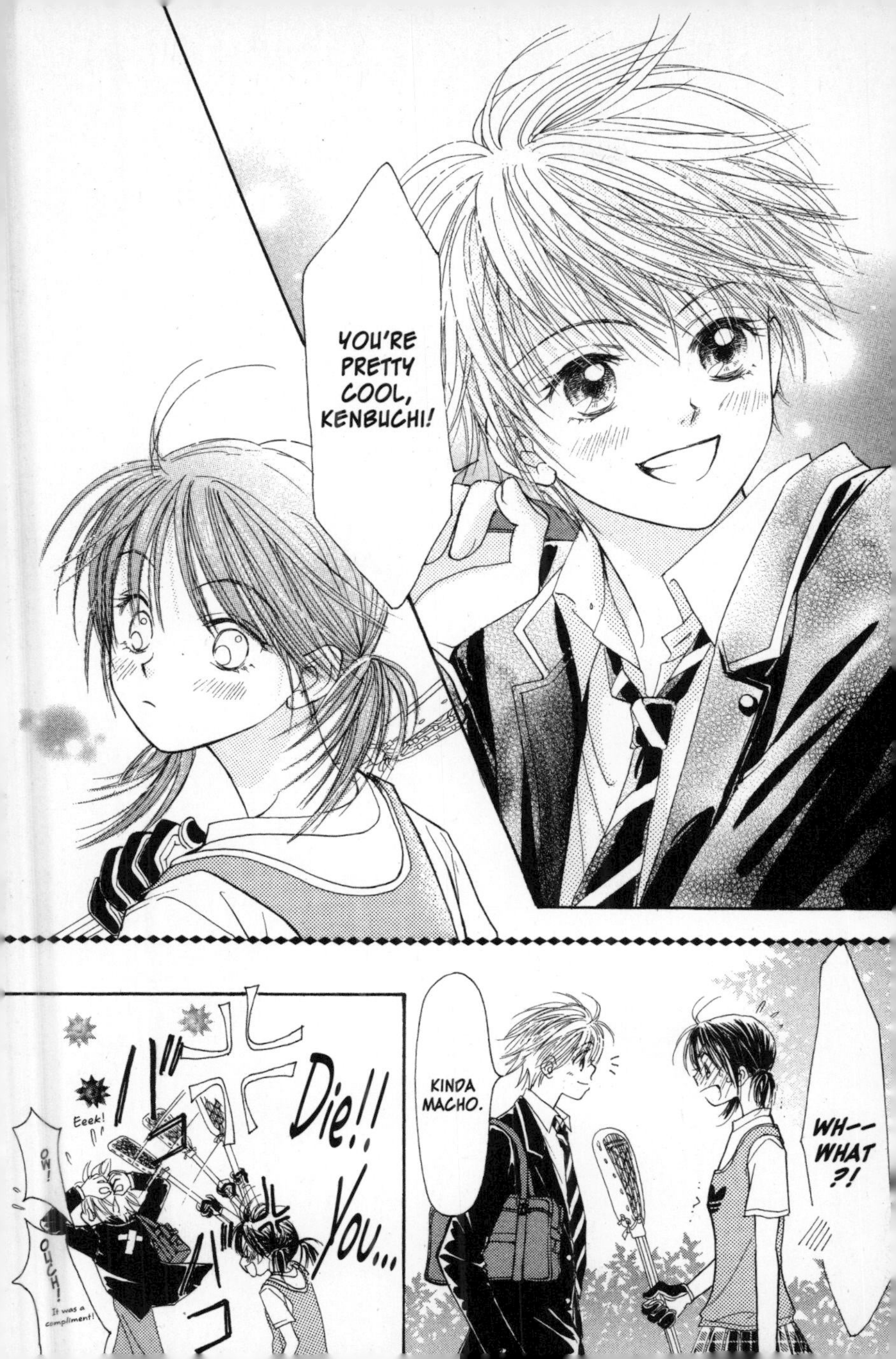
YOU'RE PRETTY COOL, KENBUCHI!
KINDA MACHO.
WH--WHAT?!
Die!! You...
Eeek!
OW!
OUCH!
It was a compliment!

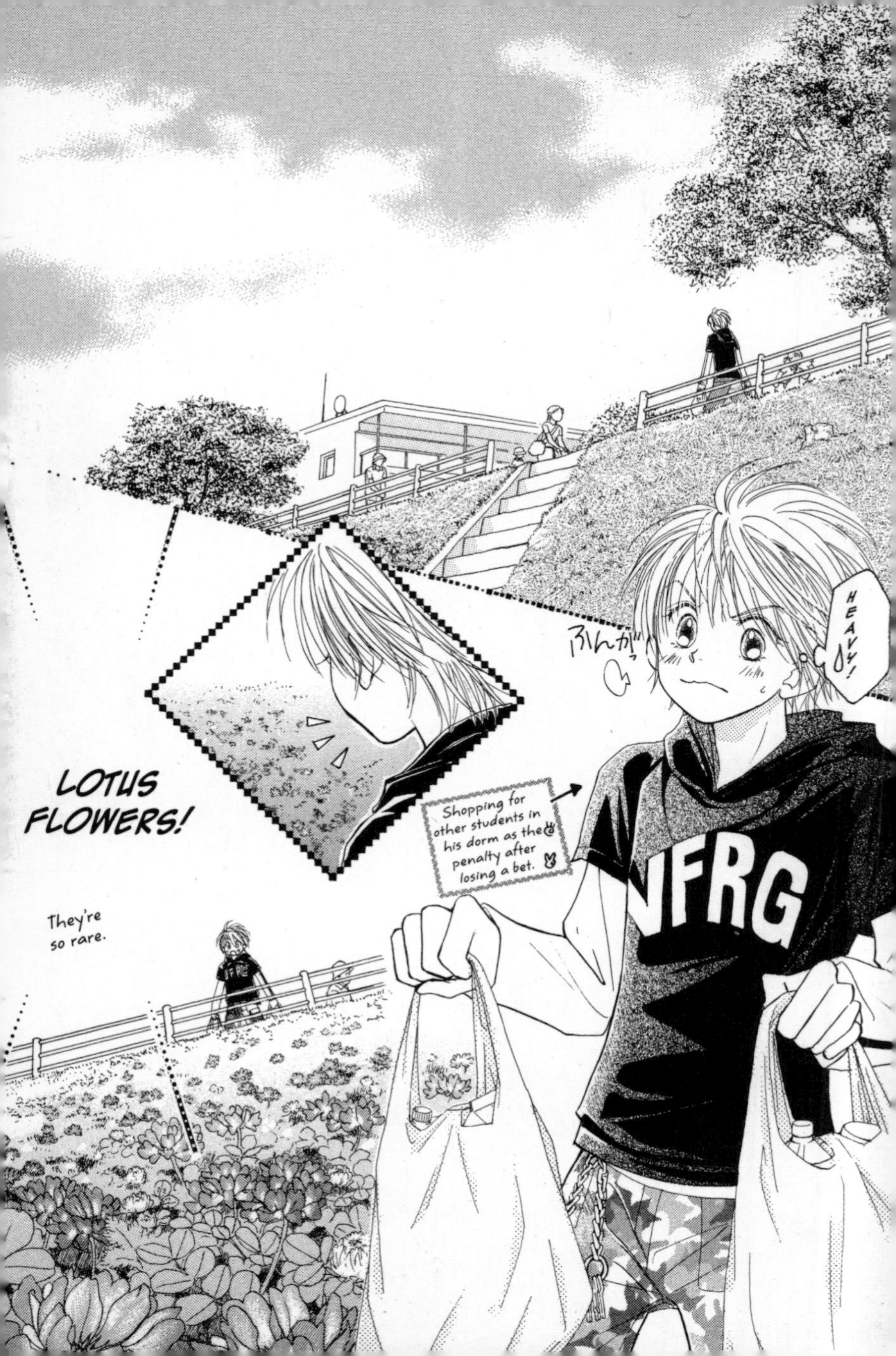
HEAVY!
ふんが!
Shopping for other students in his dorm as the penalty after losing a bet.
NFRG
LOTUS FLOWERS!
They're so rare.

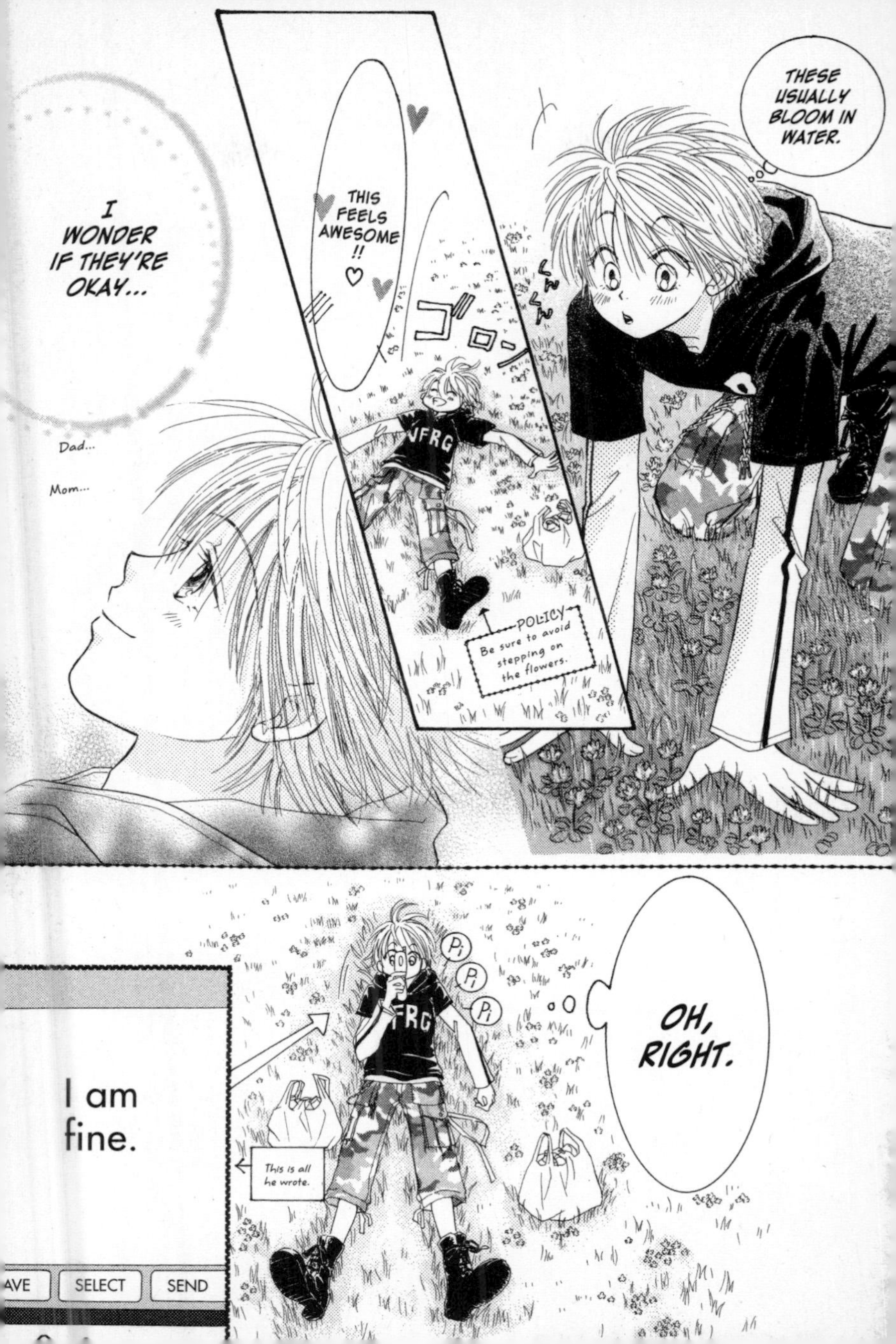
THESE USUALLY BLOOM IN WATER.
THIS FEELS AWESOME!! ♡
POLICY
Be sure to avoid stepping on the flowers.
I WONDER IF THEY'RE OKAY...
Dad...
Mom...
OH, RIGHT.
Pi
Pi
Pi
I am fine.
This is all he wrote.
AVE
SELECT
SEND

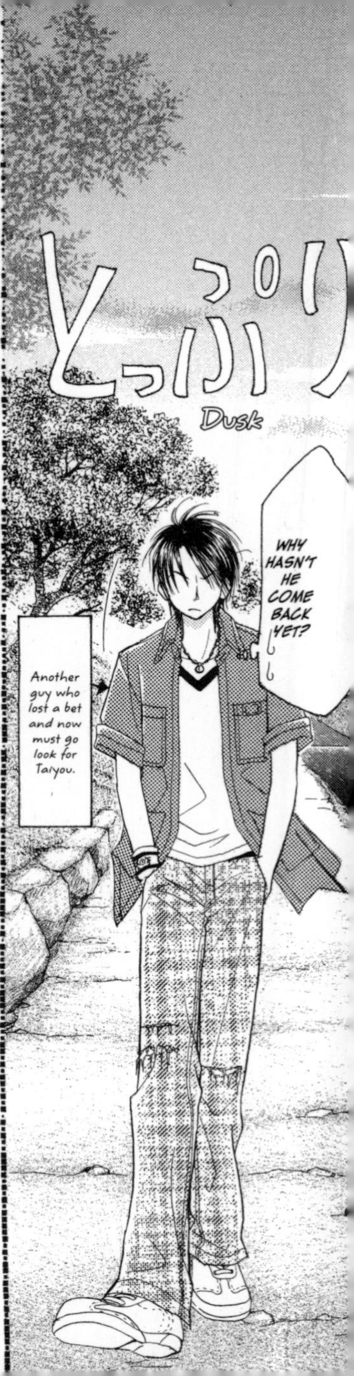
とっぷり
Dusk
WHY HASN'T HE COME BACK YET?
Another guy who lost a bet and now must go look for Taiyou.
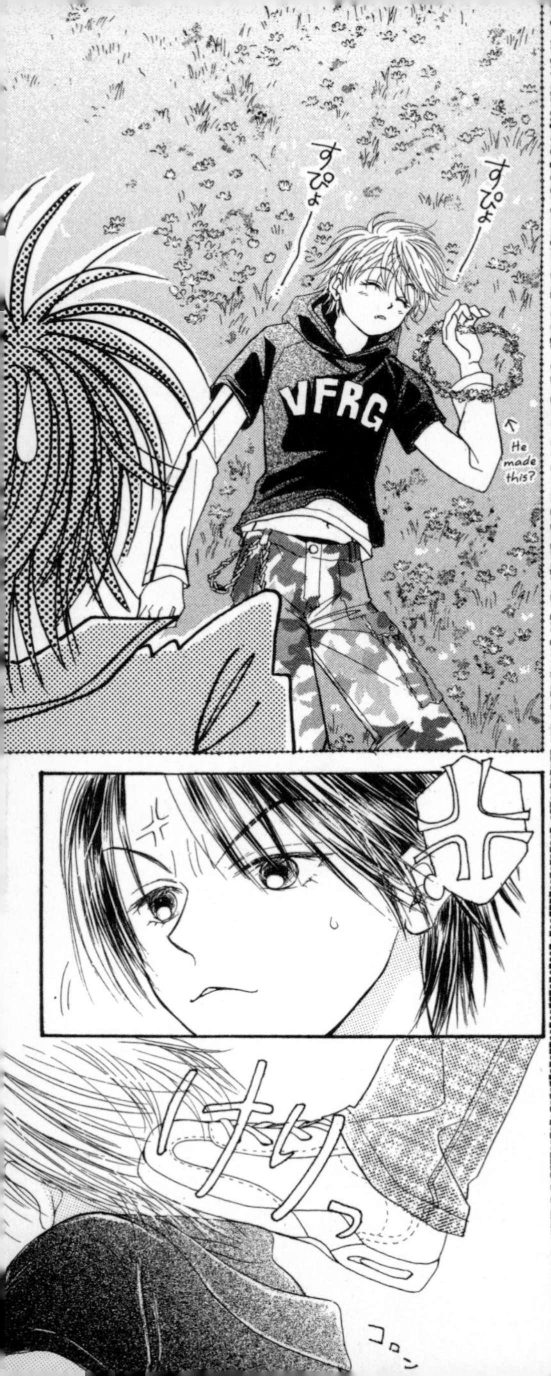
すぴょー
すぴょー
He made this?
けりっ
コロン

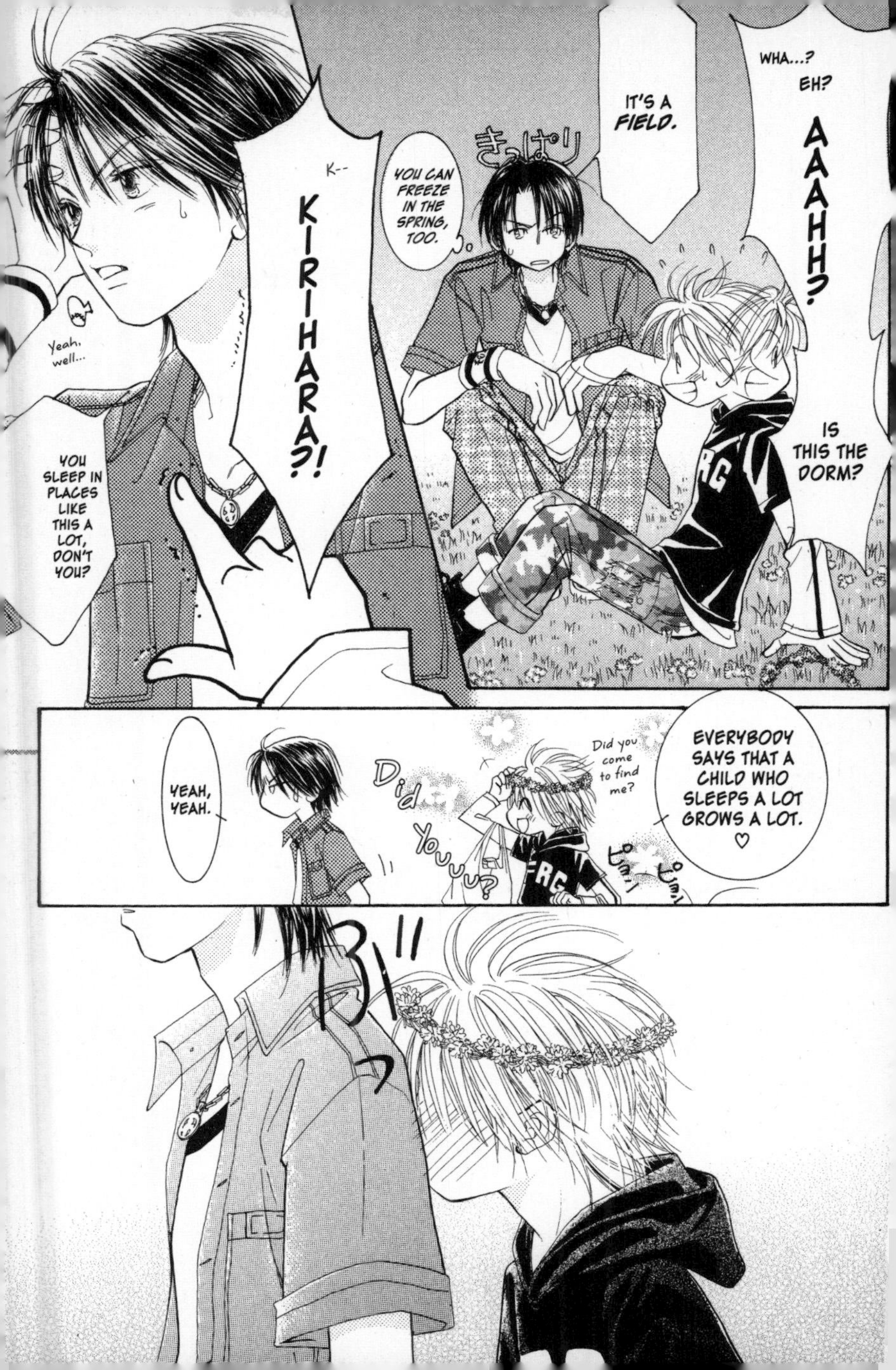
WHA...?
EH?
AAAAHH?
IT'S A FIELD.
きっぱり
IS THIS THE DORM?
YOU CAN FREEZE IN THE SPRING, TOO.
K--
KIRIHARA?!
Yeah, well...
YOU SLEEP IN PLACES LIKE THIS A LOT, DON'T YOU?
EVERYBODY SAYS THAT A CHILD WHO SLEEPS A LOT GROWS A LOT. ♡
Did you come to find me?
Did Youuuu?
YEAH, YEAH.

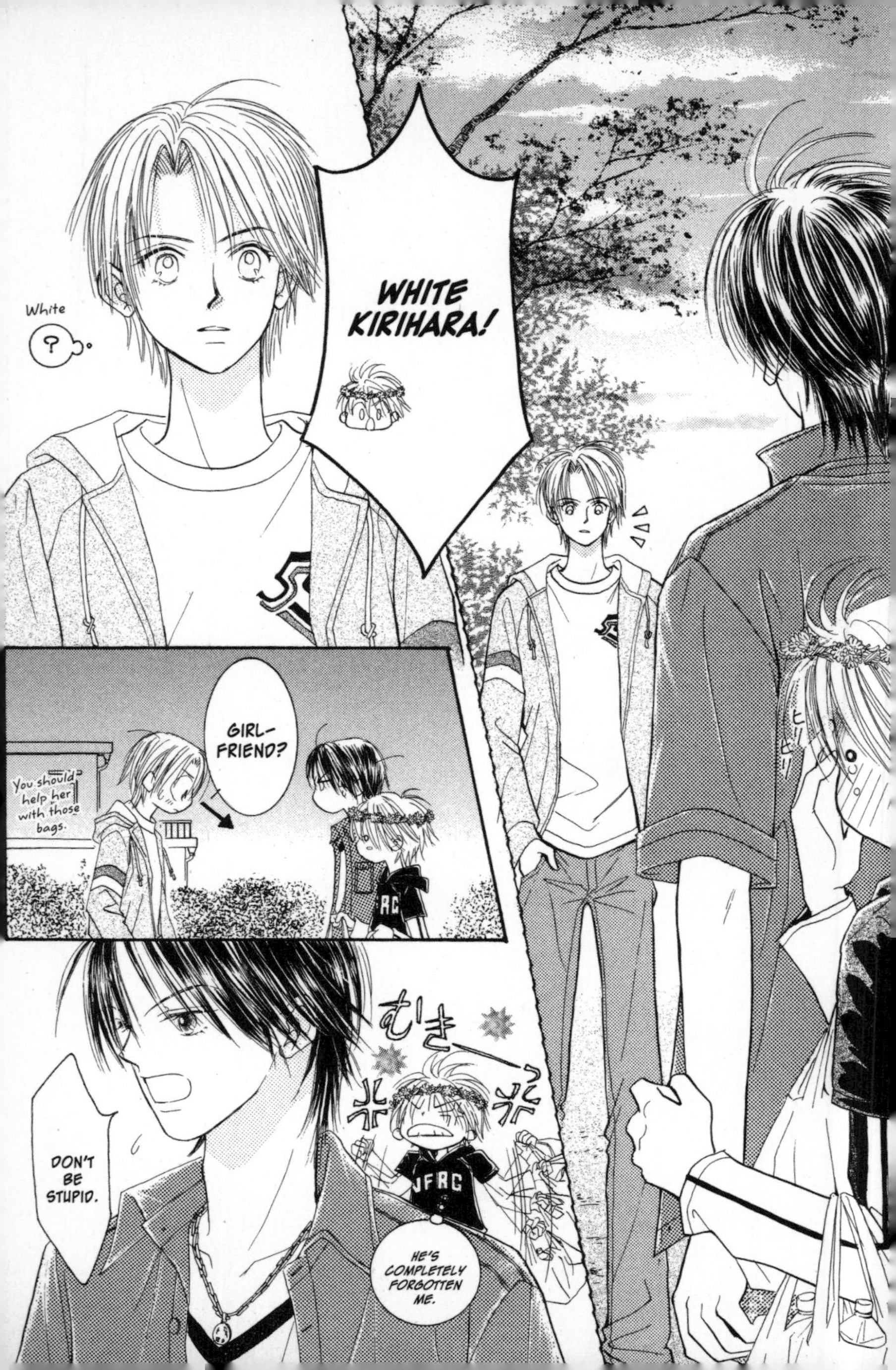
WHITE KIRIHARA!
White
?
GIRL-FRIEND?
You should help her with those bags.
DON'T BE STUPID.
むきー
HE'S COMPLETELY FORGOTTEN ME.

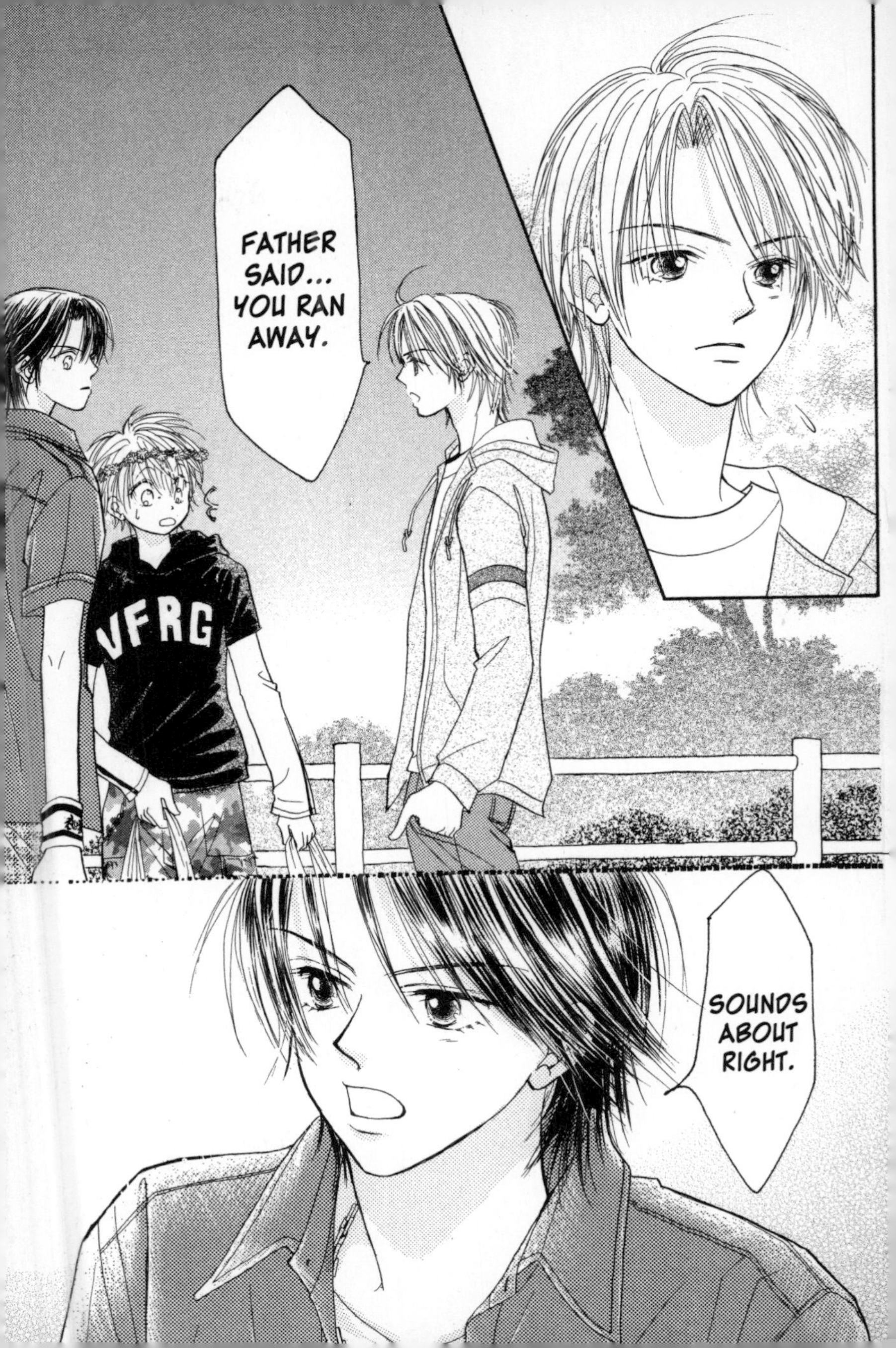
FATHER SAID... YOU RAN AWAY.
SOUNDS ABOUT RIGHT.

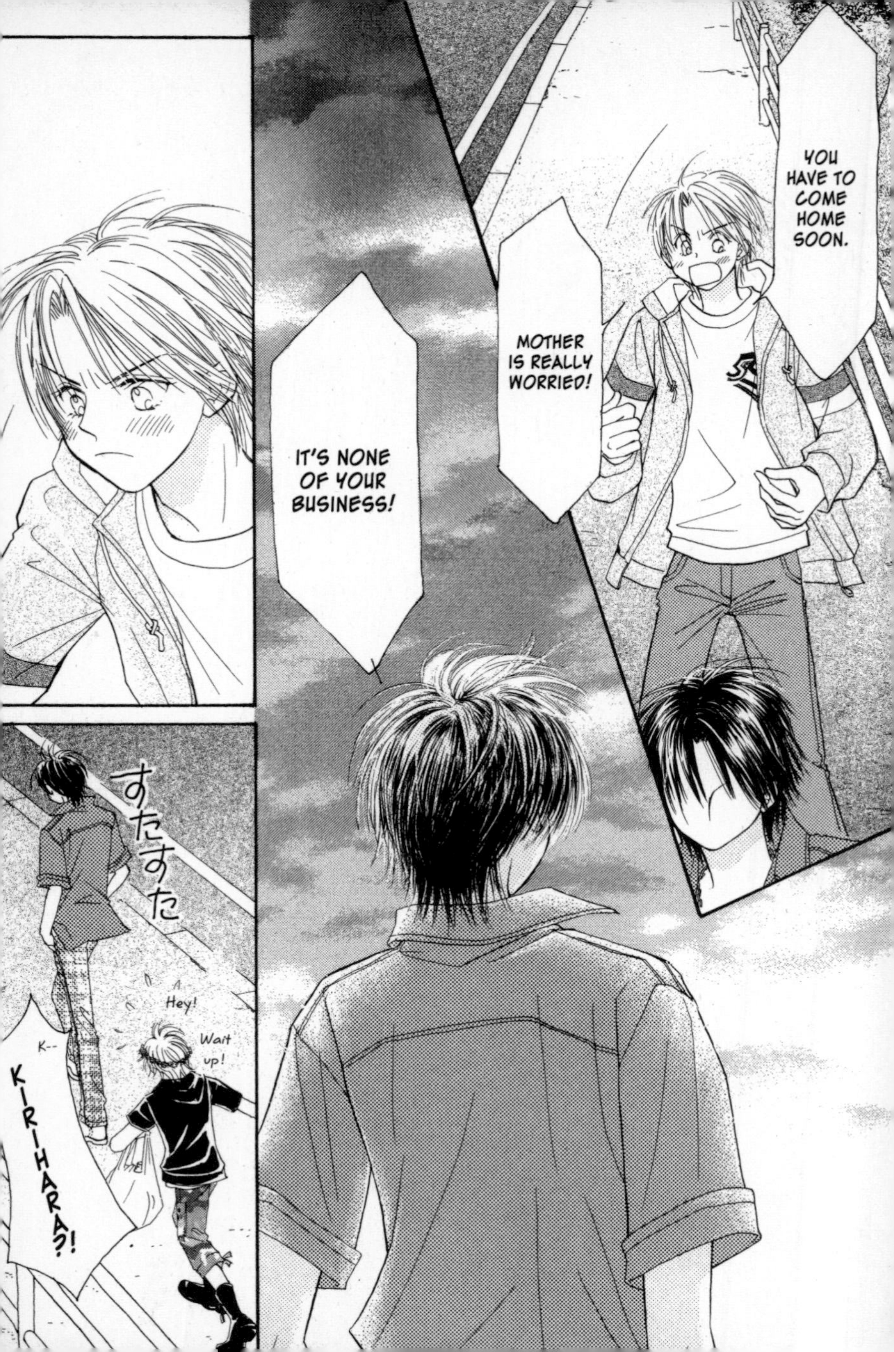
YOU HAVE TO COME HOME SOON.
MOTHER IS REALLY WORRIED!
IT'S NONE OF YOUR BUSINESS!
すたすた
Hey!
Wait up!
K--
KIRIHARA?!

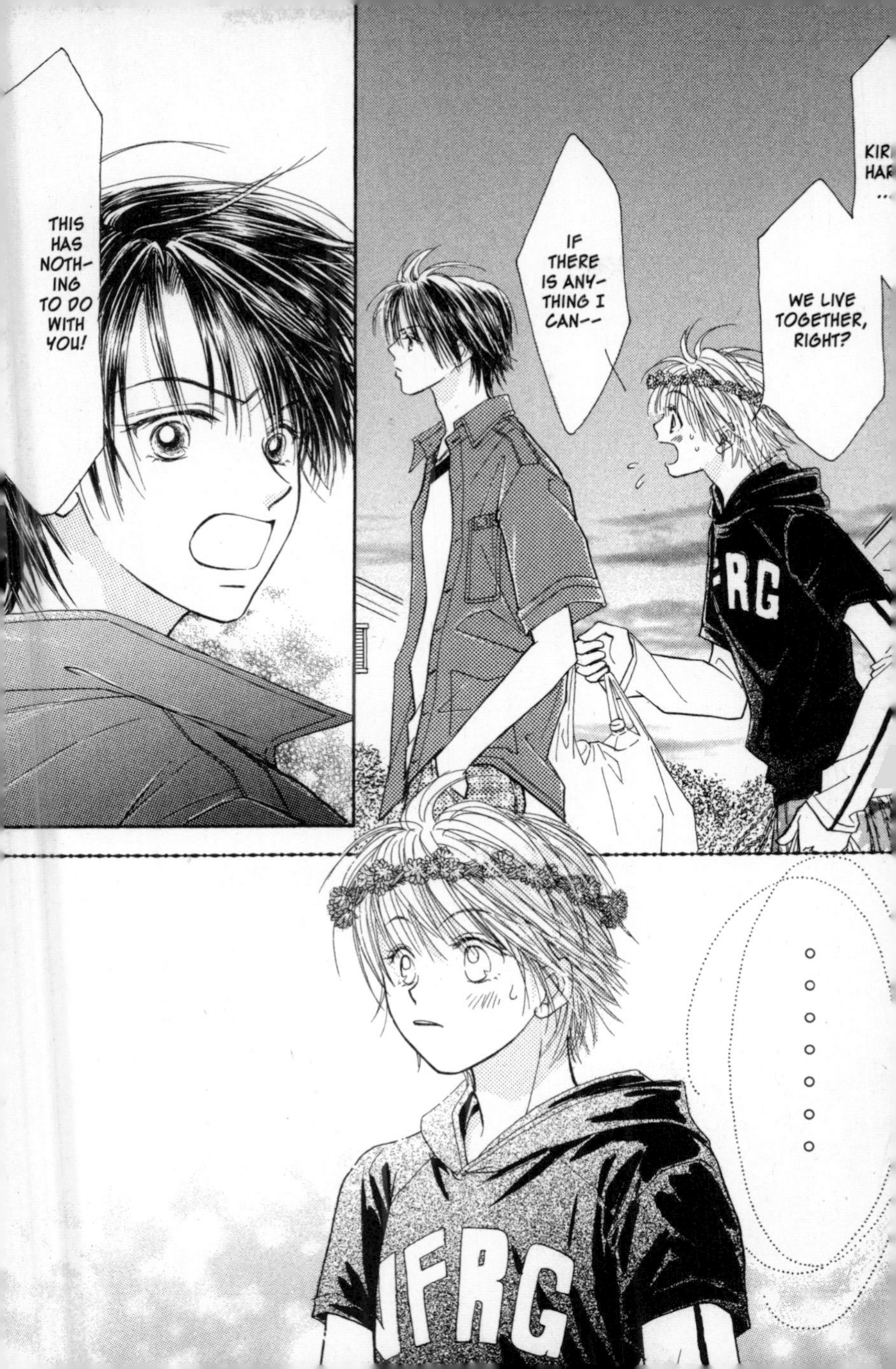
KIRI HAR ...
WE LIVE TOGETHER, RIGHT?
IF THERE IS ANY-THING I CAN--
THIS HAS NOTH-ING TO DO WITH YOU!
....

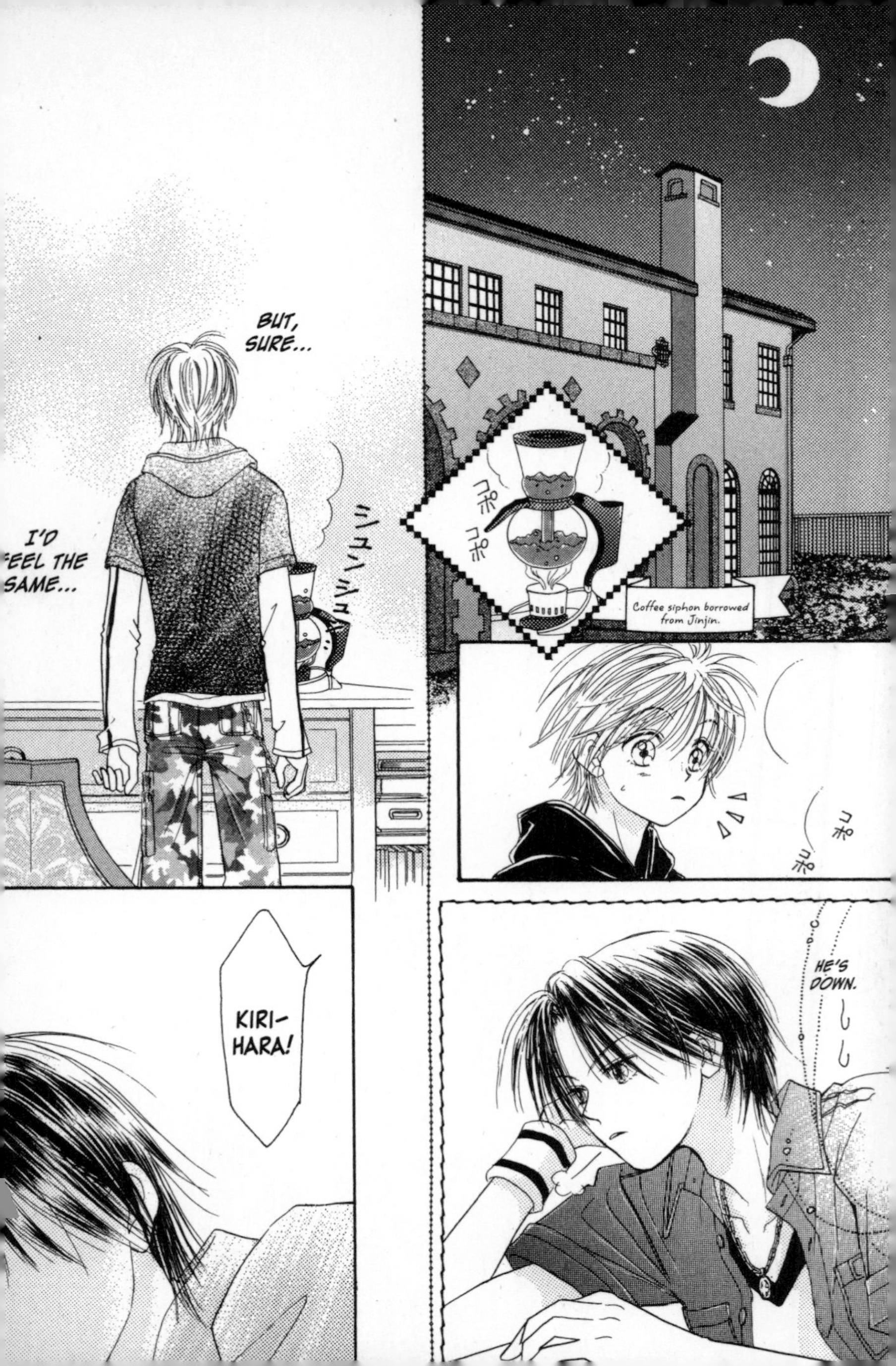
コポ
コポ
Coffee siphon borrowed from Jinjin.
HE'S DOWN.
BUT, SURE...
I'D FEEL THE SAME...
シュンシュン
KIRI-HARA!

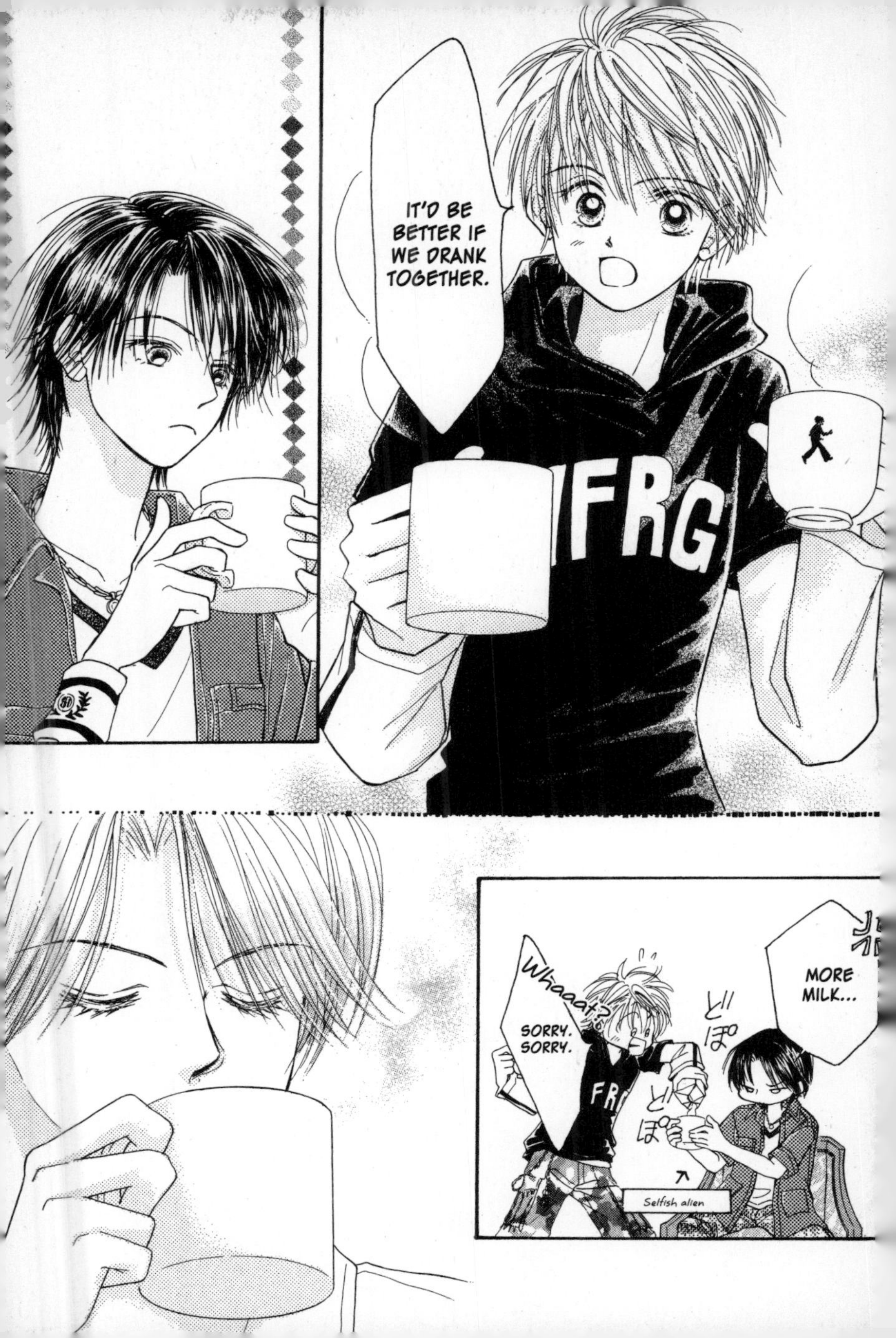
IT'D BE BETTER IF WE DRANK TOGETHER.
MORE MILK...
どぽ
Whaaat?
SORRY. SORRY.
どぽ
Selfish alien

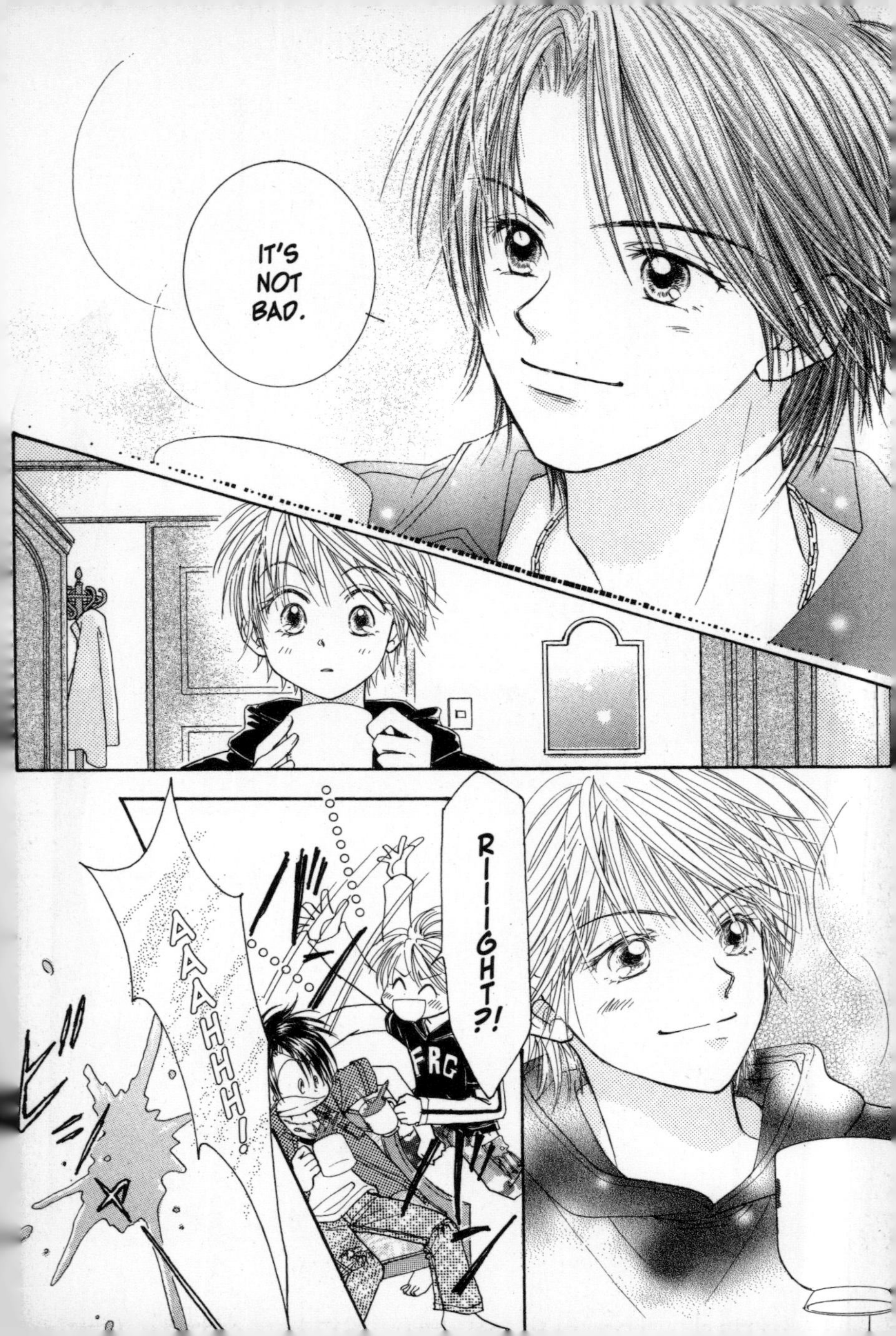
IT'S NOT BAD.
RIIIGHT?!
AAAHHHH!

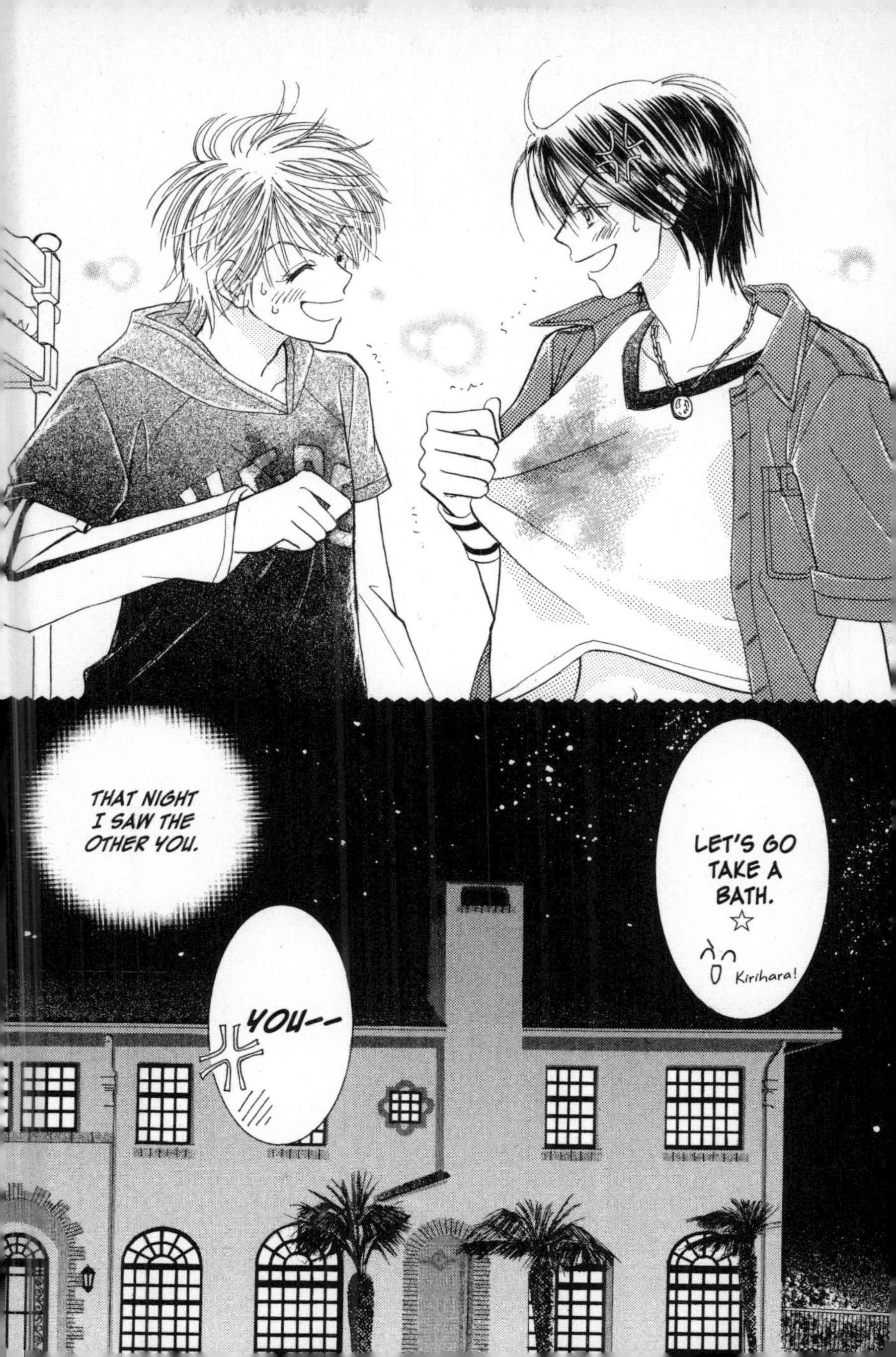
LET'S GO TAKE A BATH. ☆
Kirihara!
YOU--
THAT NIGHT I SAW THE OTHER YOU.

Chapter 3

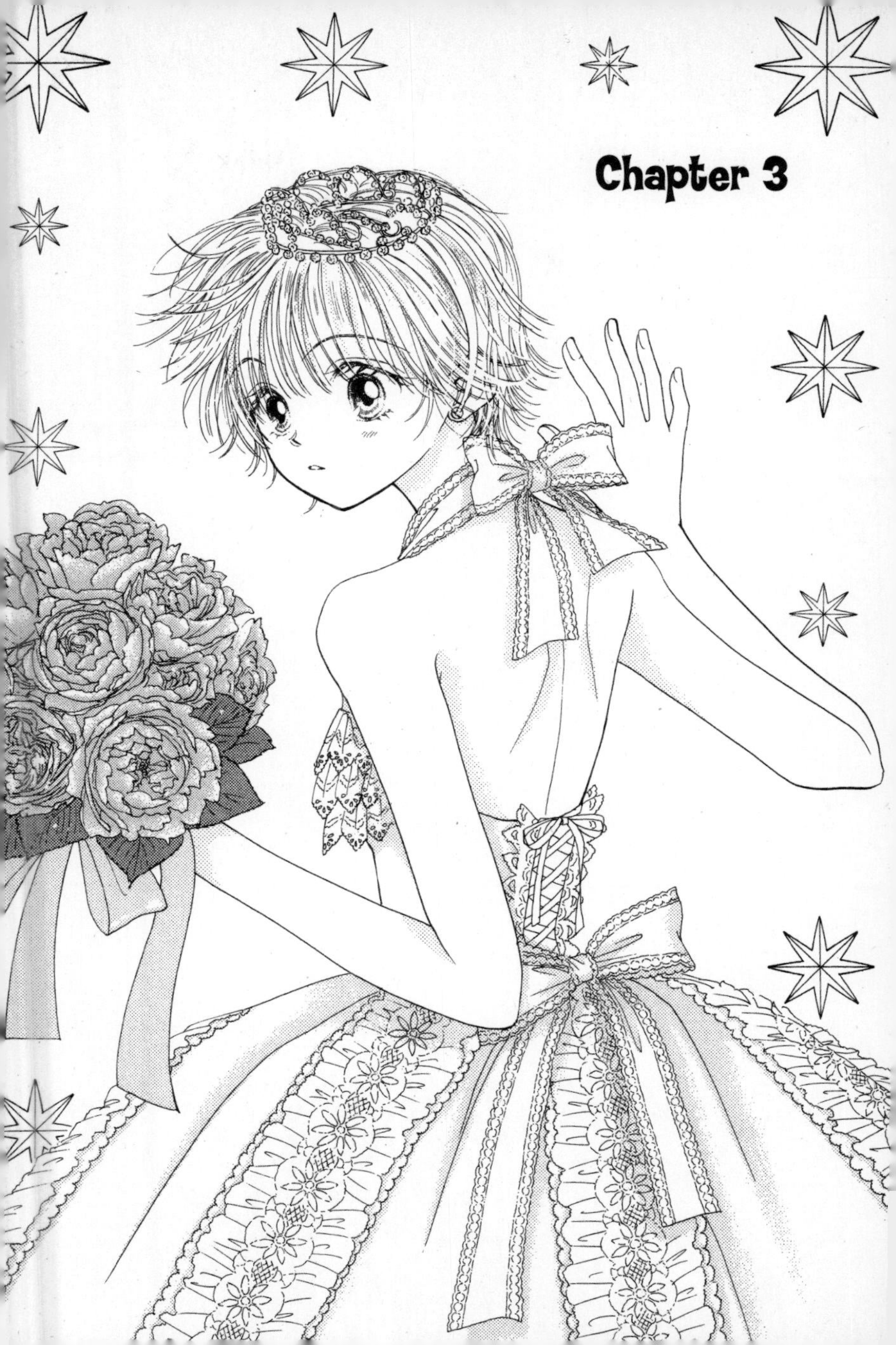

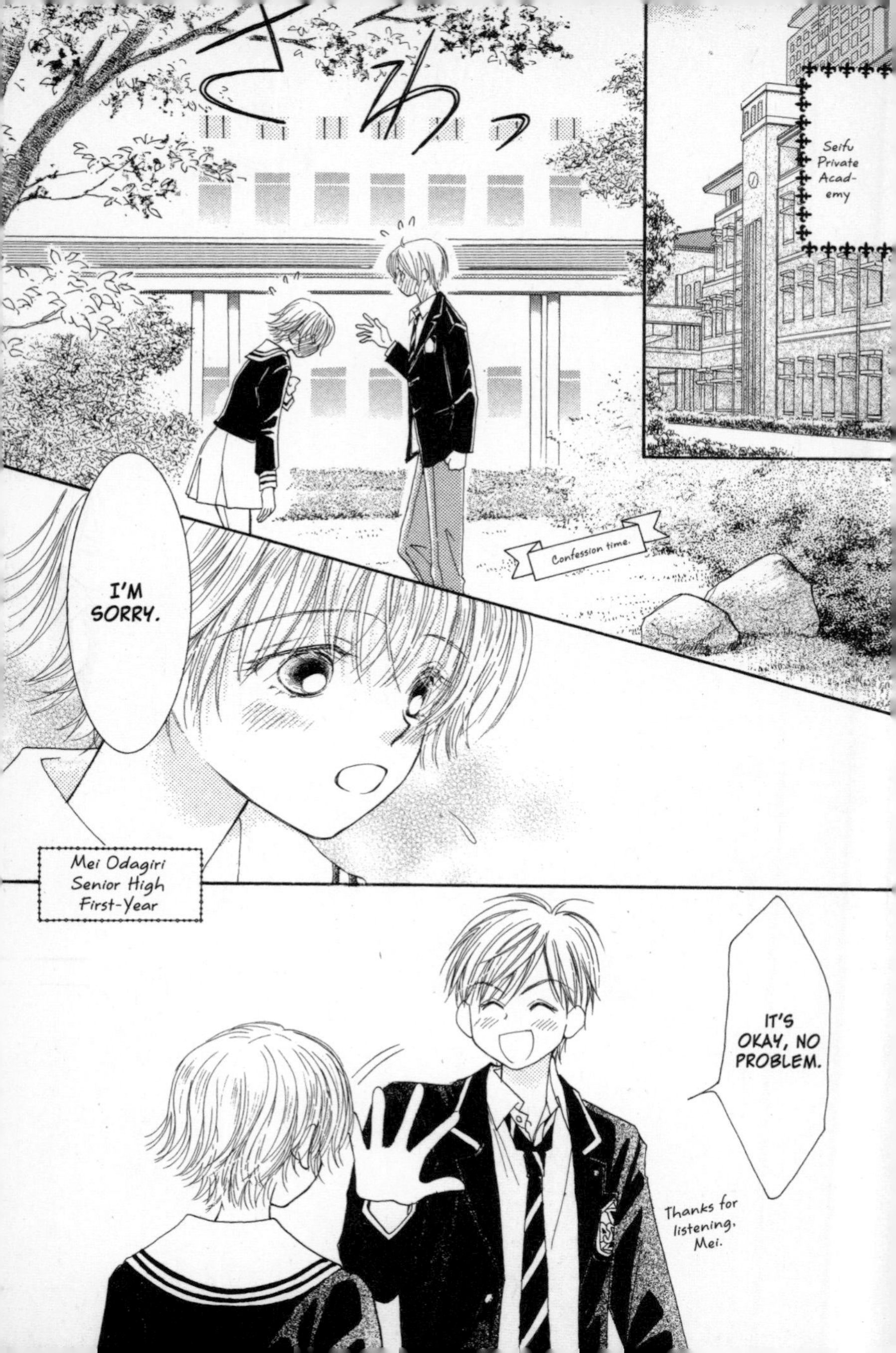
Seifu Private Academy
さわっ
Confession time.
I'M SORRY.
Mei Odagiri Senior High First-Year
IT'S OKAY, NO PROBLEM.
Thanks for listening, Mei.

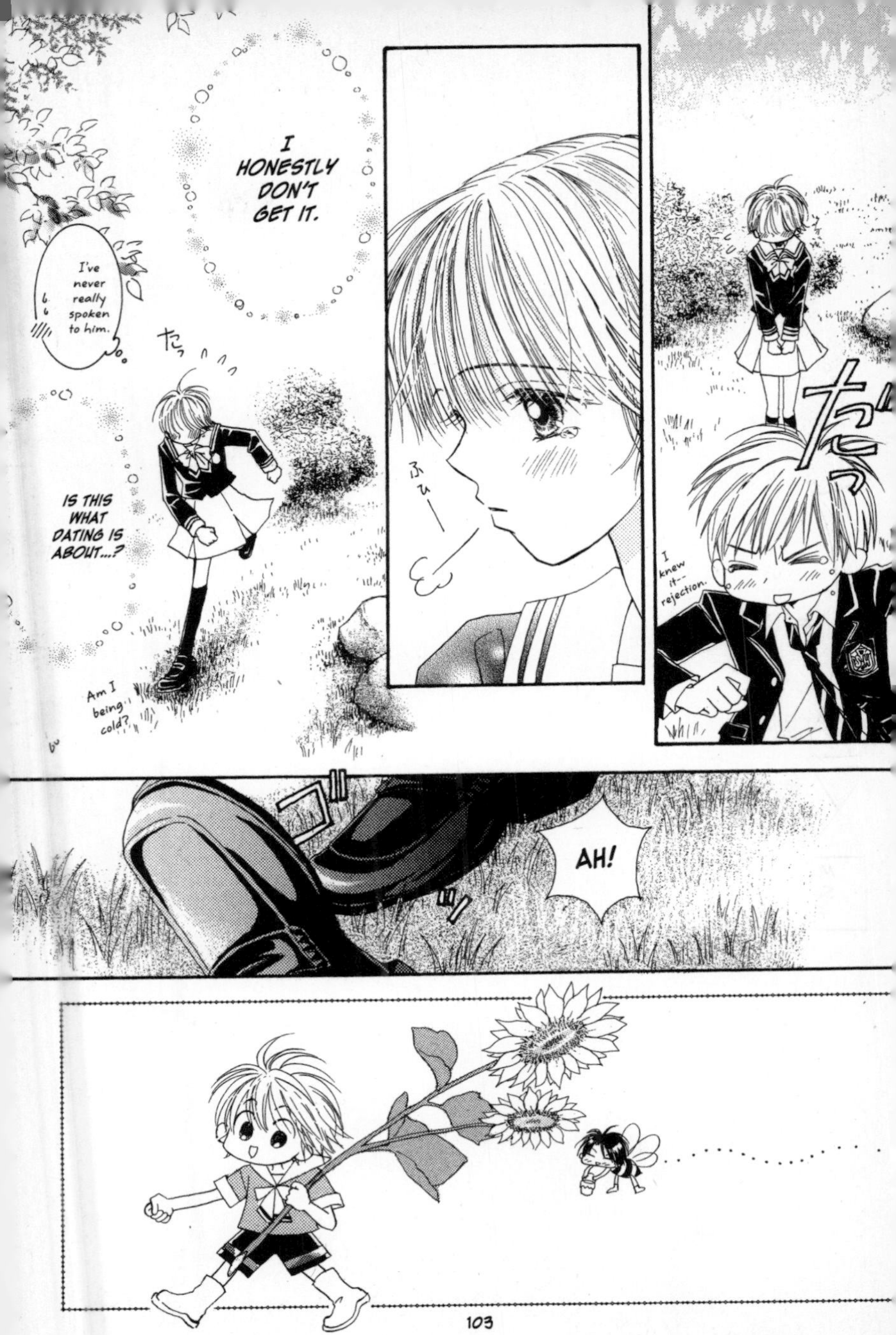
だっ
I knew it-- rejection.
ふぅ—
I HONESTLY DON'T GET IT.
I've never really spoken to him.
たっ
IS THIS WHAT DATING IS ABOUT...?
Am I being cold?
AH!

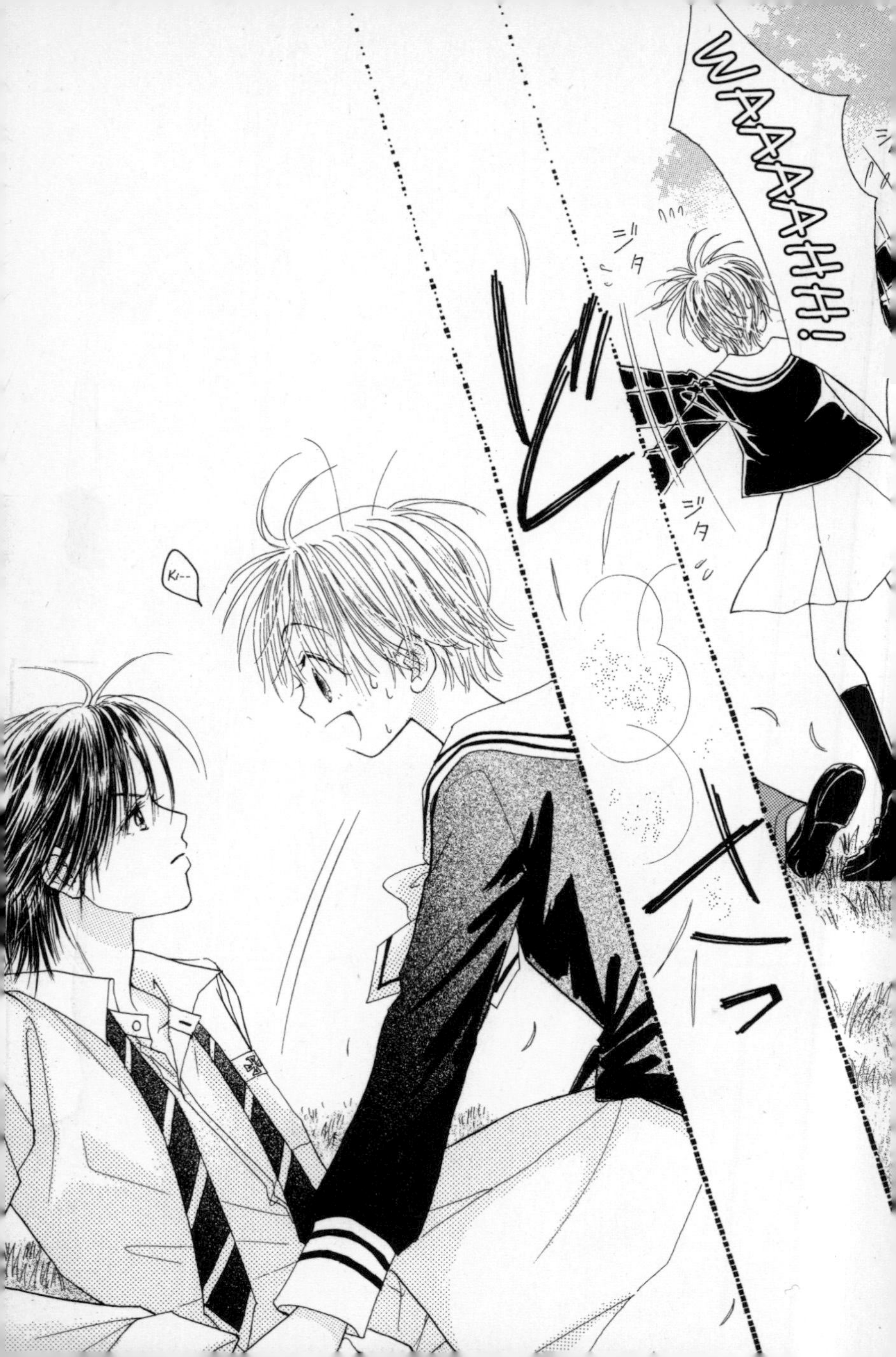
WAAAAHHH!
ジタ
ジタ
Ki--

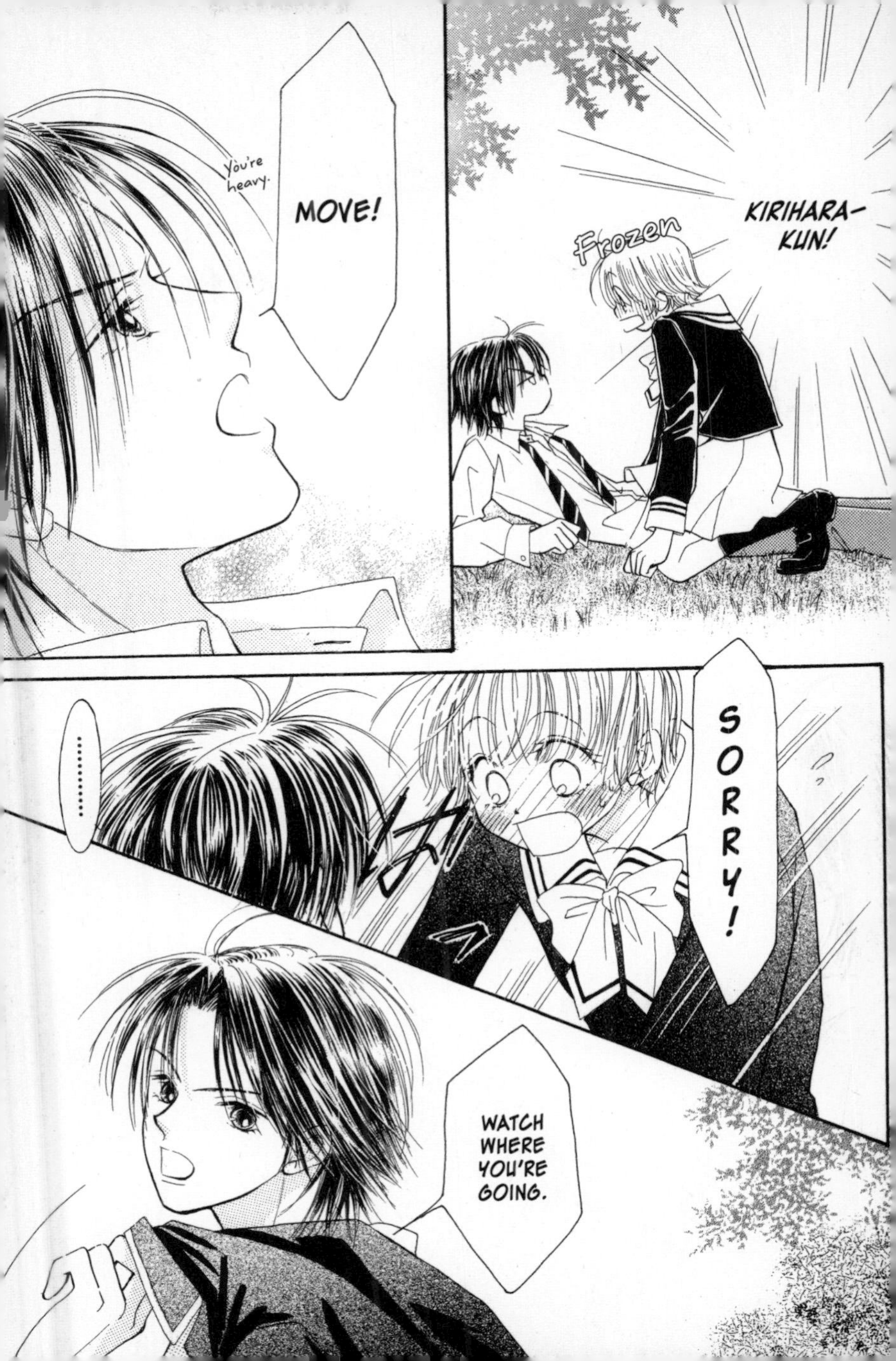
KIRIHARA-KUN!
Frozen
MOVE!
You're heavy.
SORRY!
....
WATCH WHERE YOU'RE GOING.

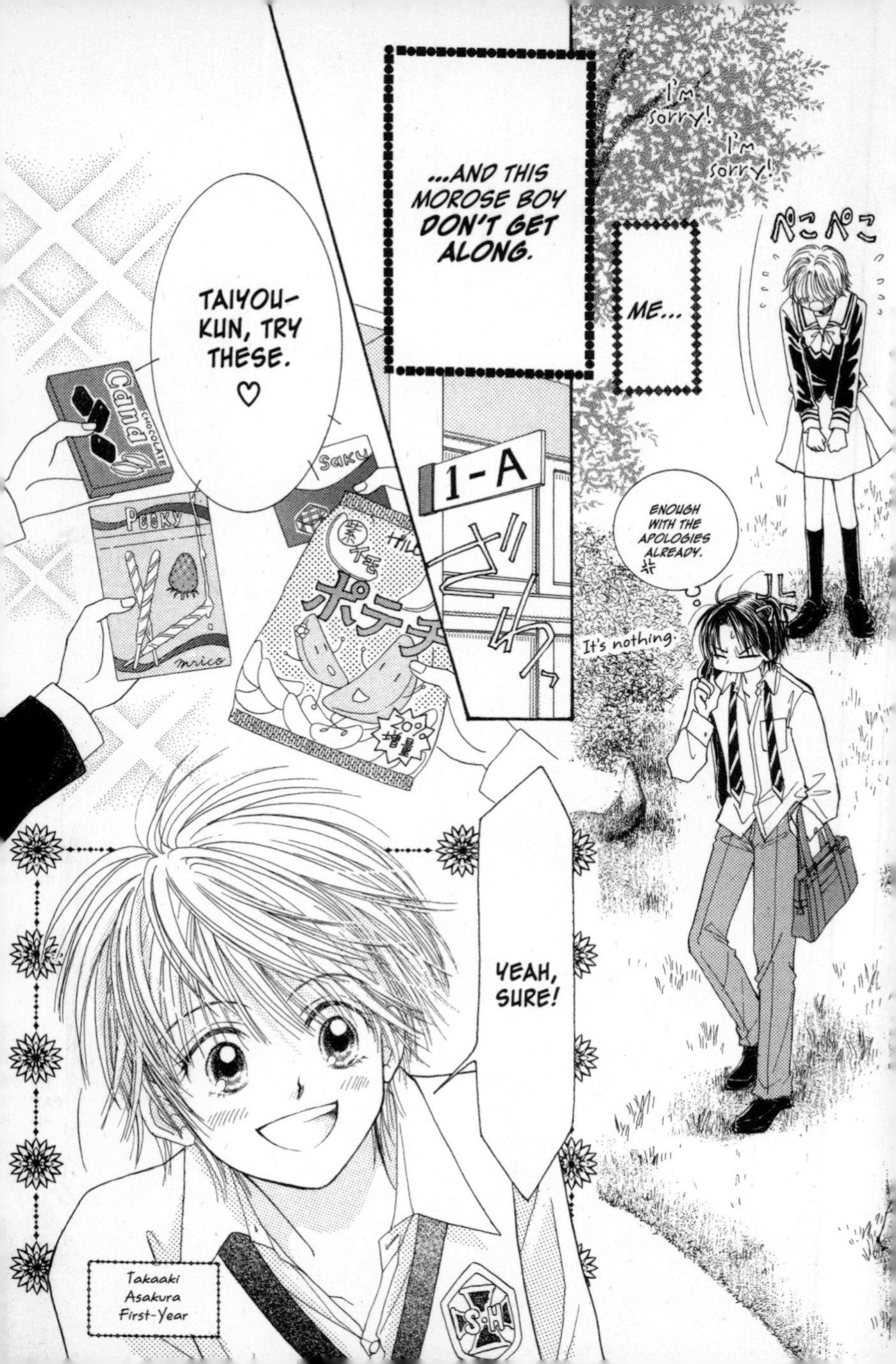
I'm sorry! I'm sorry!
ぺこぺこ
ME...
ENOUGH WITH THE APOLOGIES ALREADY.
It's nothing.
...AND THIS MOROSE BOY DON'T GET ALONG.
1-A
TAIYOU-KUN, TRY THESE. ♡
YEAH, SURE!
Takaaki Asakura First-Year

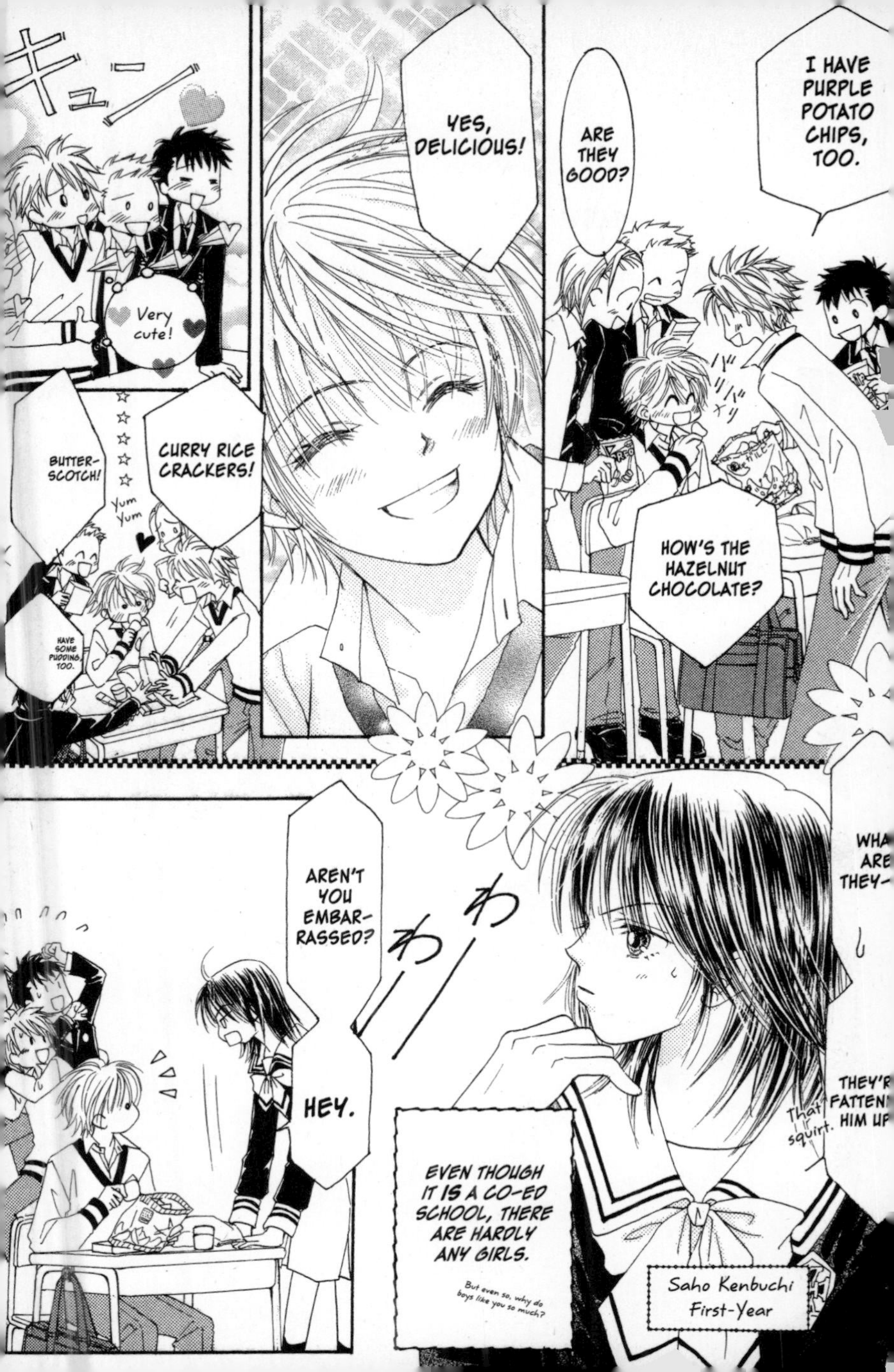
I HAVE PURPLE POTATO CHIPS, TOO.
ARE THEY GOOD?
HOW'S THE HAZELNUT CHOCOLATE?
YES, DELICIOUS!
Very cute!
CURRY RICE CRACKERS!
BUTTER-SCOTCH!
Yum Yum
HAVE SOME PUDDING, TOO.
WHA ARE THEY-
THEY'R FATTEN HIM UP
That squirt.
Saho Kenbuchi First-Year
EVEN THOUGH IT IS A CO-ED SCHOOL, THERE ARE HARDLY ANY GIRLS.
But even so, why do boys like you so much?
AREN'T YOU EMBAR-RASSED?
HEY.

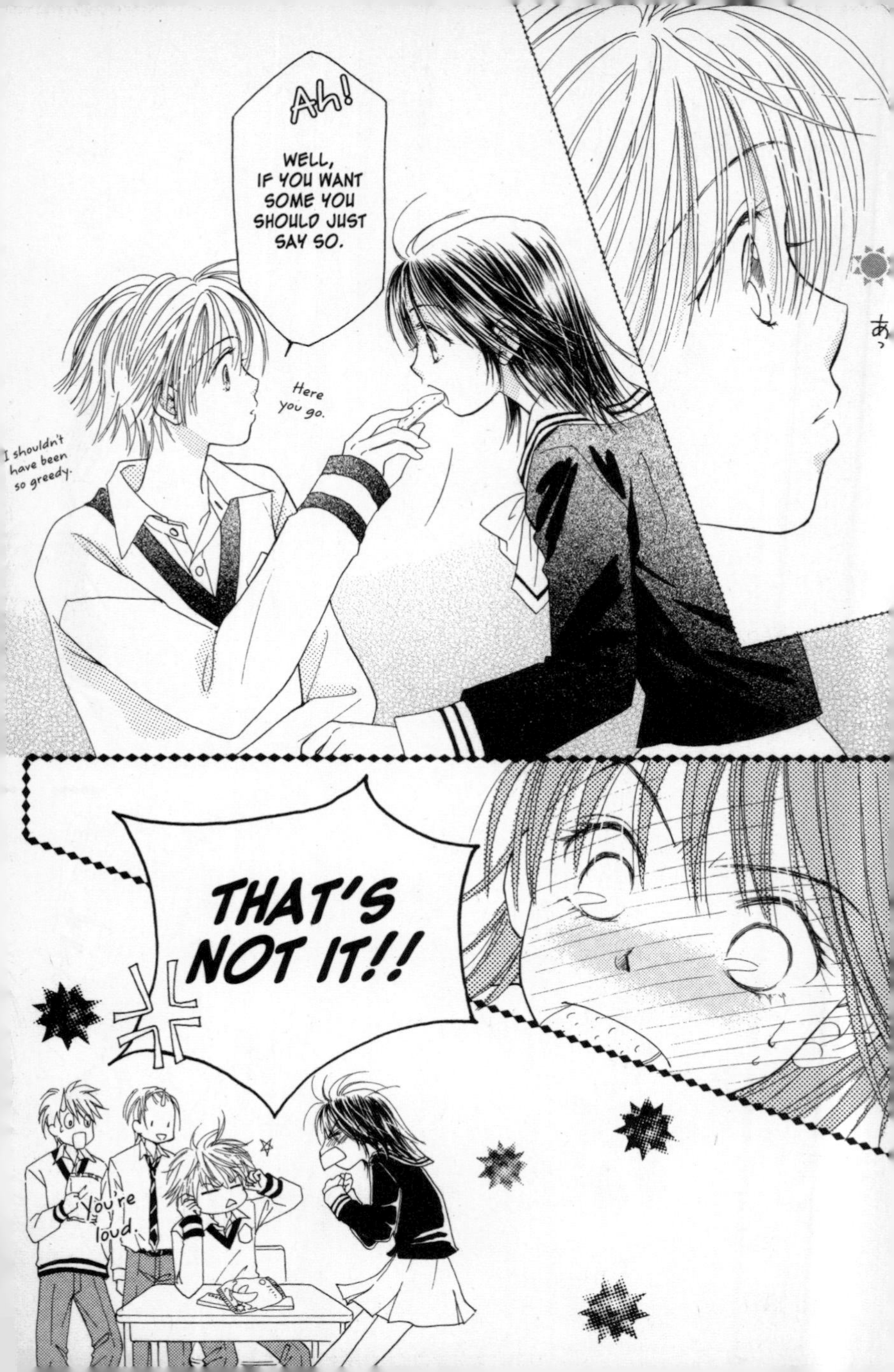
あっ
Ah!
WELL, IF YOU WANT SOME YOU SHOULD JUST SAY SO.
Here you go.
I shouldn't have been so greedy.
THAT'S NOT IT!!
You're loud.

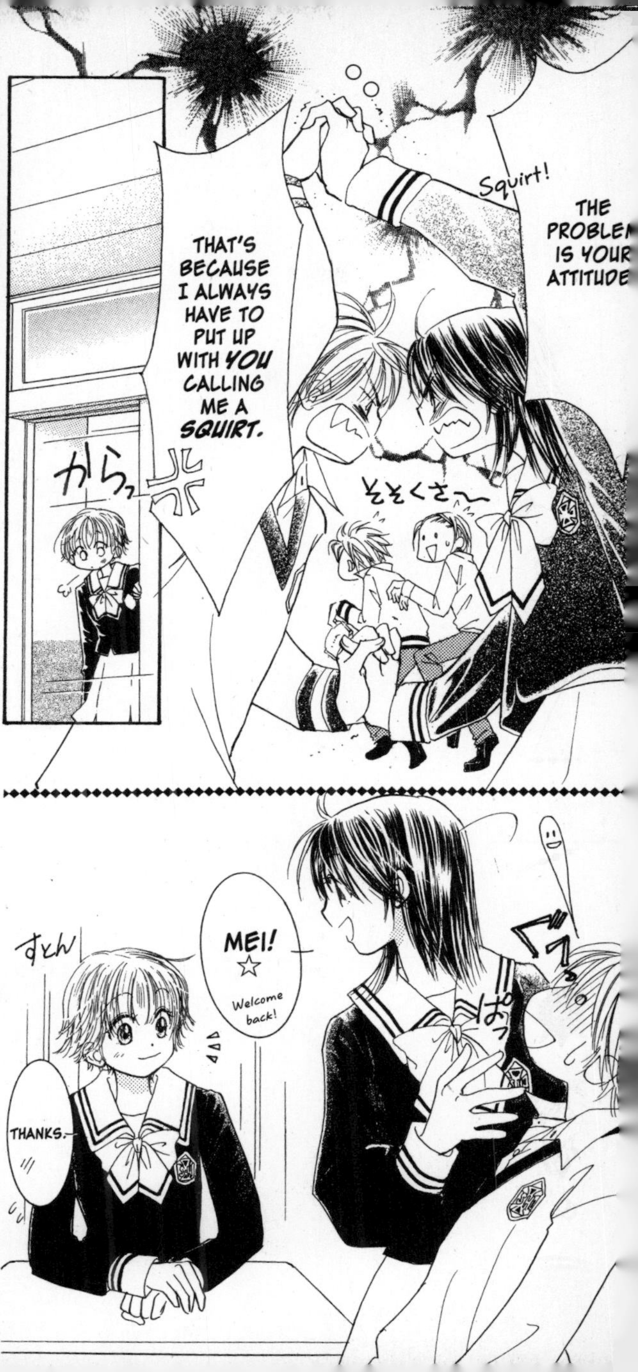
THE PROBLEM IS YOUR ATTITUDE
Squirt!
THAT'S BECAUSE I ALWAYS HAVE TO PUT UP WITH *YOU* CALLING ME A *SQUIRT*.
そそくさ～
からっ
ぱっ
MEI! ☆
Welcome back!
すとん
THANKS.

Characters who's who? ②

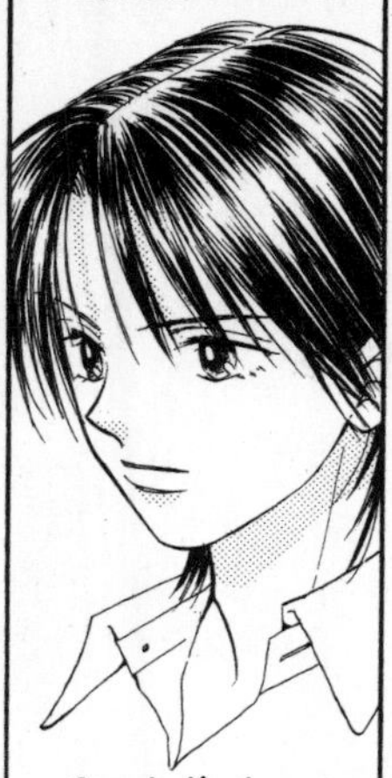

Sonoh Kirihara

First-year in high school

- Taiyou's roommate
- A twin (he's older)
- The heir to the Ikebana House of the Way of the Empress Flower
- Does everything at his own pace
- Left home (?)

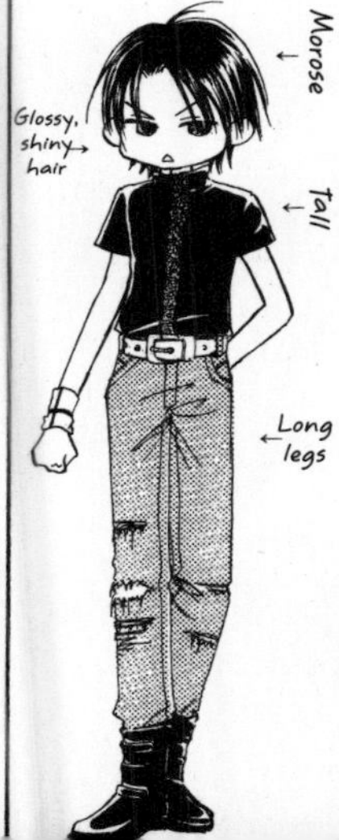
Morose
Glossy, shiny hair
Tall
Long legs

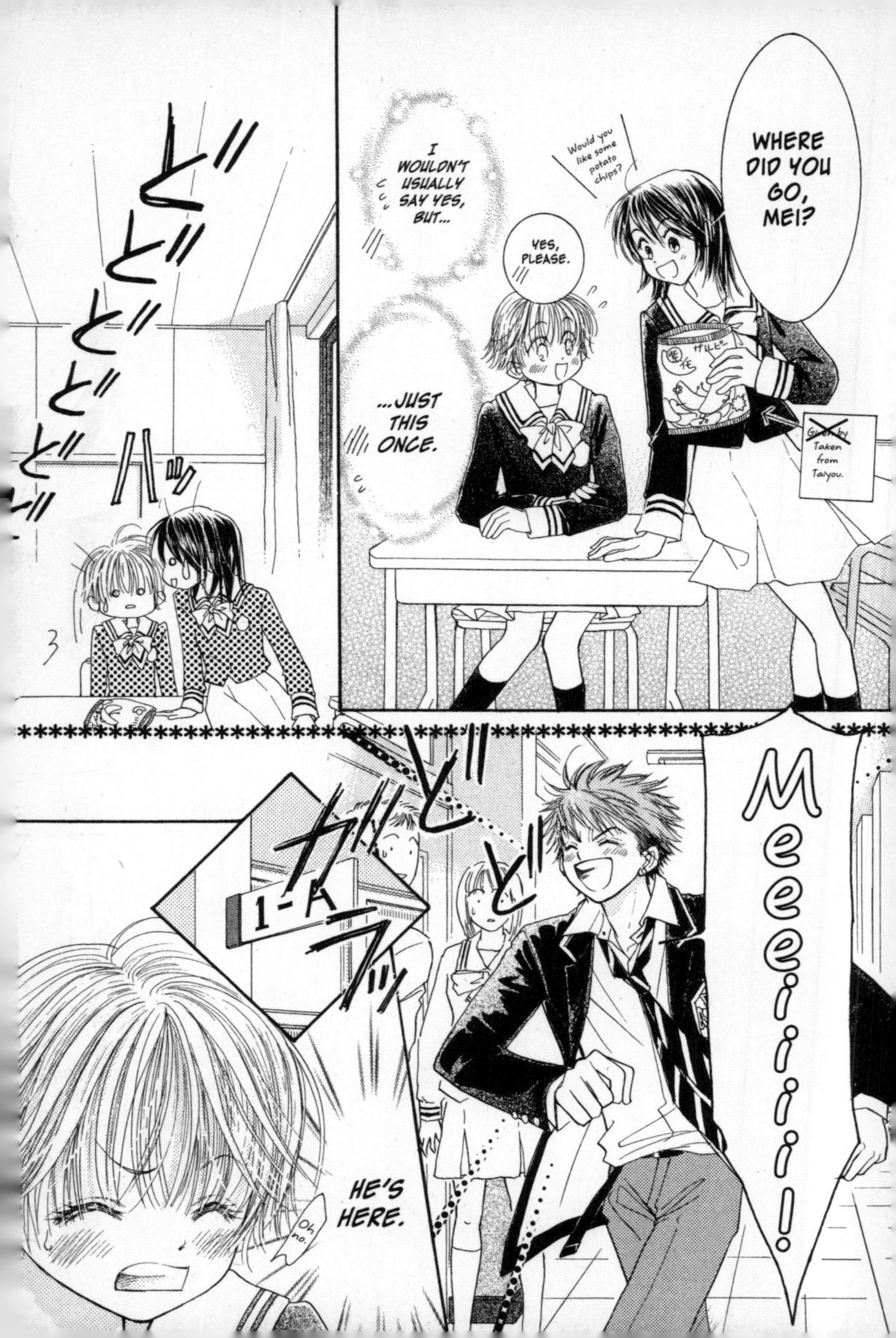
WHERE DID YOU GO, MEI?
Would you like some potato chips?
YES, PLEASE.
I WOULDN'T USUALLY SAY YES, BUT...
...JUST THIS ONCE.
~~Given~~ by Taken from Taiyou.
どどどどど
ハッ
Meeeiiiii!
どど
ガラッ
1-A
HE'S HERE.
Oh no.

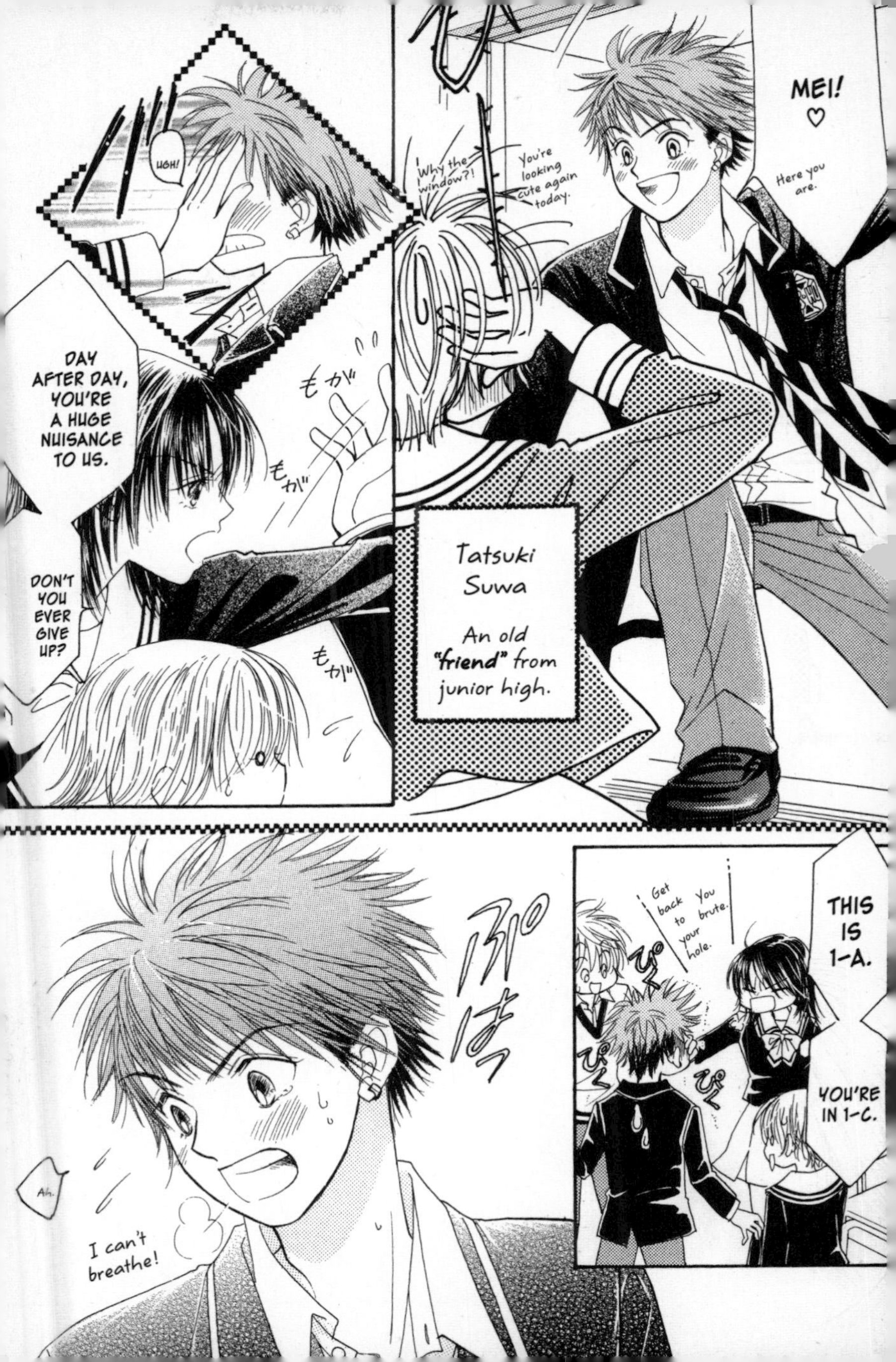
MEI! ♡
Here you are.
You're looking cute again today.
Why the window?!
もが
Tatsuki Suwa
An old "friend" from junior high.
UGH!
DAY AFTER DAY, YOU'RE A HUGE NUISANCE TO US.
もが
DON'T YOU EVER GIVE UP?
もが
THIS IS 1-A.
YOU'RE IN 1-C.
You brute.
Get back to your hole.
ぴく
ぴく
ぴく
ぷはっ
Ah.
I can't breathe!

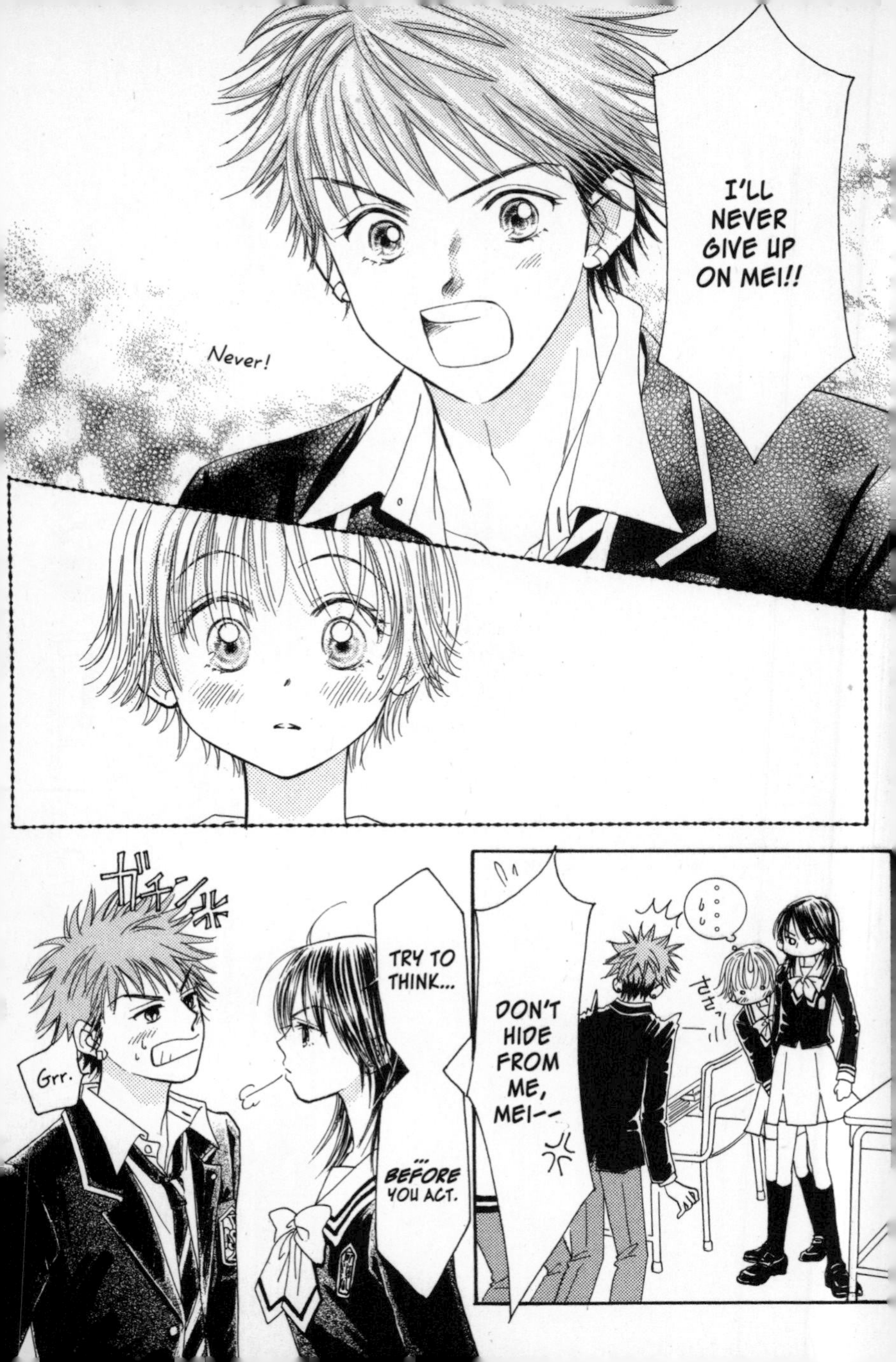
I'LL NEVER GIVE UP ON MEI!!
Never!
DON'T HIDE FROM ME, MEI--
TRY TO THINK...
...BEFORE YOU ACT.
ガチン
Grr.

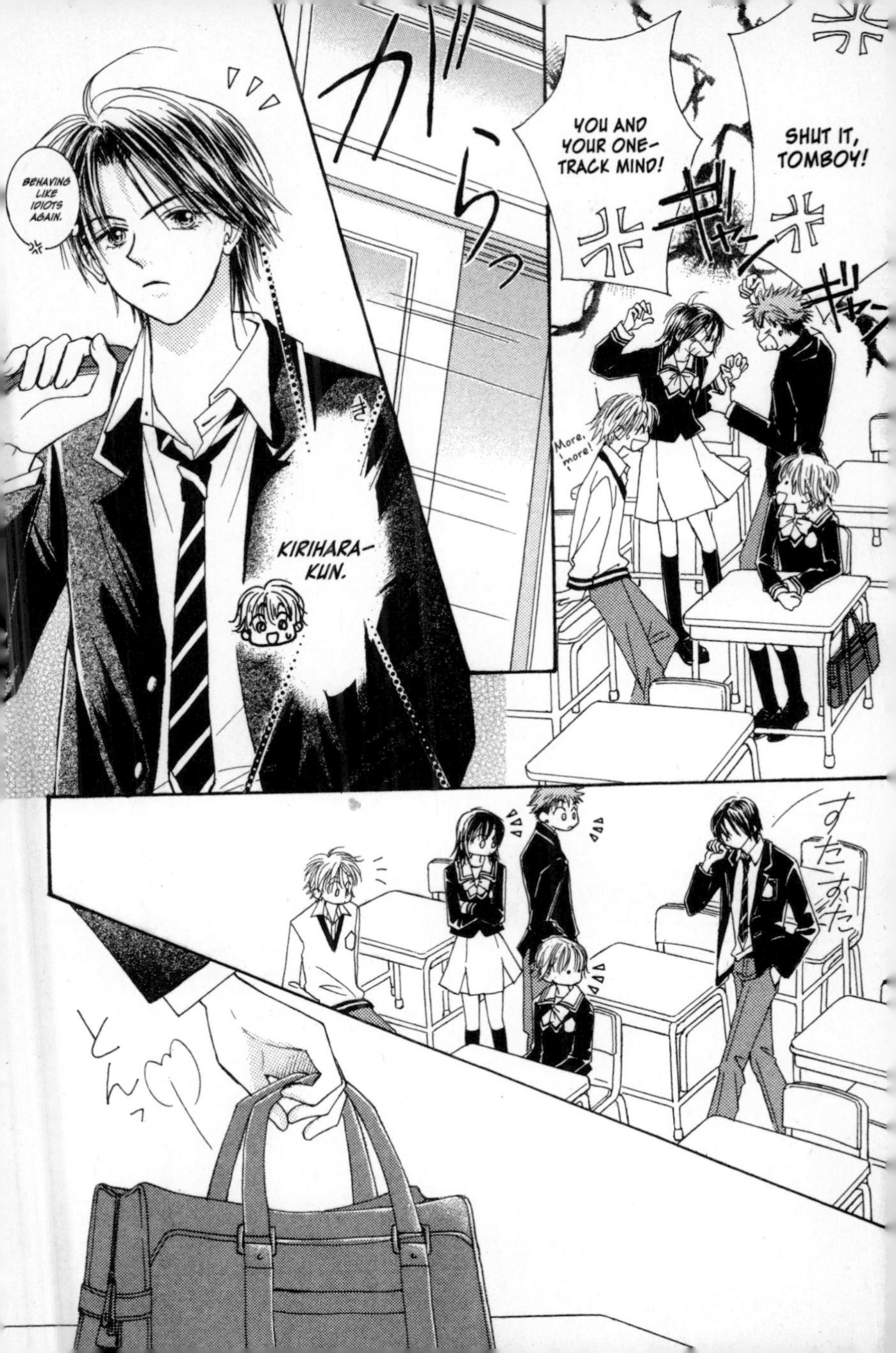
SHUT IT, TOMBOY!
YOU AND YOUR ONE-TRACK MIND!
More, more!
KIRIHARA-KUN.
BEHAVING LIKE IDIOTS AGAIN.

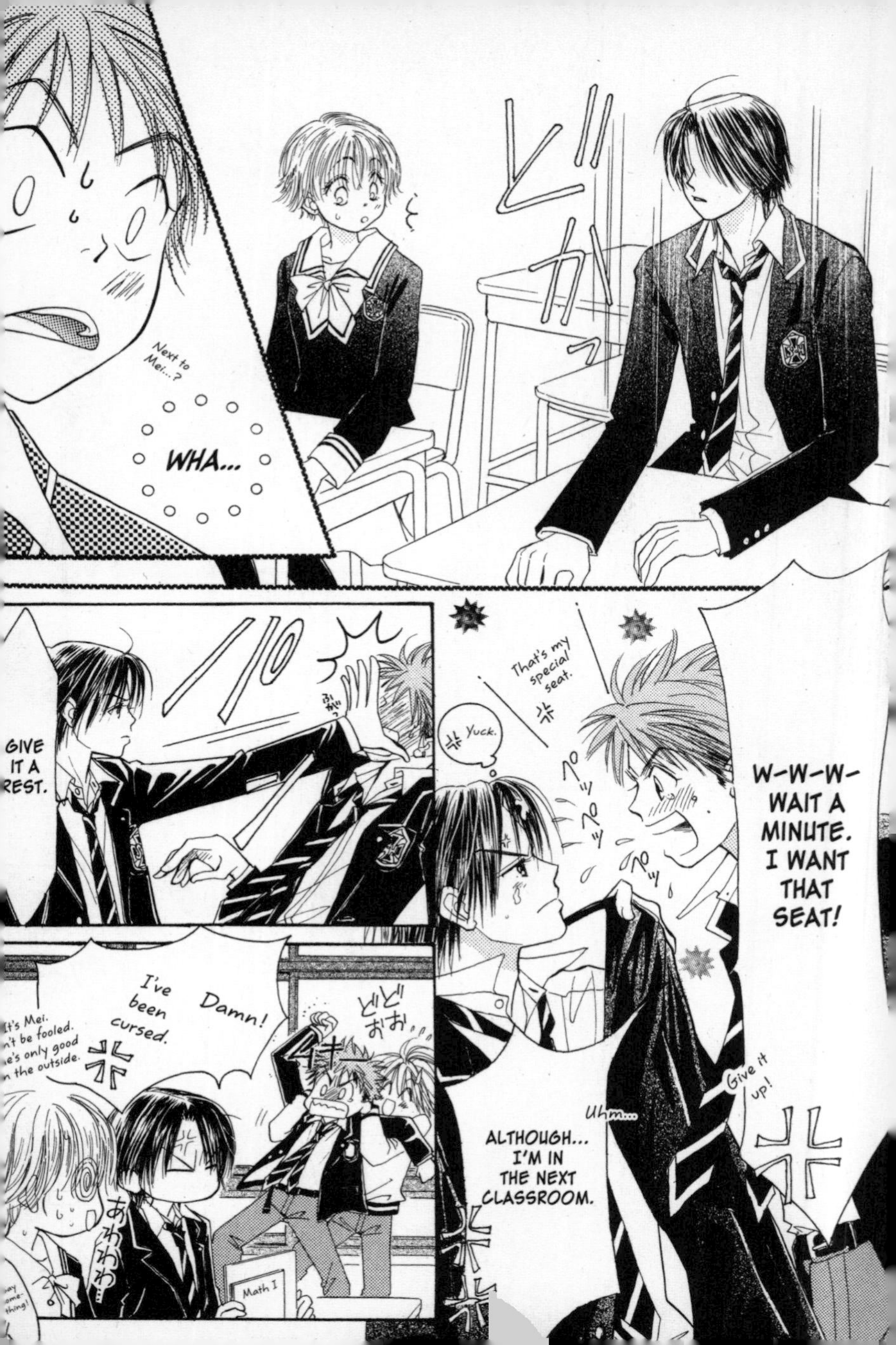

Next to Mei...?
WHA...
W-W-W-WAIT A MINUTE. I WANT THAT SEAT!
That's my special seat.
Yuck.
GIVE IT A REST.
Give it up!
Uhm...
ALTHOUGH... I'M IN THE NEXT CLASSROOM.
Damn!
I've been cursed.
It's Mei.
Math I

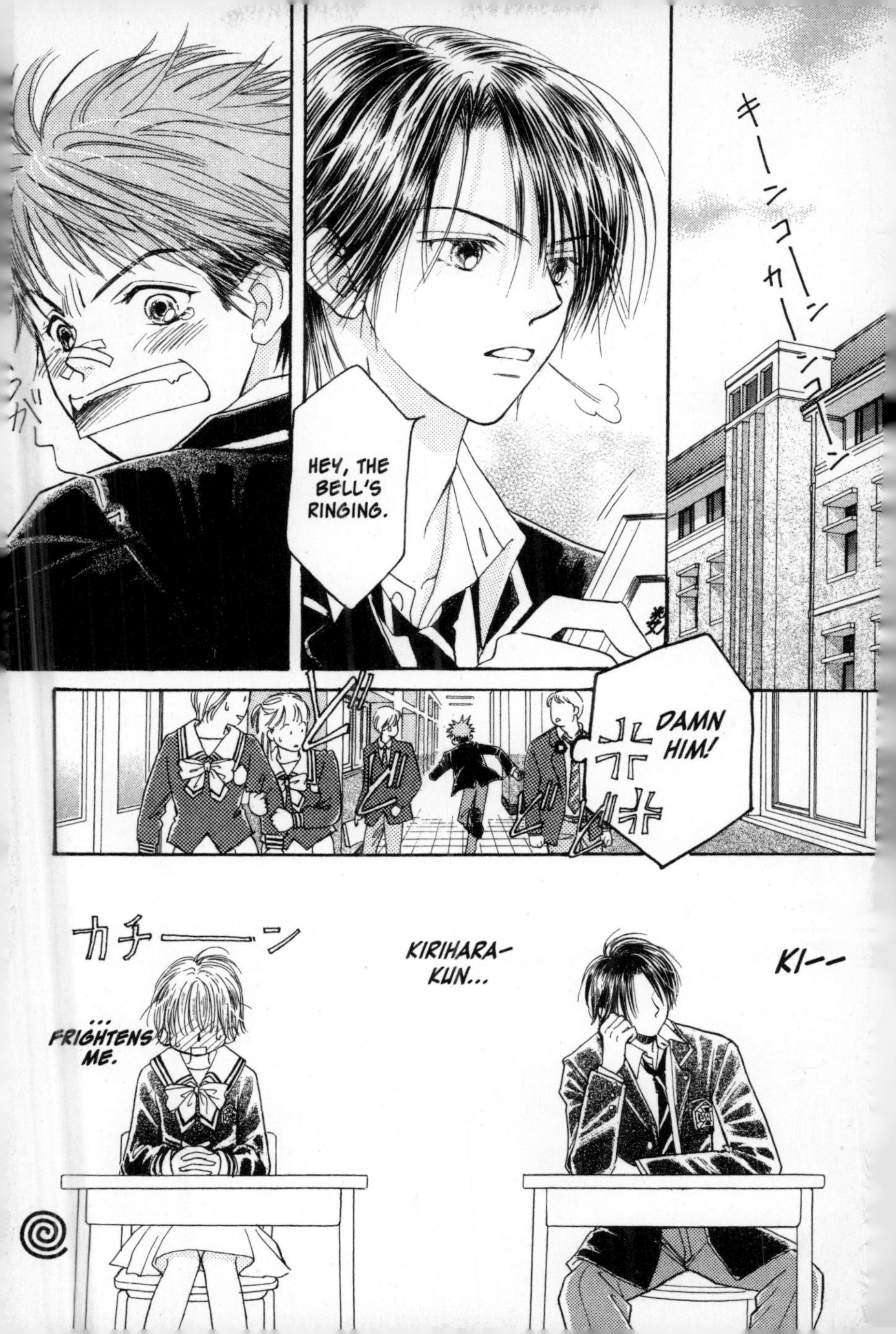
キーンコーンカーンコーン
HEY, THE BELL'S RINGING.
DAMN HIM!
KI--
KIRIHARA-KUN...
カチーーン
... FRIGHTENS ME.

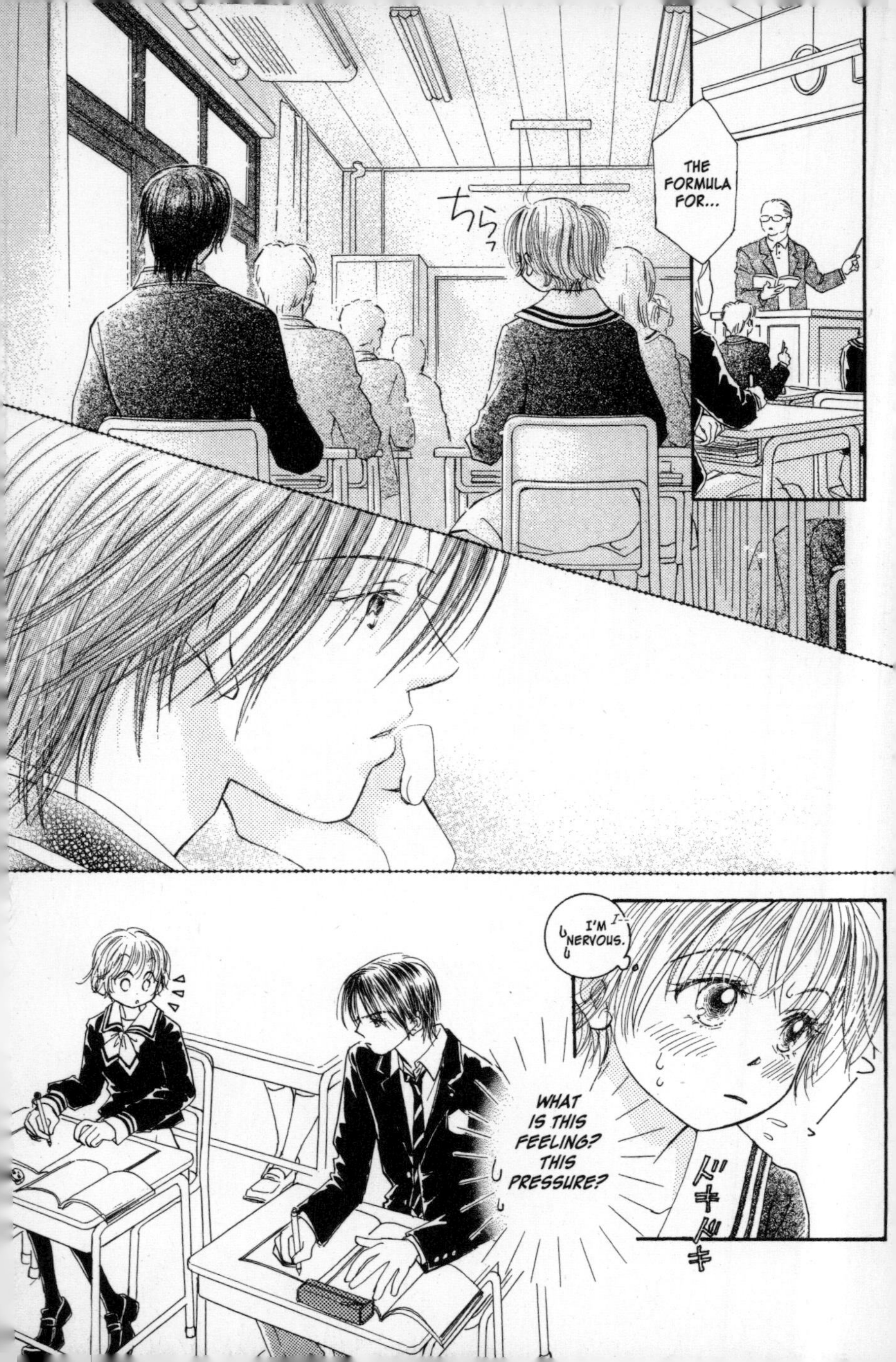
THE FORMULA FOR...
ちらっ
I-- I'M NERVOUS.
ドキドキ
WHAT IS THIS FEELING? THIS PRESSURE?

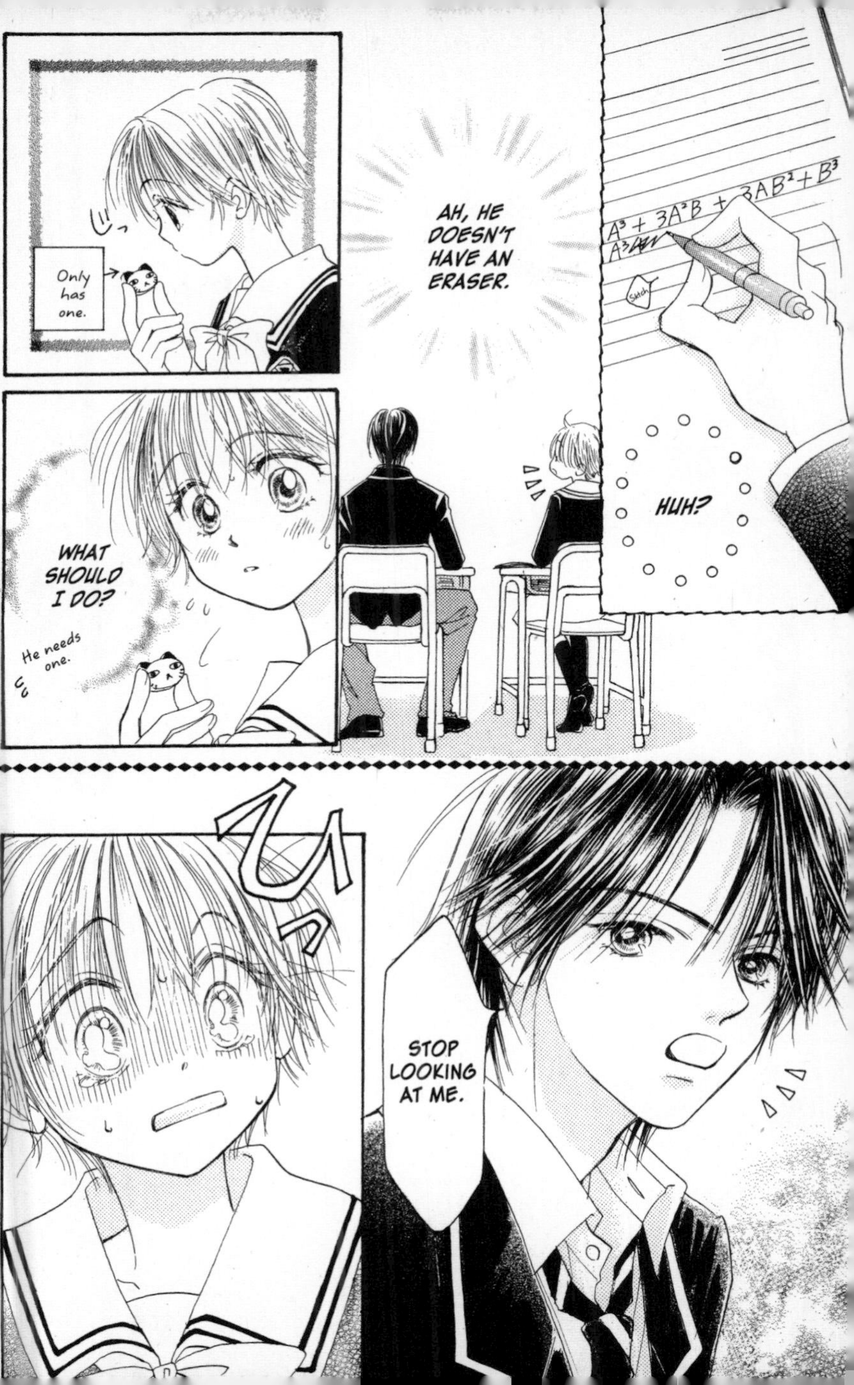
$A^3 + 3A^2B + 3AB^2 + B^3$
HUH?
AH, HE DOESN'T HAVE AN ERASER.
じっ
Only has one.
WHAT SHOULD I DO?
He needs one.
STOP LOOKING AT ME.
ひっ

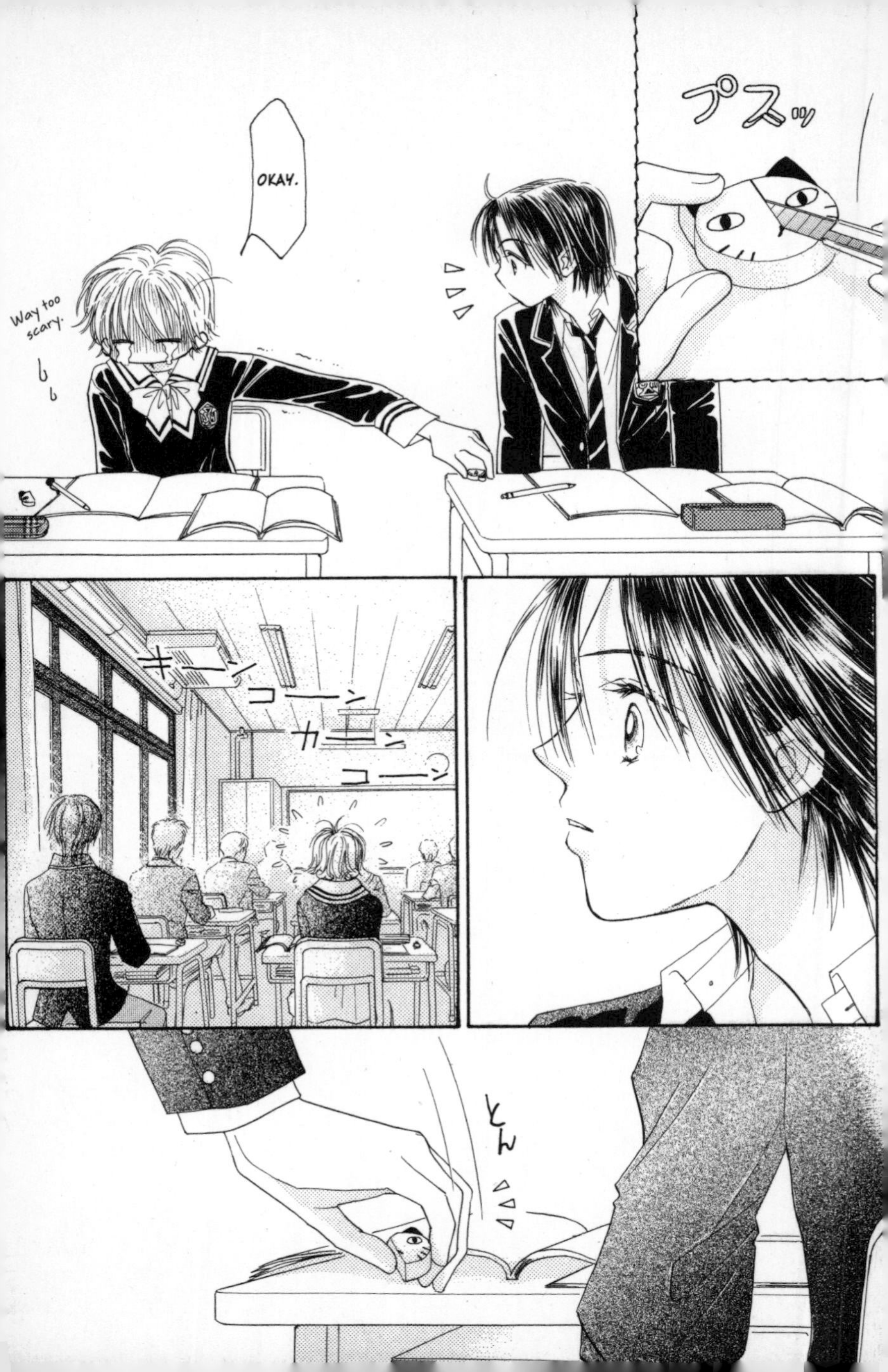
プスッ
OKAY.
Way too scary.
キーン
コーン
カーン
コーン
とん

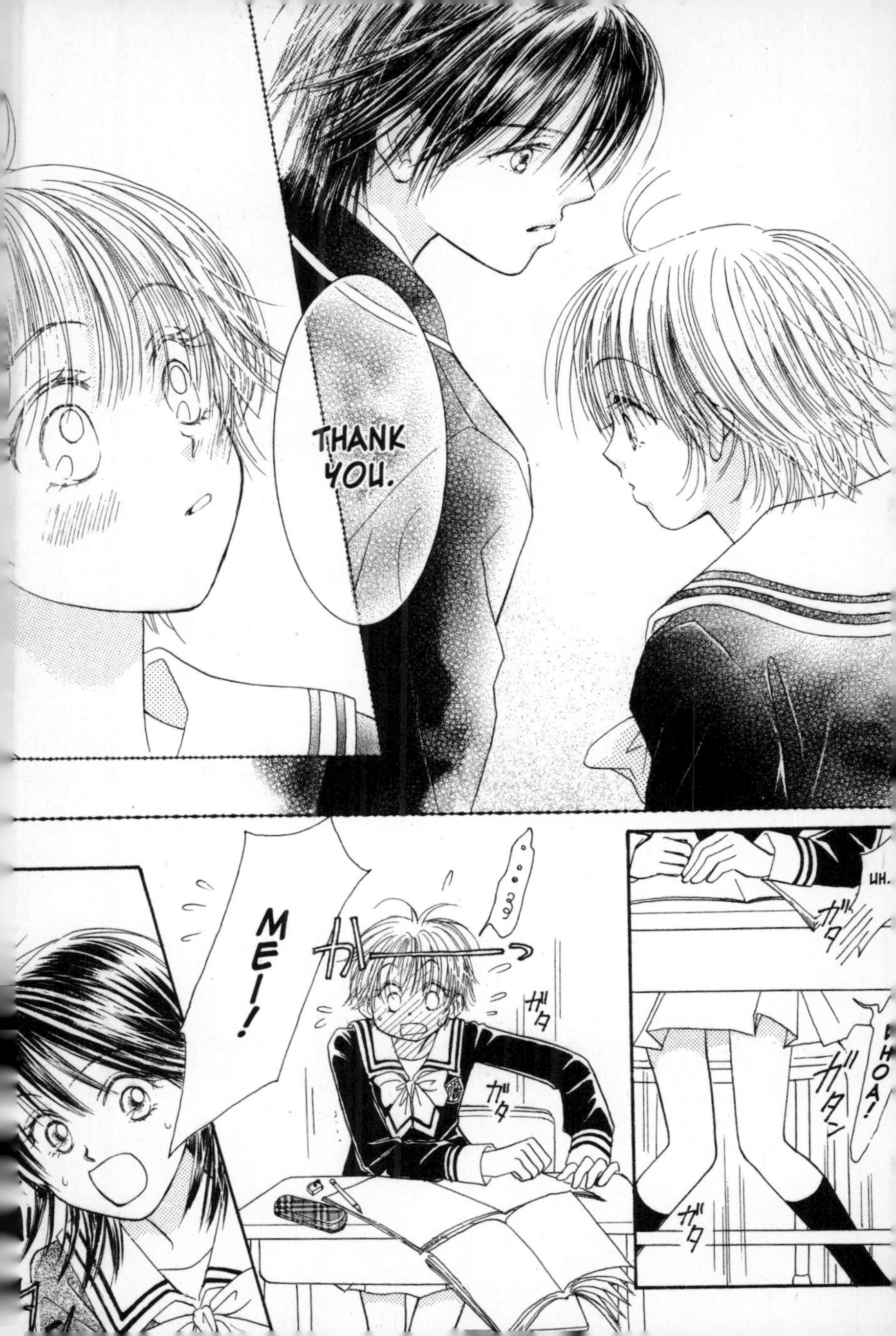
THANK YOU.
UH.
ガタ
WHOA!
ガタン
ガタ
...
わー
ガタ
ガタ
MEI!!

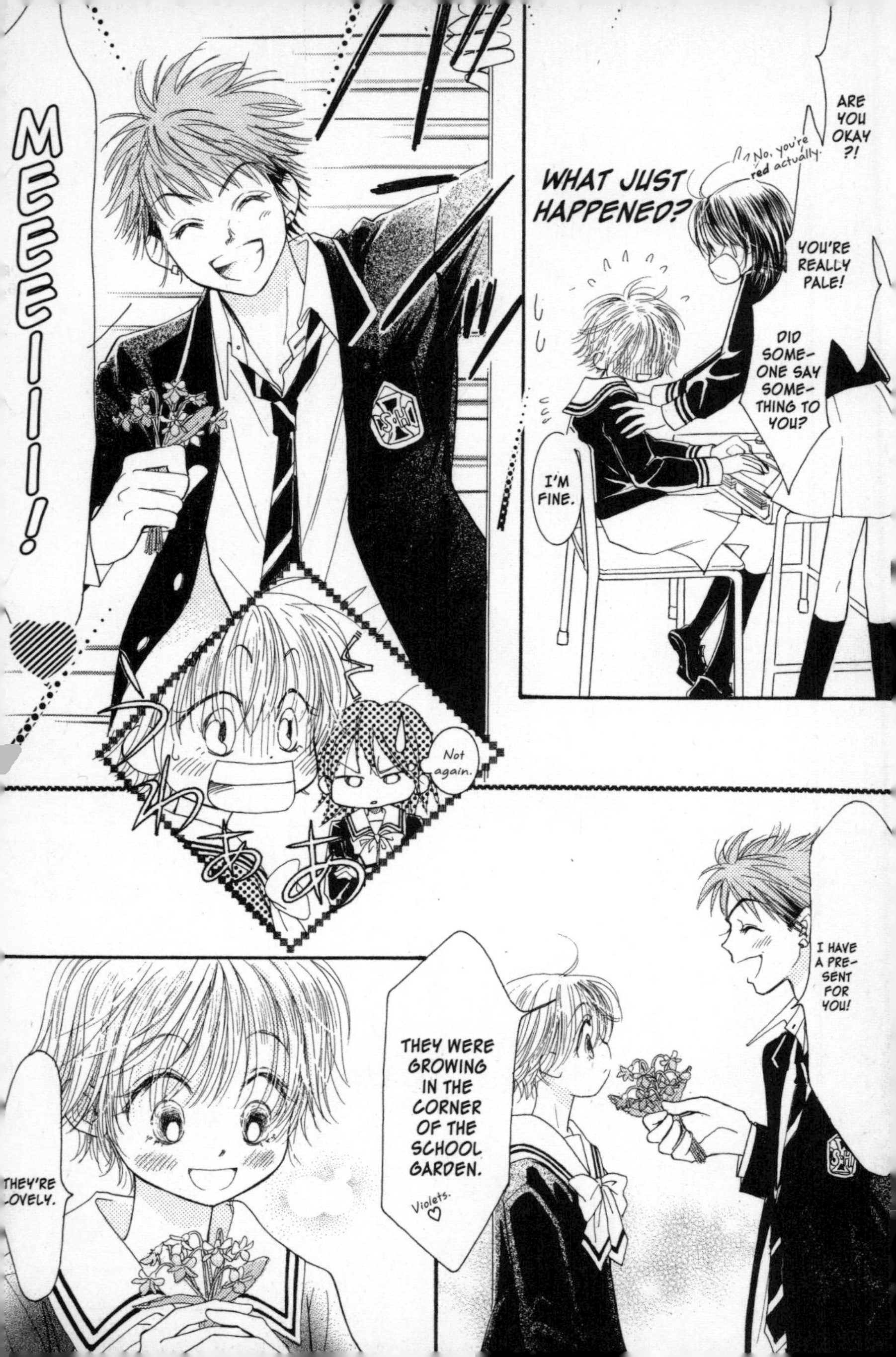

ARE YOU OKAY ?!
No, you're red actually.
WHAT JUST HAPPENED?
YOU'RE REALLY PALE!
DID SOME-ONE SAY SOME-THING TO YOU?
I'M FINE.
MEEEIIII!
Not again.
I HAVE A PRE-SENT FOR YOU!
THEY WERE GROWING IN THE CORNER OF THE SCHOOL GARDEN.
Violets.
THEY'RE LOVELY.

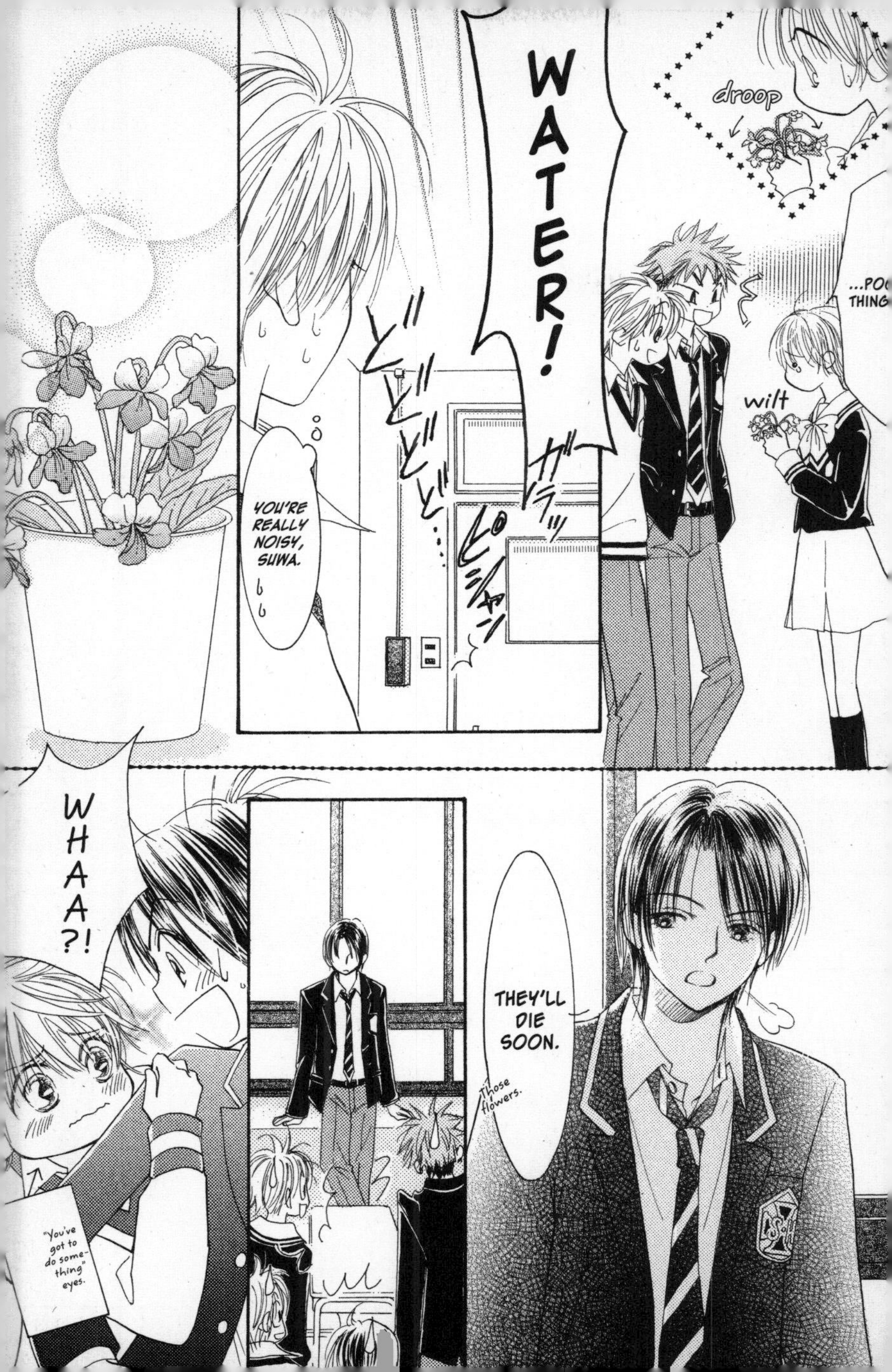
droop
...POO THING
wilt
WATER!
YOU'RE REALLY NOISY, SUWA.
THEY'LL DIE SOON.
Those flowers.
WHAAA?!
"You've got to do some-thing" eyes.

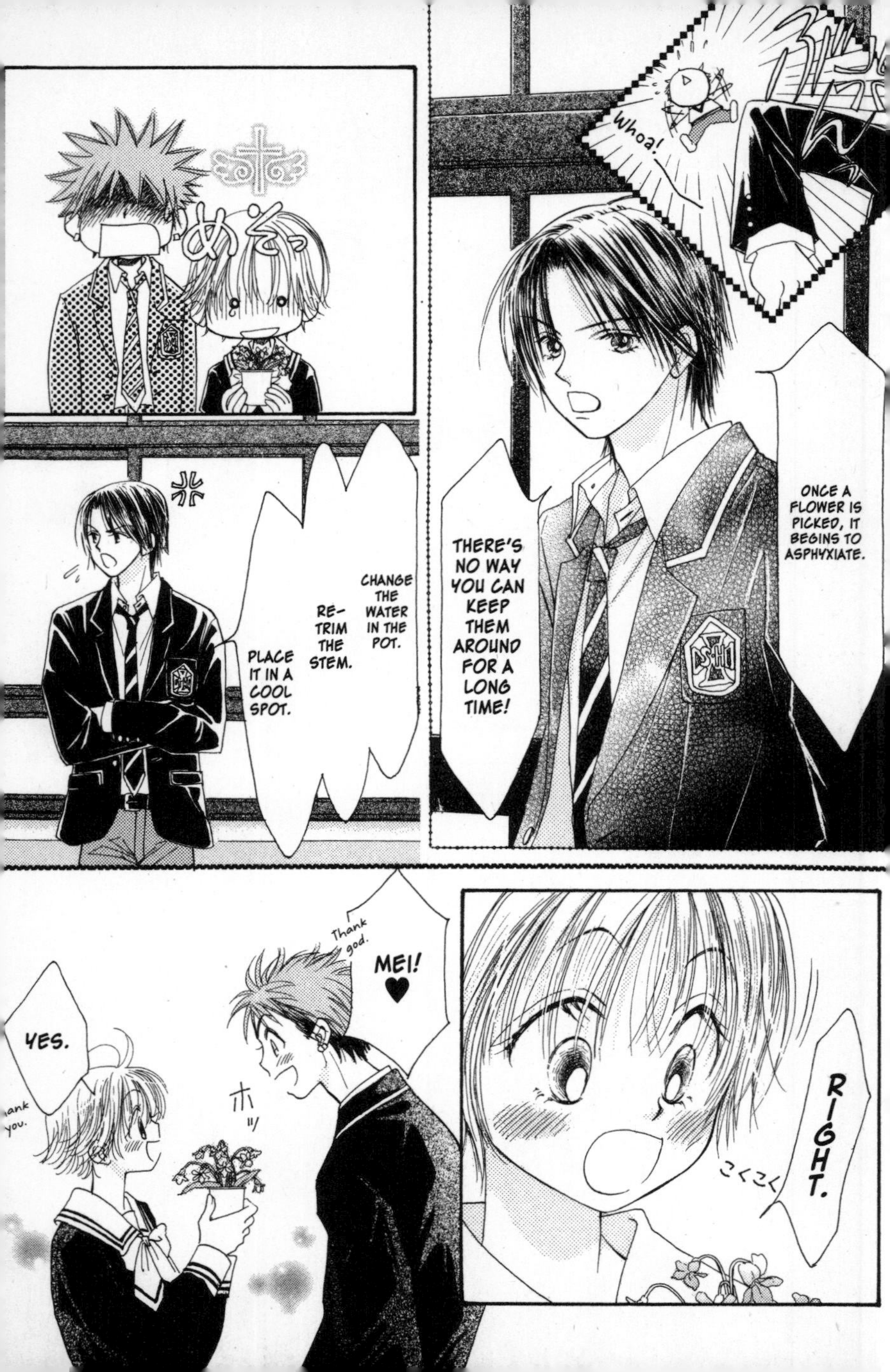
Whoa!
ONCE A FLOWER IS PICKED, IT BEGINS TO ASPHYXIATE.
THERE'S NO WAY YOU CAN KEEP THEM AROUND FOR A LONG TIME!
めそっ
CHANGE THE WATER IN THE POT.
RE-TRIM THE STEM.
PLACE IT IN A COOL SPOT.
RIGHT.
こくこく
MEI! ♥
Thank god.
YES.
hank you.
ホッ

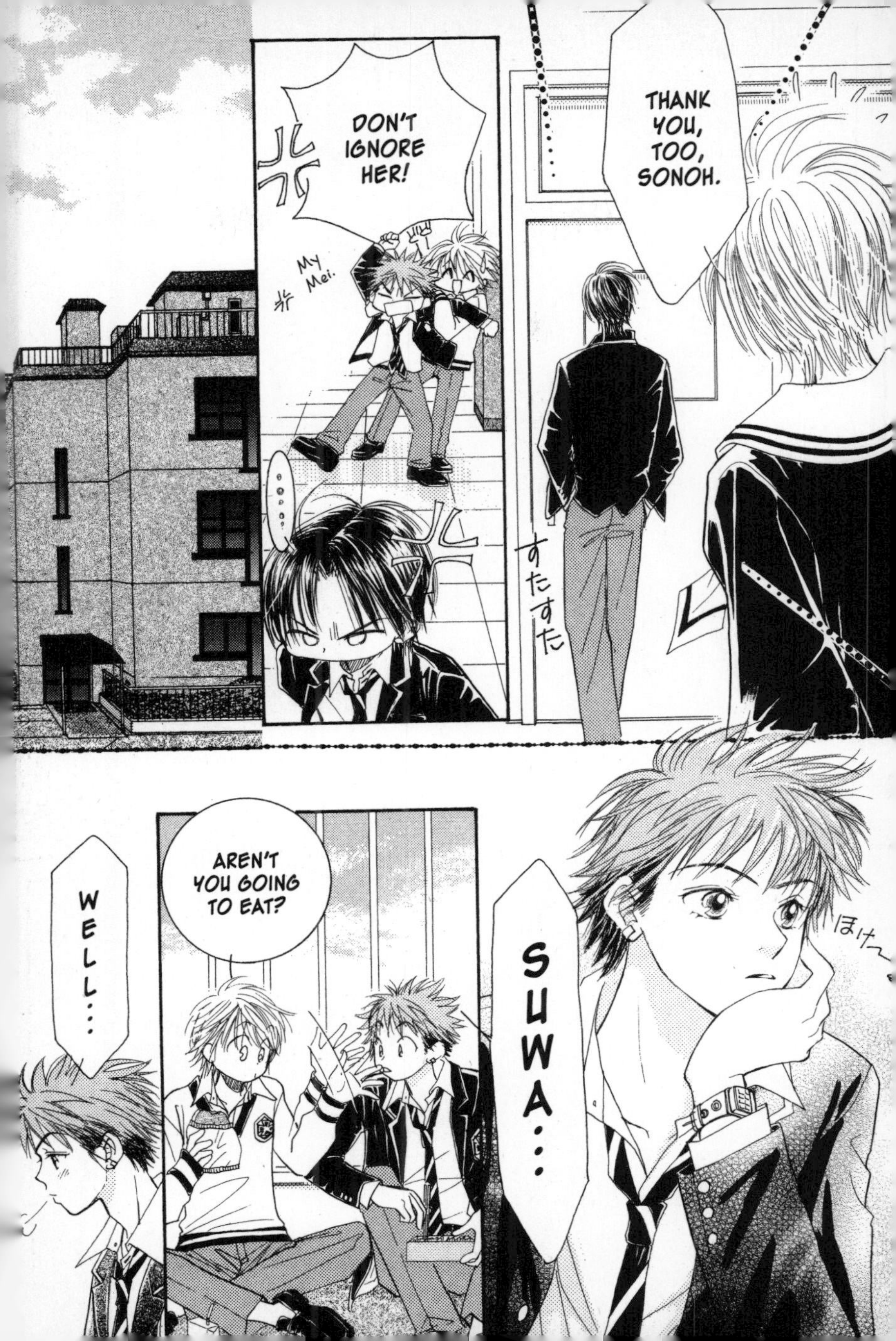
THANK YOU, TOO, SONOH.
すたすた
DON'T IGNORE HER!
My Mei.
SUWA...
ほけ~
AREN'T YOU GOING TO EAT?
WELL...

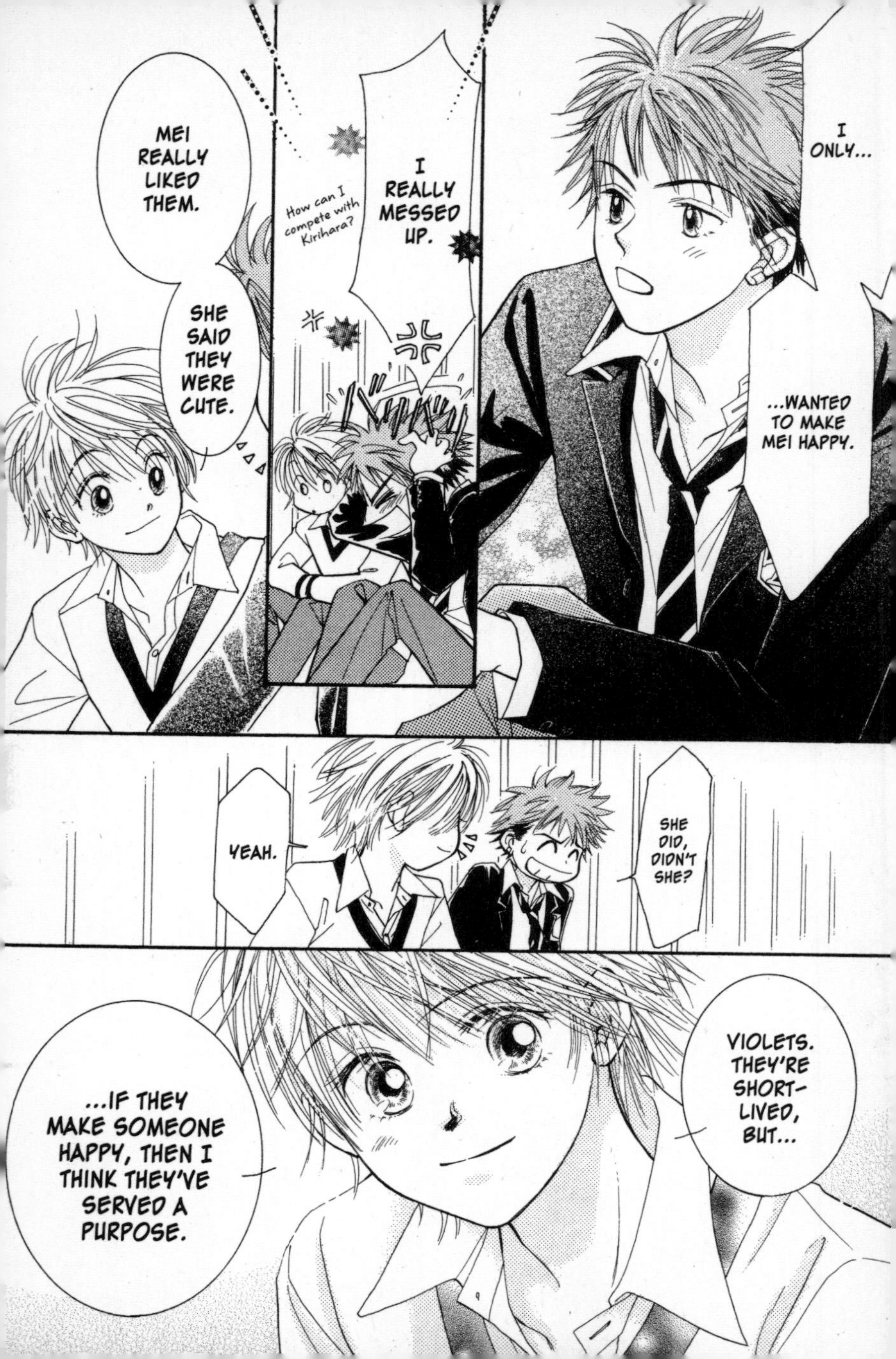
I ONLY...
...WANTED TO MAKE MEI HAPPY.
I REALLY MESSED UP.
How can I compete with Kirihara?
MEI REALLY LIKED THEM.
SHE SAID THEY WERE CUTE.
SHE DID, DIDN'T SHE?
YEAH.
VIOLETS. THEY'RE SHORT-LIVED, BUT...
...IF THEY MAKE SOMEONE HAPPY, THEN I THINK THEY'VE SERVED A PURPOSE.

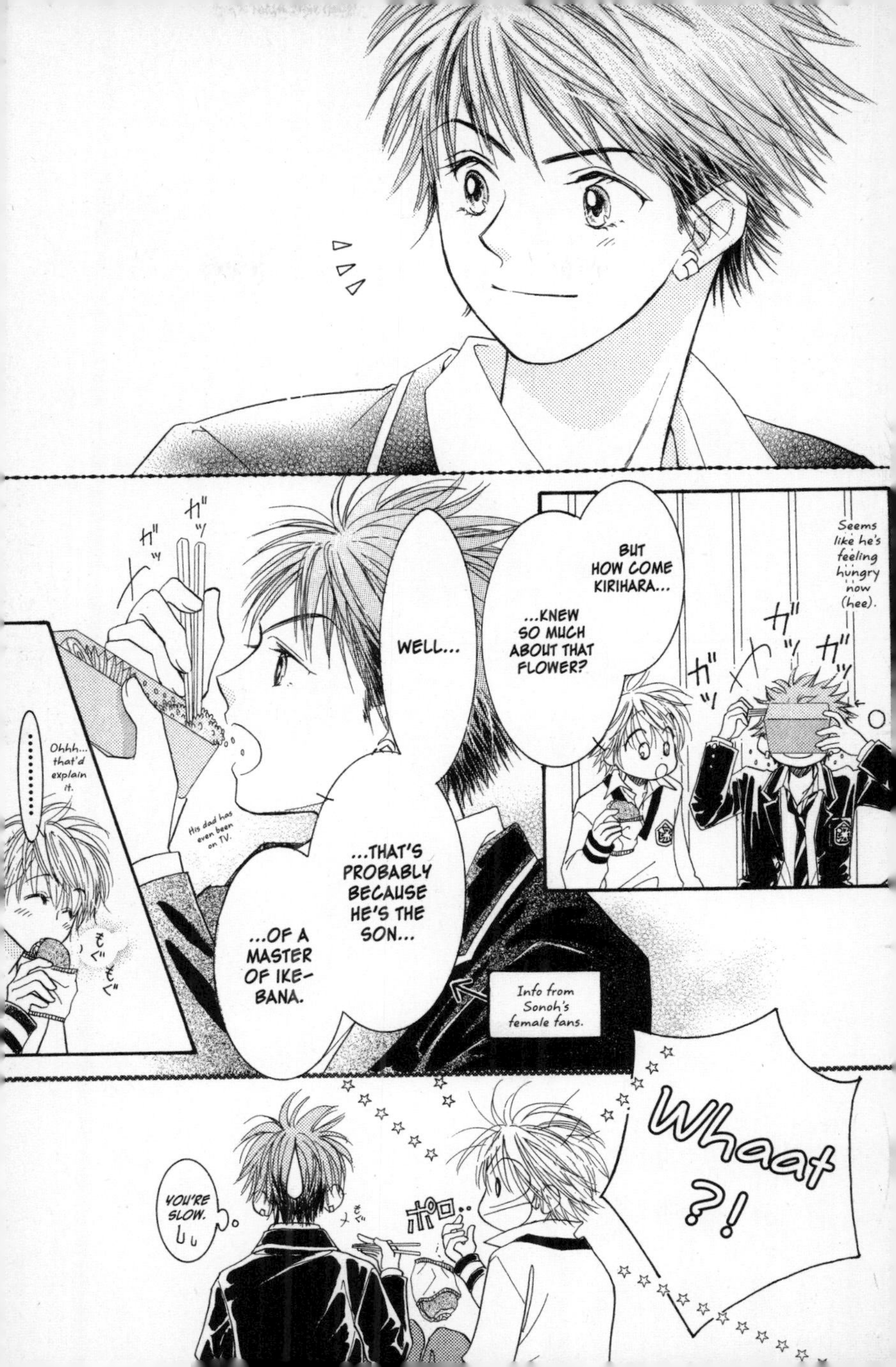
BUT HOW COME KIRIHARA...
...KNEW SO MUCH ABOUT THAT FLOWER?
Seems like he's feeling hungry now (hee).
ガツ
ガツ
ガツ
WELL...
...THAT'S PROBABLY BECAUSE HE'S THE SON...
...OF A MASTER OF IKE-BANA.
Info from Sonoh's female fans.
ガツ
ガツ
His dad has even been on TV.
......
Ohhh... that'd explain it.
もぐ
もぐ
Whaaat?!
ポロ..
YOU'RE SLOW.

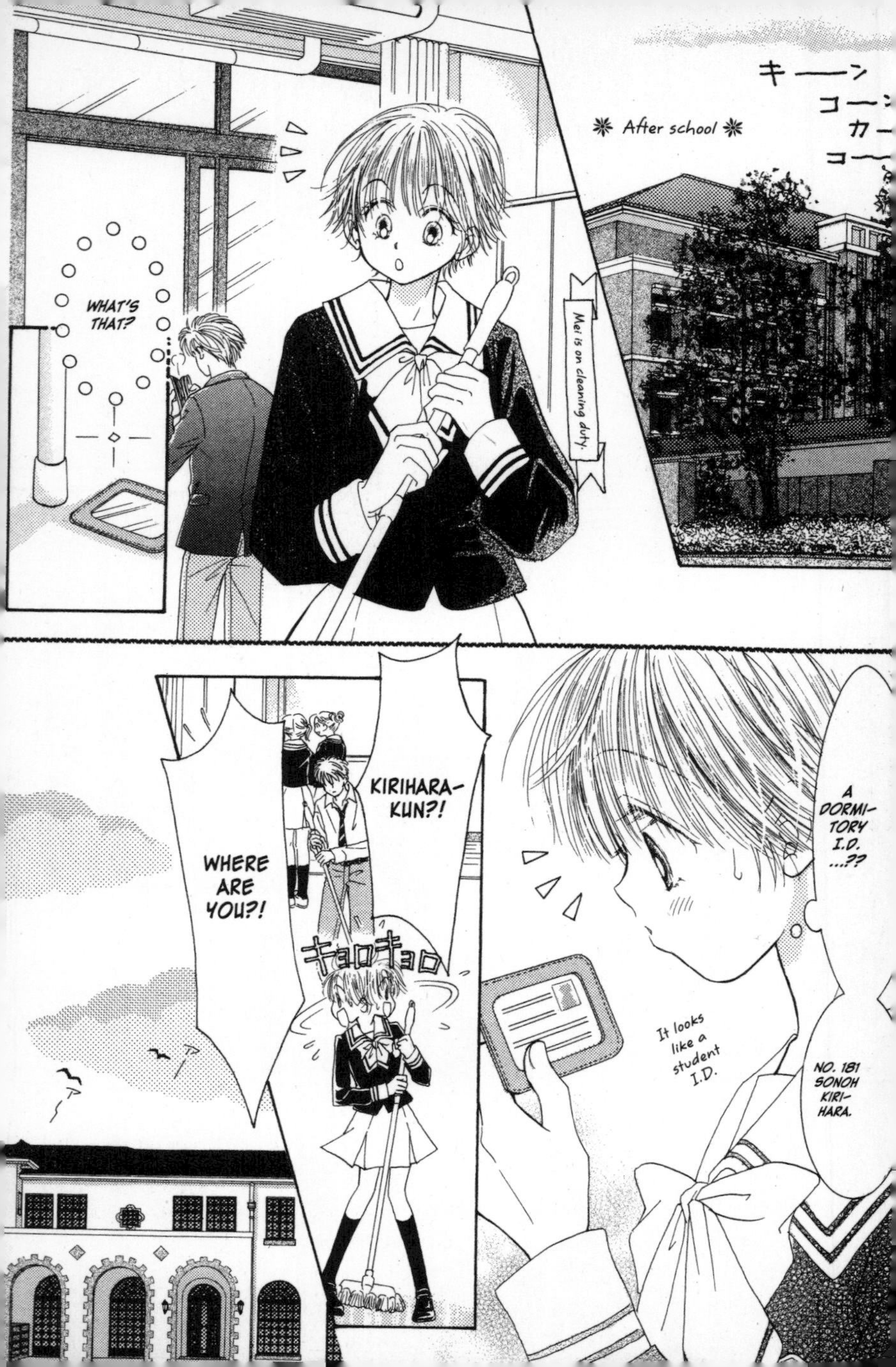

キーン
コーン
カー
コ〜
After school
Mei is on cleaning duty.
WHAT'S THAT?
A DORMITORY I.D. ...??
It looks like a student I.D.
NO. 181 SONOH KIRIHARA.
KIRIHARA-KUN?!
WHERE ARE YOU?!
キョロキョロ

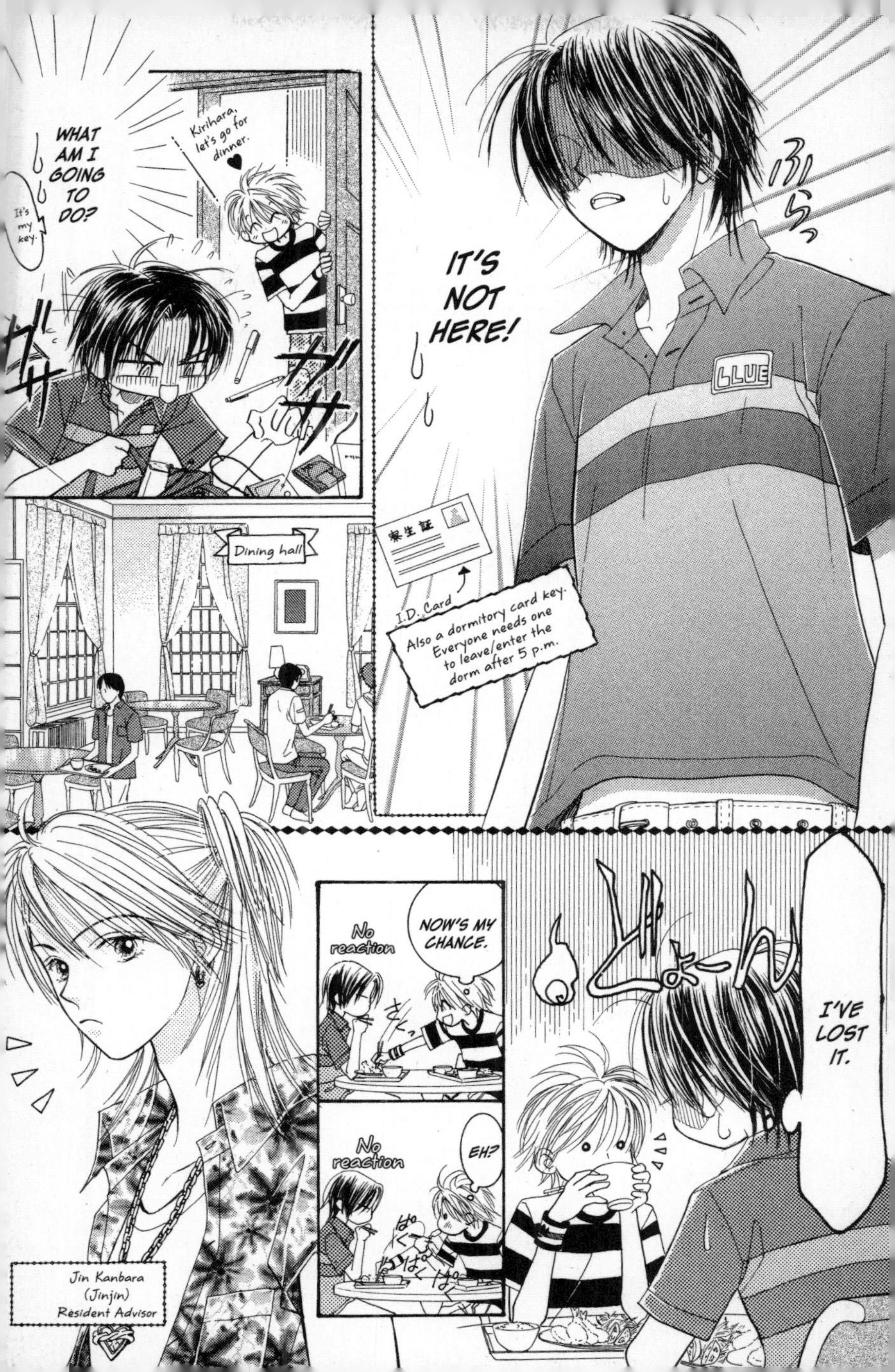

ふらっ
IT'S NOT HERE!
学生証
I.D. Card
Also a dormitory card key. Everyone needs one to leave/enter the dorm after 5 p.m.
Kirihara, let's go for dinner. ♥
WHAT AM I GOING TO DO?
It's my key.
Dining hall
I'VE LOST IT.
NOW'S MY CHANCE.
No reaction
EH?
No reaction
Jin Kanbara (Jinjin) Resident Advisor

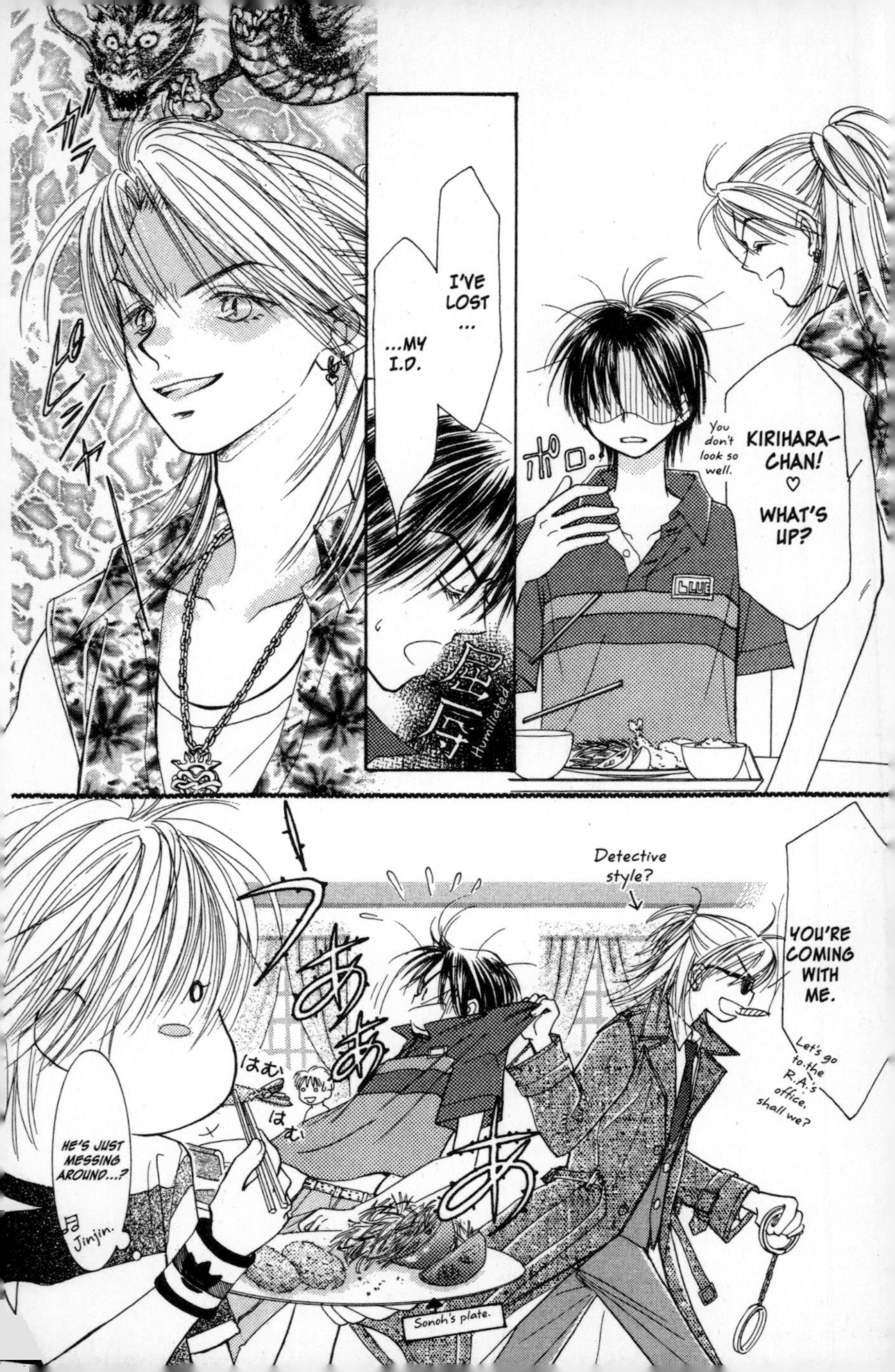
KIRIHARA-CHAN! ♡
WHAT'S UP?
You don't look so well.
I'VE LOST ...
...MY I.D.
Humiliated
Detective style?
YOU'RE COMING WITH ME.
Let's go to the R.A.'s office, shall we?
HE'S JUST MESSING AROUND...?
Jinjin.
Sonoh's plate.

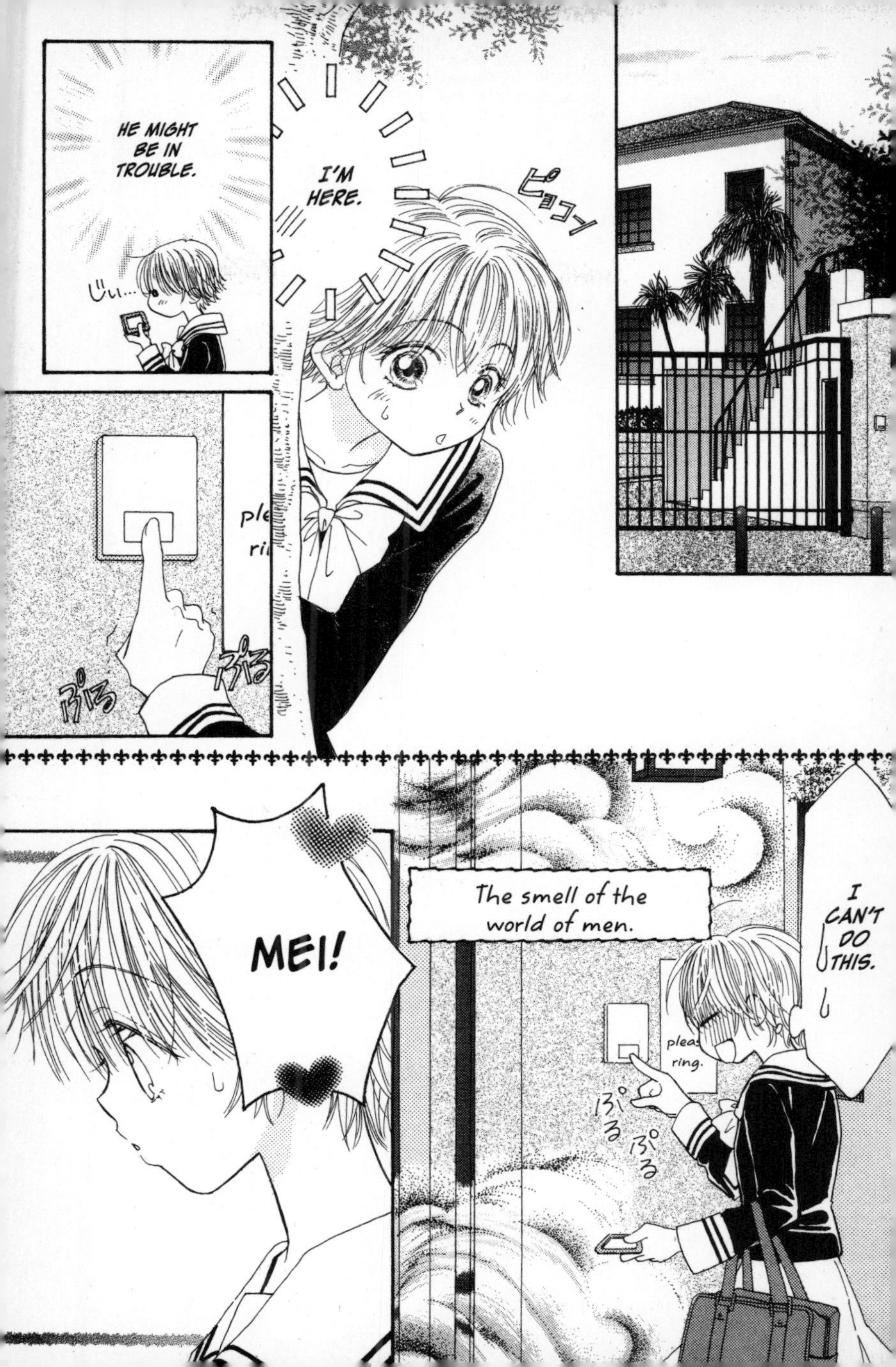

I'M HERE.
ピョコッ
HE MIGHT BE IN TROUBLE.
じぃ…
ple
ri
ぷる
ぷる
The smell of the world of men.
I CAN'T DO THIS.
pleas
ring.
ぷる
ぷる
MEI!

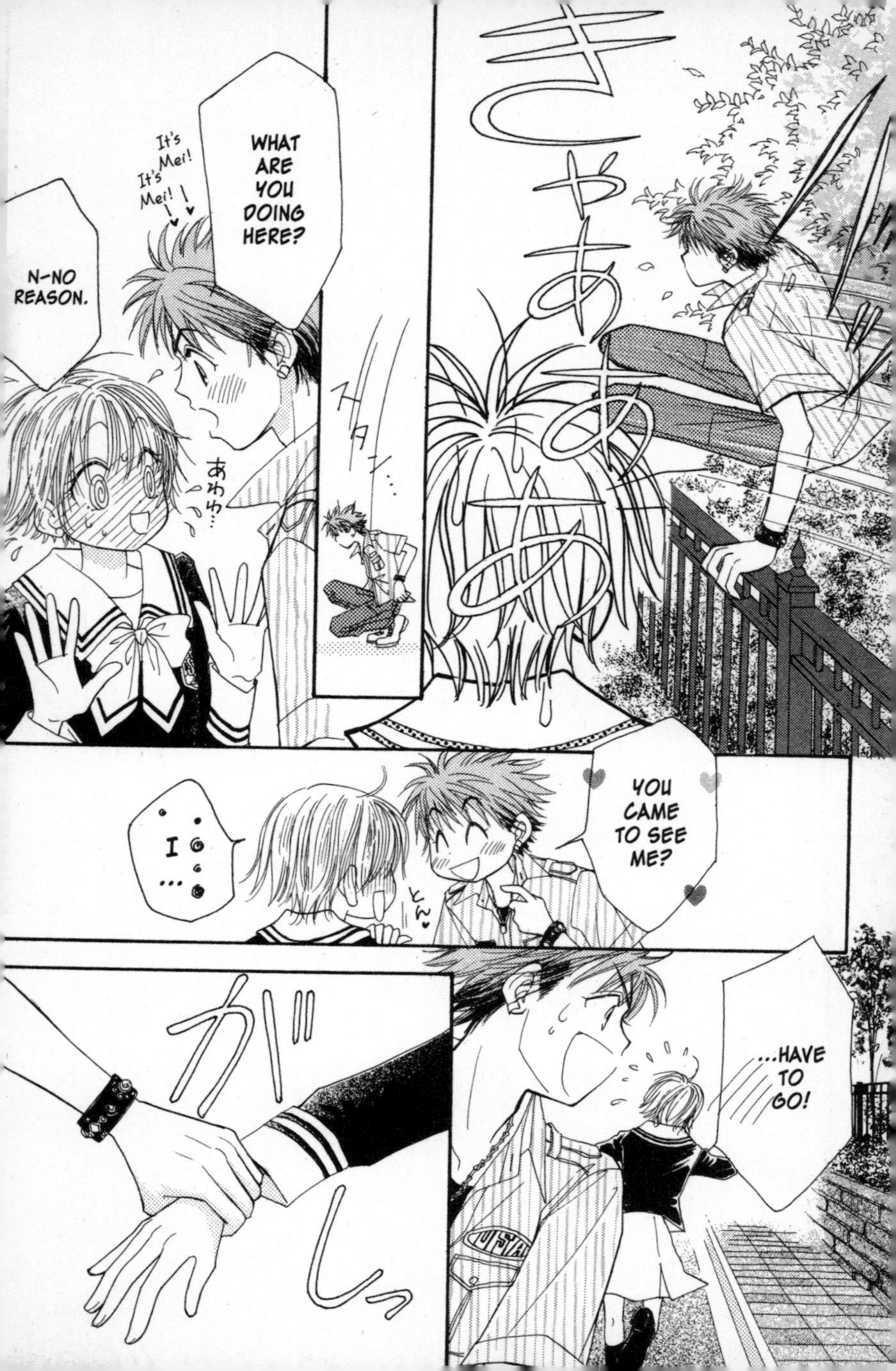
きゃあああ
スタン…
It's Mei! It's Mei!
WHAT ARE YOU DOING HERE?
N-NO REASON.
あわわ…
YOU CAME TO SEE ME?
とん
I ...
...HAVE TO GO!
がしっ

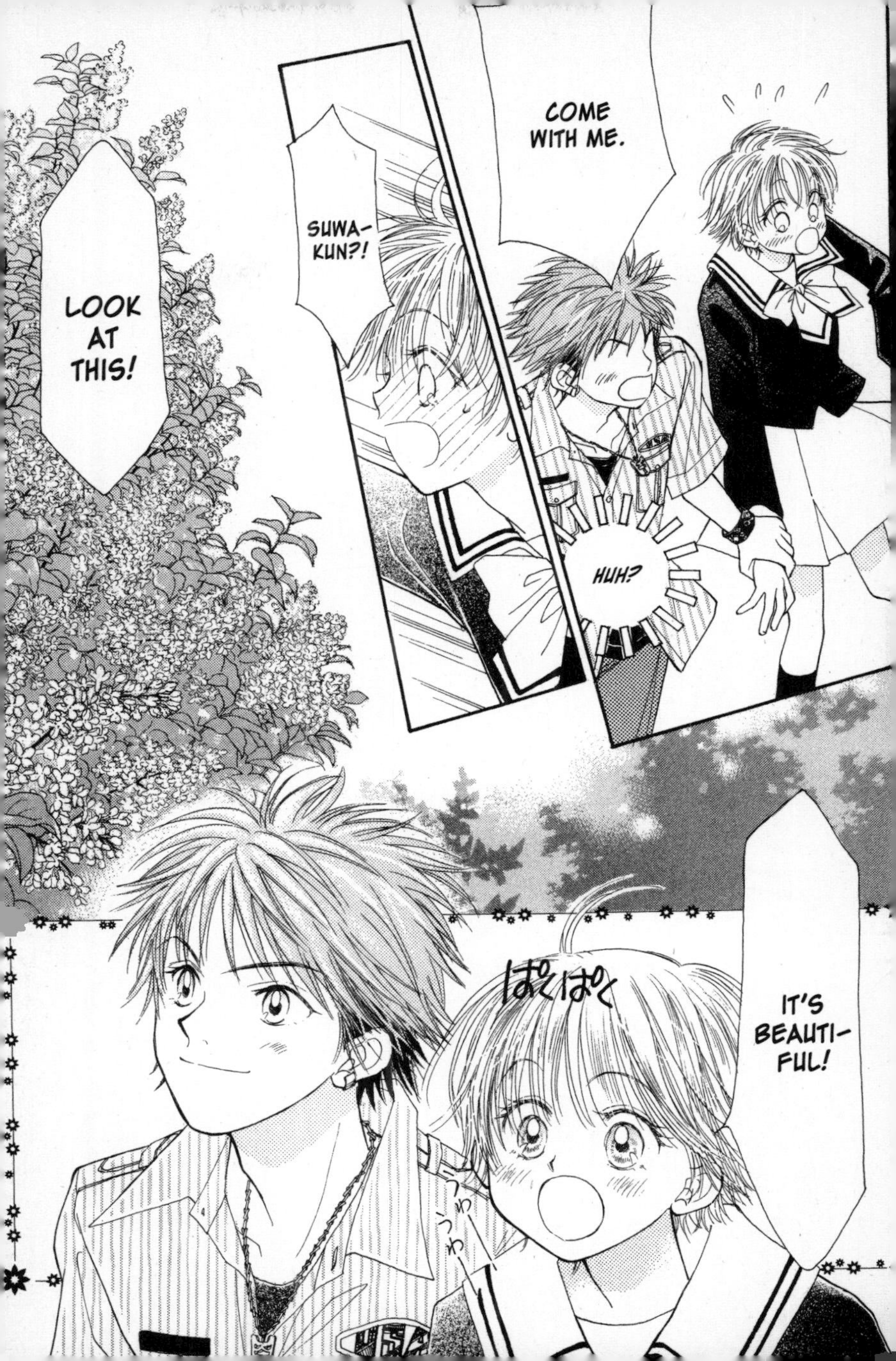

COME WITH ME.
HUH?
SUWA-KUN?!
LOOK AT THIS!
IT'S BEAUTI-FUL!
ぱくぱく
うわ うわ

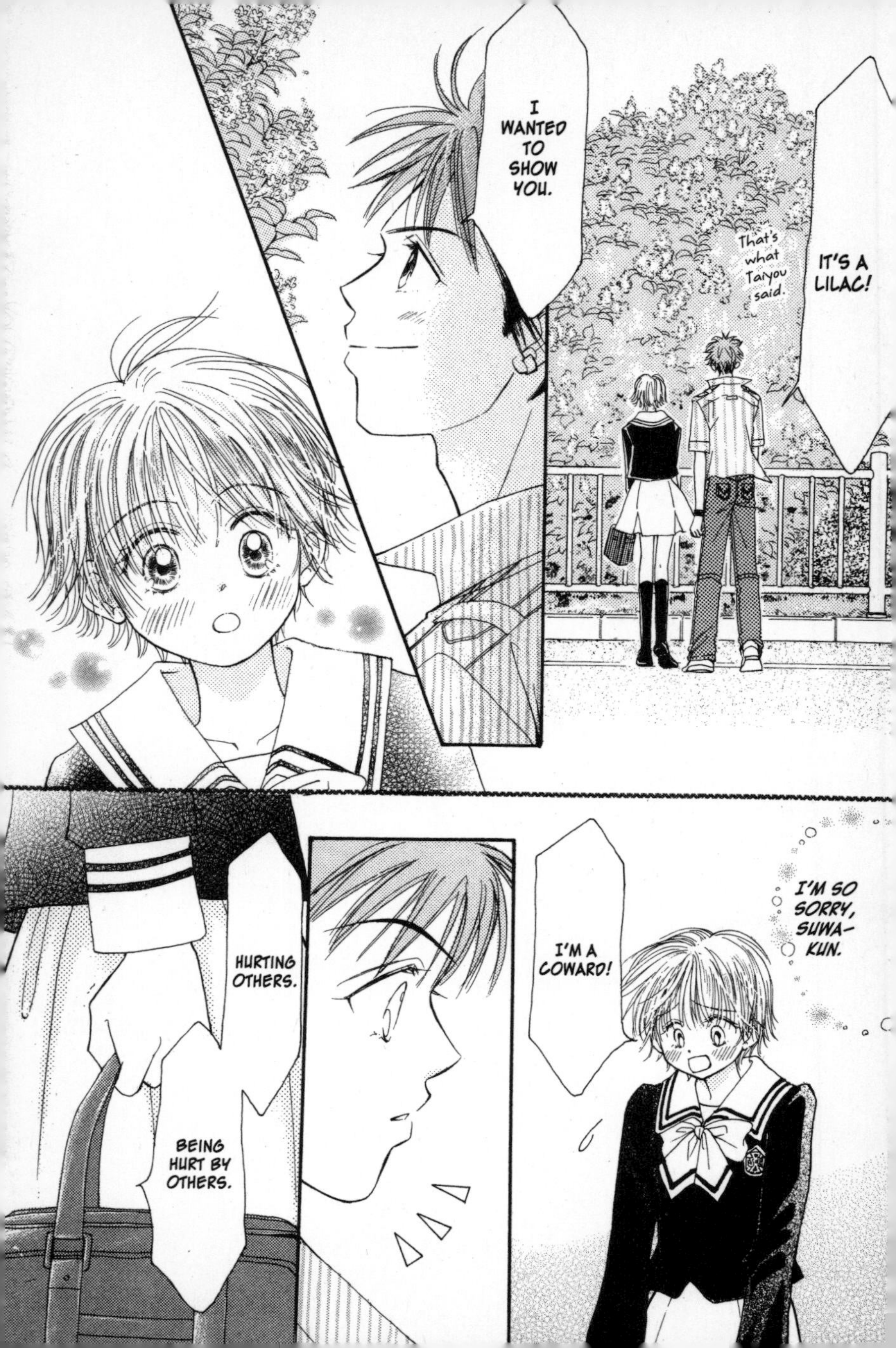
IT'S A LILAC!
That's what Taiyou said.
I WANTED TO SHOW YOU.
I'M SO SORRY, SUWA-KUN.
I'M A COWARD!
HURTING OTHERS.
BEING HURT BY OTHERS.

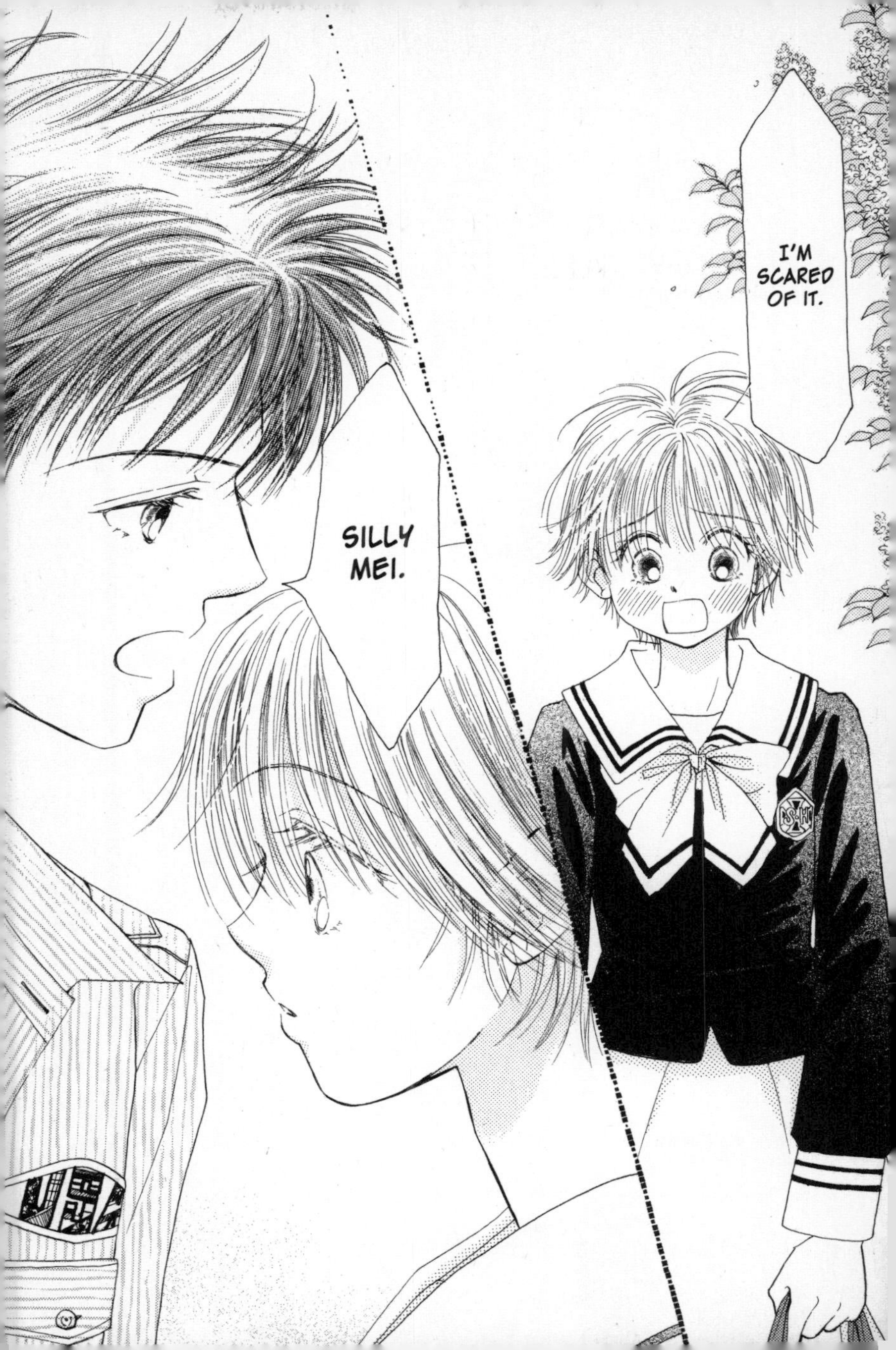
I'M SCARED OF IT.
SILLY MEI.

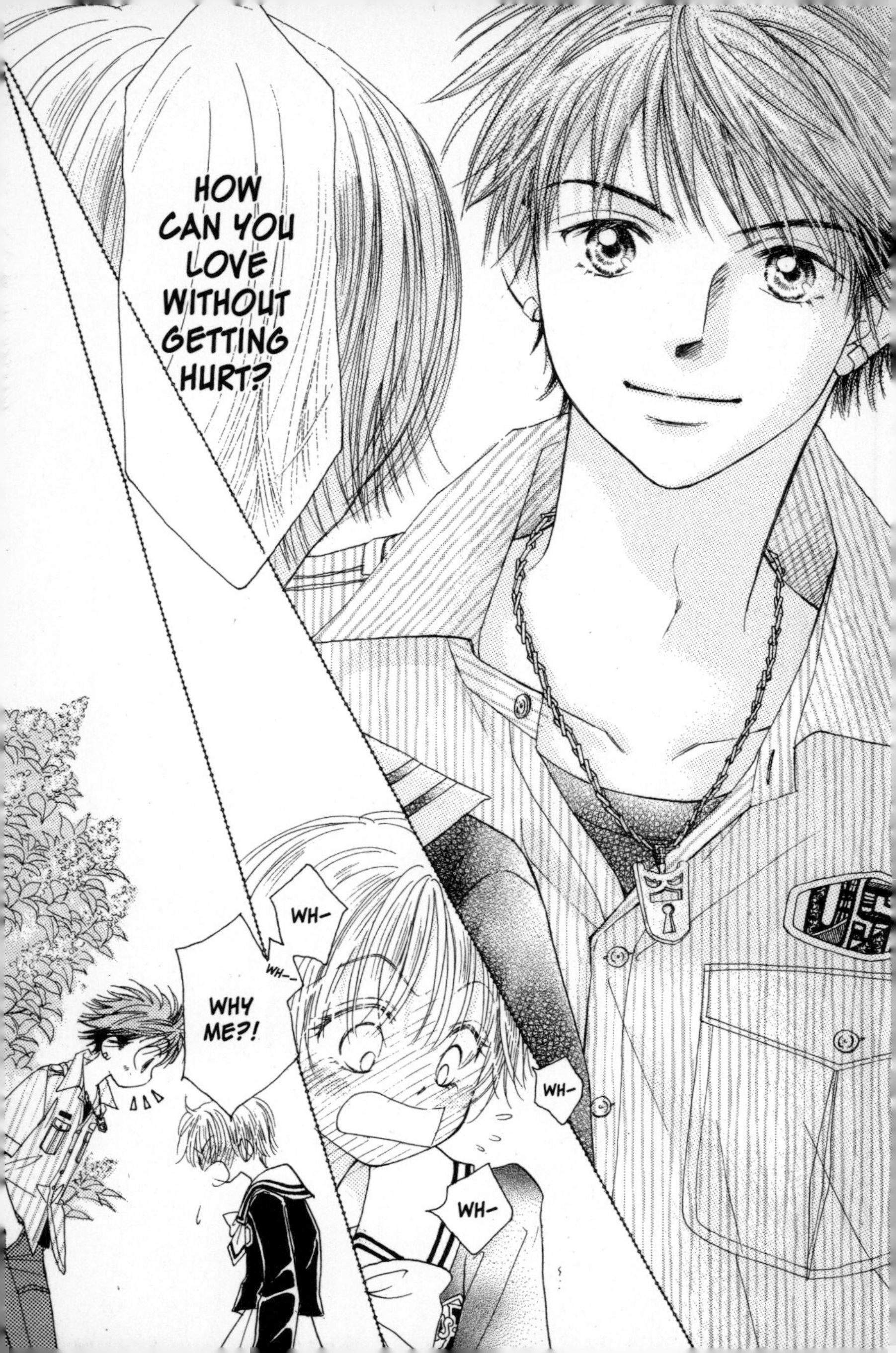
HOW CAN YOU LOVE WITHOUT GETTING HURT?
WH-
WH-
WH-
WH-
WHY ME?!

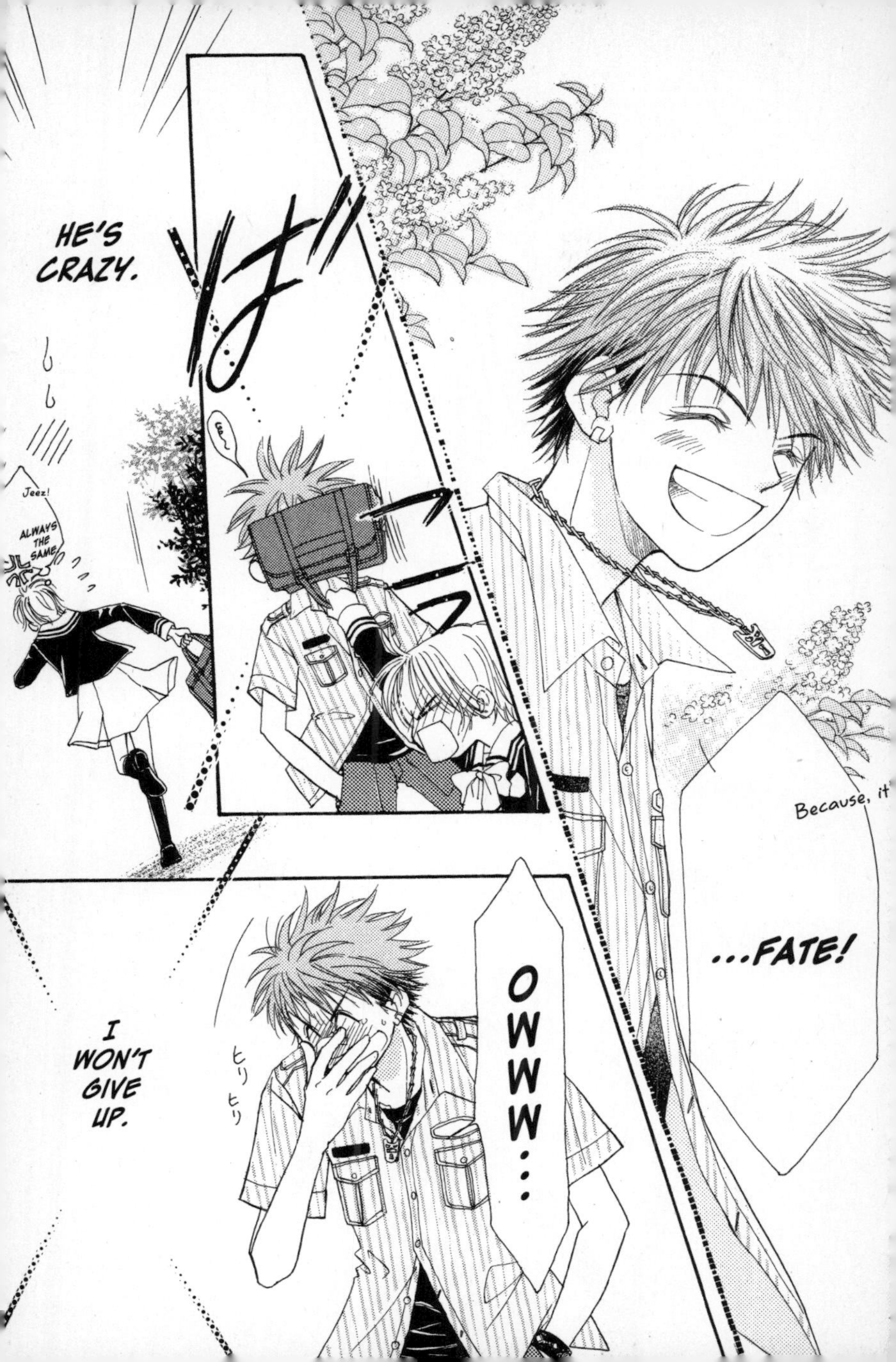

Because, it
...FATE!
HE'S CRAZY.
Jeez!
ALWAYS THE SAME
OWWW...
ヒリヒリ
I WON'T GIVE UP.

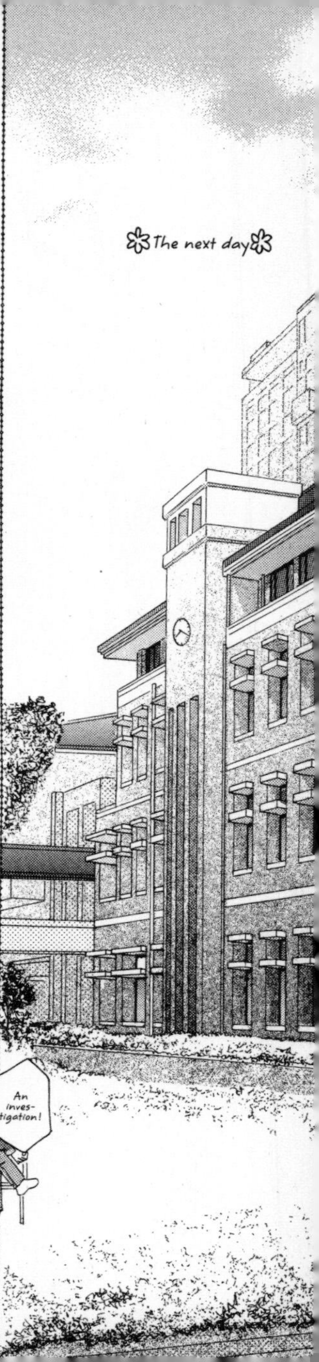
The next day

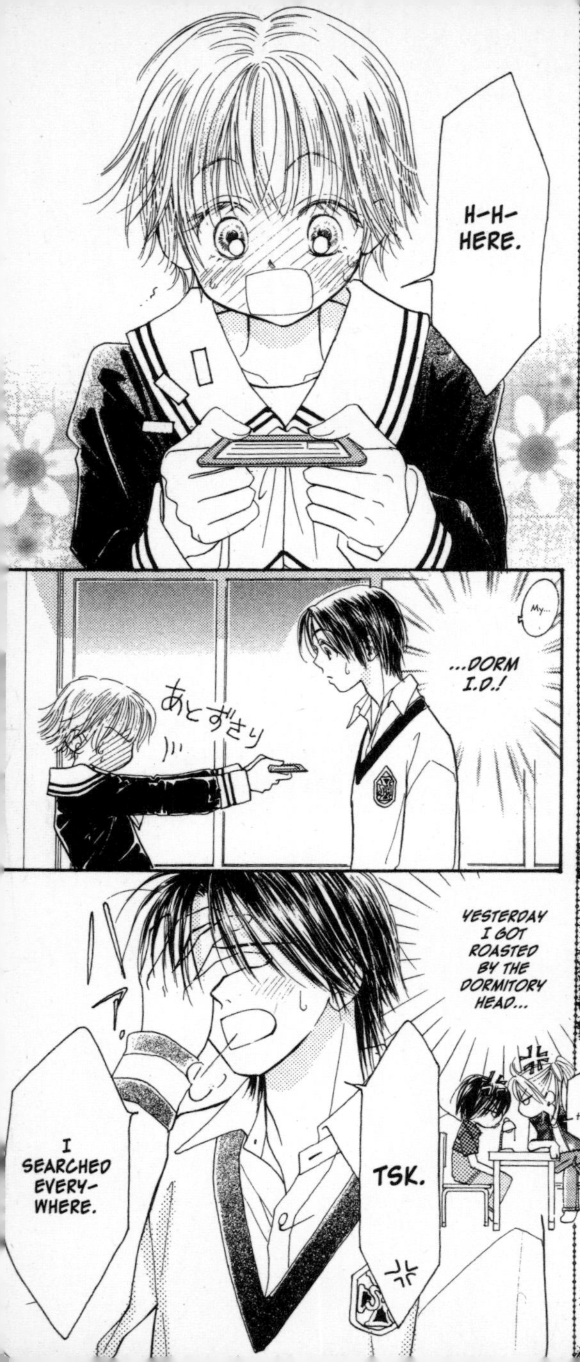
H-H-HERE.
My...
...DORM I.D.!
あとずさり
YESTERDAY I GOT ROASTED BY THE DORMITORY HEAD...
An inves-tigation!
TSK.
I SEARCHED EVERY-WHERE.

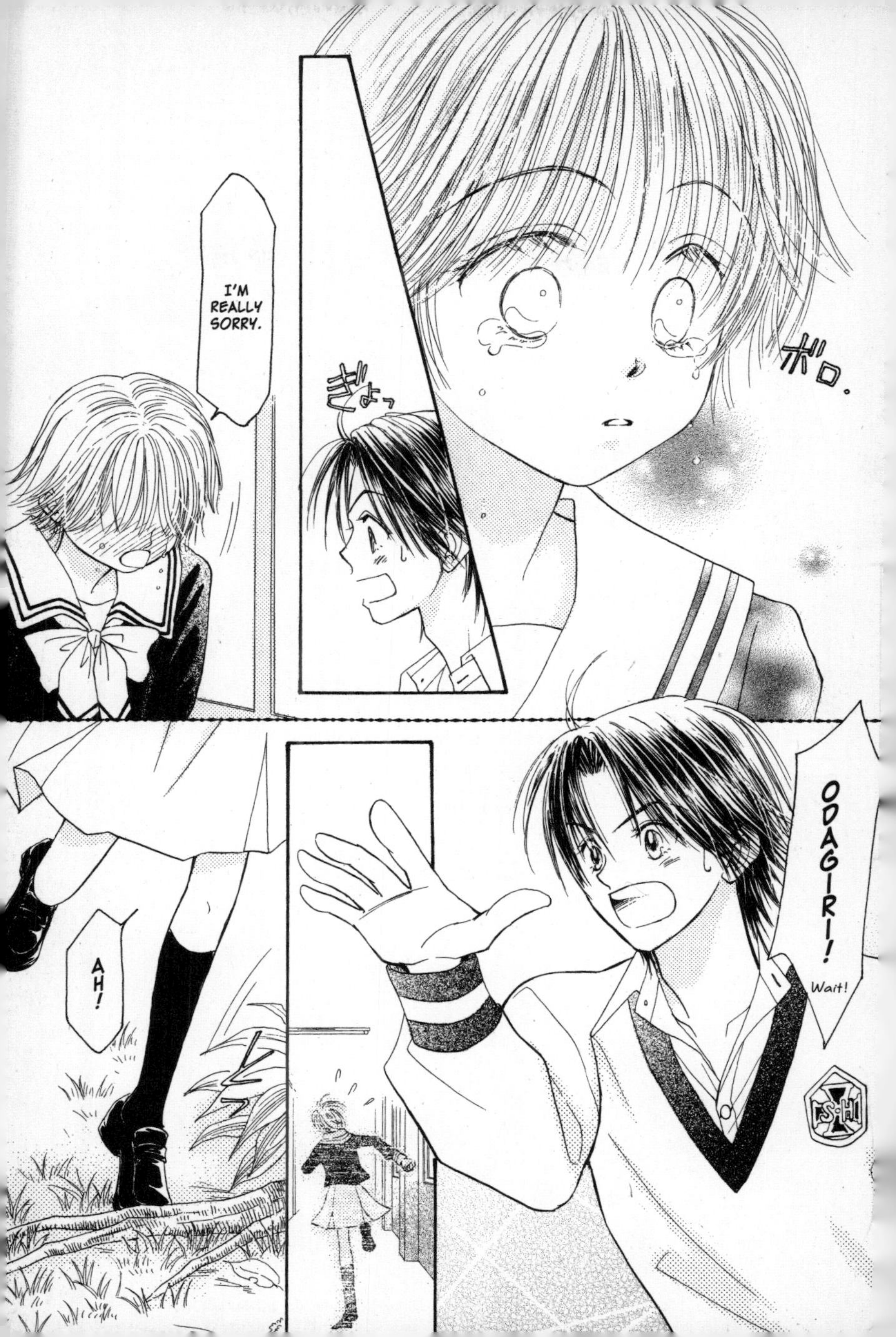
ボロ。
ぎょっ
ODAGIRI!
Wait!
I'M REALLY SORRY.
AH!

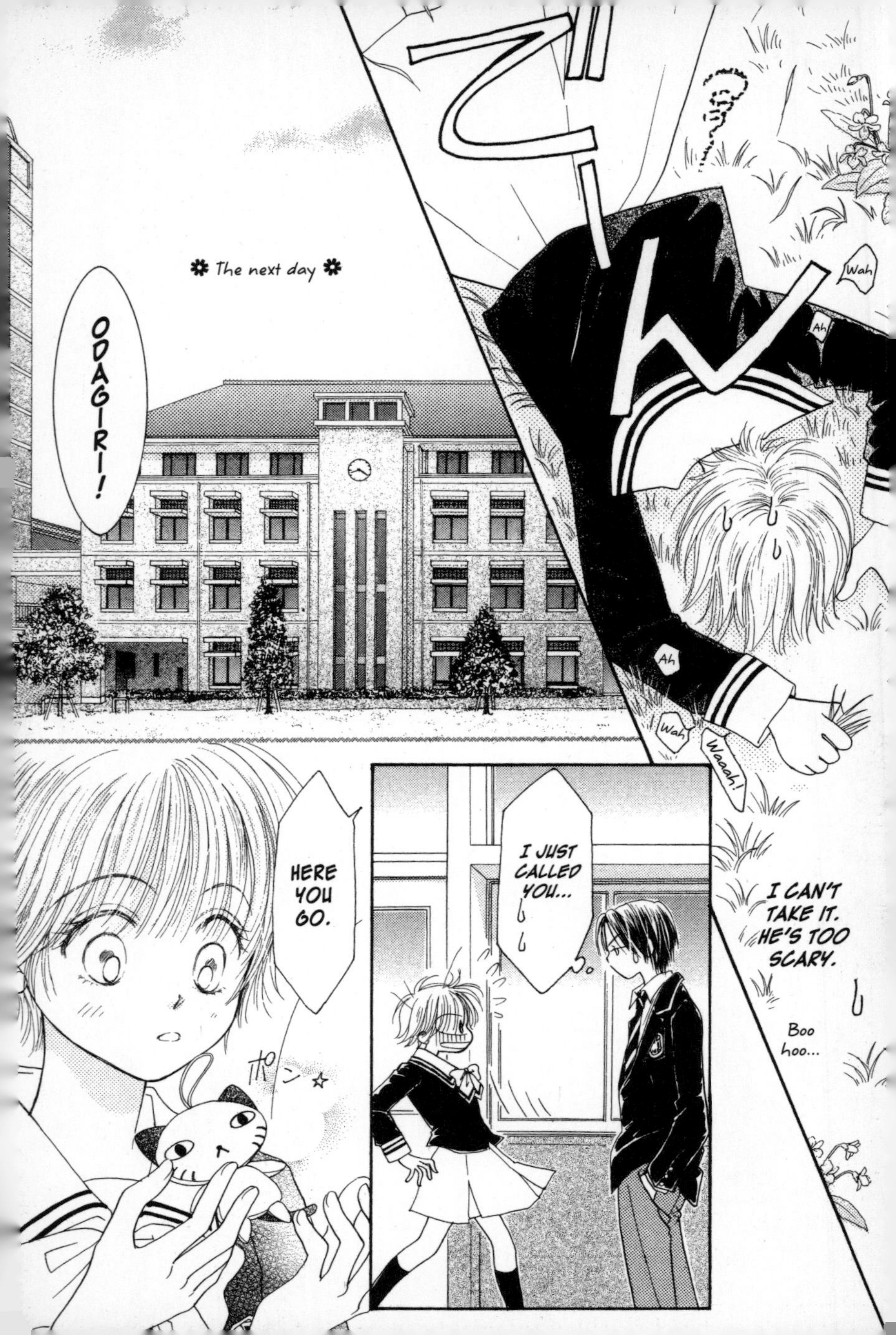
Wah
Ah
Ah
Wah
Waaah!
I CAN'T TAKE IT. HE'S TOO SCARY.
Boo hoo...
The next day
ODAGIRI!
I JUST CALLED YOU...
HERE YOU GO.
ポン☆

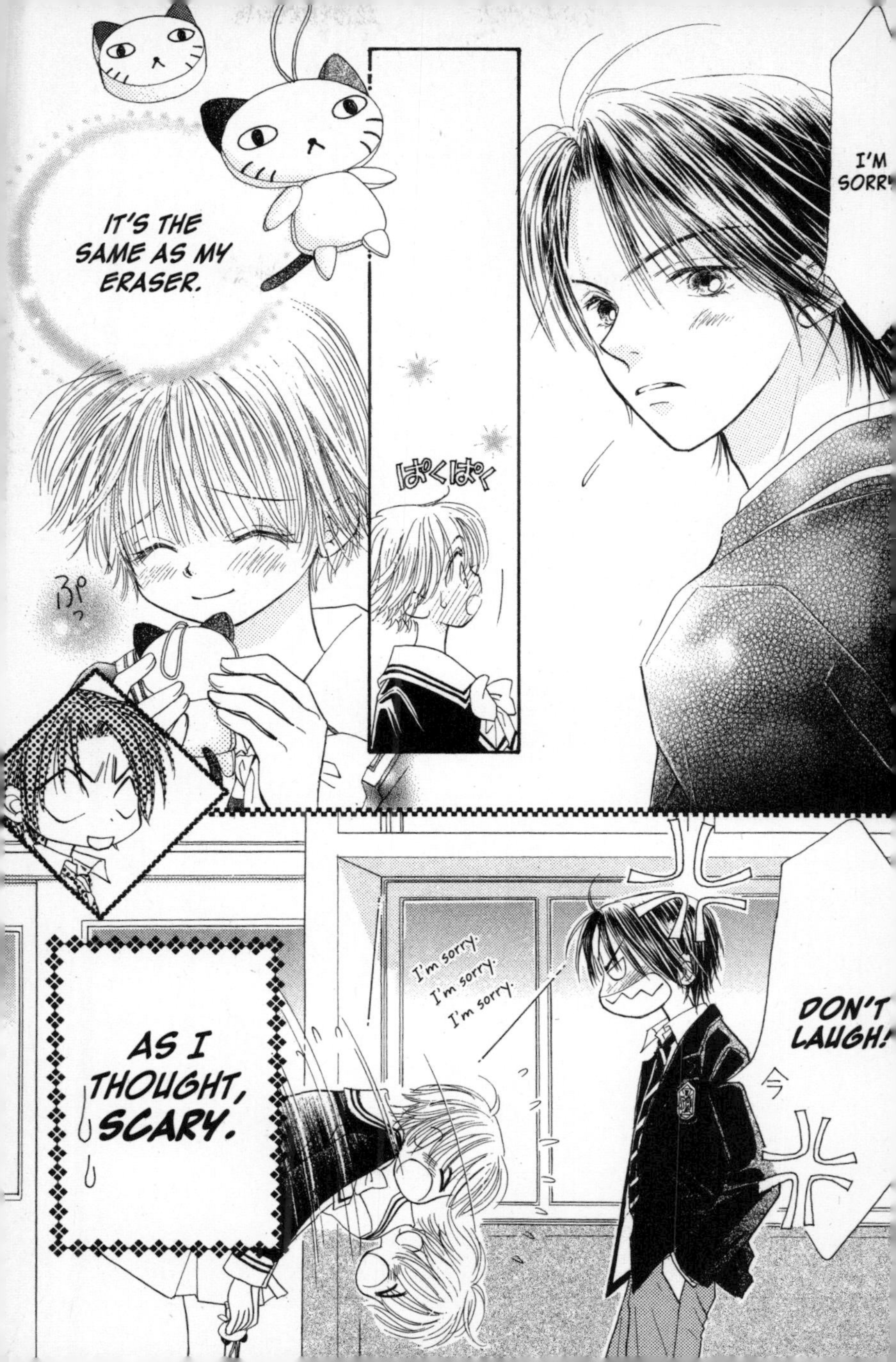
I'M SORR
ぱくぱく
IT'S THE SAME AS MY ERASER.
ぷっ
DON'T LAUGH!
今
I'm sorry.
I'm sorry.
I'm sorry.
AS I THOUGHT, SCARY.

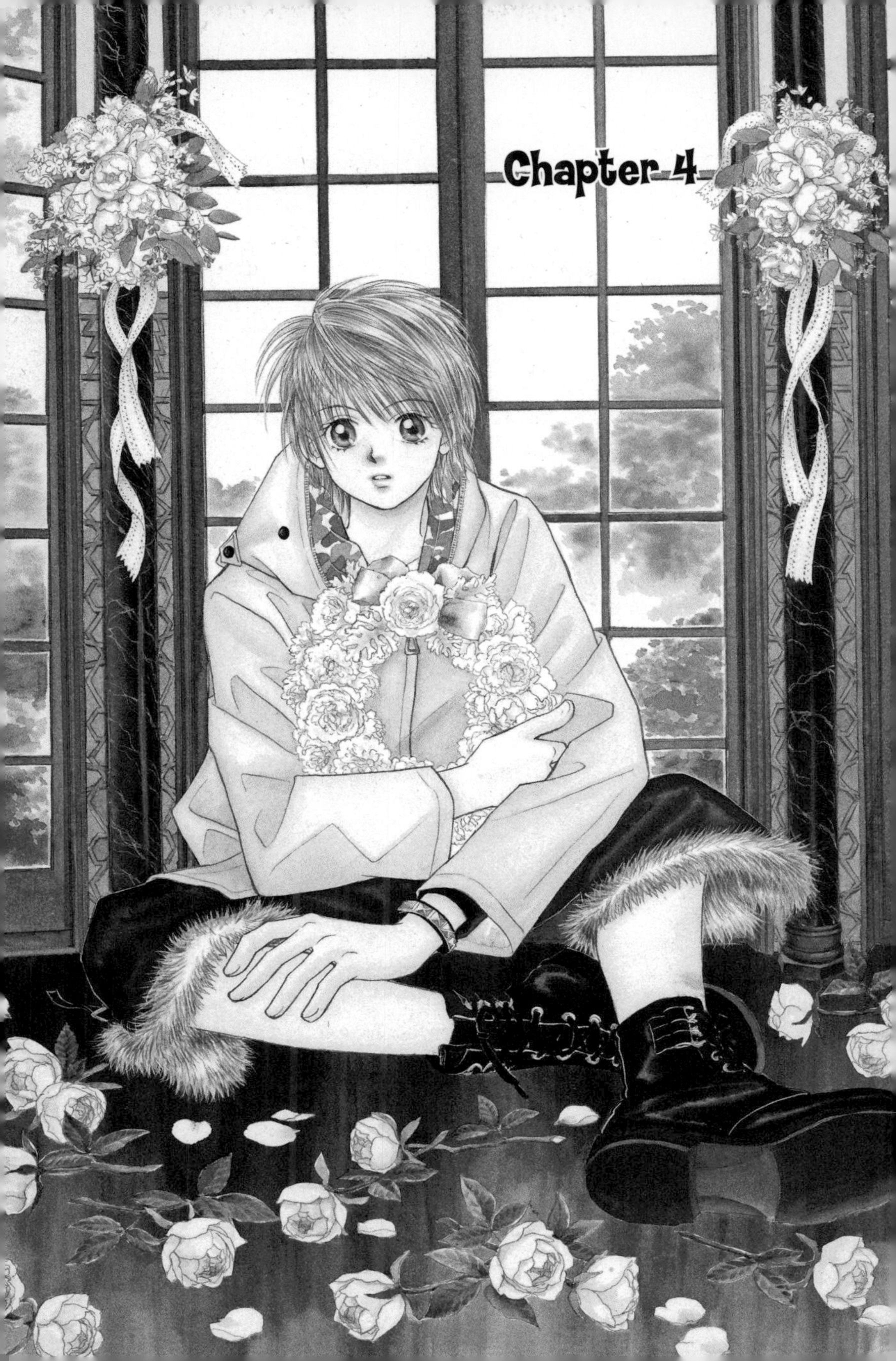
Chapter 4

ONE MONTH SINCE I MOVED IN.
THE FOOD AT THE DORMITORY IS GOOD, BUT...
...THEY DON'T SERVE LUNCH.
I wish they did.
Last night was pork cutlet curry and salad.
1—A
ぱく
Takaaki Asakura. High school First-Year.
ぱく
ぱく
niko niko
......

Accessory Road 1

Azuki chain (about 7 cm)
My current favorite! Pass the chain through the heart and it's really cute.

I love accessories! (They fascinate me). How much do I like accessories? Well, although I only have 10 fingers, right now, I own 63 rings! Although I only have two ears (three piercings), I have around 150 earrings (I know, I'm a fool). I also love bracelets, toe rings, pendants, and ankle bracelets. When I lay them all out and match them together in my head, I forget time, myself and work. ♡

(Ah, but I don't forget my cat aaaahhh

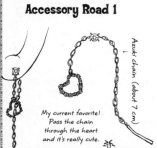

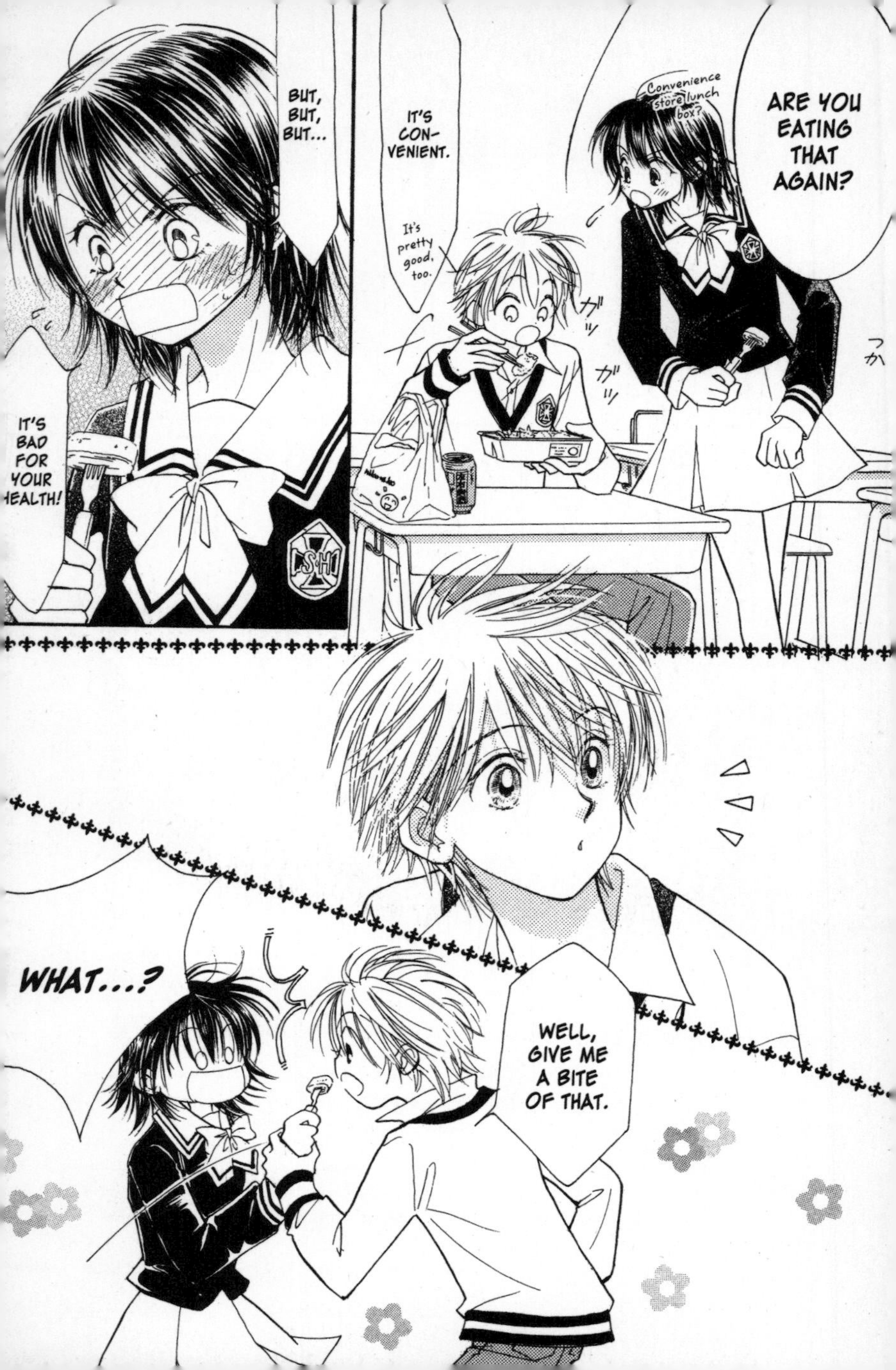
ARE YOU EATING THAT AGAIN?
Convenience store lunch box?
つか
IT'S CON-VENIENT.
It's pretty good, too.
ガツ
ガツ
BUT, BUT, BUT...
IT'S BAD FOR YOUR HEALTH!
WELL, GIVE ME A BITE OF THAT.
WHAT...?

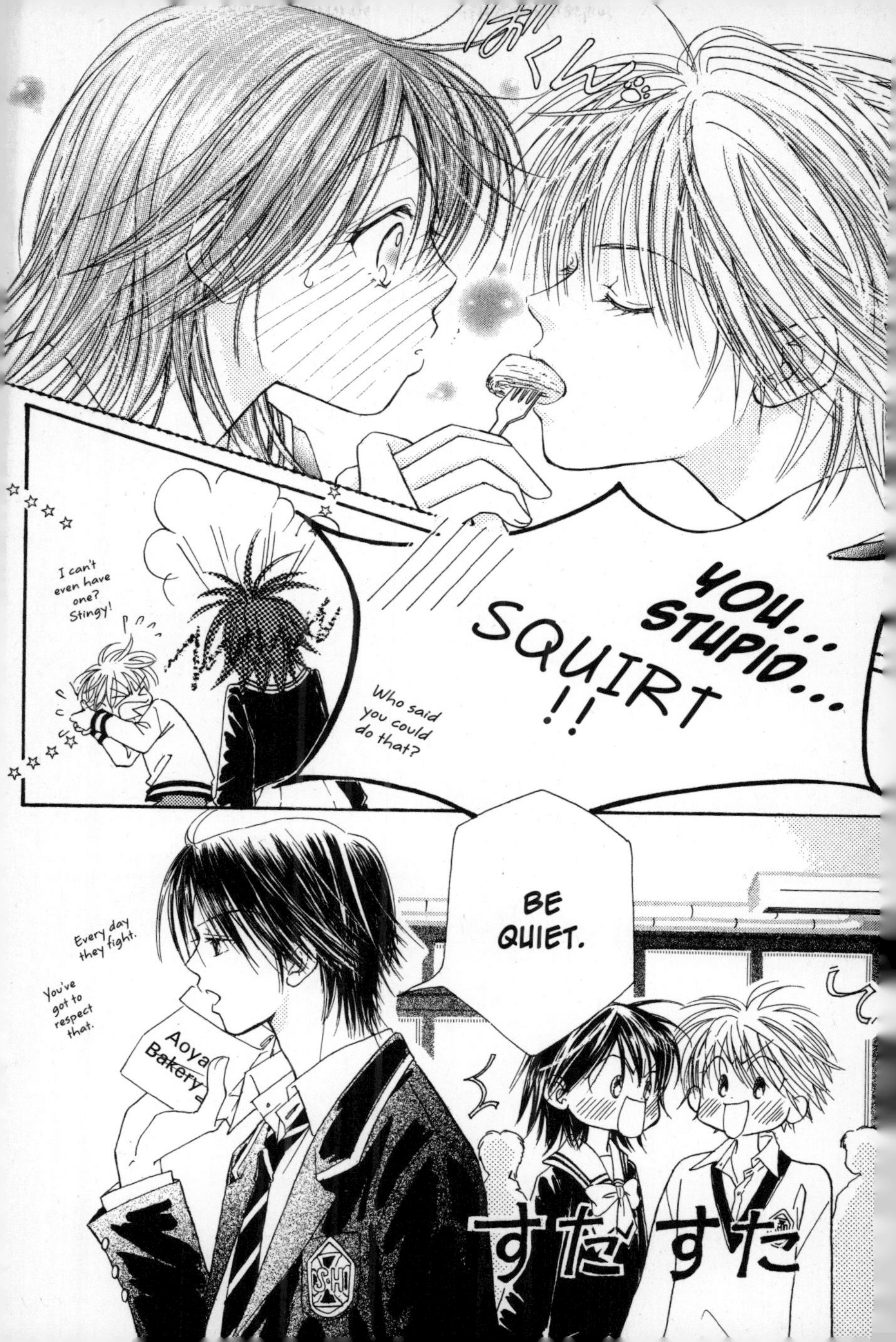
ぱくん
YOU... STUPID... SQUIRT!!
Who said you could do that?
I can't even have one? Stingy!
BE QUIET.
Every day they fight.
You've got to respect that.
Aoya Bakery
すたすた

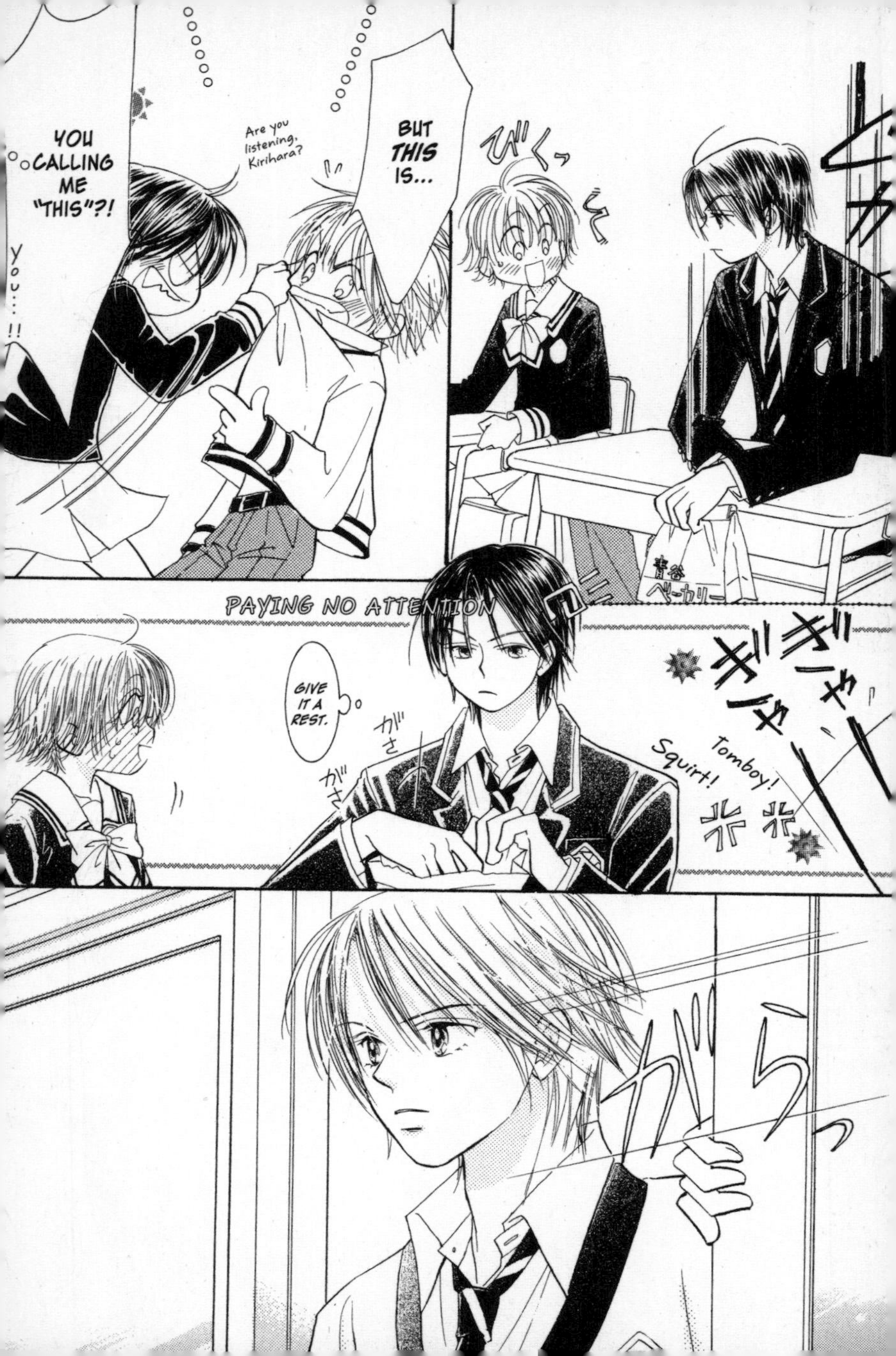

びくっ
BUT THIS IS...
Are you listening, Kirihara?
YOU CALLING ME "THIS"?!
You...!!
PAYING NO ATTENTION
Tomboy!
Squirt!
GIVE IT A REST.
がさ
がさ
がらっ

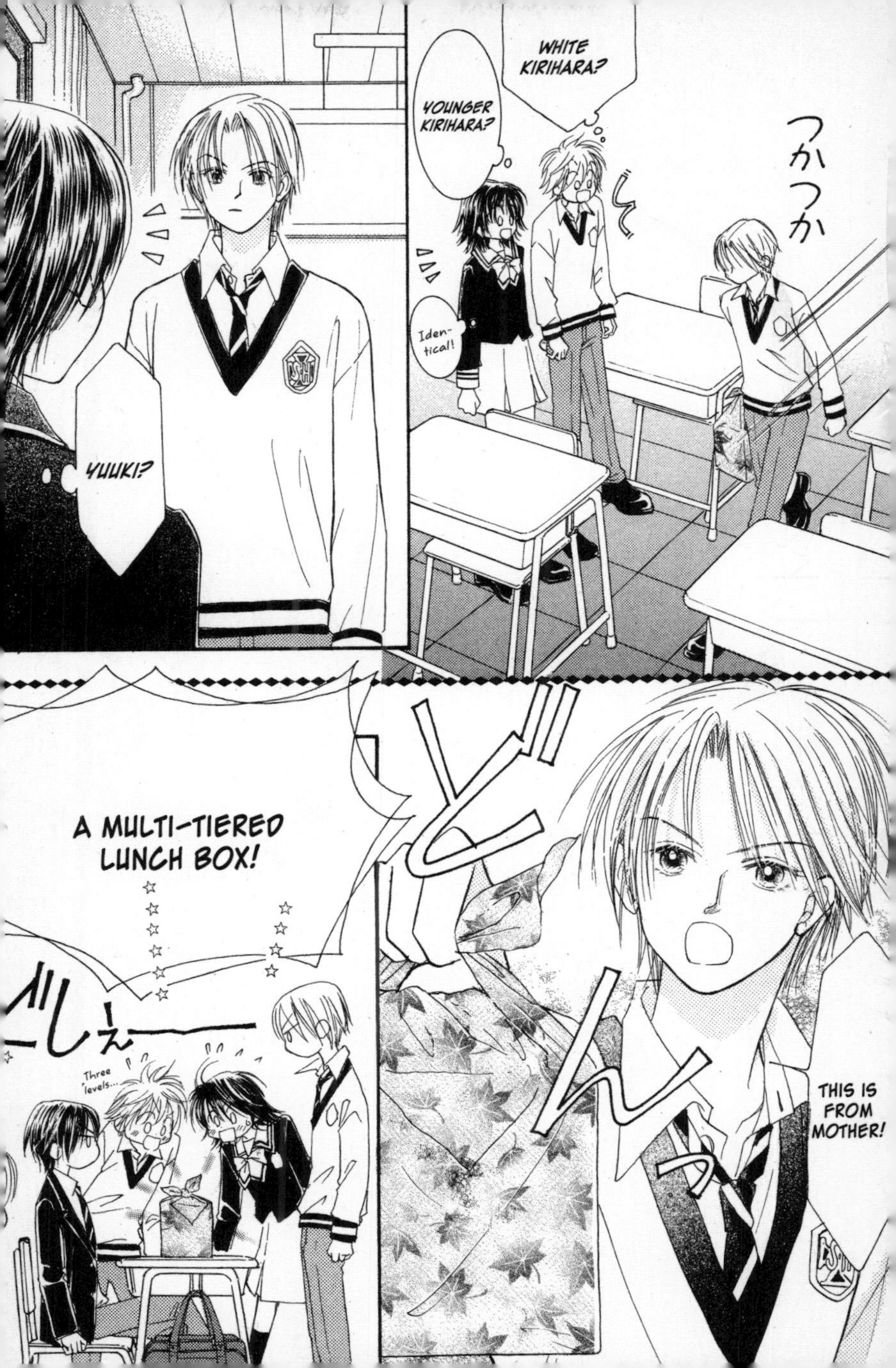
WHITE KIRIHARA?
YOUNGER KIRIHARA?
Iden-tical!
つかつか
YUUKI?
THIS IS FROM MOTHER!
A MULTI-TIERED LUNCH BOX!
Three levels...

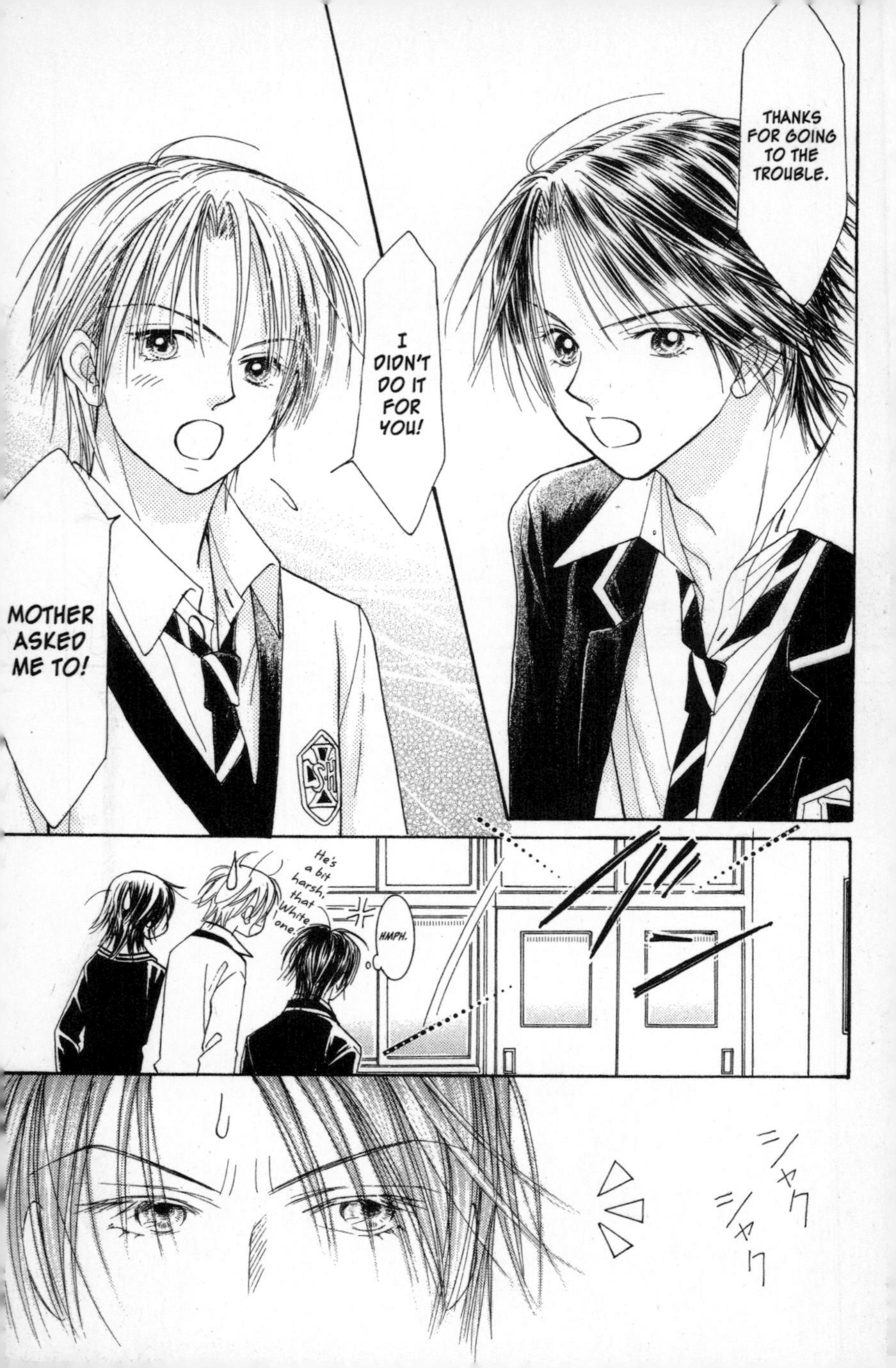
THANKS FOR GOING TO THE TROUBLE.
I DIDN'T DO IT FOR YOU!
MOTHER ASKED ME TO!
HMPH.
He's a bit harsh, that White one.
シャク
シャク

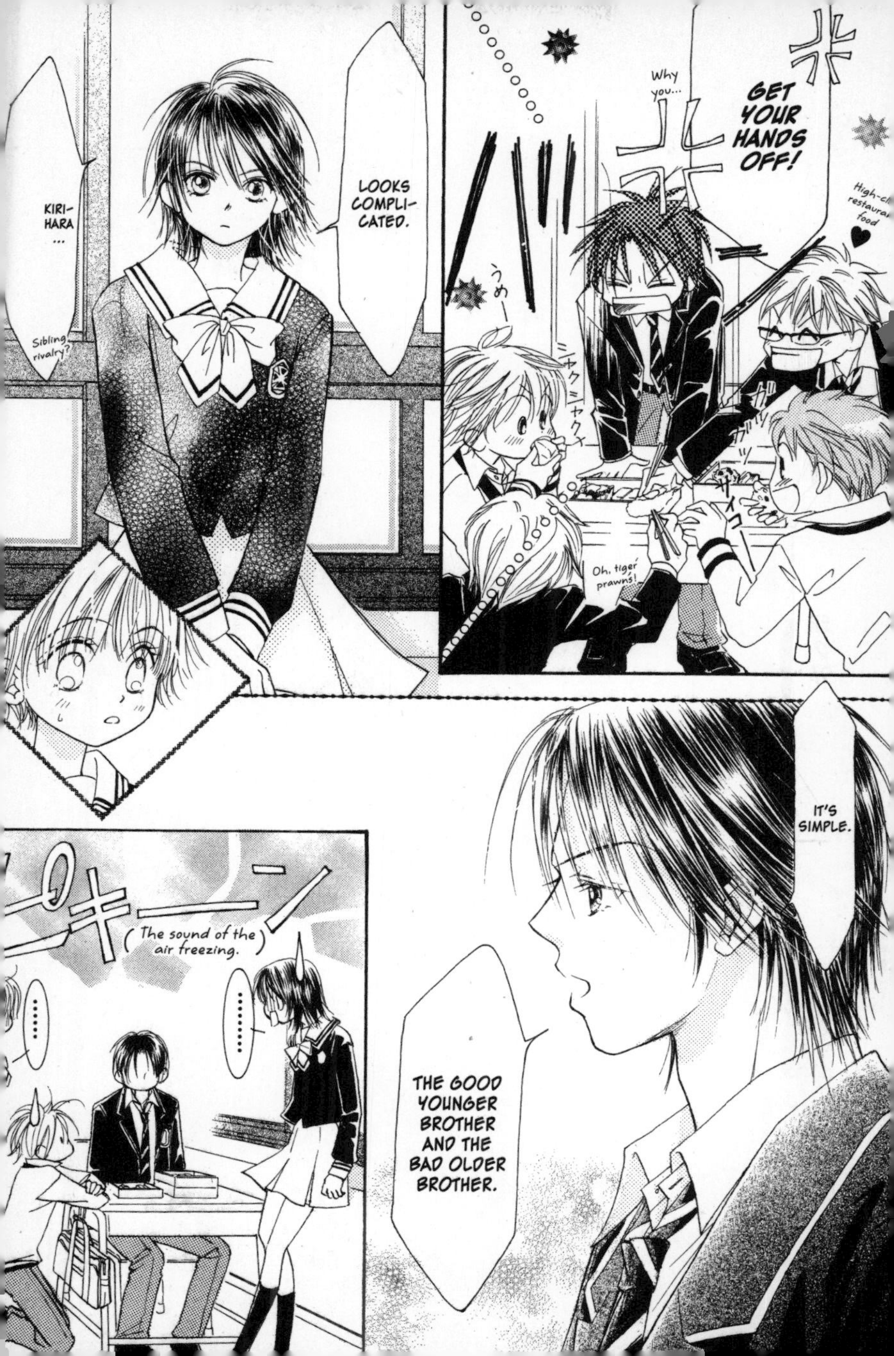
Why you...
GET YOUR HANDS OFF!
High-cl restaura food
うめー
シャクシャク
Oh, tiger prawns!
KIRI-HARA ...
LOOKS COMPLI-CATED.
Sibling rivalry?
IT'S SIMPLE.
THE GOOD YOUNGER BROTHER AND THE BAD OLDER BROTHER.
(The sound of the air freezing.)
......
......

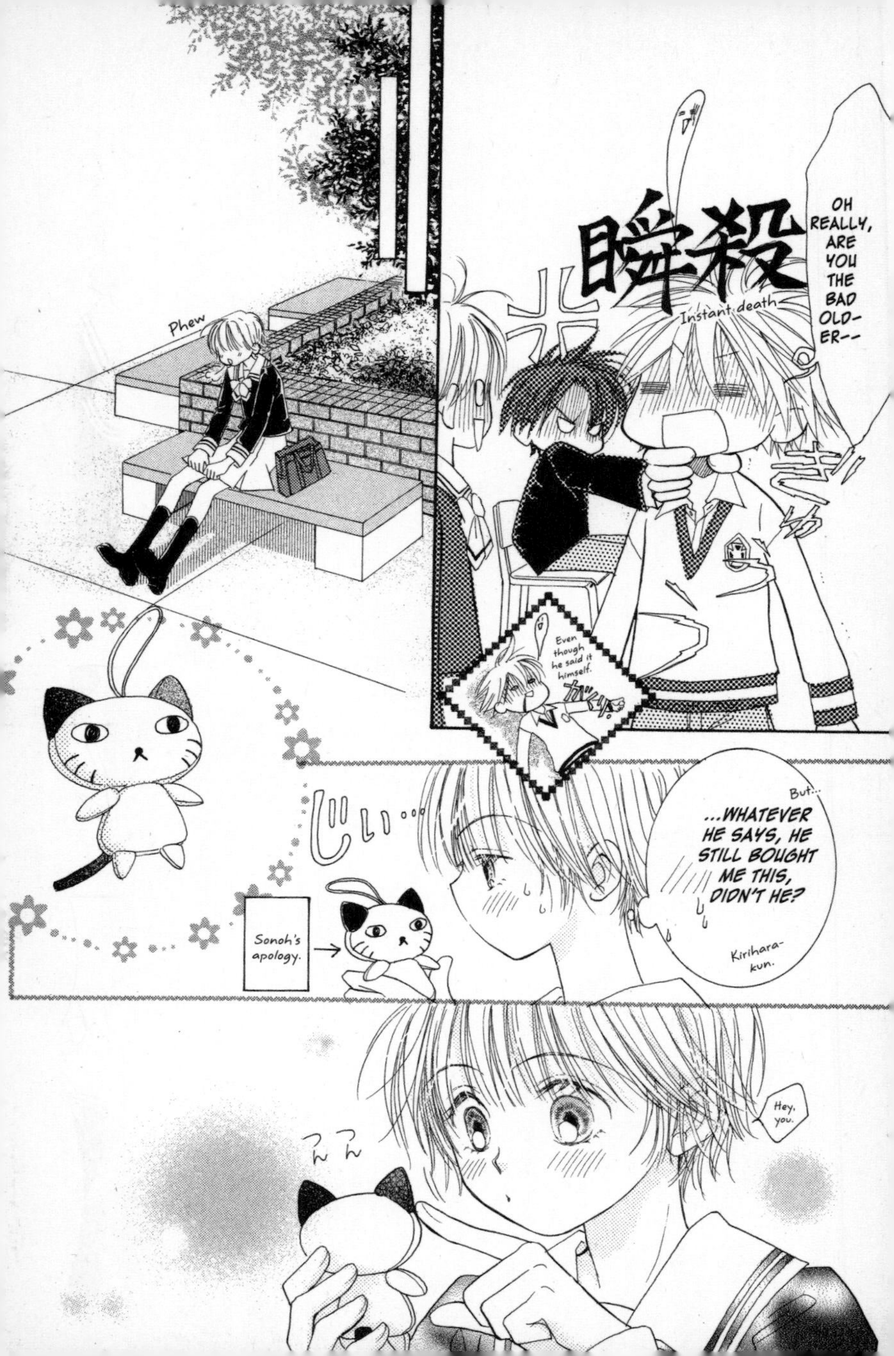

OH REALLY, ARE YOU THE BAD OLDER--
瞬殺
Instant death
Even though he said it himself.
Phew
But...
...WHATEVER HE SAYS, HE STILL BOUGHT ME THIS, DIDN'T HE?
Kirihara-kun.
じぃ…
Sonoh's apology.
Hey, you.

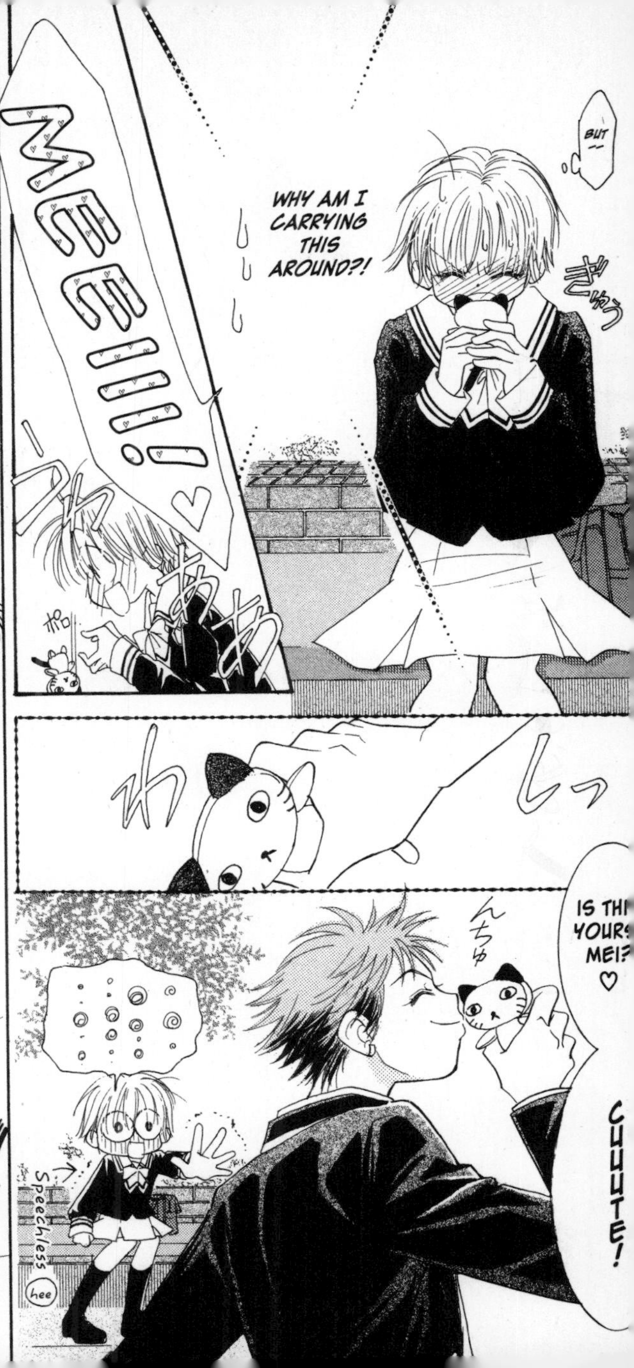
BUT—
WHY AM I CARRYING THIS AROUND?!
ぎゅう
MEEIII!
うわああ
ポロ
しっ
IS THI YOURS MEI? ♡
んちゅ
CHUUTE!
Speechless
hee

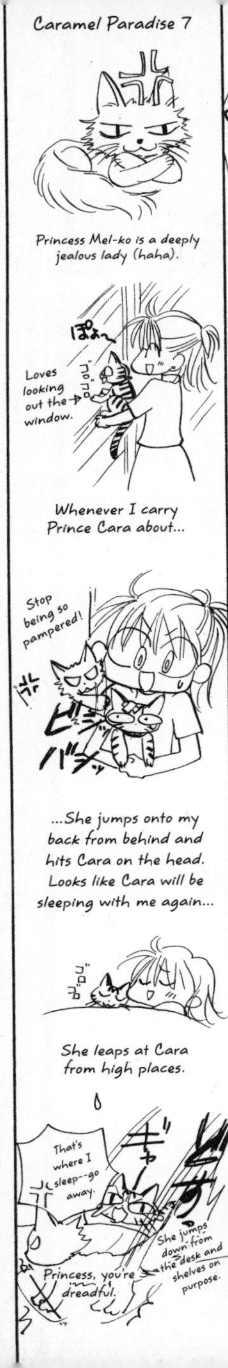
Caramel Paradise 7
Princess Mel-ko is a deeply jealous lady (haha).
Loves looking out the window.
ゴロゴロ
Whenever I carry Prince Cara about...
Stop being so pampered!
バシッ
...She jumps onto my back from behind and hits Cara on the head. Looks like Cara will be sleeping with me again...
ゴロゴロ
She leaps at Cara from high places.
That's where I sleep--go away.
ギャー
She jumps down from the desk and shelves on purpose.
Princess, you're dreadful.

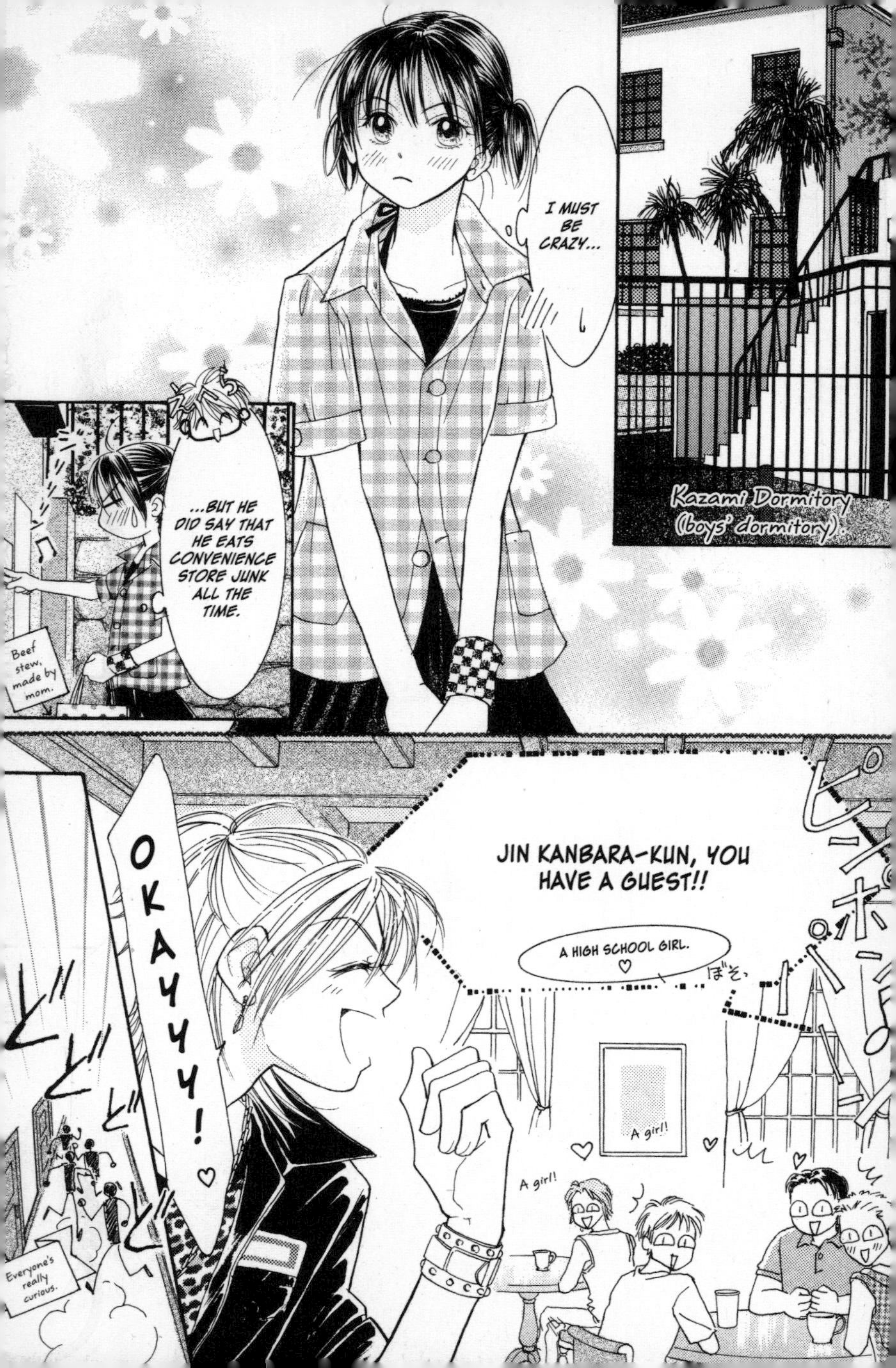
Kazami Dormitory (boys' dormitory)
I MUST BE CRAZY...
...BUT HE DID SAY THAT HE EATS CONVENIENCE STORE JUNK ALL THE TIME.
Beef stew, made by mom.
JIN KANBARA-KUN, YOU HAVE A GUEST!!
A HIGH SCHOOL GIRL. ♡
ぼそっ
A girl!
A girl!
OKAYYYY!
Everyone's really curious.

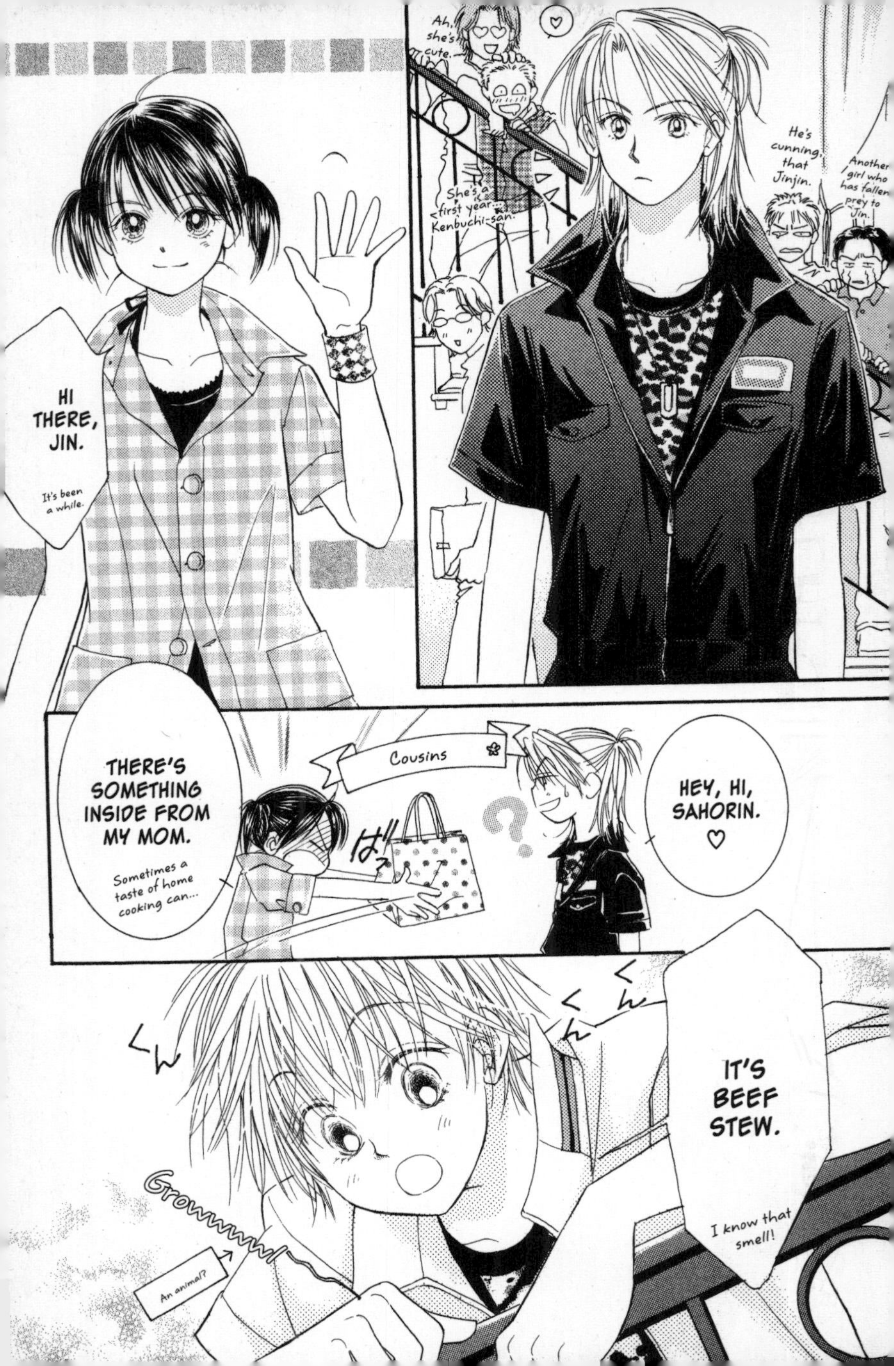

Ah, she's cute.
♡
She's a first year... Kenbuchi-san.
He's cunning, that Jinjin.
Another girl who has fallen prey to Jin.
HI THERE, JIN.
It's been a while.
HEY, HI, SAHORIN. ♡
Cousins
THERE'S SOMETHING INSIDE FROM MY MOM.
Sometimes a taste of home cooking can...
ぱっ
IT'S BEEF STEW.
I know that smell!
くん くん
くん
Growwwwl
An animal?

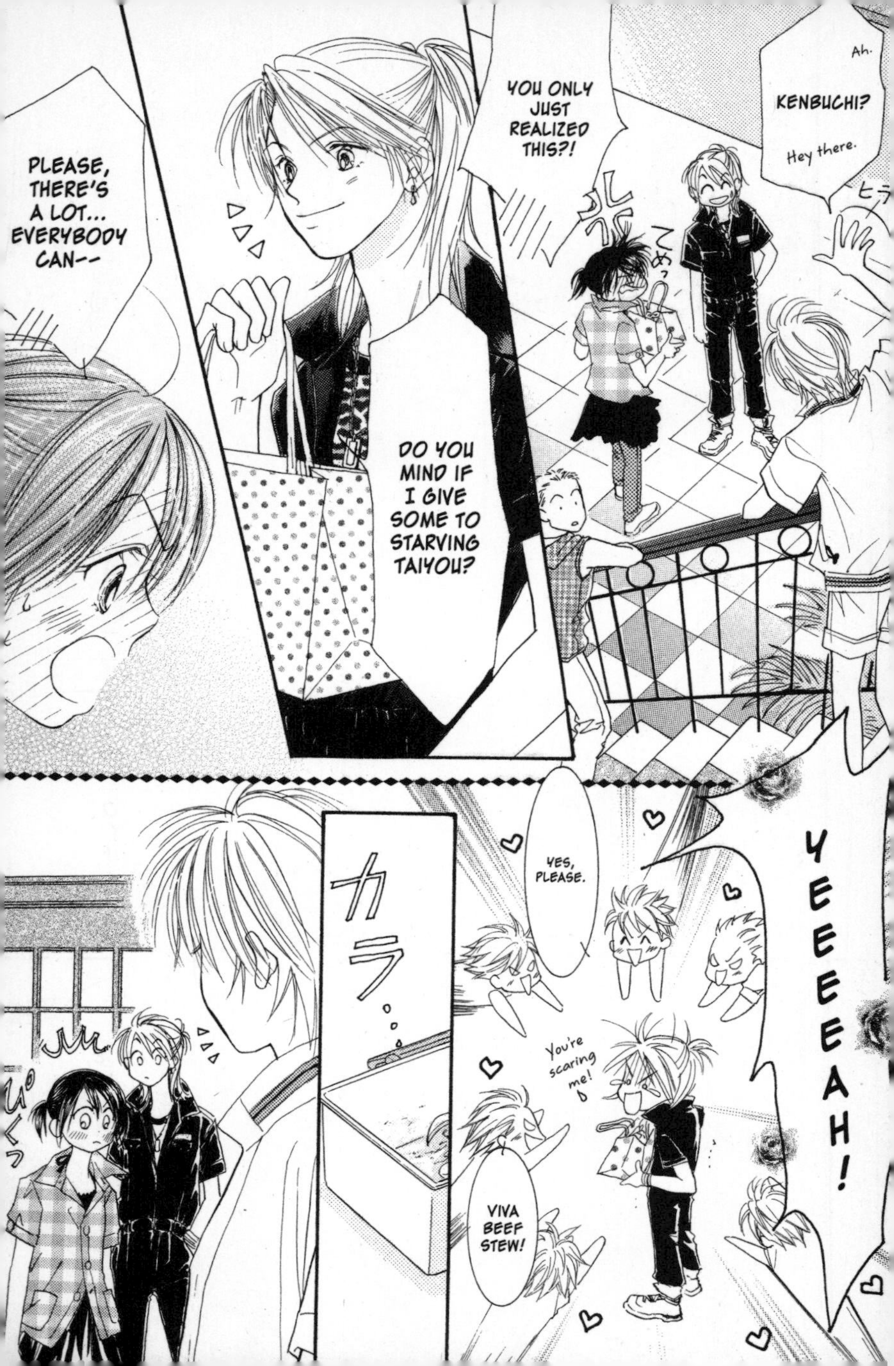
Ah.
KENBUCHI?
Hey there.
ヒラ
YOU ONLY JUST REALIZED THIS?!
てめっ
DO YOU MIND IF I GIVE SOME TO STARVING TAIYOU?
PLEASE, THERE'S A LOT... EVERYBODY CAN--
YEEEEAH!
YES, PLEASE.
You're scaring me!
VIVA BEEF STEW!
カラ
ぴくっ

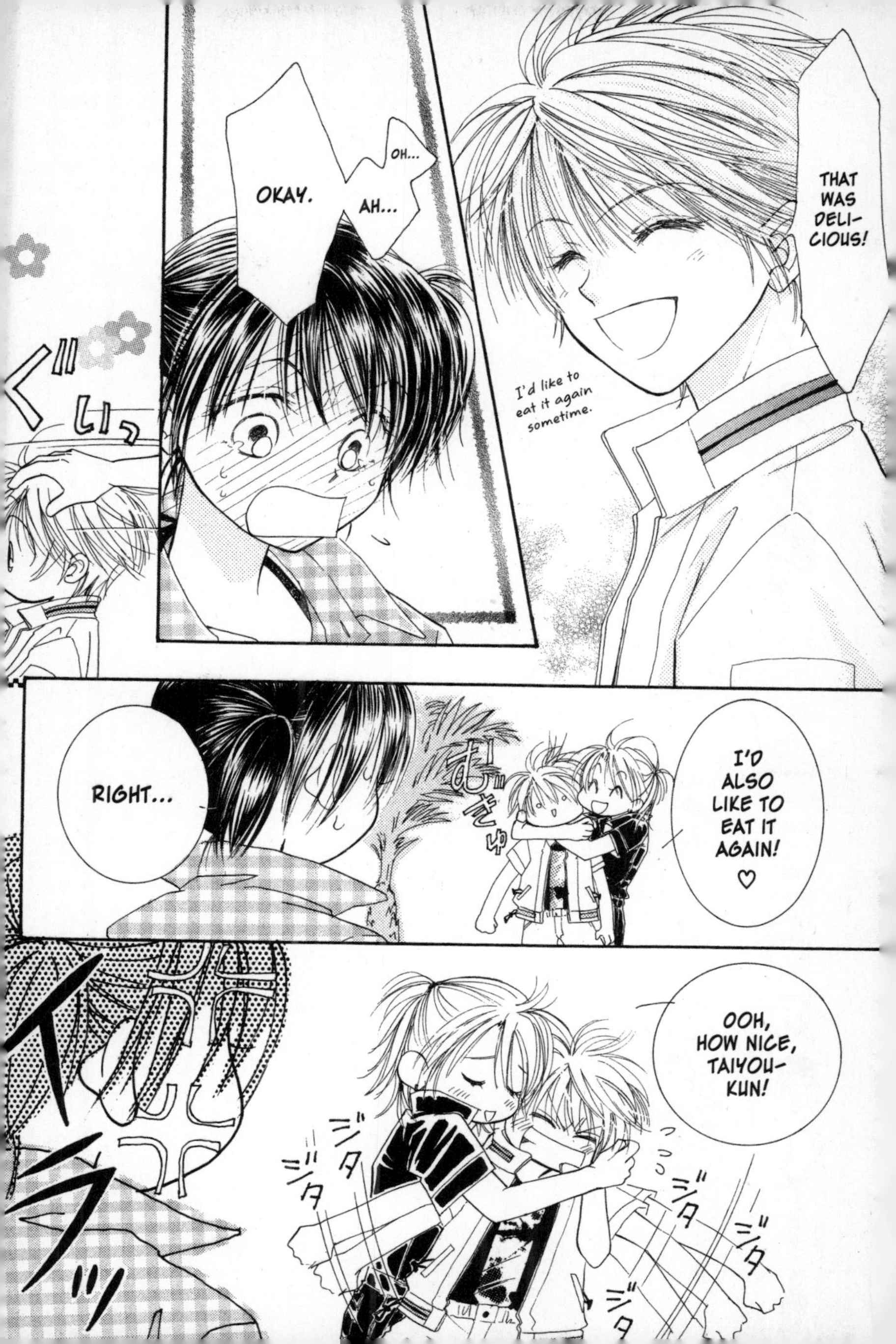

THAT WAS DELICIOUS!
I'd like to eat it again sometime.
OH...
AH...
OKAY.
ぐいっ
I'D ALSO LIKE TO EAT IT AGAIN! ♡
むぎゅ
RIGHT...
OOH, HOW NICE, TAIYOU-KUN!
ジタ ジタ
ジタ ジタ
イラッ

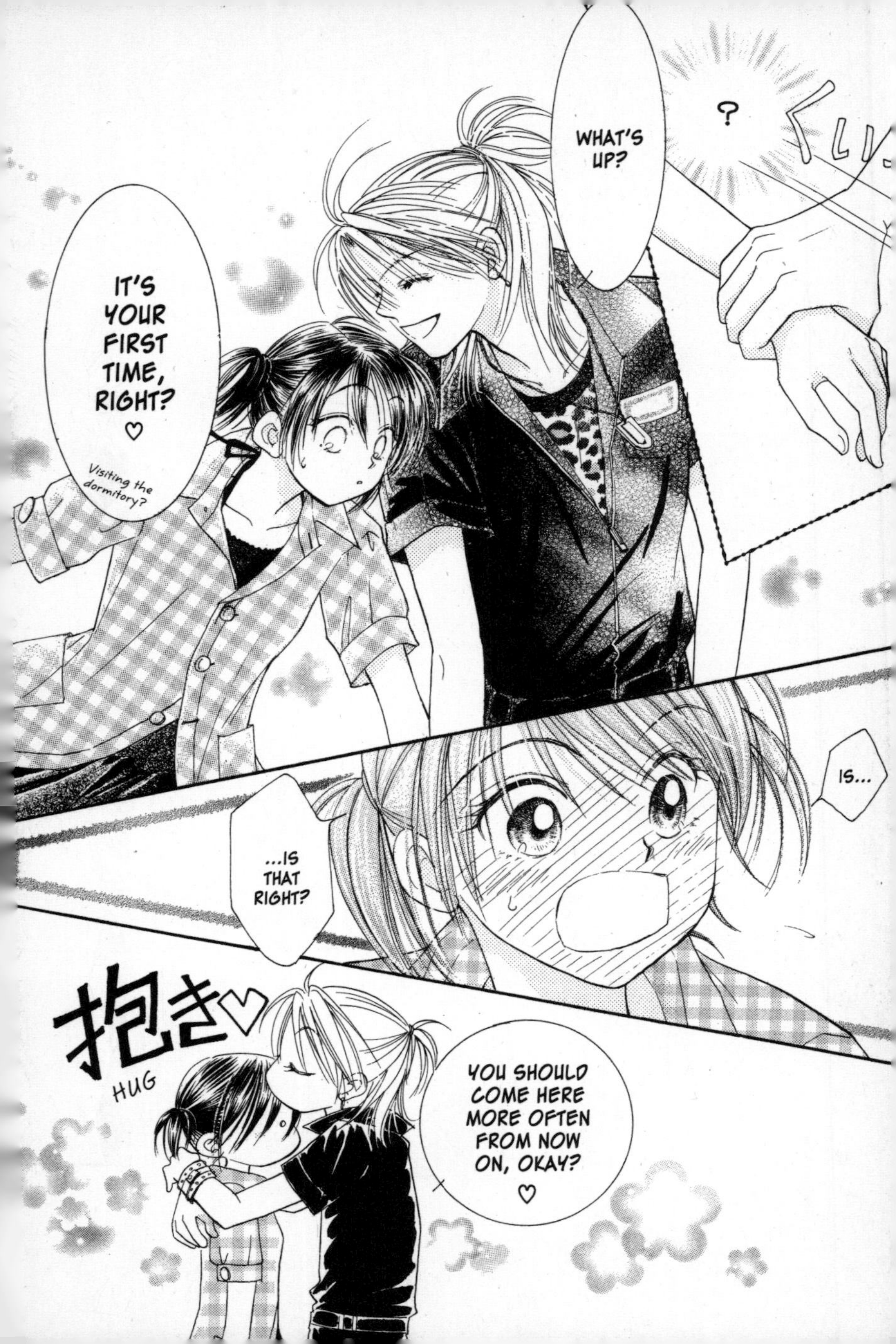
?
くい
WHAT'S UP?
IT'S YOUR FIRST TIME, RIGHT? ♡
Visiting the dormitory?
IS...
...IS THAT RIGHT?
YOU SHOULD COME HERE MORE OFTEN FROM NOW ON, OKAY? ♡
抱き♡
HUG

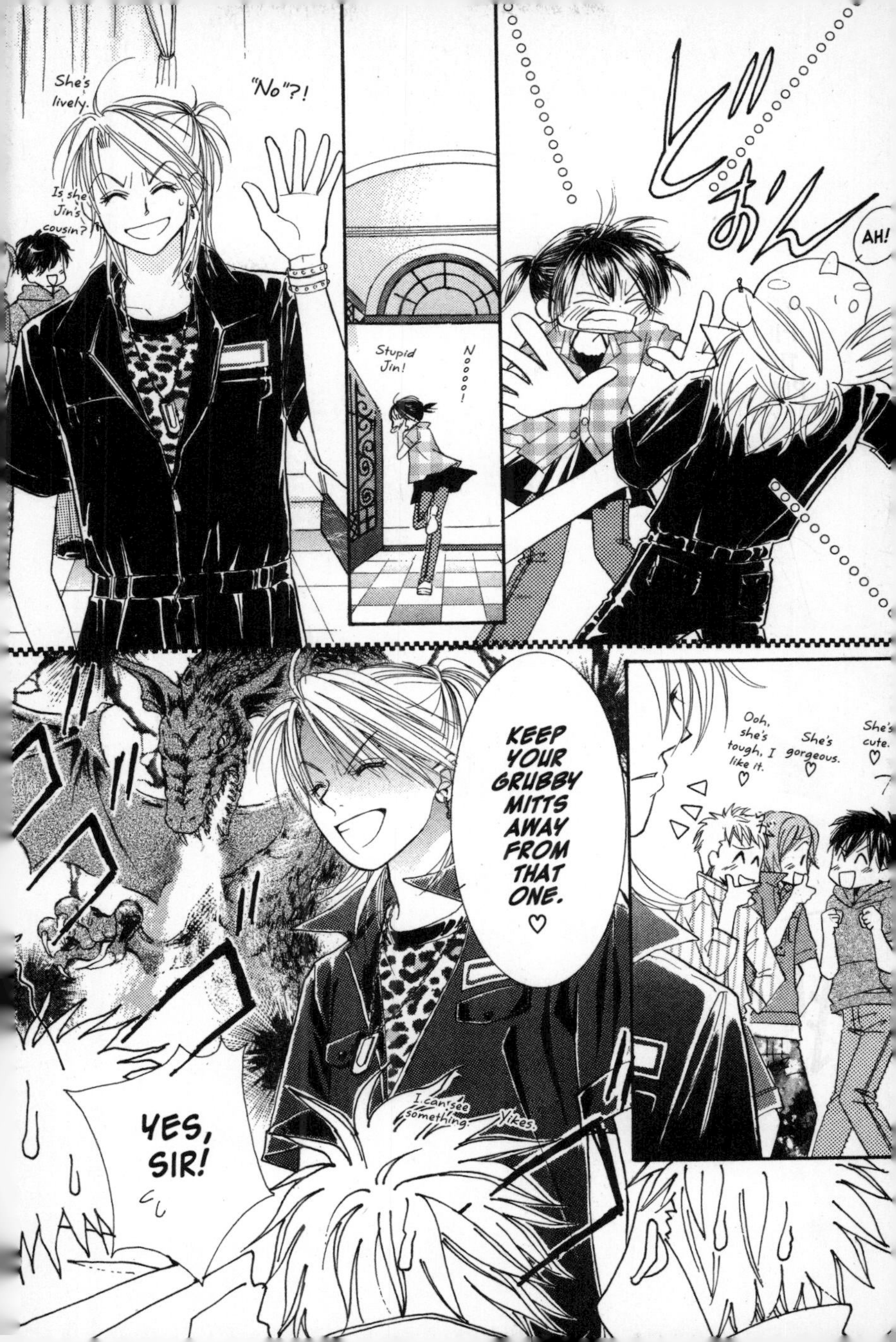
AH!
Noooo!
Stupid Jin!
"No"?!
She's lively.
Is she Jin's cousin?
She's cute.
She's gorgeous.
Ooh, she's tough, I like it.
KEEP YOUR GRUBBY MITTS AWAY FROM THAT ONE. ♡
Yikes.
I can see something.
YES, SIR!

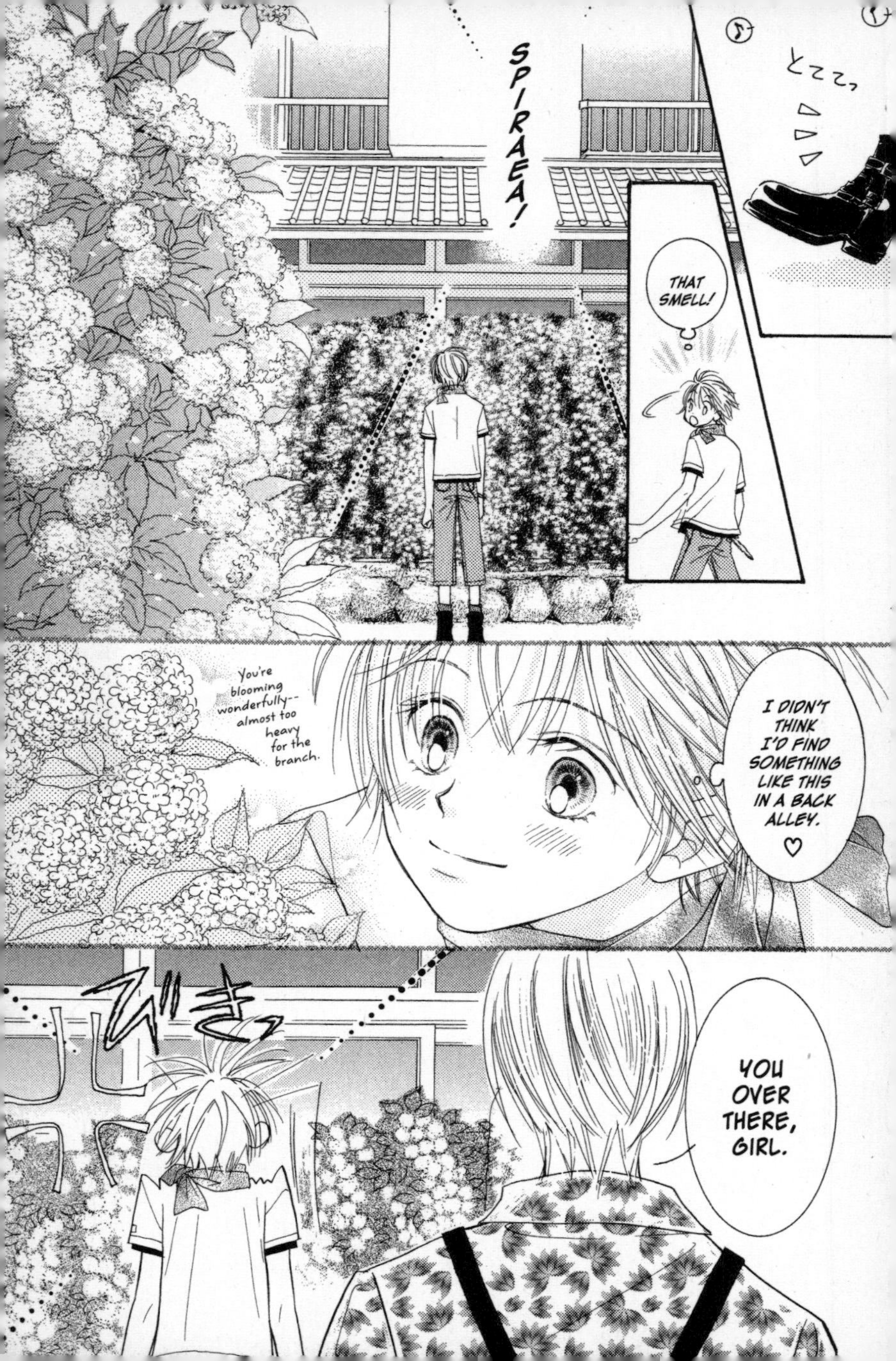
とととっ
THAT SMELL!
SPIRAEA!
I DIDN'T THINK I'D FIND SOMETHING LIKE THIS IN A BACK ALLEY. ♡
You're blooming wonderfully--almost too heavy for the branch.
YOU OVER THERE, GIRL.

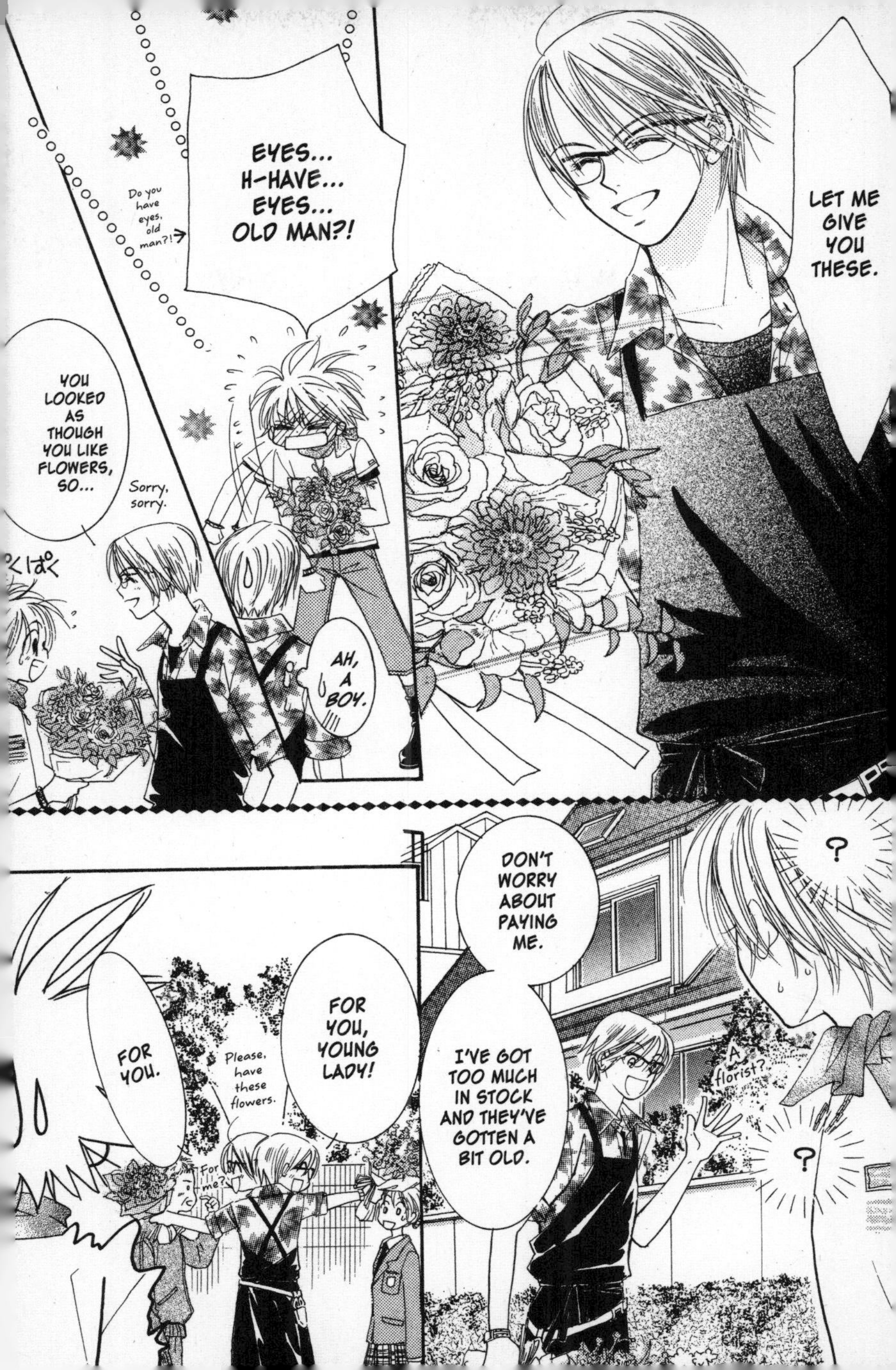
LET ME GIVE YOU THESE.
EYES... H-HAVE... EYES... OLD MAN?!
Do you have eyes, old man?!
AH, A BOY.
YOU LOOKED AS THOUGH YOU LIKE FLOWERS, SO...
Sorry, sorry.
くぱく
?
?
A florist?
DON'T WORRY ABOUT PAYING ME.
I'VE GOT TOO MUCH IN STOCK AND THEY'VE GOTTEN A BIT OLD.
FOR YOU, YOUNG LADY!
Please, have these flowers.
For me?
FOR YOU.

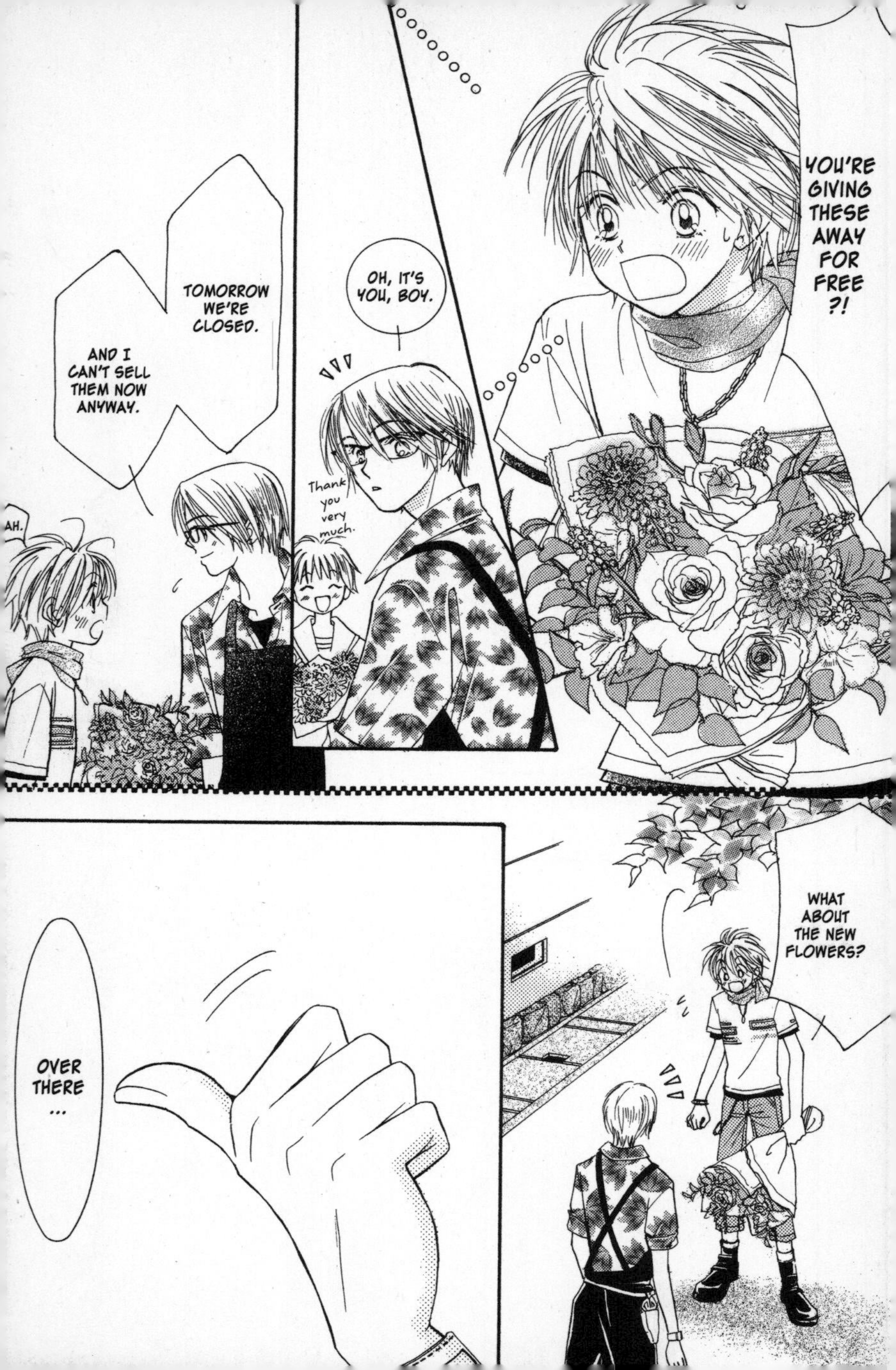
YOU'RE GIVING THESE AWAY FOR FREE ?!
OH, IT'S YOU, BOY.
Thank you very much.
TOMORROW WE'RE CLOSED.
AND I CAN'T SELL THEM NOW ANYWAY.
AH.
WHAT ABOUT THE NEW FLOWERS?
OVER THERE ...

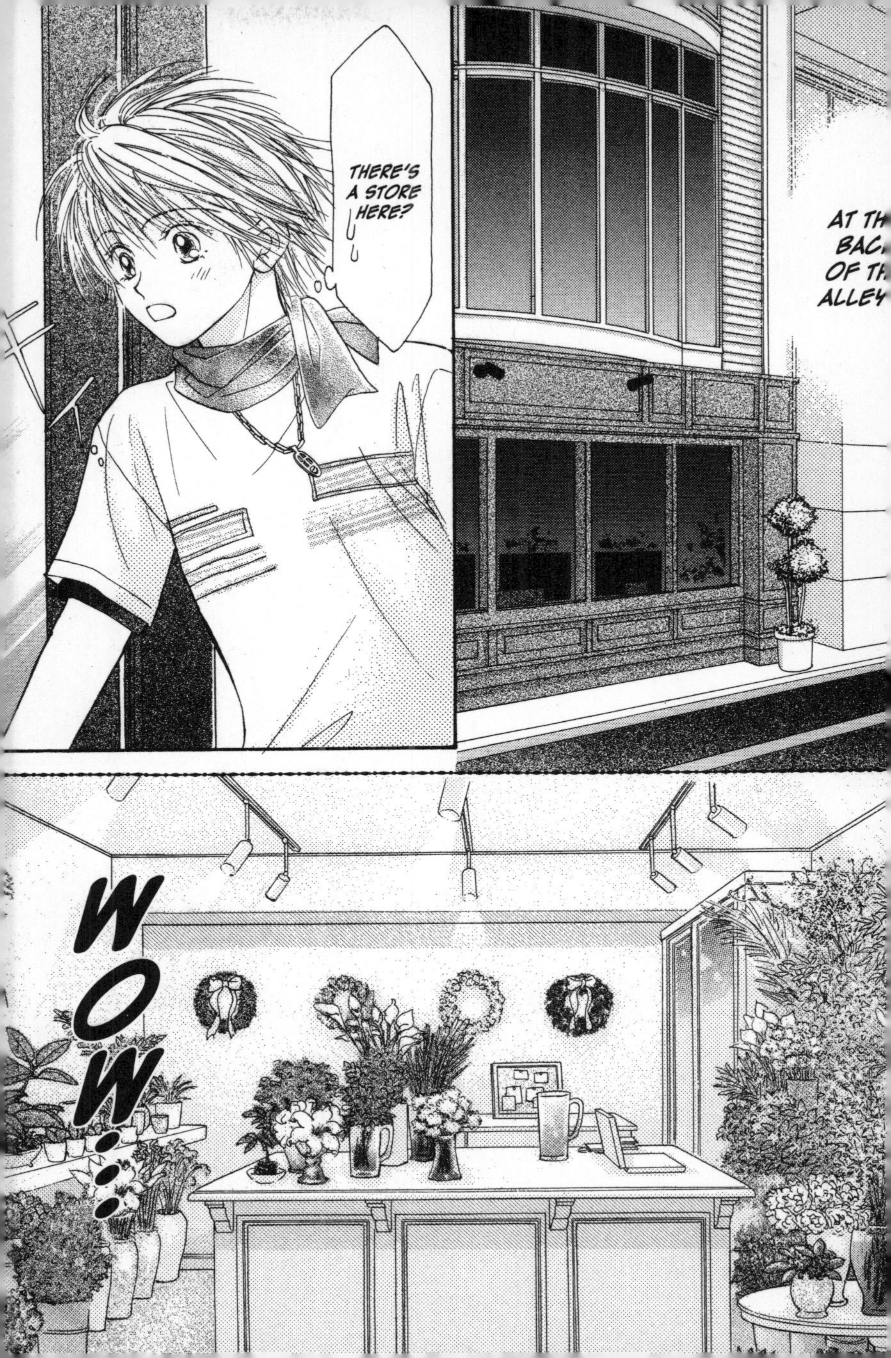

AT TH BAC OF TH ALLEY
THERE'S A STORE HERE?
WOW...

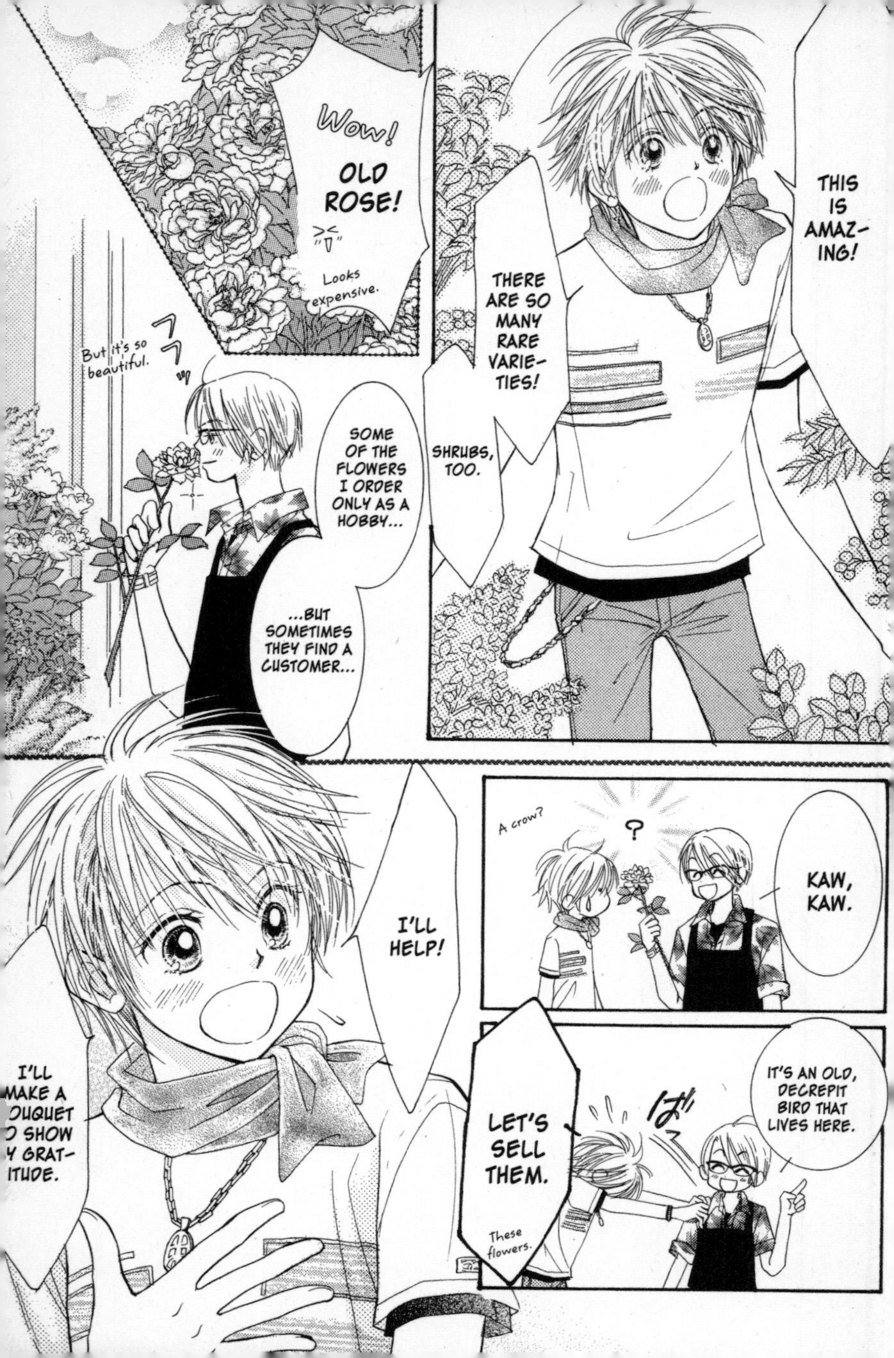
THIS IS AMAZ-ING!
THERE ARE SO MANY RARE VARIE-TIES!
SHRUBS, TOO.
Wow!
OLD ROSE!
Looks expensive.
But it's so beautiful.
SOME OF THE FLOWERS I ORDER ONLY AS A HOBBY...
...BUT SOMETIMES THEY FIND A CUSTOMER...
KAW, KAW.
?
A crow?
IT'S AN OLD, DECREPIT BIRD THAT LIVES HERE.
LET'S SELL THEM.
These flowers.
I'LL HELP!
I'LL MAKE A OUQUET O SHOW Y GRAT-ITUDE.

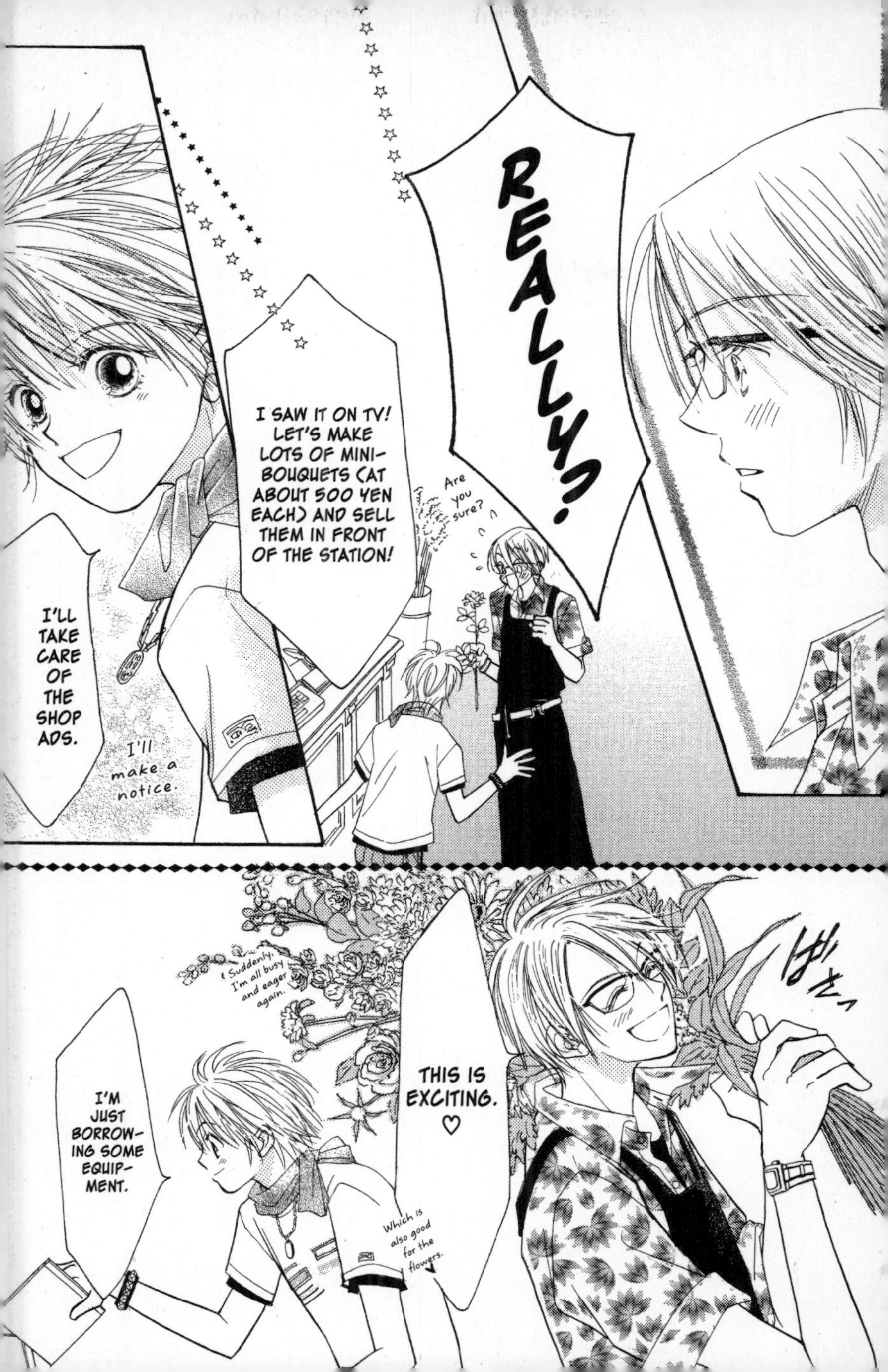
REALLY?
Are you sure?
I SAW IT ON TV! LET'S MAKE LOTS OF MINI-BOUQUETS (AT ABOUT 500 YEN EACH) AND SELL THEM IN FRONT OF THE STATION!
I'LL TAKE CARE OF THE SHOP ADS.
I'll make a notice.
ばさっ
THIS IS EXCITING. ♡
Which is also good for the flowers.
Suddenly, I'm all busy and eager again.
I'M JUST BORROWING SOME EQUIPMENT.

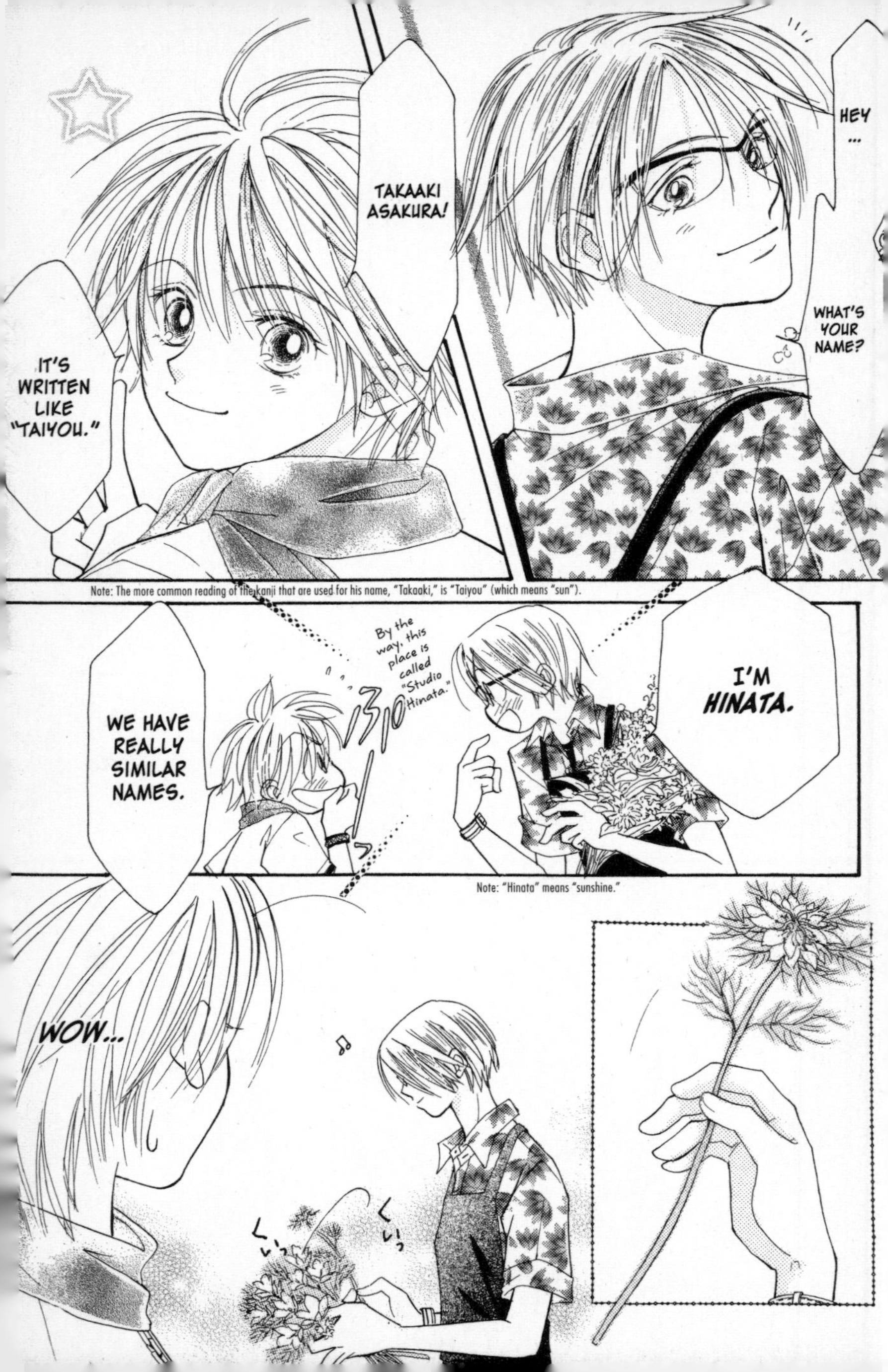
HEY ...
WHAT'S YOUR NAME?
TAKAAKI ASAKURA!
IT'S WRITTEN LIKE "TAIYOU."
Note: The more common reading of the kanji that are used for his name, "Takaaki," is "Taiyou" (which means "sun").
I'M HINATA.
By the way, this place is called "Studio Hinata."
WE HAVE REALLY SIMILAR NAMES.
Note: "Hinata" means "sunshine."
WOW...

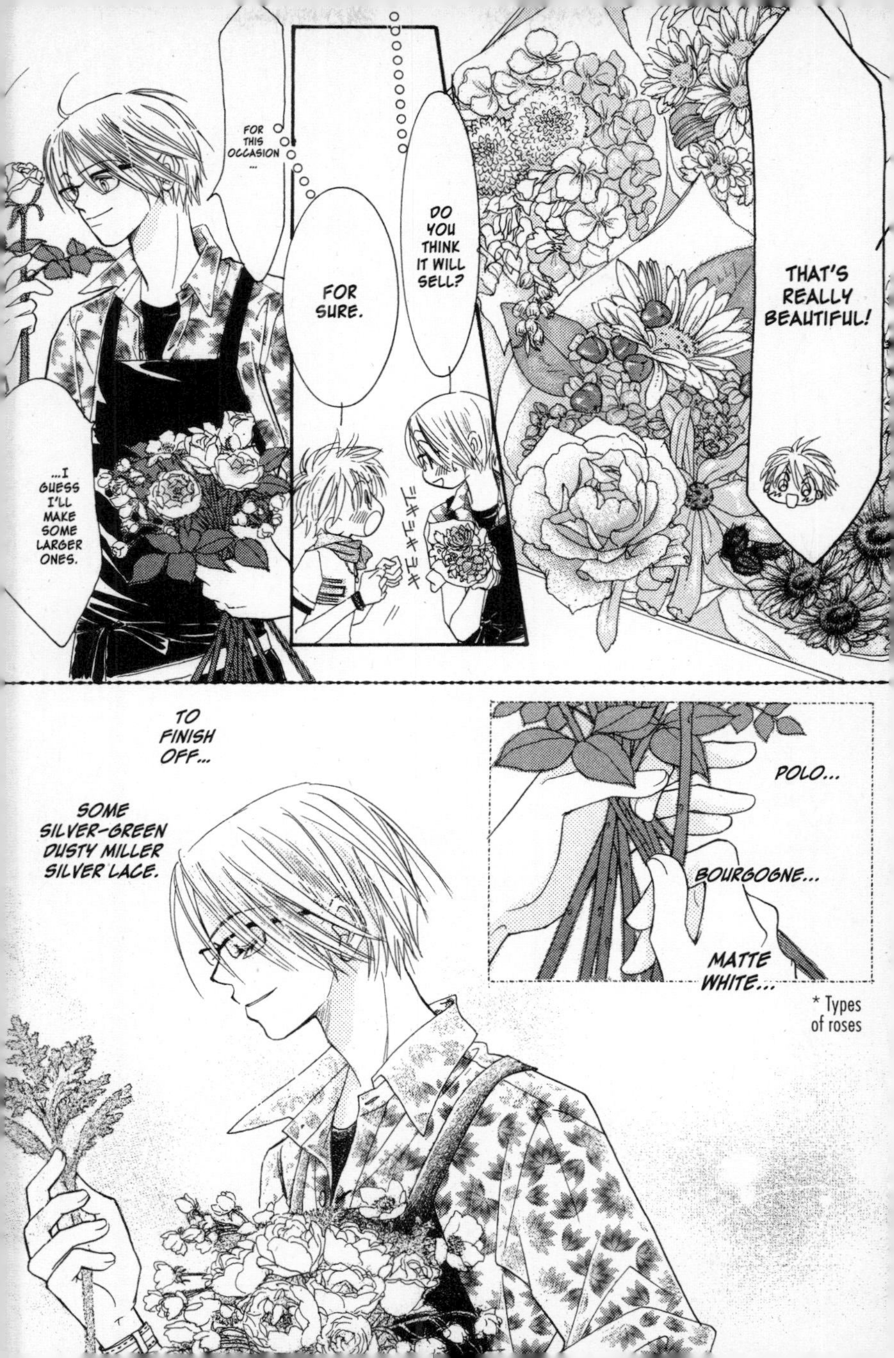
THAT'S REALLY BEAUTIFUL!
DO YOU THINK IT WILL SELL?
FOR SURE.
FOR THIS OCCASION...
...I GUESS I'LL MAKE SOME LARGER ONES.
POLO...
BOURGOGNE...
MATTE WHITE...
* Types of roses
TO FINISH OFF...
SOME SILVER-GREEN DUSTY MILLER SILVER LACE.

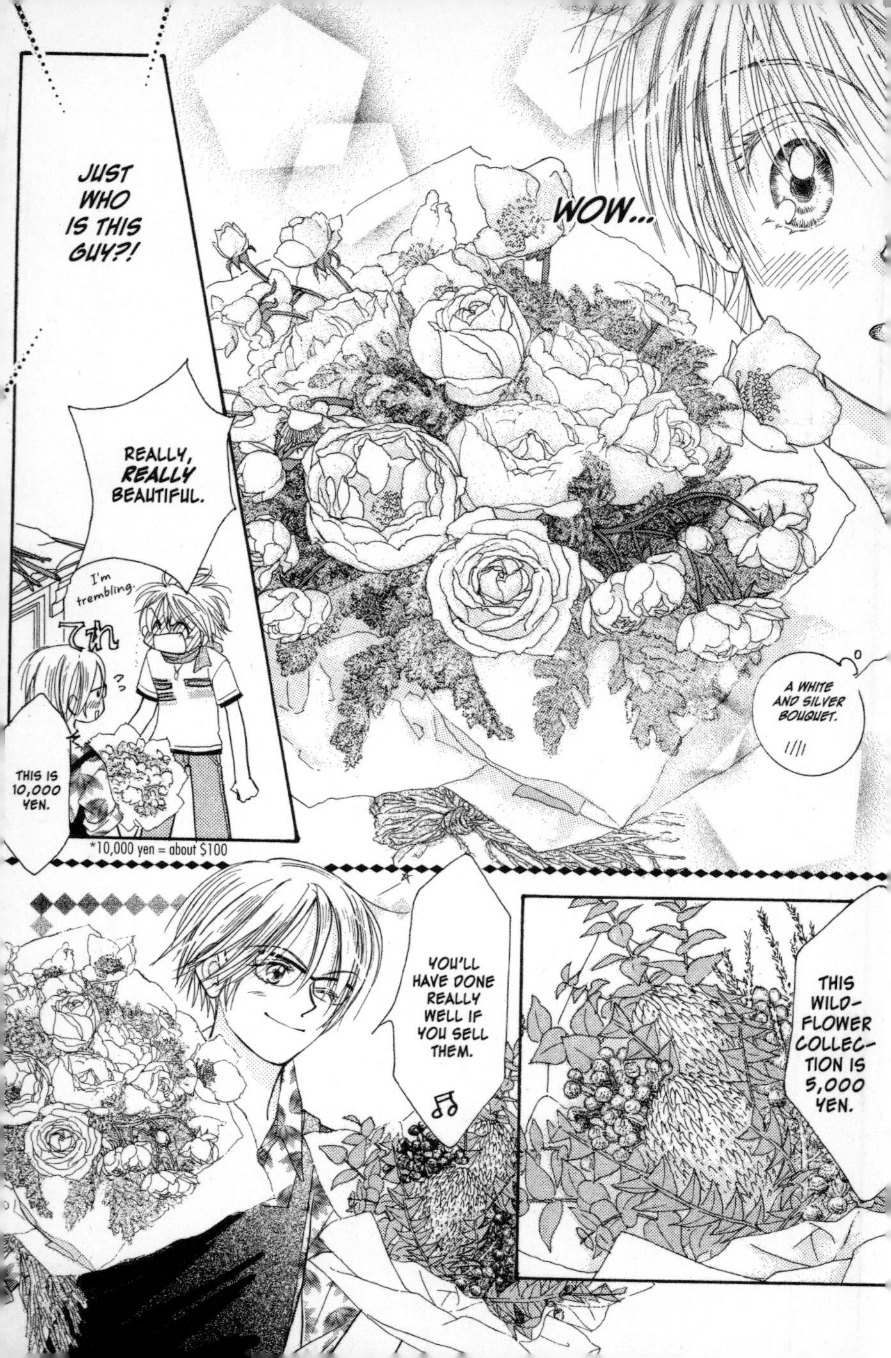
WOW...
A WHITE AND SILVER BOUQUET.
JUST WHO IS THIS GUY?!
REALLY, REALLY BEAUTIFUL.
I'm trembling.
てれ
THIS IS 10,000 YEN.
THIS WILDFLOWER COLLECTION IS 5,000 YEN.
YOU'LL HAVE DONE REALLY WELL IF YOU SELL THEM.
*10,000 yen = about $100

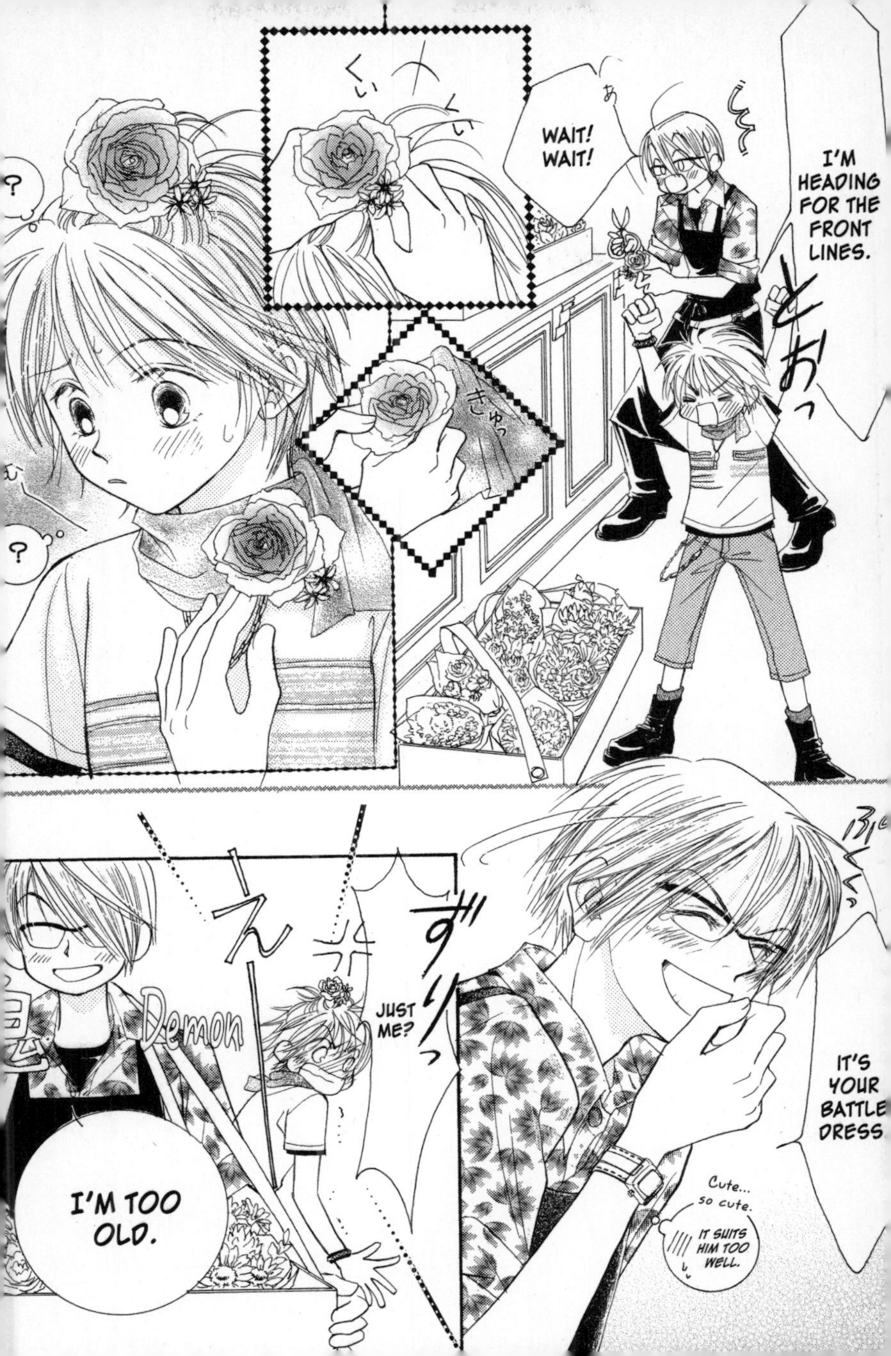
I'M HEADING FOR THE FRONT LINES.
とおっ
あ
WAIT! WAIT!
くい
くい
きゅっ
?
?
IT'S YOUR BATTLE DRESS
ぷくくっ
Cute... so cute.
IT SUITS HIM TOO WELL.
ずりっ
JUST ME?
ん
Demon
I'M TOO OLD.

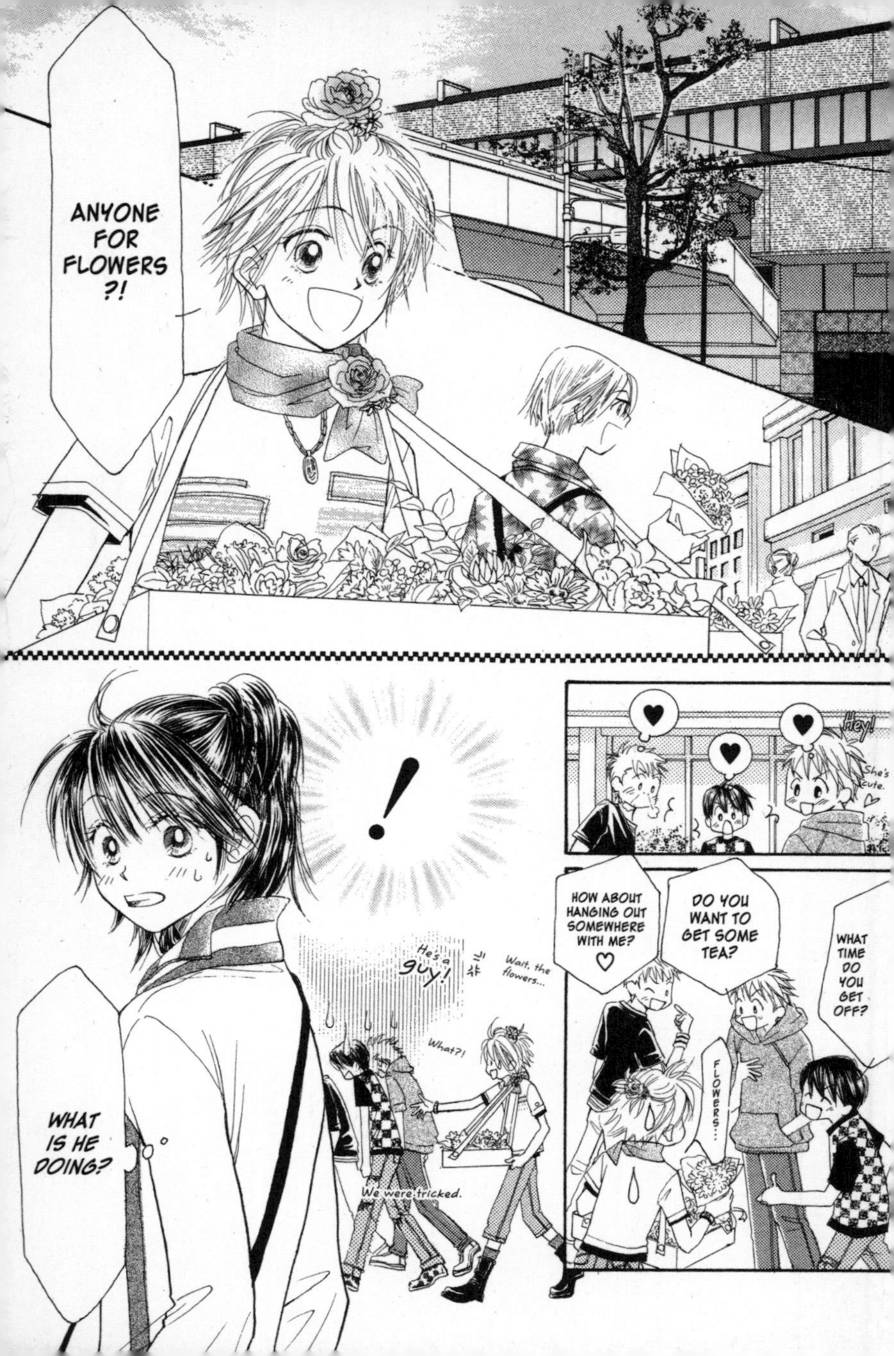
ANYONE FOR FLOWERS?!
Hey!
She's cute.
WHAT TIME DO YOU GET OFF?
DO YOU WANT TO GET SOME TEA?
HOW ABOUT HANGING OUT SOMEWHERE WITH ME? ♡
FLOWERS...
!
Wait, the flowers...
He's a guy!
What?!
We were tricked.
WHAT IS HE DOING?

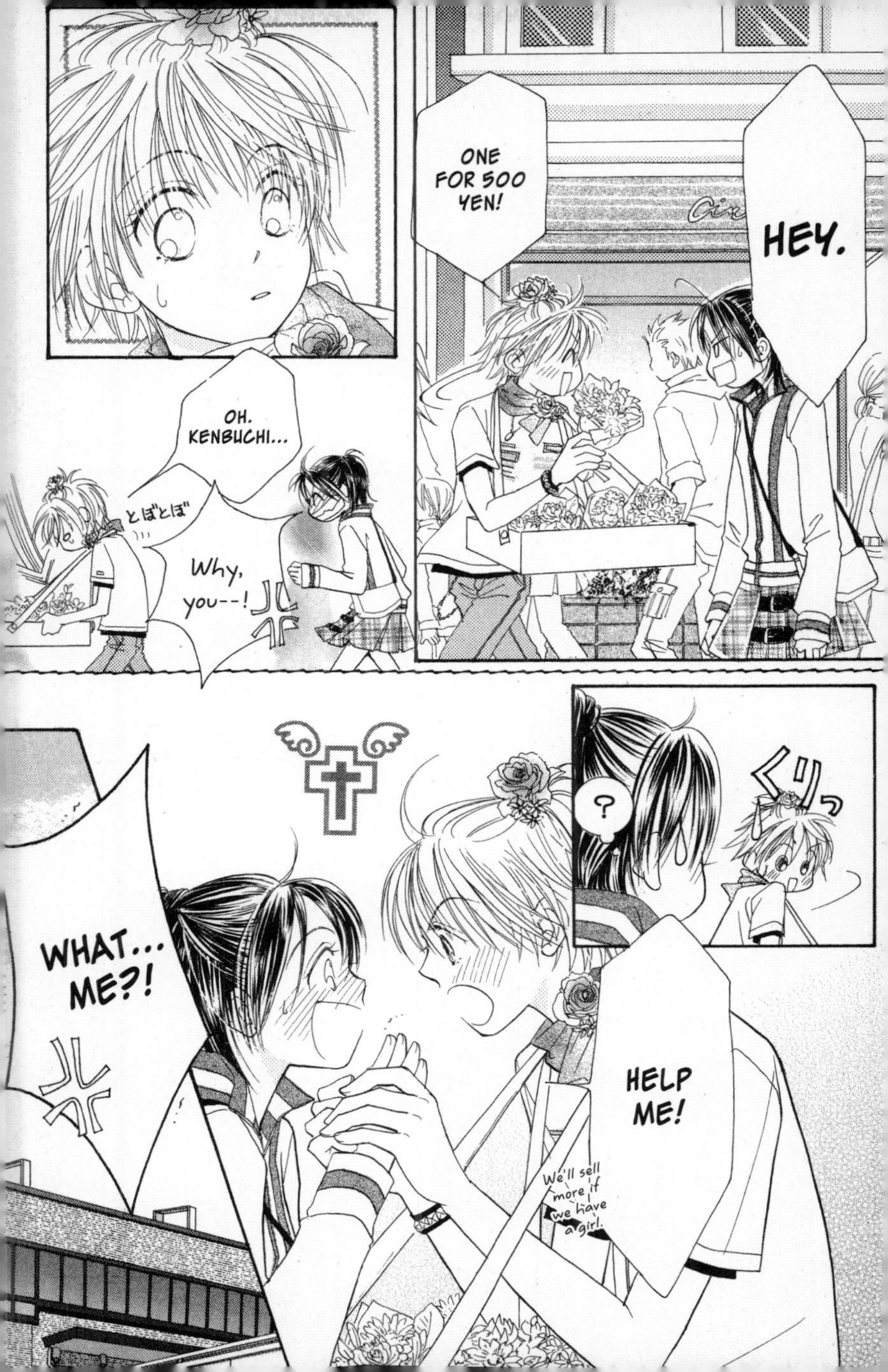
HEY.
ONE FOR 500 YEN!
OH. KENBUCHI...
とぼとぼ
Why, you--!
?
くりっ
HELP ME!
We'll sell more if we have a girl.
WHAT... ME?!

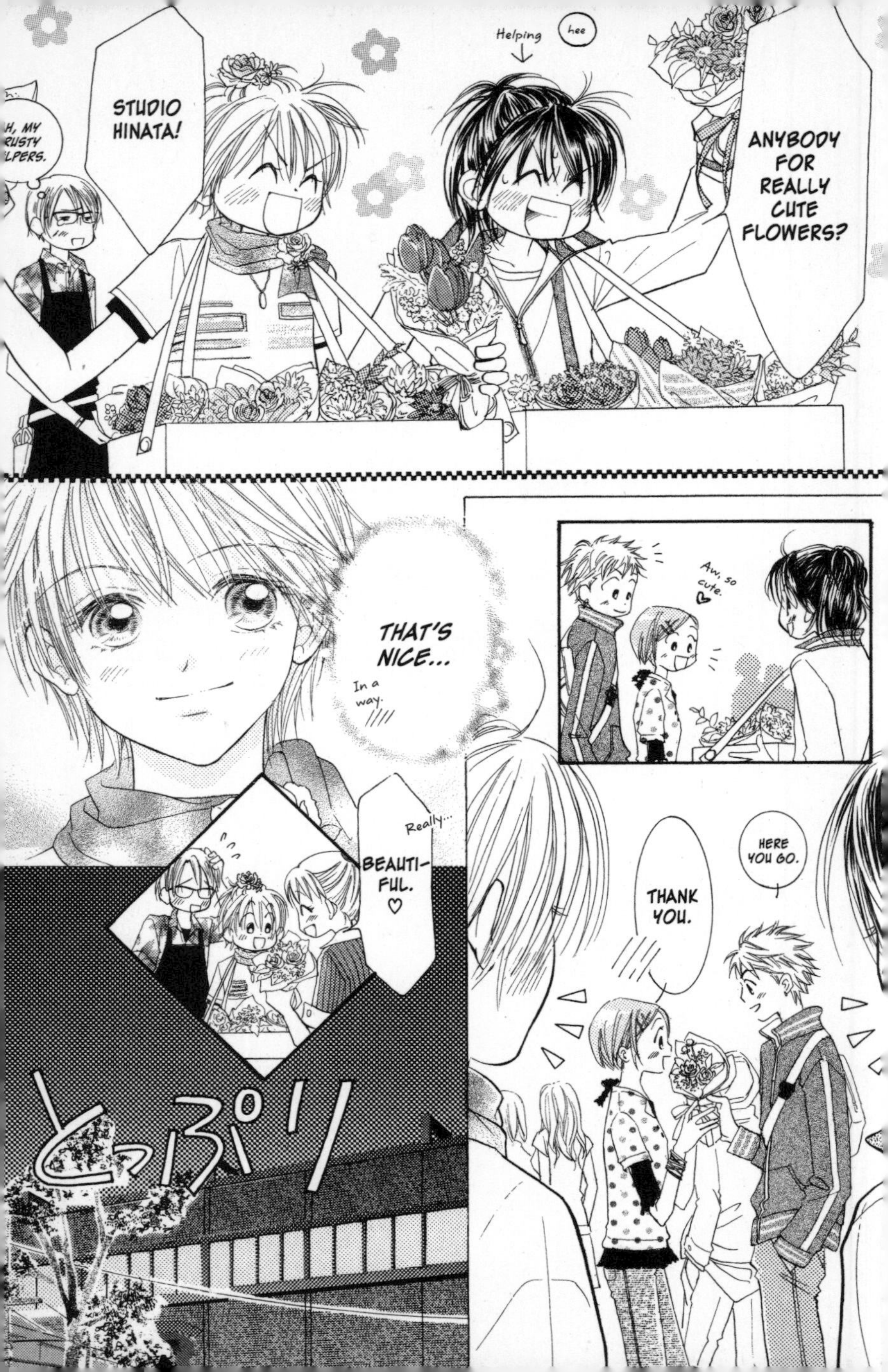
ANYBODY FOR REALLY CUTE FLOWERS?
hee
Helping
STUDIO HINATA!
H, MY RUSTY LPERS.
Aw, so cute. ♡
HERE YOU GO.
THANK YOU.
THAT'S NICE...
In a way.
Really...
BEAUTI-FUL. ♡
とっぷり

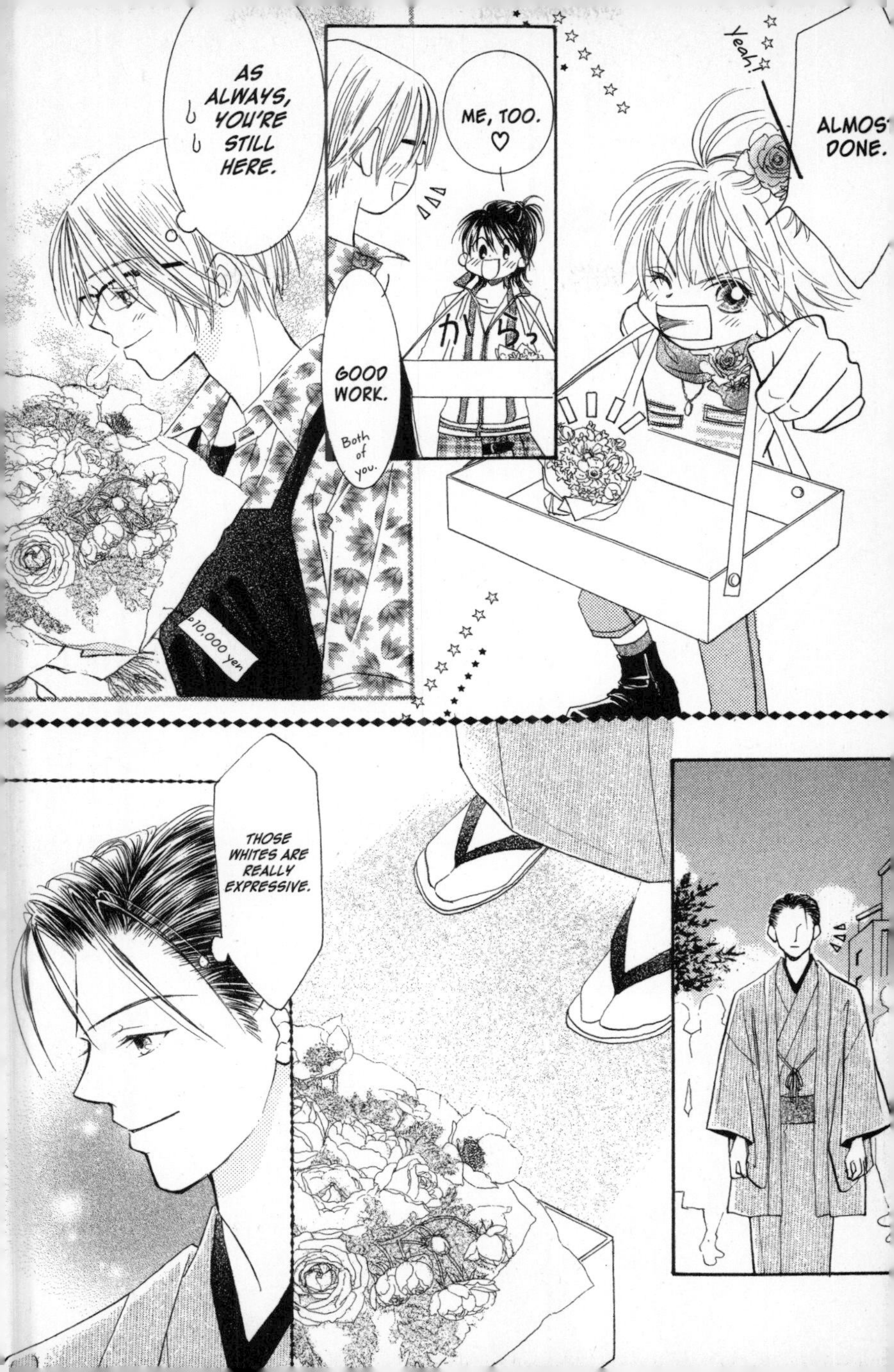
Yeah!
ALMOST DONE.
ME, TOO. ♡
からっ
GOOD WORK.
Both of you.
AS ALWAYS, YOU'RE STILL HERE.
10,000 yen
THOSE WHITES ARE REALLY EXPRESSIVE.

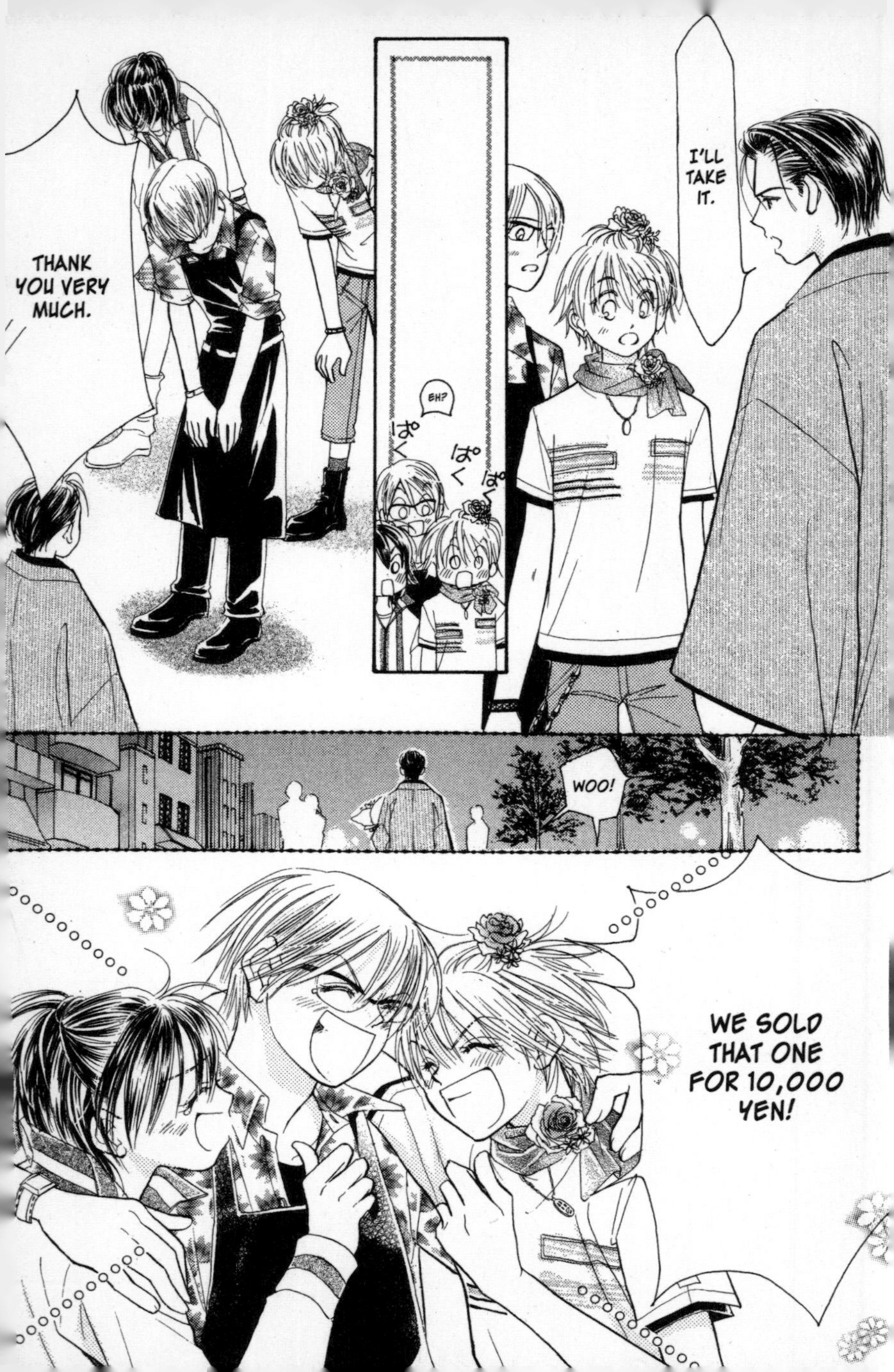
I'LL TAKE IT.
EH?
ぱく
ぱく
ぱく
THANK YOU VERY MUCH.
WOO!
WE SOLD THAT ONE FOR 10,000 YEN!

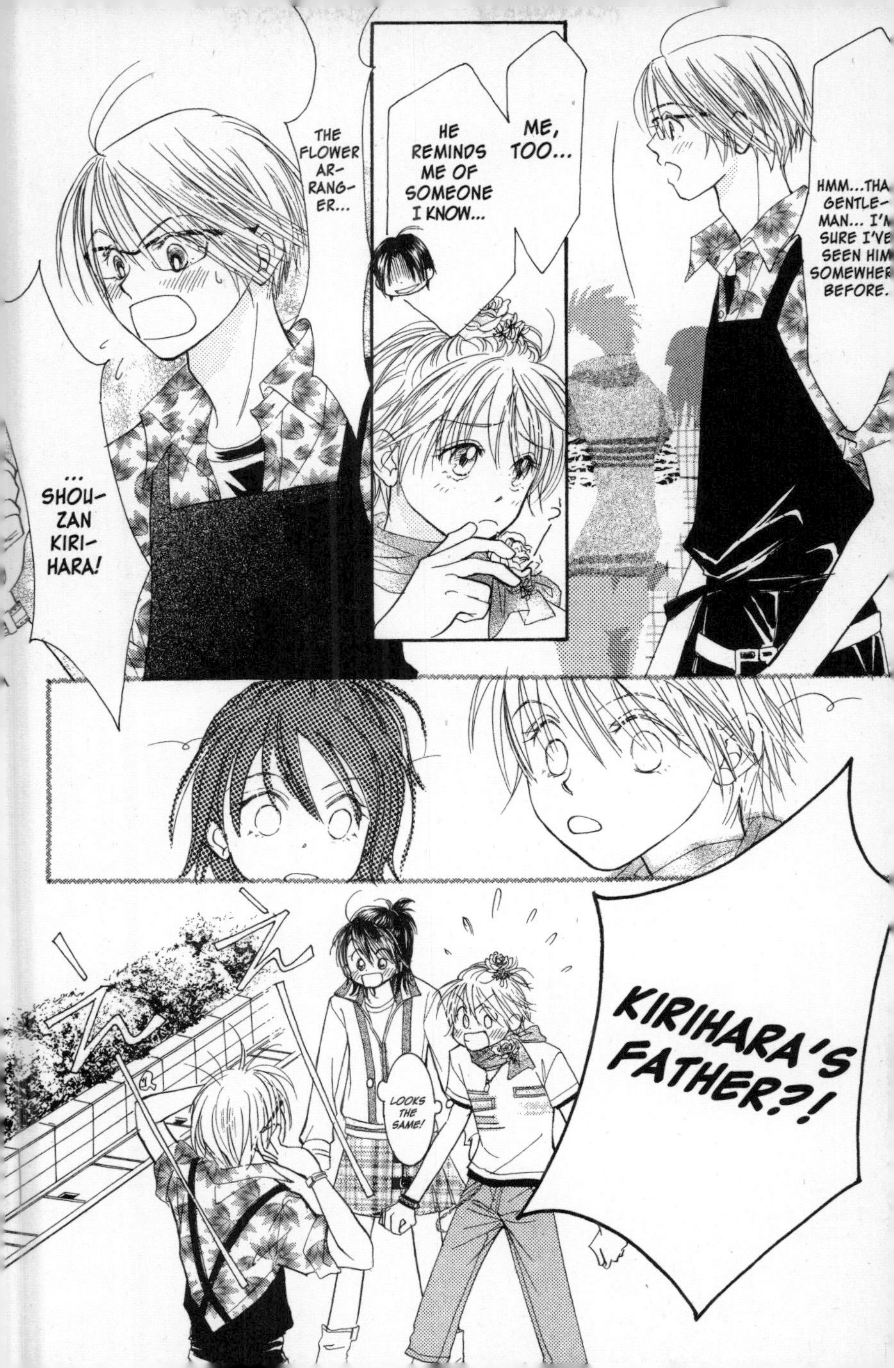
HMM...THA GENTLEMAN... I'M SURE I'VE SEEN HIM SOMEWHER BEFORE.
ME, TOO...
HE REMINDS ME OF SOMEONE I KNOW...
THE FLOWER ARRANGER...
...SHOUZAN KIRIHARA!
KIRIHARA'S FATHER?!
LOOKS THE SAME!

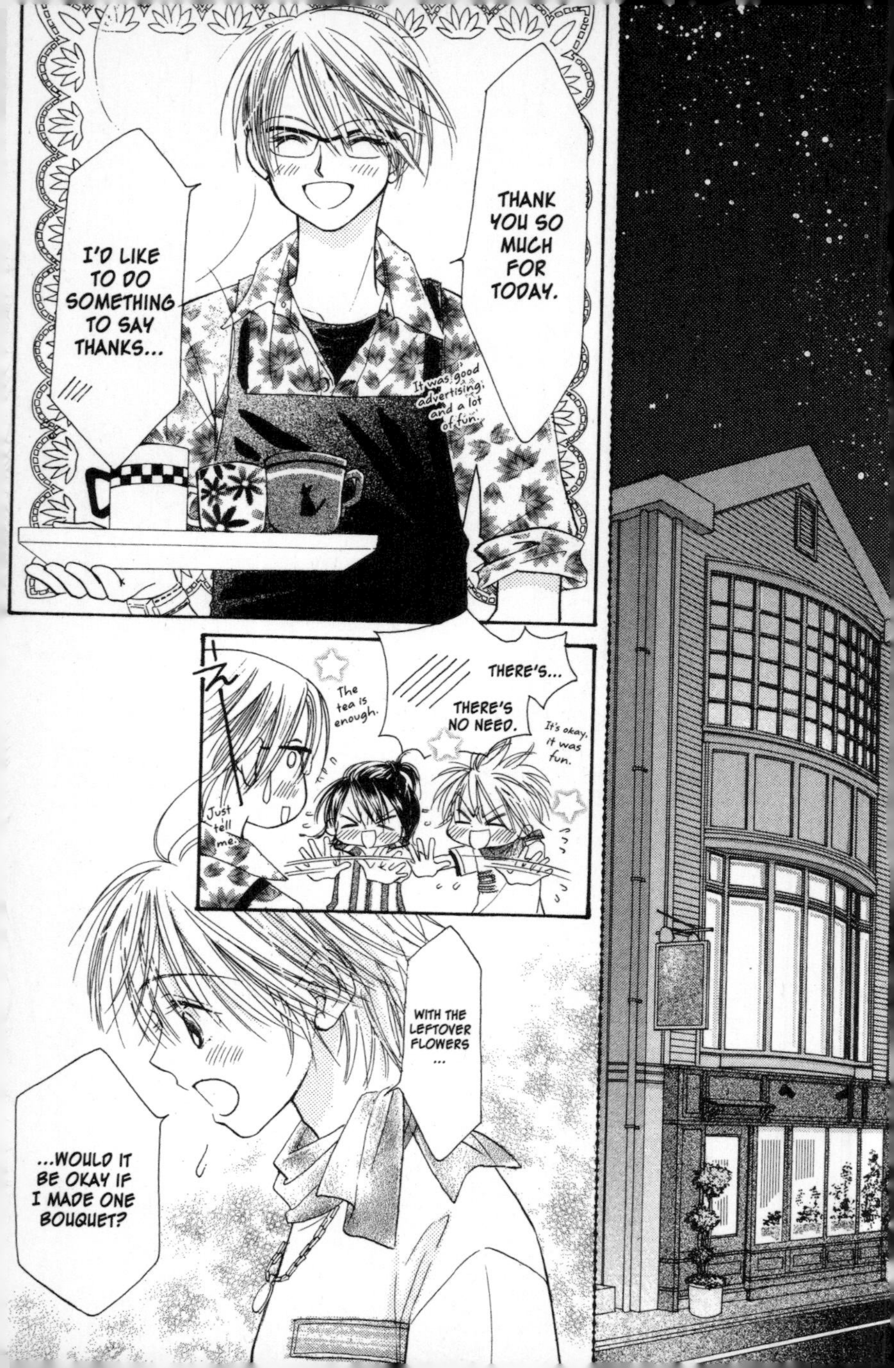
THANK YOU SO MUCH FOR TODAY.
It was good advertising, and a lot of fun.
I'D LIKE TO DO SOMETHING TO SAY THANKS...
THERE'S...
THERE'S NO NEED.
It's okay, it was fun.
The tea is enough.
Just tell me.
WITH THE LEFTOVER FLOWERS...
...WOULD IT BE OKAY IF I MADE ONE BOUQUET?

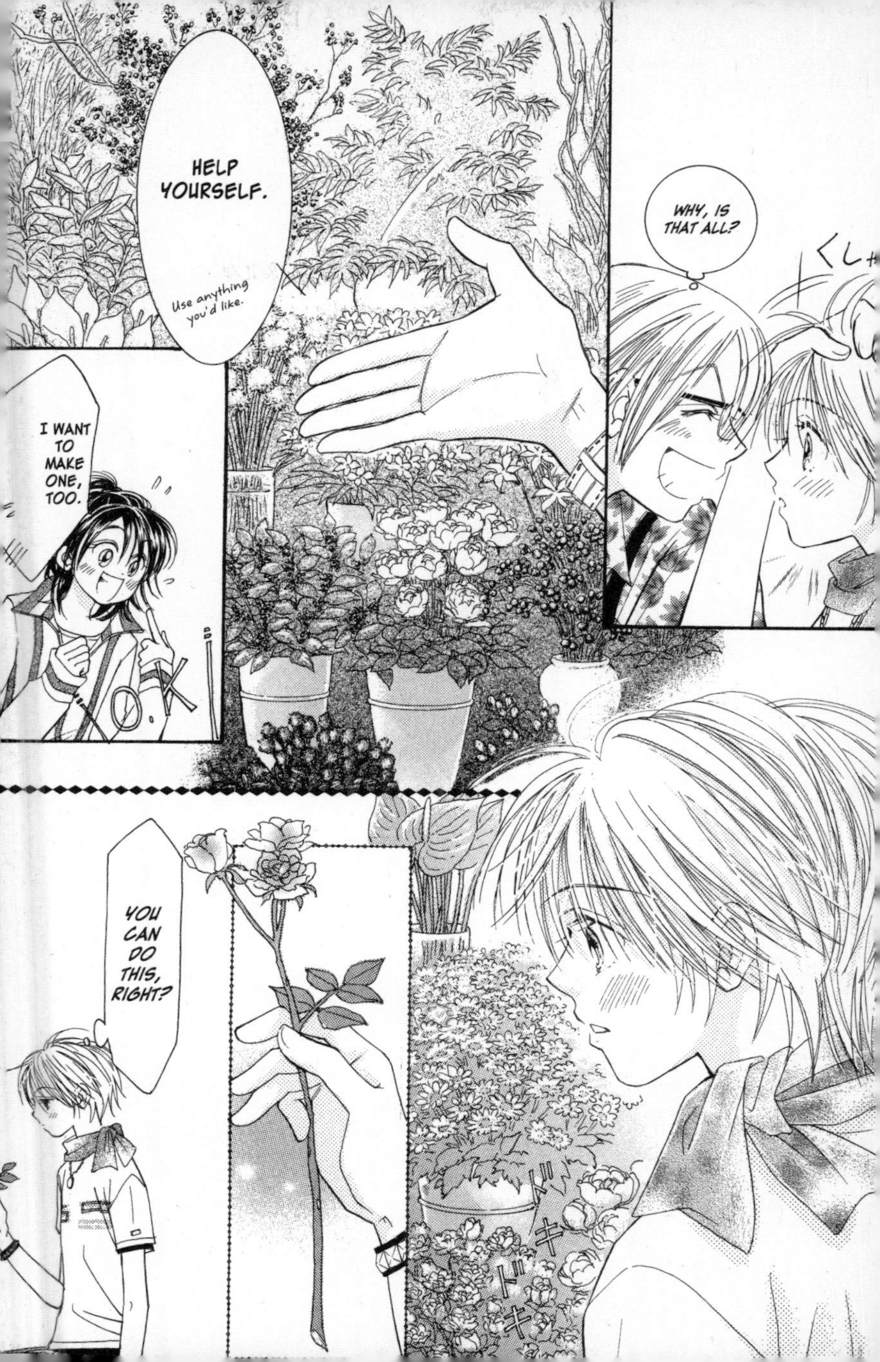
WHY, IS THAT ALL?
くし
HELP YOURSELF.
Use anything you'd like.
I WANT TO MAKE ONE, TOO.
OK
ドキドキ
YOU CAN DO THIS, RIGHT?

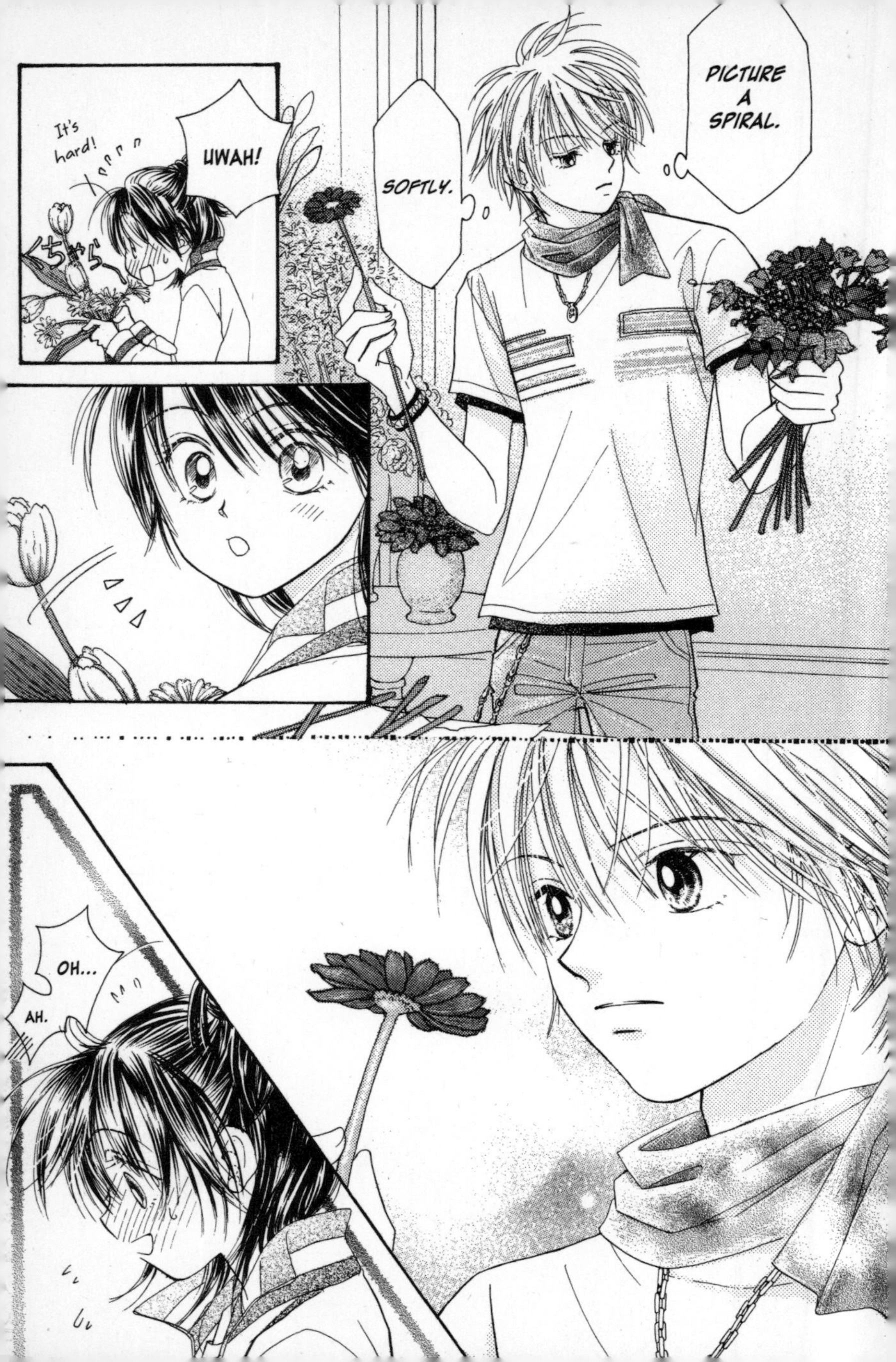
PICTURE A SPIRAL.
SOFTLY.
UWAH!
It's hard!
くちゃら〜
OH...
AH.

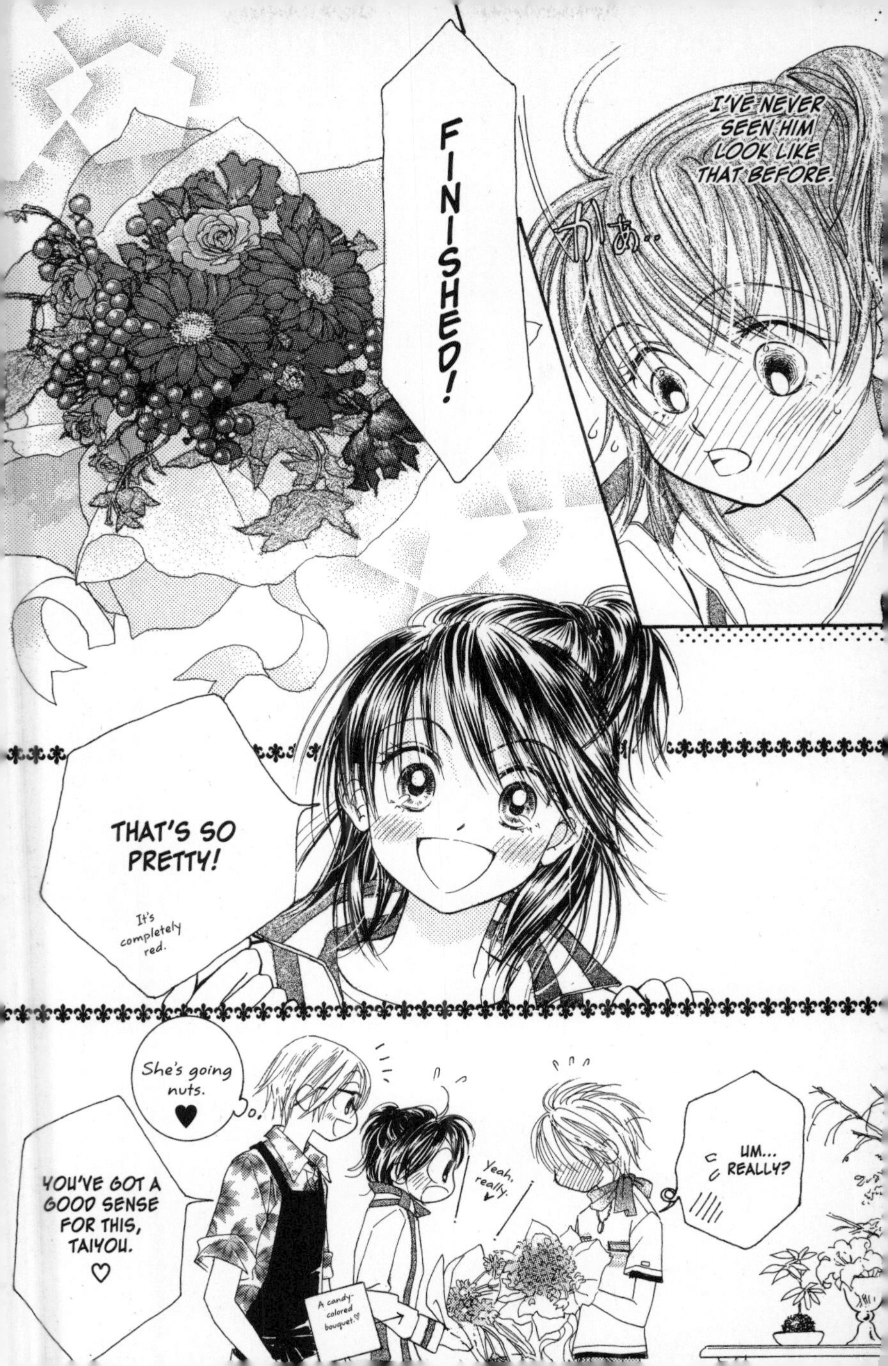

I'VE NEVER SEEN HIM LOOK LIKE THAT BEFORE.
わあ..
FINISHED!
THAT'S SO PRETTY!
It's completely red.
UM... REALLY?
Yeah, really.
She's going nuts.
YOU'VE GOT A GOOD SENSE FOR THIS, TAIYOU.
A candy-colored bouquet.

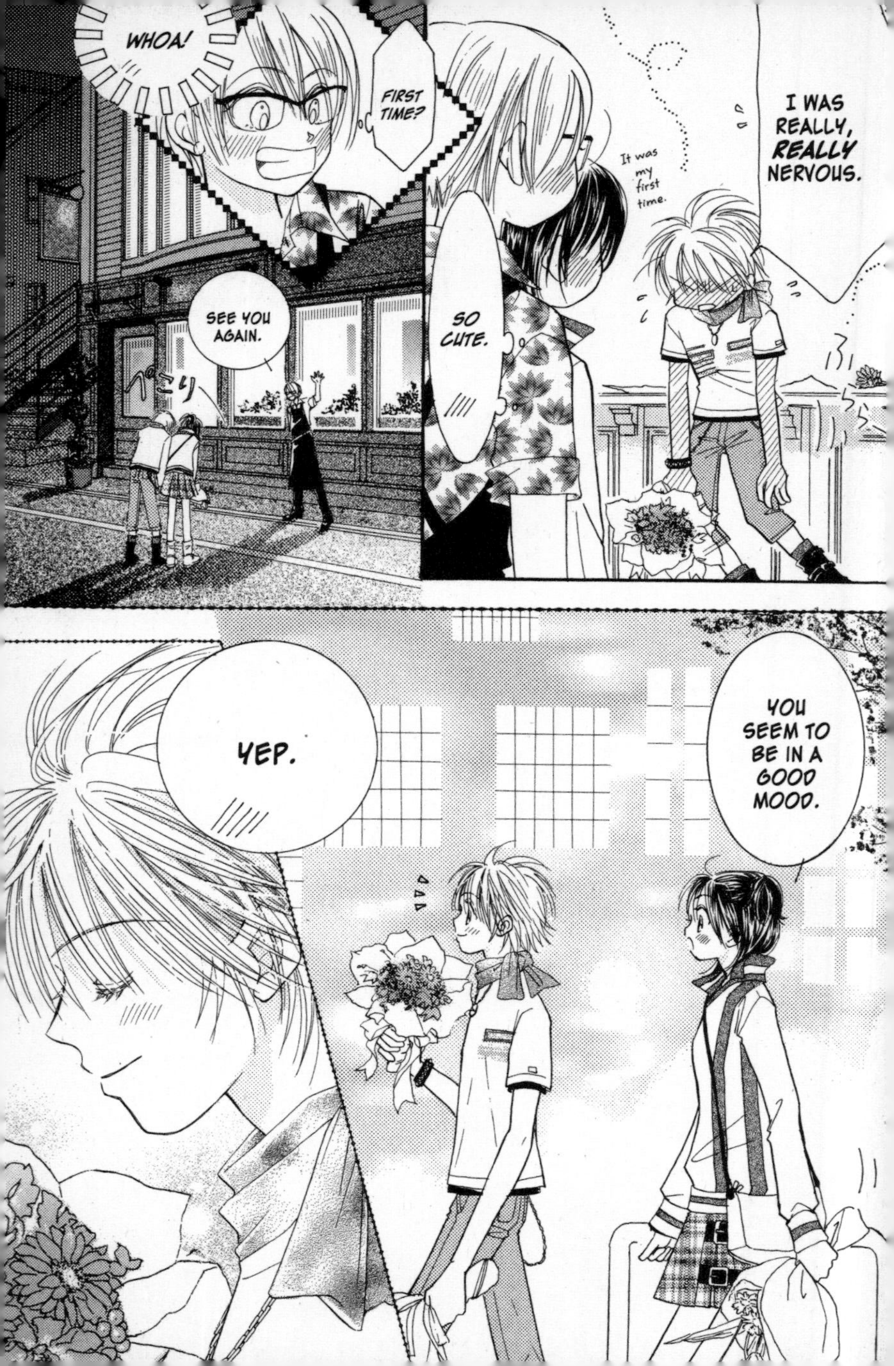
I WAS REALLY, REALLY NERVOUS.
It was my first time.
SO CUTE.
WHOA!
FIRST TIME?
SEE YOU AGAIN.
ぺこり
YOU SEEM TO BE IN A GOOD MOOD.
YEP.

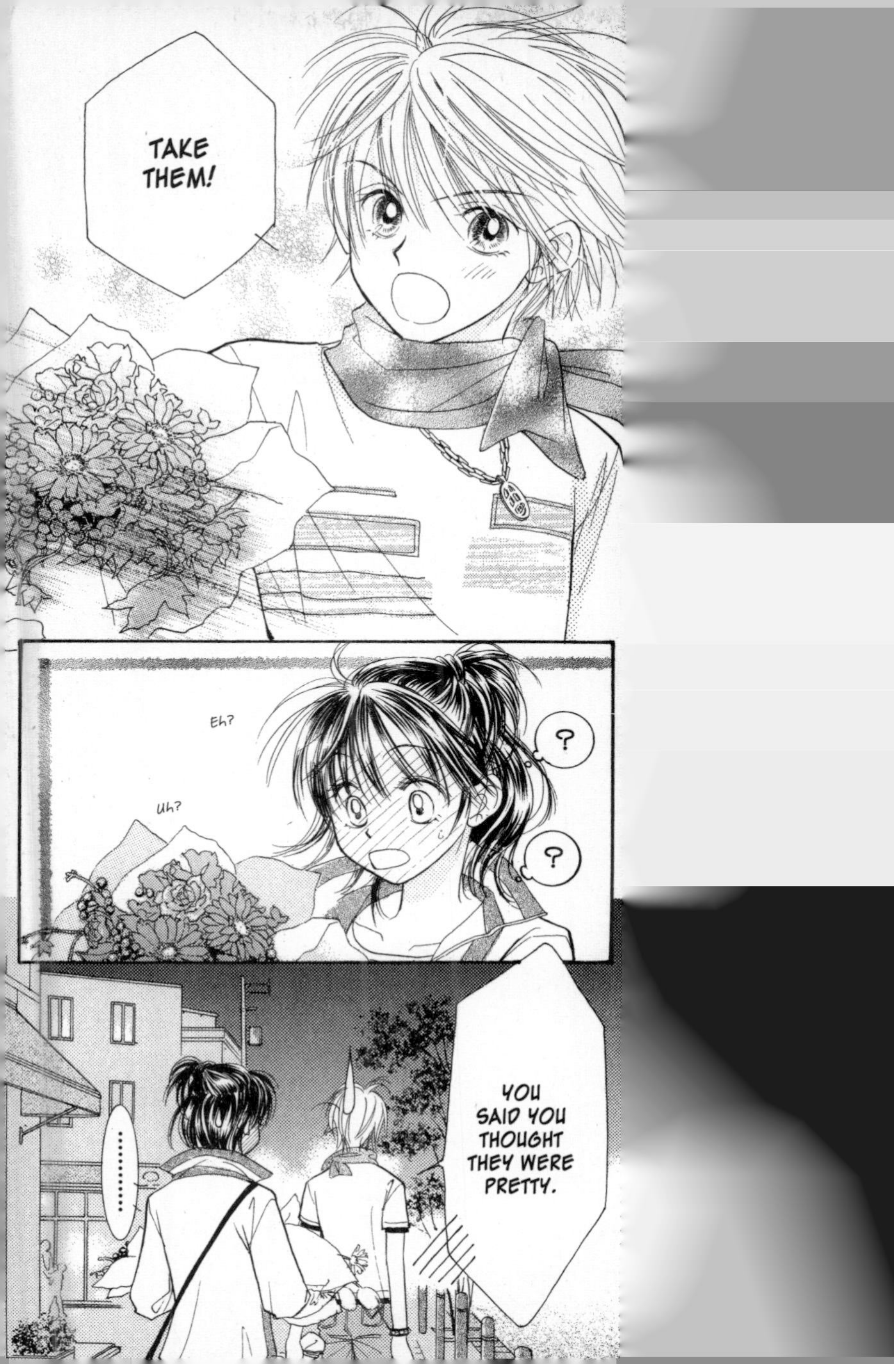
TAKE THEM!
?
?
Eh?
Uh?
YOU SAID YOU THOUGHT THEY WERE PRETTY.
....

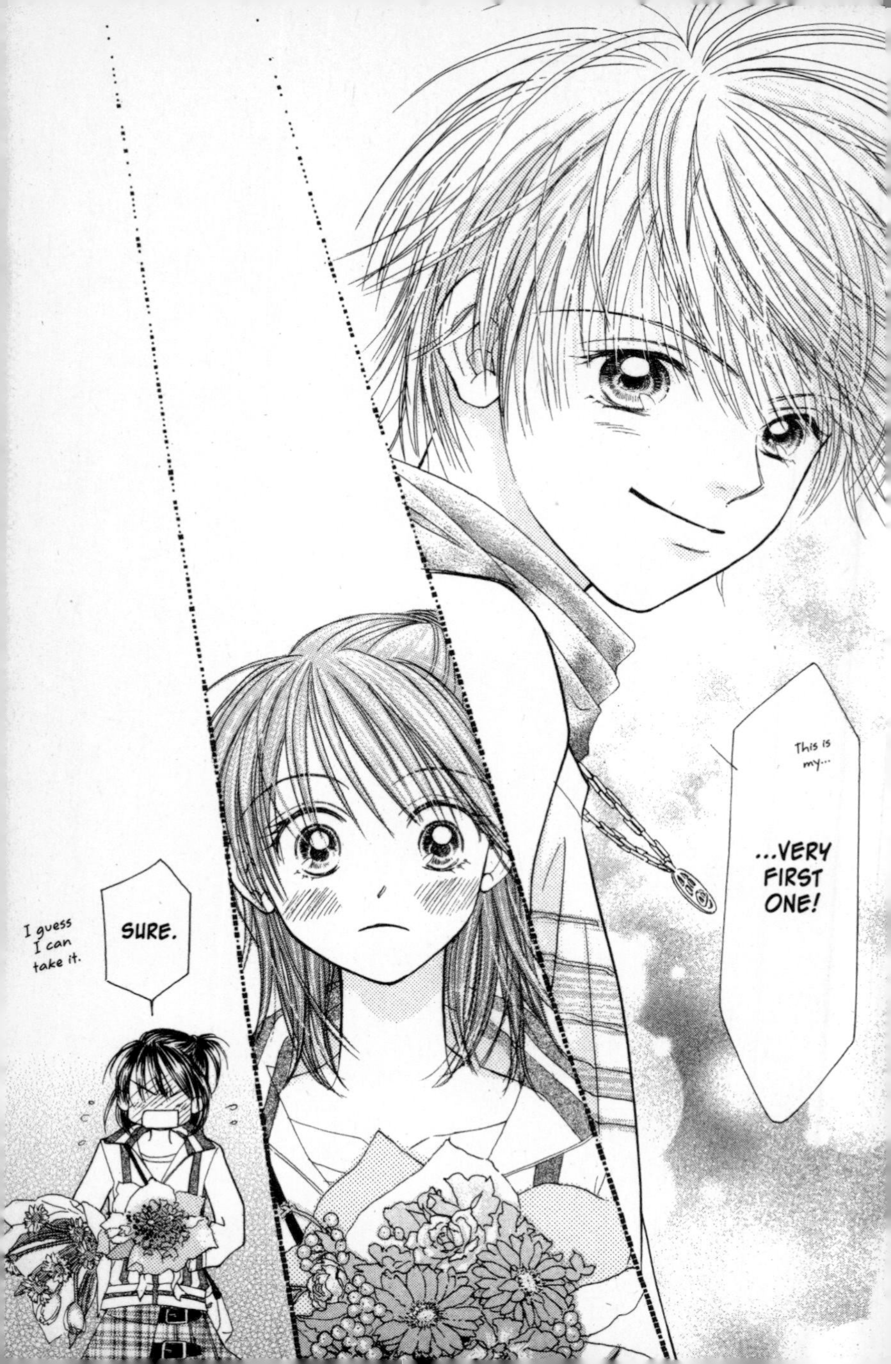
This is my...
...VERY FIRST ONE!
SURE.
I guess I can take it.

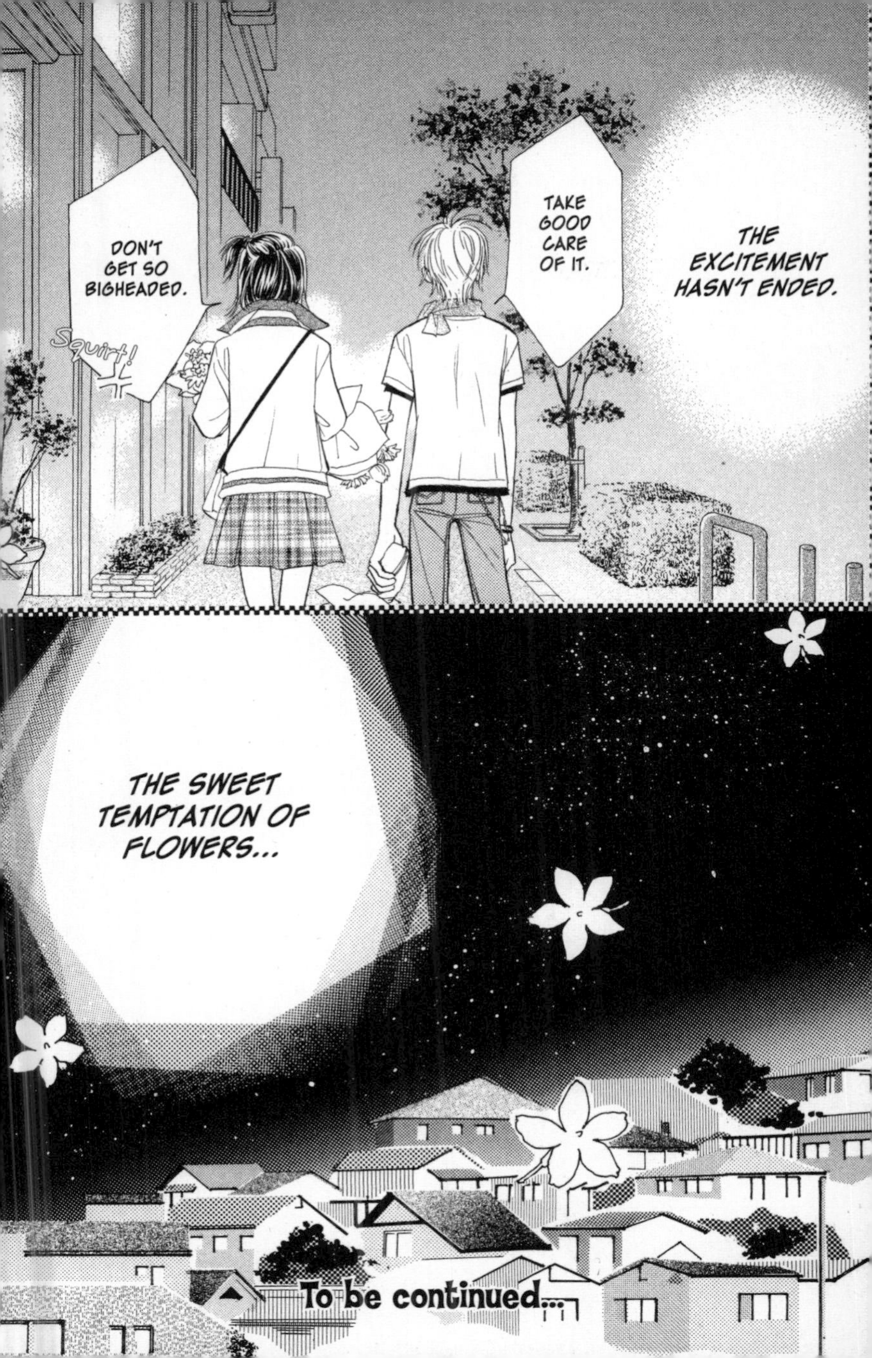
THE EXCITEMENT HASN'T ENDED.
TAKE GOOD CARE OF IT.
DON'T GET SO BIGHEADED.
Squirt!
THE SWEET TEMPTATION OF FLOWERS...
To be continued...

Caramel
Photo Studio III

(Enter the room of my hobbies and loves. There's no going back! Ha ha!)

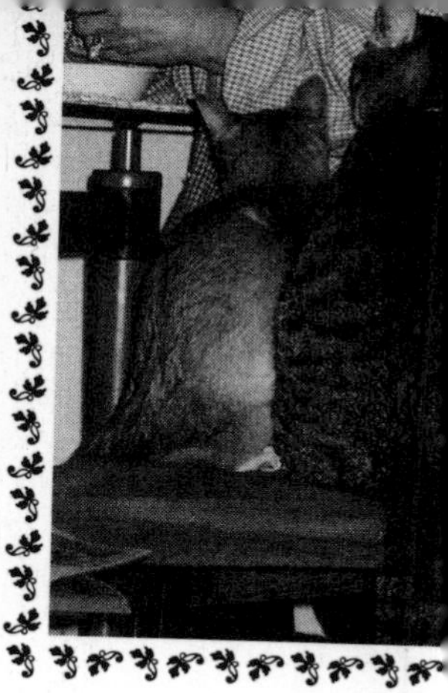

Cara and Mel waiting anxiously for their mommy to carefully unwrap their treats.

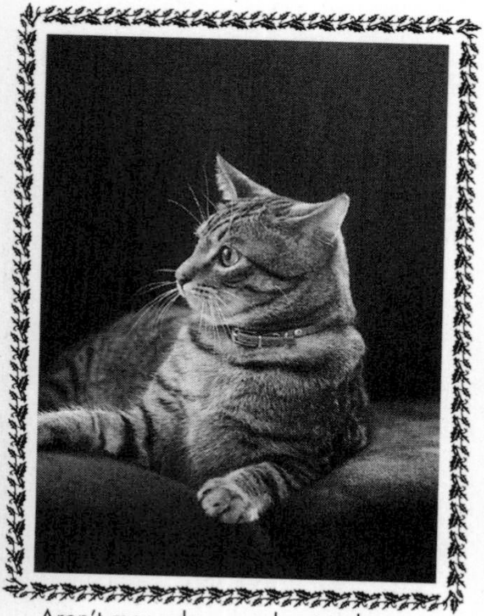

Aren't men who are about to have a showdown always profiled in movies? Oh, Cara, you're so manly!

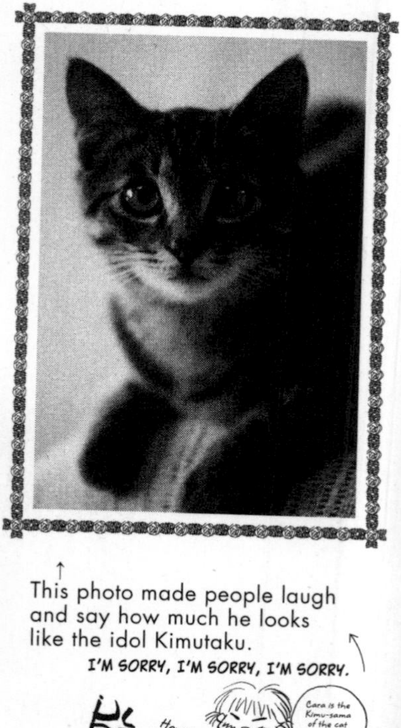

↑ This photo made people laugh and say how much he looks like the idol Kimutaku.

I'M SORRY, I'M SORRY, I'M SORRY.

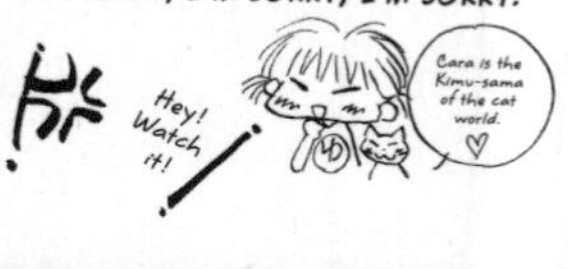
Hey! Watch it!
Cara is the Kimu-sama of the cat world. ♥

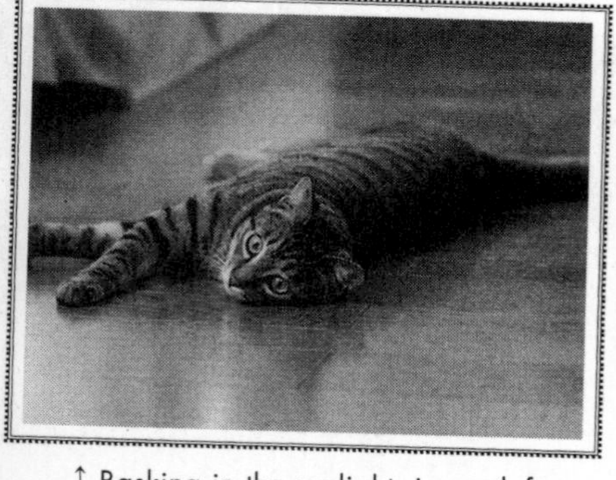

↑ Basking in the sunlight, in our loft.

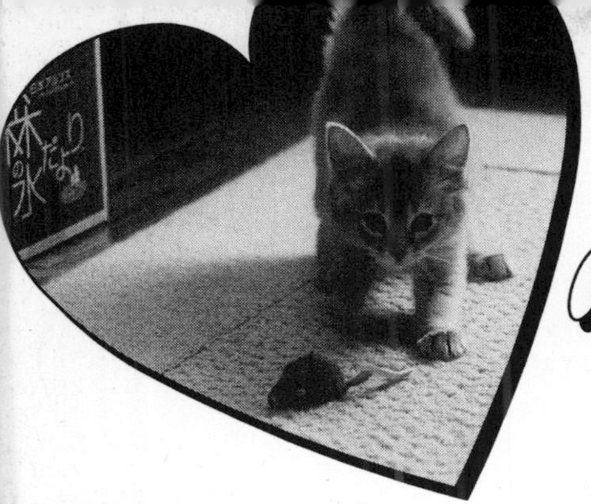

Itty-bitty Mel as a
← baby! She's just toooo
cute!! I'm melting!

Girls are even sexier from
↓behind... ♡ Her tail's sooo fluffy!

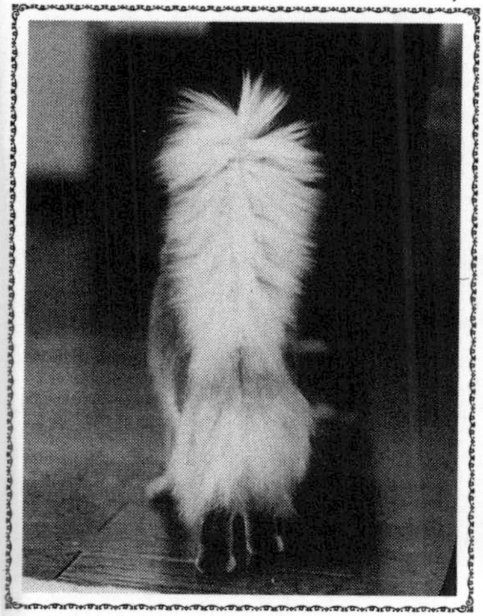

All dressed up for
Christmas... She's one
pissed-off looking princess.
↓ But still so beautiful! Ha!

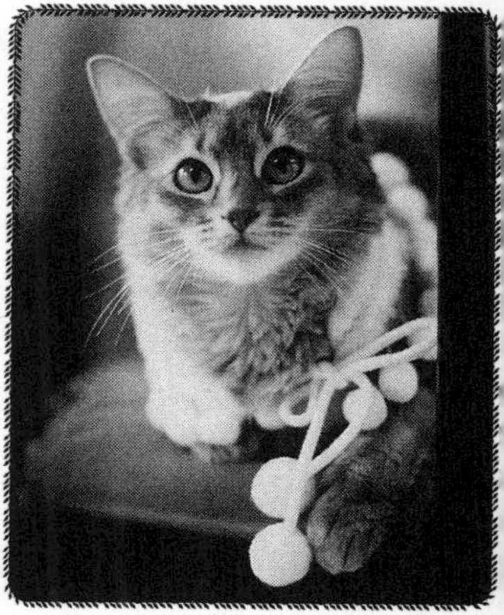

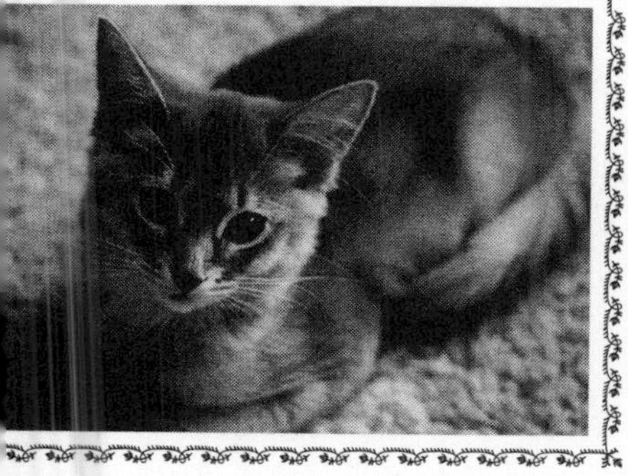

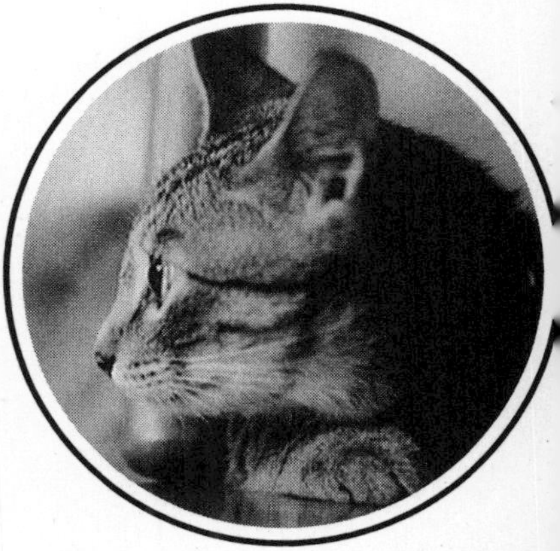

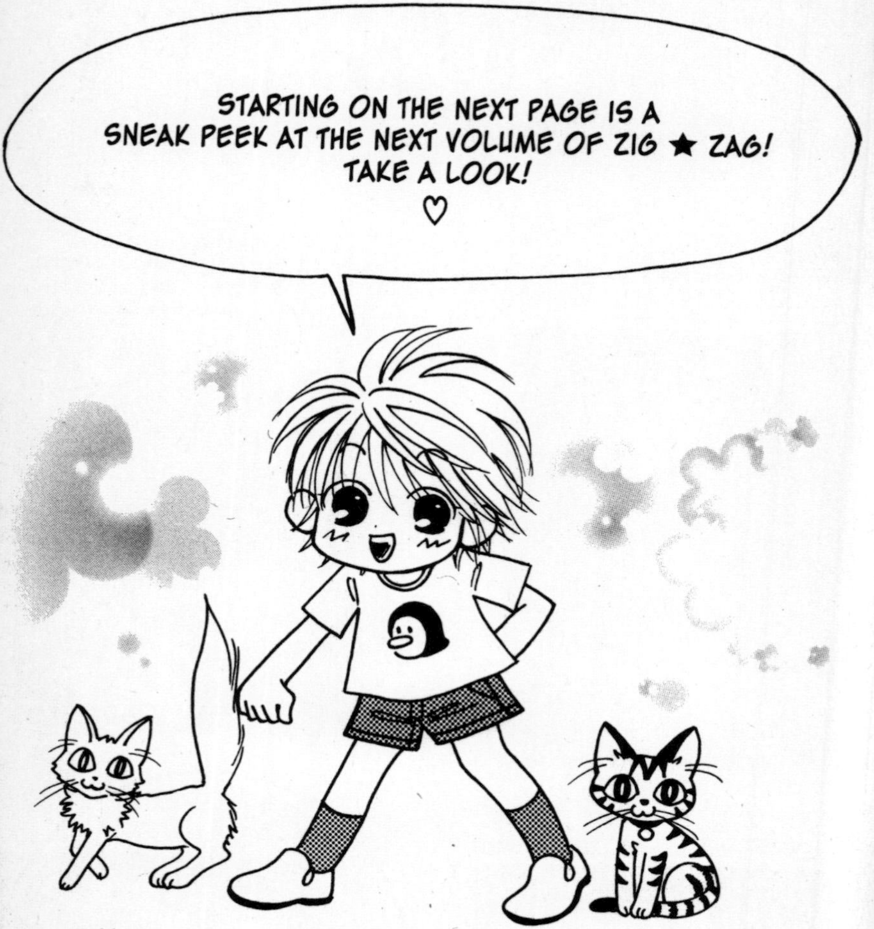
STARTING ON THE NEXT PAGE IS A SNEAK PEEK AT THE NEXT VOLUME OF ZIG ★ ZAG! TAKE A LOOK! ♡
Mel
Taiyou
Cara

Update on Yuki Nakaji's Newest Series! ♥

WHAT ARE FLOWERS TO YOU?
FAIRY?! BOY
SOMETHING TO LOVE!
WHAT WILL BECOME OF THESE THREE BOYS WHO ARE CHARMED BY FLOWERS?
Hi
WHATEVER.
COOL?! BOY
ENJOY THE SWEET AND SLIGHTLY BITTER STORY...
HOT?! BOY
YOU CAN'T EVEN EAT 'EM.
...OF THIS FLOWERY HIGH SCHOOL LIFE!

In the next

ZIG★ZAG

After coming face to face with the Ikebana master Shouzan Kirihara and learning that he is in fact the father of his enigmatic roommate, Sonoh, Taiyou lends his energies toward trying to bring them closer together. It's a process that proves to be, in more ways than one, more painful than he imagined. Also, Saho starts to realize the extent of her feelings for Taiyou, but he's still stuck on Marika. Are they on a collision course with heartbreak?

Quiz time: Their hair isn't colored.
Which one's black and which one's white? (hee)

Special Thanks xxx

EDITOR
T. KONDOU

and everyone.

STAFF
H. SUE
M. YOKONO
M. TANAKA
K. INOUE
Y. OKADA

N. AKINO

VOLUME 2: SILENT NOISE

TRINITY BLOOD
RAGE AGAINST THE MOONS

THE TRINITY BLOOD FRANCHISE RAGES ON!

Nothing is quite as it seems...

A mysterious weapon called Silent Noise destroys
Barcelona and threatens Rome... Abel Nightroad
battles personal demons... And the Duchess of Milan is in
more danger than she knows... The next volume of the
thrilling Pop Fiction series rages with sound and fury!

"INSTANTLY GRIPPING."
—*NEWTYPE USA*

POP
FICTION

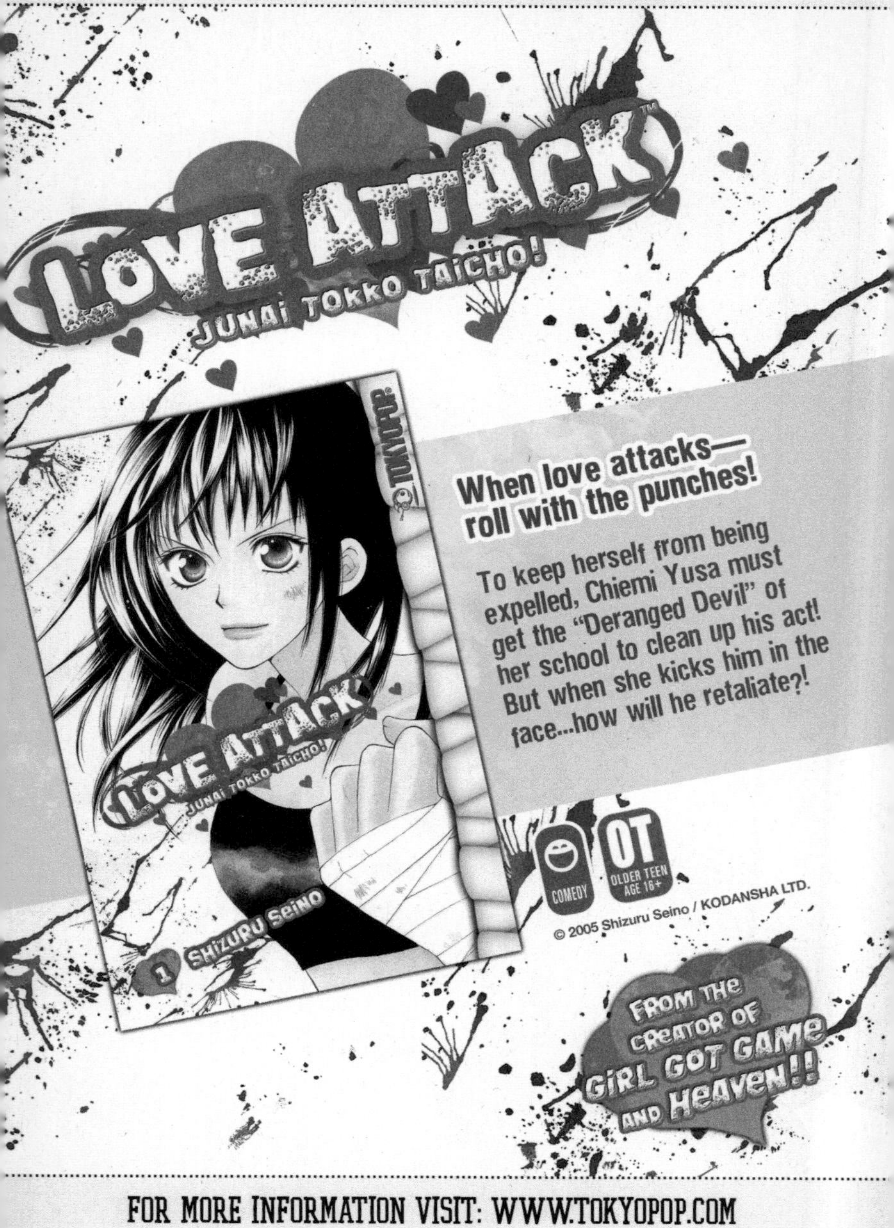
LOVE ATTACK™
JUNAI TOKKO TAICHO!
TOKYOPOP
When love attacks—
roll with the punches!
To keep herself from being expelled, Chiemi Yusa must get the "Deranged Devil" of her school to clean up his act! But when she kicks him in the face...how will he retaliate?!
LOVE ATTACK
JUNAI TOKKO TAICHO!
1 SHIZURU SEINO
COMEDY
OT
OLDER TEEN AGE 16+
© 2005 Shizuru Seino / KODANSHA LTD.
FROM THE CREATOR OF GIRL GOT GAME AND HEAVEN!!

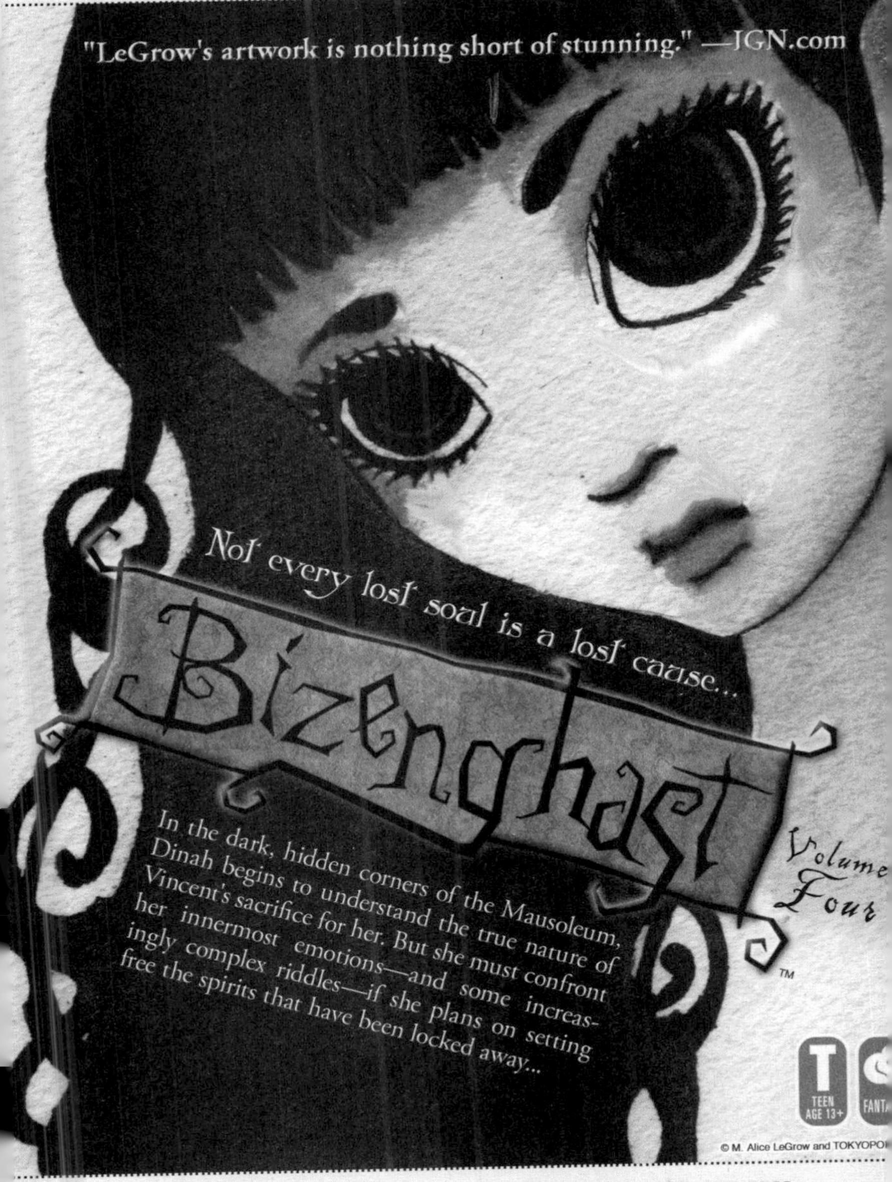
"LeGrow's artwork is nothing short of stunning." —IGN.com
Not every lost soul is a lost cause...
Bizenghast
Volume Four
TM
In the dark, hidden corners of the Mausoleum, Dinah begins to understand the true nature of Vincent's sacrifice for her. But she must confront her innermost emotions—and some increasingly complex riddles—if she plans on setting free the spirits that have been locked away...
T
TEEN AGE 13+
© M. Alice LeGrow and TOKYOPO

STOP!

This is the back of the book.
You wouldn't want to spoil a great ending!

This book is printed "manga-style," in the authentic Japanese right-to-left format. Since none of the artwork has been flipped or altered, readers get to experience the story just as the creator intended. You've been asking for it, so TOKYOPOP® delivered: authentic, hot-off-the-press, and far more fun!

DIRECTIONS

If this is your first time reading manga-style, here's a quick guide to help you understand how it works.

It's easy... just start in the top right panel and follow the numbers. Have fun, and look for more 100% authentic manga from TOKYOPOP®!

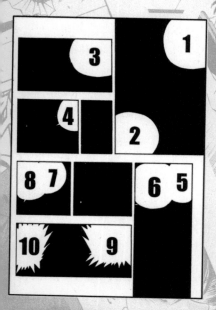